P9-ASF-355

BREAD

**Social, Nutritional and Agricultural
Aspects of Wheaten Bread**

*International Symposium organised by Rank Prize Funds
and held at Selsdon Park Hotel, Croydon, Surrey, UK*

BREAD

Social, Nutritional and Agricultural Aspects of Wheaten Bread

Edited by

ARNOLD SPICER

Scientific Adviser to R H M Research Ltd,
and
Chairman of the Advisory
Committee on Nutrition
to the Rank Prize Funds

APPLIED SCIENCE PUBLISHERS LTD

LONDON

APPLIED SCIENCE PUBLISHERS LTD
RIPPLE ROAD, BARKING, ESSEX, ENGLAND

ISBN: 0 85334 637 2

WITH 74 TABLES AND 45 ILLUSTRATIONS

© APPLIED SCIENCE PUBLISHERS LTD 1975

All rights reserved. No part of this publication may be reproduced,
stored in a retrieval system, or transmitted in any form or by any
means, electronic, mechanical, photocopying, recording, or otherwise, without the prior written permission of the publishers, Applied
Science Publishers Ltd, Ripple Road, Barking, Essex, England

Printed Offset Litho in Great Britain by Cox & Wyman Ltd, London, Fakenham and Reading

Foreword

The international symposium, of which the proceedings form the subject matter of this book, was the first major activity in the nutritional field of the Rank Prize Funds. The Funds, initiated shortly before the death of the founder, Lord Rank, were constituted to encourage further research into and provide awards for significant advances in the fields of human and animal nutrition, crop husbandry (but not animal husbandry) and opto-electronics and nearly related phenomena.

This first symposium brought together scientists from a wide variety of disciplines, and technologists and industrialists from sixteen of the major wheat producing and bread consuming countries of the world. Plant breeders, agronomists, millers, bakers, nutritionists, sociologists and economists discussed the important factors in their contributions towards providing the world with one of its most important staples, viz. bread.

Over recent years there has been a growing interest, not least on the part of the consuming public, in the nutritional content, quality and acceptability of wheaten bread. It is also a subject which is able to raise the strongest passions, as well as being one about which there are many misconceptions, frequently based on inadequate or inaccurate information.

It is no coincidence, of course, that the subject is one that would have been dear to Lord Rank's heart, and the proceedings of this symposium are offered here as an up-dated and authoritative record of the latest thinking in the many disciplines involved in the manufacture and distribution of wheaten bread. It is hoped that this book will not only serve as an instructive document, but as a lasting tribute to the memory of the founder of the Rank Prize Funds.

JAMES HADLEY,
Executive Director,
Rank Prize Funds

Contents

SESSION III—YIELD FACTORS
(*Chairman:* Professor Sir Ernst Chain)

SESSION VII—SUMMING UP
(*Chairman:* Professor F. Lynen)

The History of Wheat and Bread

ARNOLD SPICER

Scientific Adviser to R H M Research Ltd,
The Lord Rank Research Centre,
High Wycombe, Bucks, U K

The art and craft which stood at the cradle of the Science and Technology we are going to discuss during the next few days, existed at the outset of recorded history and predates it, documented by excavations undertaken in many parts of the world. Archaeological explorations on Swiss lake habitations dating back to 4000 BC found a fermented type cake, whilst we have clear evidence of the art of bread baking being practised at that time and before in Egypt. The Bible, which has now become a dearly loved book for early references, mentions bread on a number of occasions. In one place God says to Adam 'In the sweat of thy brow shall thou eat bread' a statement of such profound wisdom, that it dominated men's life for thousands of years. Whilst bread so referred to in early references may not necessarily mean wheaten bread, acorns, nuts, millet, barley, rye and oats were all used and are used to some extent today to produce bread-like products, also the early wheat was not the type we know today, it was Emmer or Spelt wheat with narrow and rather pointed grains. Linnaeus, or Carl van Line, as he was known after receiving his knighthood in 1761, published in 1736 after a visit from his native Sweden to England, his 'Genera Plantarum' followed the next year by his 'Classes Plantarum', which must be regarded as the starting point of modern systematic botany. In 'Species Plantarum', written in 1753, he set out to classify the vast number of wheats, recognising five species, and this attempt has been followed by many botanists since his days. Dr Flaksberger and colleagues in the Soviet Union then published a comprehensive classification of the wheats of the world. For my historical review it will suffice to give you merely a broad outline sketch in order not to bore the many experts assembled here with too much detail, and yet enabling us during the next few days to fill in this sketch with distinct colours and detail. Modern taxonomy divides wheat into three groups by chromosome number. Group I, chromosome number 14, includes the wild and cultivated 'Einkorn' wheats, *Triticum aegilopoides* and *T. monococcum*. Group II, chromosome number 28, the wild and cultivated 'Emmer' wheats, *T. dicoccoides*; Durum wheat; Abyssinian wheat; Rivet or Cone wheat;

1

Persian wheat; Polish wheat; and *T. timopheevi*. And Group III, chromosome number 42, Spelt wheat (*T. spelta*); common or bread wheat (*T. aestivum*); Indian Dward wheat; and Macha wheat. These classifications are mainly though not exclusively based on morphological differences, details of which may well be filled in by one or two other speakers. One point I should mention though, even if it appears superfluous with all the expertise represented here, that the most important and most widely distributed of all varieties mentioned is the bread wheat. It grows in the most widely differing forms, with variations in length and density of ear, habit of growth, period of ripening, resistance to disease, adaptation to different climatic conditions and yields ranging from 15 cwt per acre to 3 ton per acre due to different agronomical conditions. The ancestry is shrouded in some obscurity and on this point Professor Riley may well shed some more light in his paper, from his vastly greater knowledge. Some workers in this field believe that bread wheats are derived from a wheat of the Emmer group (*Triticum dicoccoides*) through hybridisation with the genus Aegilops, a wild grass found in southern Europe and Asia, and these wheats have been manipulated from very early times on to give improved yields, show better disease resistance or mature earlier. The Romans already practised mass selections, taking the best ears and largest grains as seed for their next crop. It is said that some of the world's best known wheats have been selections of single ears or plants exhibiting desirable characteristics found growing casually on roadsides, in hedges or in other crops on cultivated ground. Hybridisation of plants, to obtain through crossing, a great varying offspring was also practised, and this work received an enormous impetus when the Bohemian Abbott T. G. Mendel in 1866 propagated the scientific theory relating to the distributive mechanism of organic inheritance now known as Mendelism. By the painstaking selection of the progeny of succeeding generations it became possible to produce plants that breed true and combine certain characteristics such as the strength and high yield of the original parents. So men received the scientific tools to prepare for an era of progress of which we are still witnesses today.

Though the highest yielding varieties today in our country with a crop per acre nearly double of that 20 years ago are a remarkable achievement of our Plant Breeding Institute in Cambridge, their grain quality is unfortunately poor and they do not qualify as suitable for breadmaking. Dr Irvine is going to address us on the baking qualities of wheat, the particular points millers and bakers stress today in their selections of wheats for the bread grist. This selection system is a scientific procedure, today fully computerised by the very large operator, and it enables the plant baker to produce a bread of uniform volume and crumb structure. In fact uniformity becomes so pronounced that many critics of our present bread maintain, it is this uniformity which causes to some extent the lack of appeal of sliced and wrapped bread which represents about 80–85% of all bread sold today. Yet this science of breadmaking of today only started in 1950, as Dr Amos said in a Symposium in March, but the dawn that heralded the revolutionary breakthrough went back some 25 years before that. It was in 1926 that two research workers at the Kansas State Agricultural College designed a laboratory mixer, which combined a pack-squeeze-pull-tear action and demonstrated that such a mixer could produce good bread without bulk fermentation. Then in 1950 the Wallace and Tiernan Do-Maker used mechanical Dough Ripening in its continuous breadmaking process where flour, shortening and a precultured yeast broth were metered continuously into a premixer, which feeds the resulting dough into a mechanical developer that ripens the dough in about 90 s instead of 3–4 h bulk fermentation. But the size and the cost of these automatic bread producing plants restricted their use to very large companies only. A few years later the then British Baking Industries Research Association's Laboratories in Chorleywood, which we are going to visit on Friday, picked up the threads and a team led by Dr Chamberlain under the then Director of Research, Dr Elton researched into the basic chemical and physical principles of mechanical dough development. In 1961 we saw the Chorleywood Bread process defining precisely the conditions for energy and time requirements and the chemical modifications needed to achieve dough ripening in high speed batch mixers in about 4 min. At the same time we saw research workers in the USA perfecting the so-called activated dough development process, which employed conventional slow speed mixers, but relied on an ingenious mixture of reducing and oxidising agents plus fat of a specified slip point to achieve ripening without lengthy bulk-fermentation. L-cysteine hydrochloric was the reducing agent and ascorbic acid with potassium bromate the oxidising agent. We are fortunate in having Dr Chamberlain on Thursday giving us a detailed account of all these advances, which put paid to the many thousand years old art of breadmaking. At the very beginning of this art heated convex stones prepared the bread from flour or parch grain, with hot ashes sometimes thrown over the cake. The ancient Egyptians carried this rudimentary art to high perfection. Herodotus says of them 'they knead their dough with their feet, but their clay with their hands'. A common shape for Egyptian bread revealed by ancient monuments or in excavated tombs is a small round loaf like a muffin or elongated rolls, sprinkled on top with seeds like modern Vienna bread. Classical Greece and Italy continued the development of breadmaking and soon after the war with Perseus (171–168 BC) public bakehouses came into use, though the Romans continued to regard breadmaking as a housewife's art. The ruins of Pompeii reveal several home mills and ovens. In that same city round loaves though were found stamped with the maker's name, fixing responsibility for purity and weight on the owner of a public bakehouse. These public bakehouses were under the control of the Aediles, grain was delivered to the public granaries by the Saccarii and another body called the Catabolenses distributed the grain to the baker. Bakers were known as pistories, or 'pounders' reminiscent of the primitive time when grain was pounded by a pestle in a mortar. About AD 100 the Emperor Trojan founded the College of Pistores, leading Juvenal in his famous satire to make the remark that Romans only needed two things, panem et circenses, bread and circuses.

In London the bakers formed a brotherhood as early as 1155 and were incorporated in 1307 into two distinct bodies, the Company of White Bakers and the Company of Brown Bakers, not referring to their skin but to the colour of their bread. The art prospered and from dough made in a large wooden trough, divided by hand and set by peel into the oven, mechanisation gradually took over towards the end of the 19th century. Better wheats, flour improvers taking over from atmospheric oxidisation, diastatic correctives ensuring satisfactory gas production during fermentation evolved the technology but did not revolutionise it. Baking remained an art craft, with many uncertainties plaguing the Baker until 25–30 years ago. The dawn of today's breakmaking science radically altered the whole situation. In the next few days a galaxy of speakers are going to present us with the details of the contribution science and technology has made to one of the major nutritional sources of ancient and modern man. I am sure we are going to explode many a myth, correct many false impressions, and present in our ultimate documentation to the world an up to date, unbiased picture of a good, healthy and nutritious food.

Session I

FUNDAMENTALS

The Sociology of Bread

MARY DOUGLAS

Department of Anthropology,
University College, London, UK

One object of this paper is to demonstrate that a better knowledge of the social uses of food would be helpful to nutritionists and food experts of all kinds. It is well known that the place of bread is declining in importance in the total food consumption of western European countries. The explanations for this are not difficult. Much more challenging is the fact that in Britain over the last 5 years, while demand for bread and flour show downward trends, and cakes also decline slightly, purchases of biscuits remain steady during the same period. Why do biscuits hold their place against the trend for other farinaceous foods? The increased demand for slimming biscuits may account for something. But the increased demand for slimming bread has not changed that general trend. An explanation of change in the amount expended on a particular food is often given in terms of a change in consumer preferences. This explains very little. It merely says that changes in price and incomes do not account for the change in demand. For example: take the demand for potatoes as shown in the Report of the National Food Survey Committee. Between 1966 and 1970 potatoes as a whole showed a very slight downward trend; but potato products (quick-frozen, canned, dried) doubled. 'About four-fifths of the growth of the latter', says the Report, 'can be attributed to a change in consumer preferences, about a sixth to a decrease in their real price, and the remainder to the rise in real incomes' (p. 21, par. 43). As to cakes, the Report says that the decline in average purchases of cakes and buns, scones, teacakes and pastries is 'due mainly to a weakening in the underlying demand' (par. 53). Another suggestion, about why biscuits go against the trend, is that 'Biscuits appear to behave as expensive foods, perhaps because they are relatively costly in comparison with other cheap sources of energy' (Marr and Berry, 1974, p. 47). The implication here is the general principle that, as the country gets more prosperous, the cheaper forms of food are dropped in favour of luxuries.

Thus we have two non-explanations. The first is that a change in demand is explained by a change in consumer tastes—a tautology. The other is that a change in demand is explained by the total cost structure.

7

Since prices themselves are partly determined by demand, the explanation of demand in terms of costs in the long run is circular. A third explanation hardly worth considering in this case is that demand is manipulated by the advertisers of the big combines. If the flour millers knew how to keep up the demand for bread we perhaps would not be here today. A fourth explanation, even less serious, is that some foods are just more palatable than others: if the bakers would only make good bread, there would be no problem. To the anthropologist this makes least sense of all. It is not true that there is a universal human criterion of palatability. Tribe by tribe, nation by nation, the tastes and smells and textures that are regarded as delicious or horrible overlap and contradict each other. The rules of edibility even (a different subject from palatability) go deep into the symbolic structure of each culture. What is disgusting and dangerously toxic here is regarded as a splendid treat somewhere else. The examples I will give suggest that the general direction of anthropological criticism is negative. I hope that this will be corrected. But first it is necessary to accept a fully relativistic view of how labels of edibility and inedibility are culturally determined.

Whenever I ask English friends why fox is not eaten, I am told that it is a carnivorous animal, that its flesh would be rank and that no carnivores are edible. In Russia foxes are (or were) reckoned a delicacy; likewise dogs in China, but both are carnivorous. I have never met anyone who has eaten either, nor human flesh for that matter. Repugnances arise from deep symbolic associations to which anthropology has paid some attention from time to time. Here are three illustrations to the argument that an idea about a food being inedible is always part of a complex system of classifications. The first is the classification of living creatures to which villagers in Thailand subscribe. Basically all birds and all land animals are edible: the main exceptions are the animals in the house, dogs, cats, mice and lizards, and their wild counterparts. Avoid pets and vermin, whether tame or wild, is roughly the rule. The attitudes which are excited towards the species in daily contact is extended to its members in the wild. The article by S. J. Tambiah (1969) develops the very interesting idea that this culture is strongly structured on spatial boundaries; humans who trespass on other humans and animals which invade the habitat of other species are suspect or disapproved. So the strongest feelings of physical aversion to the very idea of contact with certain animals, to say nothing of eating them, are roused by amphibians which come on to the land, the monitor lizard, the otter.

This kind of approach to palatability undermines the value of psychological theories. Psychology tries to find the universal human characteristics. Anthropology shows that where food is concerned, culture is the governing factor. By this means we have been able to make sense of the Mosaic dietary rules. The ancient Jewish universe was divided into the three elements, water, land and air. Each had its proper kind of denizens which were edible for humans. Each also had some denizens which didn't properly fit into the classification. Living things were classed as unfit for contact, fit for the table, or fit for the altar as sacrifice. Ultimately the whole universe was divided between those living beings which came under the protection of God's covenant, and all others. So the quadruped flocks and herds of the Israelites (which observed the Sabbath day of rest and the rule of consecrating the first born) were the model of the most sacrificable and most edible kinds of meat. Wild animals related to domestic sheep, cattle and goats were also edible: but that was all. As the Thailand system projects domestic inedibility on to the wild, the Hebrew system only projected edibility from domestic to wild. I have written much about this elsewhere; also about Lele rules of edibility. The Lele are a tribe in Zaïre who are extraordinarily fastidious about what they will and won't eat. In the full analysis it turns out that every social category in their society is represented by a special dietary rule. Women never eat this animal, pregnant women can't eat that one, men have to be initiated before they can safely eat carnivorous animals. Basically all land animals were edible, as were all air creatures, including squirrels, monkeys and birds, so long as they were not predatory, burrowing, nocturnal or water-frequenting. Each set was edible for a specific set of humans. Most sickness is diagnosed as due to breach of these dietary rules. Obviously their idea of toxicity in food is based on their social categories more than on the natural properties of the food. It is as if we regarded children as mince and rice-pudding classes, adolescents as ice-cream and coke classes, women as tea and bun classes, men as meat and alcohol classes, and then attributed illness to a person's having strayed into the wrong gastronomic class.

If palatability depends on the classifying system of the whole culture, and if our culture is a mixture in this respect, it follows that we cannot do the same analysis of edible classes at home that explains palatability in the homogeneous cultures of small, isolated peoples. But there are other ways of discovering the causes of consumers' preference than by an appeal to palatability. One is to study the general system of trends in which the declining demand for bread is a part.

Bread has a declining share in total UK expenditure on food. Rice shows the same trend; so do potatoes. So there is a general trend, of which the bread case is an example, for carbohydrates to have a declining share in total expenditure on food. But this itself is part of a bigger trend. Food as a group has a declining share of total expenditure. This pattern of demand is known as the demand for necessities. As real income goes up, the proportion spent on staple foods and on the staples of existence shows a relative decline. Bread is essentially a staple, it shares the destiny of other necessities, which is to give way in face of a demand for a wide

variety of non-necessities or luxuries when the standard of living goes
up.

It is worth pausing to note how the categories of necessities and
luxuries are defined. They are purely descriptive terms which describe
the movement of demand. Therefore the terms cannot without circularity
be used to explain the shifts in demand.

'A common definition of a luxury is that it is a "good", the income
elasticity of which is greater than unity; correspondingly, for a necessity
it is less than unity. An alternative procedure . . . is to define a "good" as
a luxury if its consumption decreases with an increase in household size'
(Prais and Houthakker, 1973, p. 90). These definitions arise out of the
study of how expenditure on a particular commodity varies with the
income level of the household. An Engel curve shows how the proportion
of expenditure devoted to the commodity varies with the size of total
expenditure. For the smaller household the curve flattens much more
quickly than for the larger one. Ernest Engel, whose name is given to the
curve, over a century ago studied family budgets systematically seeking
for regularities. His findings that the proportion of expenditure devoted
to food decreases as the standard of living in the household rises is known
as Engel's law, and has practically unchallenged applicability.

Engel's law holds good for us too. The report of the National Food
Survey Committee (1973) shows that between 1966 and 1971 total food
expenditure in this country as a percentage of total consumers' expenditure
on goods and services declined steadily (Table 1, p. 5). The extra income
was being spent on a wide variety of other things, which would be cut out
if income declined. The same pattern holds within food expenditures.
With rising income, the curve for necessities flattens out and a wide variety
of other foods comes in to the diet. This appears clearly in the consumption patterns of different income groups. The National Food Survey
uses its own classification as follows: groups are designated A1, A2, B,
C, D according to the size of the income of the head of the household.
For example, in 1971 group A1 covered households with a gross income
of £69 or more weekly and 3% of households in the sample was drawn
from this top group; A2, between £66 and £45, 8% of households in the
sample; B, £45–£27 and 31·9% of households in the sample; C, £27–£14
and 35·4% of households in the sample; D, under £14 and 21·8% of the
sample.

The National Food Survey (1973) compares three of these different
income groups over the period 1955–71 (see Table I). For the top incomes,
there was a dramatic rise in expenditure in meat and fruit, and a dramatic
decline in potatoes, bread and sugar; biscuits more than held their own
with a 7% increase. For class C there was a rise in the purchase of meat
and fruit, sugar declined a little, potatoes and bread a lot, but biscuits
increased by 21%—I will refer to biscuits again later.

If we want to understand better what has happened to bread in the national diet we have to look more closely at trends in the consumption of calories. The National Food Survey Report (1973) shows that over the period 1955–71 the percentage of energy derived from eating protein has hardly changed, for any of the six income groups. But very funny things have been happening to the proportion of fats to carbohydrates.

TABLE I
OUNCES OF FOOD/WEEK PER 1000 DAILY (KCAL)

		Income groups		
		A	B	C
Cheese in oz	1955	1·11	1·06	1·07
	1962	1·31	1·20	1·13
	1971	1·67 (+50%)	1·47 (+39%)	1·33 (+24%)
Meat in oz	1955	13·73	12·99	12·69
	1962	15·38	14·30	14·16
	1971	17·09 (+24%)	15·30 (+18%)	14·86 (+17%)
Total milk and cream in pints	1955	2·24	1·95	1·82
	1962	2·28	2·05	1·89
	1971	2·31 (+3%)	2·09 (+7%)	1·94 (7%)
Total fats in oz	1955	4·61	4·50	4·46
	1962	4·64	4·57	4·50
	1971	4·50 (−2%)	4·60 (+2%)	4·55 (+2%)
Potatoes in oz	1955	20·27	23·75	23·85
	1962	18·30	20·75	21·06
	1971	14·40 (−29%)	19·67 (1−7%)	21·16 (−11%)
Bread in oz	1955	17·53	20·40	21·88
	1962	13·56	16·06	17·67
	1971	11·47 (−35%)	13·52 (−34%)	15·36 (−30%)
Biscuits in oz	1955	2·12	2·01	1·88
	1962	2·24	2·23	2·13
	1971	2·27 (+7%)	2·30 (+14%)	2·28 (+21%)
Sugar and preserves in oz	1955	8·21	8·17	8·17
	1962	8·20	8·05	8·17
	1971	6·41 (−22%)	7·09 (−13%)	7·61 (−7%)
Total fruit in oz	1955	14·56	10·79	8·91
	1962	15·67	12·00	9·49
	1971	18·46 (+27%)	13·10 (+21%)	10·61 (+19%)

For class A1 until 1964 the two lines were converging, a larger proportion of fats and a declining proportion of carbohydrates. After 1965 the two lines cross and the two trends continue. Incomes A2 are doing exactly the same thing with a lag of 5 years, 1970 is the year the lines cross. Incomes in B have not shown the convergence yet; with C and D the gap is larger still.* Marr and Berry (1974) have investigated this more closely and find that the foods we are choosing are generally expected to have a higher proportion of fat in them.

Over the 16 years 1955–71 the proportion of energy consumption contributed by fats consumed in the home increased in this nation from 36% to 42·2% while that contributed by carbohydrates declined from 51·7% to 46%.† In case there is any doubt left that we are observing very steady long term trends, as shown in Fig. 1 (Marr and Berry, 1974, p. 44) which depicts class C as just 9 years behind class A in the transfer from carbohydrates to fats.

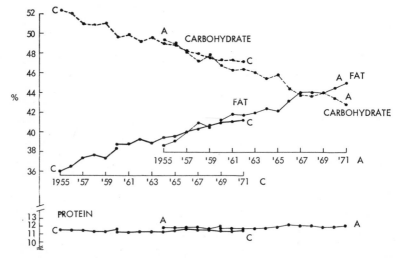

FIG. 1. Percentage energy from carbohydrate, fat and protein, income groups A and C, 1955–71. Income group C plotted with a 9-year time lag behind group A showing the same trends—a decreased percentage of energy from carbohydrate and an increase from fat.

The experience of anthropologists suggests a social reason for this movement and I do not doubt that a physiological one can be found to support it. Humans, like animals, know what they like to eat, but unlike animals, they don't know when to stop. Repletion is somehow not clearly signalled as a stop sign. Consequently the trend to eat more and more fats and oils in relation to other foods is not a healthy one and

* Figures show how the number of children in a household affect this relation in the same way as size of income.

† These figures only relate to food consumed in the home.

Marr and Berry are uncompromising in their disapproval of it. They would like us to go back to more plain bread. Therefore the straight physiology of what is good for us does not explain the switch. There may be a physiological factor in the fact that we can only take in a given amount of dry foods. If we want to take more we normally wash them down with liquids and ease them down with oils. Why should we want to eat more than is good for us? The answer is that food is only partly for nutrition and very largely for ceremonial and other social purposes. The more ceremonial the occasion, the more the tendency to lard the food, butter it and serve it with oil.

When Tikopia experienced famine for two successive bad seasons, life did not stop, but ceremonies came to a standstill, because, as they said, there couldn't be any real ceremonies without coconut butter and coconut cream (Firth, 1960). The upshot is that we need more thorough research into the social uses of food; particularly the part it plays in ceremonials. The National Food Survey stopped taking information over Christmas. If it had not done so, how much more impressive would the figures for fats and oils have been.

The anthropological approach assumes that food-taking is a social event, and like other social events it is structured by clear-cut categories. At this point it may be useful for nutritionists and others interested in diet to be introduced to some of the other assumptions which the anthropologist normally makes in analysing cultural regularities. Behaviour in respect to food is assumed to be not random. First, it is a prior assumption of cultural anthropology (and one that would lie under all sociological study) that human behaviour is patterned activity. Secondly, it is assumed that the tendency to fall into patterns is affected by economic and political concerns. Consequently, and thirdly, the patterns that are sufficiently stable to be identified in research are assumed to be adapted to an equally stable distribution of power in the social dimension. As the distribution of power changes so will the cultural patterns affected by it. When these assumptions which are almost too deep to be explicit in tribal studies are brought to the fore and applied to our own family life, they shed an unfamiliar light upon the family and its food. We assume easily enough that within given budgetary constraints and within widely agreed cultural standards of hygiene and nourishment it makes sense to speak of a family food system. That is, within these constraints, each family works out a regular pattern of food, mealtimes, children's food and drink, men's food and drink, women's, celebratory and ordinary food. To call it a food system implies that if one part varies, other linked variations can be expected. A recent piece of research which I directed for the Department of Health and Social Security was focused on the problem of finding a method for recognising acceptable and unacceptable innovations. We imagined a dietician in an unknown Papuan or African tribe wondering how to introduce a new reinforcing element into their diet. We assumed that the dietician's first task would be to discover how they structure their food, and to identify the more and the less highly structured parts of the food system. By the end of the research we had formed the hypothesis that the highly structured parts of the diet would only be receptive to improved quality in the traditional foods. Improvements in quality have to depend on native criteria. But in the less structured parts there would be scope for introducing completely new kinds of food, new tastes and smells, cheap substitutes. If the hypothesis is correct, it should make a difference to the fate of innovations in food. But it can only be tested by further research.

What is striking to the anthropologist, a newcomer to this field of inquiry, is that enormous changes have taken place in society at large in the last 50 years, a period which includes a modern world war and great technical developments in every field. One would expect food habits to have changed commensurately. But the literature of dietary inquiry and market research emphasises the very opposite. It seems to be taken as axiomatic that the British public is conservative in its food habits. The same would seem to be true of any dietary system that we care to name. Those who would promote a new food are conscious of strongly entrenched attitudes. To read the reports one gets the impression that when everything else changes, food systems are stable. However open-minded a population may, after the event, prove to have been in its readiness to adopt new crops, clothes and transport, in matters of food it is said to be likely to display a die-hard conservatism (Elliston, 1968). If this is true, then food is a part of culture which is well chosen for the study of stabilising factors. But we would question whether the alleged conservatism is not an optical illusion caused by a two-fold focus upon continuity. On the one hand, the eye of the investigator lights upon any continuity which enables him to perceive a steady pattern in the flux of material he is studying. Thus it is reassuring to find that the British traveller in 19th-century Paris was disdaining foreign cookery and calling for plain fish and potatoes (Aron, 1973, p. 59). On the other hand the housewife who is composing a meal and her family who will be sitting in gastronomic judgement upon it are themselves conscious of the need for past models to guide them as to just what it is they are supposed to be serving or receiving. Parts of the meal may in fact reflect new economies or daring experiment on her part, but usually the meal has to be recognisably a meal of a certain known kind. The variations take place within a known matrix. Within that framework there may be minor changes but everything conspires to imply that at least the frame is steady. It is impossible to start a meal in the British food system with Hungarian pink cherry soup. Pastel colours and sweet liquids and fruits are ending gambits in this system, not starters. It is unthinkable in the British food system to start with a potato, go on to another potato and end with another 'for sheer greed' like the supper of the Curé d'Ars. Variation and sequence are required but both are under the governance of some kind of restrictive patterning. To find a way of identifying that patterning was our task.

Instead of a worked-out survey asking the public about their attitudes to food and about the contents of their most recent meal, we eschewed all interpretive and other questions completely. The researcher found four families in which he was accepted as a lodger and he stayed in them for varying periods (the shortest was one month), watching every mouthful and sharing whenever possible. Finding the families and gaining admission to them was the hardest part of the research. Establishing a role of student-lodger engaged on a history of British food was surprisingly less difficult. The rule of not asking questions was taxing at first, but since every time that it was breached in the smallest way the menu showed a directly responsive change, the value of this rule was continually in our minds. Once the North London hostess was asked whether she liked frozen peas and next day they appeared on the table. One question about the relative merits of real cream and custard and next day real cream took the place of the latter. The period of stay was much longer than previously undertaken in nutritional research. We reckon that after 10 days of such a discreet and incurious presence the most nervous and sensitive housewife, busy with her children, settles down to her routine menus, making special allowance for the lodger in ways that are perfectly obvious, a cooked breakfast for instance. The second way in which this study tried to meet the problems of imported assumptions was by making our assumptions completely explicit to ourselves. Therefore what we imparted to the research is clearly visible in the structure of our attention. We knew what we were looking for. In brief, we expected to find correlations between the structure of the food and that of the social relations between people who habitually ate the food together. We were looking for regularities that might appear between social and dietary behaviour. It is possible that the smallness of sample may have allowed us to imagine regularities which would have disappeared in a welter of new facts if the research had been more extensive or prolonged. To protect ourselves against this objection, each family study was followed by a street survey to control for idiosyncrasy. Our assumptions caused us to be specially interested in the capacity of food to mark social relations and to celebrate big and small occasions. Therefore we needed as big a gamut of celebration as could be achieved. It was an integral part of our method, required by these assumptions, that the researcher be present on feast days, Sundays, Bank holidays, Christmas, weddings and christenings whenever possible.

After some experiment we finally fastened attention upon sculptural and sensory qualities of the food and compared its arrangement in the following dimensions which seemed regularly used and valued: savoury/

sweet, hot/cold, liquid/dry. Under this grosser classification, the food served on the table was able to be correlated with the kinds of regular social events which marked a meal.

The researcher, Michael Nicod, introduced and defined for his purpose certain terms: food event, structured event, snack, meal. A food event is an occasion when food is taken, without prejudice as to whether it constitutes a meal or not. A structured event is a social occasion which is organised according to rules prescribing time, place and sequence of actions. If food is taken as part of a structured event, then we have a meal. The latter is distinguished from the snack according to the following definition: A snack is an unstructured food event in which one or more self-contained food items may be served. The event is unstructured in so far as there are no rules to prescribe which items should appear together and there is no strict order of sequence when more than one item appears. Snacks may be sweet or savoury, separable from but capable of accompanying a drink. The meal by contrast has no self-contained food items and is strongly rule-bound as to permitted combinations and sequences. Together with the distinction between special and common food events, these terms constitute the tools of the analysis whereby the structuring of social relations was found to be related to the structuring of the food. Simple Venn diagrams were used to record which members of the family and which categories of visitors were present for each kind of meal.

THE STRUCTURE OF FOOD

The food system that we discovered poses problems of notation. Michael Nicod's full report (1974) describes the daily common menus and the special menus of each of the families and summarises the response to the street questionnaires. When it comes to abstracting from the full report a set of rules we are conscious of creating our own conventions and anxious not to reify what are in fact no more than practical devices.

Between the week and the weekend different kinds of meals are taken regularly at different times of the day. Ignoring the names for the meals, and concentrating only on what is served, there emerge three kinds of meals: the major hot meal, at roughly 6 p.m. on weekdays and early afternoon at weekends; the minor meal usually follows this, at 9 p.m. on weekdays and about 5 at weekends; a still less significant meal, a tertiary food event consisting of a sweet biscuit and a hot drink, is available in the system to be used at different times, say at 4 on return from the factory on weekdays, at bed-time at weekends. Breakfast does not enter into the system as a meal. If asked, our subjects said they never had breakfast, just a cup of tea, just a piece of toast, etc. But this research has so much eschewed the evidence of question and answer that it has to rest upon observations and its own definitions. Breakfast stands as a snack according to our definition of the word. The three meal system is broken by a major division between potato and cereal. The important family meal is centred upon hot potatoes and their accompaniments. This is more plentiful and more ceremonious than the other meals. The minor meal starts with bread and may go on to cake and biscuits accompanied by tea. The tertiary meal consists of biscuits and tea or coffee.

The structure of the meal system starts to emerge with criteria of ranking: A is the main meal, B the second meal and C the third meal on the criteria of complexity, copiousness and ceremoniousness. The latter is expressed by plate-changes and extra utensils, spoons, forks as well as

TABLE II

Week	12.30 p.m.	4.30 p.m.	6.30 p.m.	9.30 p.m.
	B	C	A	B
Weekend	1–2 p.m.	5–6 p.m.		9.30 p.m.
	A	B		C

knives. Inversely correlated with rank is the progressive segregation of liquids from solids as the meals become less important. On weekdays this clear ranking in order of importance does not govern the times of serving. At first sight the sequence of meals is a matter of convenience. On an ordinary weekday when the family assemble after work, they sit down to meal C at 4.30 p.m., have their main meal soon after 6 p.m. and meal B at 9 or 10 p.m. On a Sunday, however, a match between the time sequence and the rank order is to be seen. Table II shows that the pattern has to be observed at least across the week and does not appear in any weekday sequence in its full significance, still less in any single meal.

TABLE III
FIRST CORRESPONDENCE

1st	2nd	3rd	Sunday time order
A	B	C	Meal rank order

In one of the four families the father came home for his midday meal, but whether he did or not it is interesting to see that the family crams the whole of the Sunday meal system into the last part of its day, after return from work. In some parts of England it is being reported that the working

class family which enjoys a hot potato meal at the canteen is less and less
inclined to cook one again for itself in the evening. This just happened
not to be the case in our four families. The weekday meals repeat the
Sunday sequence in a modified timetable. A close correspondence
between the structure of the Sunday dinner and that of the weekday main
meal 'A' is very evident. Take the main course, which is generally called
the dinner. It always consists of a serving of potato, a 'centrepiece'
which on Sundays is always meat, 'trimmings' (which word designates
one or two green vegetables) and a sousing in rich brown thickened gravy
(here called 'liquid dressing'). The difference between this course in a
special meal (say Sunday or Christmas Day) compared with a common
meal (say a weekday evening) is that the number of trimmings are increased. So the rules of combination are the same: one staple, one centrepiece, one liquid dressing, one trimming in all cases; the special meal
may have more than one dressing and more than one trimming. Archi-
tecturally speaking it is as if the difference between the doorway of a
humble home and that of a grand mansion when it consists always of two
uprights and a cross-beam is entirely in the decoration on the main
structure. The first course is the main course and it is always hot and
savoury. The rules of sequence require this. When the second course is
examined we find a repetition of the rules of combination for course one,
except that everything is sweet (Table IV). There is more freedom to

TABLE IV

MEAL A. SECOND CORRESPONDENCE
(COURSE TWO REPEATS STRUCTURE OF
COURSE ONE IN DIFFERENT MATERIALS)

	Mode	Structure	Elements
Course 1	Hot	Staple	Potato
	Savoury	Centre	Meat, fish, egg
		Trimming	Green vegetable, stuffing
			Yorkshire pudding
		Dressing	Thick brown gravy
Course 2	Hot or cold	Staple	Cereal
	Sweet	Centre	Fruit
		Dressing	Liquid custard or cream

serve one element and omit another from the three prototypes of Christmas
pudding, trifle and fruit tart. The puddings vary freely upon the theme of
cereal, fruit and cream: on the one hand the fruit may be diminished to
a thin layer of jam or a streak of colour in the jelly of a trifle which consists mostly of juice-soaked cake and custard, and it may disappear

completely in a rice pudding; on the other hand the fruit may dominate over everything else as in the fruit pie, or the cereal may be omitted as in tinned fruit and custard. Whether the cereal be omitted on a weekday second course or not, the Christmas Day pattern is staple, centre (fruit) and two dressings (brandy and cream), and in the case of a common meal the most simplified formula is centrepiece and dressing. The liquid dressing, the custard or cream, is poured over the plate in the same way as the liquid dressing, gravy, is used in the first course. When this course is nearly finished preparations are made for the third part of the meal, the hot drink and biscuits. Hitherto only cold water has been drunk with the food. The variations of liquid and solid are carried out upon the plate of food. Now, in the third course, a total segregation of liquids from solids appears: in the cup is the hot brown drink, on the plate the cold dry solid, a reversal of the hot–cold pattern of the first course, when the cold drink is in the glass and the hot food upon the plate.

TABLE V
MEAL A. THIRD SET OF CORRESPONDENCES SHOWS OVERALL PATTERN

1	*2*	*3*
Savoury	Sweet	Sweet
Potato staple	Cereal staple	Cereal staple
No discretion to omit elements	Some discretion	Solid optional
Liquid dressing runny	Liquid dressing thick	Dressing solid
Other sensory qualities of food dominate over visual pattern	Visual pattern dominates until serving	Visual pattern dominates until eating
Solids not segregated from liquids		Solids and liquids segregated

The rules for structuring course one are absolutely strict. There is no possibility of recognising the event as a meal in the system unless its first course is constituted on these rules. Some elements can be duplicated, but none omitted. It is impossible to start with something sweet, say grapefruit. There is more scope for fantasy in the composition of course two. It is possible to serve a sweet cake with custard, doing homely week-day service for the trifle, or to serve a tin of fruit in its syrup, with cream, in the one case leaving out the fruit, in the other leaving out the cereal.

This scope for fantasy in the pudding course allows a formal pattern to be imposed upon the elements before they are served on to individual plates, an option which is not necessarily taken up on weekdays. Another difference is that the second course is served from the table whereas the first course is always served straight from cooking vessels on to plates. Pattern making is not at all required or even appropriate for the first course. A third difference is that the liquid dressing of the second course is thicker than for the first. We find that these three differences between course one and course two themselves become reinforced in course three so that their effect is of themes which extend over all the courses (Table V).

It is no surprise to the native Englishman that the distinction between hot and cold is much valued in this dietary system. For the third course the teapot is heated before the water is poured in, actually on the boil, the plates for the first course are kept stacked on the rack above the cooker so that they are carried to the table warm. Apart from the bottled sauces no addition of cold foods to a hot plate is permitted, nor vice versa.

TABLE VI
FOURTH CORRESPONDENCE. MEAL B REPEATS A IN COURSE SEQUENCE, BUT KEEPS TO THE STAPLE OF COURSE TWO

Meal B	Course 1	Savoury, hot or cold	Staple: bread
			Centre: meat, fish or
			    egg or baked
			    beans
			Trimmings: optional

	Course 2	Sweet, cold	Staple: bread Centre: jam Trimming: butter
	Course 3	Hot sweet drink	Optional cake for Sundays or biscuits

Looking again at Table VI we can see that the three courses of the main meal, in their due sequence and rules of combination, present the same structure as do the three meals of Sunday. This becomes clearer when we consider the rules governing meal B (Table VI).

The rules which govern the main meal acquire more significance when we find them governing the second meal and even more when certain of them carry through systematically over the two meals. The regularity of the pattern is so strong that it can be made to bear some weight of explanation. For example, before seeing the structure laid out, one could have asked reasonably why they never serve potatoes in meal B. The answer now would be that potatoes are the staple for meal A, course one. That part of the pattern would lose its distinctiveness and the pattern would lose its shape if potatoes were served in course two or meal two (Table VII).

TABLE VII
FIFTH CORRESPONDENCE. RULES CONTROLLING RELATION OF MEAL A AND MEAL B

Between meal A and meal B through courses 1, 2, 3, the following rules hold:
  (a) increasing segregation of liquids
  (b) increasing dominance of visual pattern
  (c) decreasing scale of quantity
  (d) non-reversibility: (i) of staple order
                          (ii) of savoury/sweet order
                          (iii) of desiccation order
                          (iv) of scale order

On to the three courses of the main meal are mapped the sequence, ranking and rules of the three meals of Sunday. First the potato meal, second the main cereal meal, third the last cereal, sweet and dry. Scanning the diagrams in the report we see that the last course of the first two meals and the only solid of the third meal is exactly the same item except that it is progressively drier. The lavish liquid dressing of sweet custard has been poured over a cake, whether plum cake or jam sponge and dried in the form of icing sugar. The option to select any of the possible ingredients of a second course in the main meal is given even more latitude in the minor meal, but working through the menus, week by week and month by month the prototype puddings and custard in the second course of the main meal are recognisable in the minor meal in their dry forms as plum cake and jam sponge cake. When it comes to the final course of the main meal or the last meal on Sunday night, the range of sweet biscuits reveals the pudding again, in its most desiccated forms: currant biscuits, sugar-coated biscuits, jam-centred biscuits. Nowhere else in the world is there a steady demand for small geometrically shaped sweet biscuits with a layer of jam or cream in the middle and coated with icing, at a sufficiently modest price to permit them a regular place in the daily menu. In so far as the sweet biscuit eaten last thing at night on Sunday is a dry version of the cake, and the cake a dry version of the pudding, we can regard it not merely as a coda nor as an irrelevant conclusion, but as a summary form, literally, of those courses. The biscuit is capable of standing for all the sequences of puddings through the year and of wedding cakes and christening cakes through the life cycle (Table VIII). Our analysis is beginning to reveal in the dietary system, with undeniable economy of means, the mimetic and rhythmic qualities of other symbolic systems. The capacity to recall the whole by the structure of the parts is a well-known technique in music and poetry for arousing attention and sustaining interest.

TABLE VIII
THE BISCUIT AS A CONDENSED SYMBOL

Course 3	Meal A	Meal B	Meal C
	Pudding ——————→ cake ——————→ biscuit		
			↘ wedding cake

The same recurring theme is visible in the sequence from thick gravy to thicker custard to solid icing sugar. One of the structural rules of this food system is progressive desiccation and geometrification of forms through the day. The first course of the main meal is presented in what appears to the uninitiated as a slushy indistinguishable mixture in which it is difficult to distinguish the trimmings and solid dressings from the meat and potatoes under their lavish coat of rich brown gravy. The second course, though still wet and viscous, has an undeniable sculptural form, whether it be the sphere of the Christmas pudding, or the trifle decorated with fruit.

TABLE IX
COURSE THREE UNDER TRANSFORMATION

	Course 1	Course 2	Course 3
Meal A	wet	wet	dry
Meal B	less wet	less wet	dry
Meal C			dry

We can summarise the rules transforming the elements of the sweet part of any meal, through the sequence of meals as in Table IX.

This progressive desiccation allows of the shift from forks and spoons to fingers.

The movement from wet food to dry food through the day involves a shift in utensils; fingers can take up dry food, but forks and spoons lift wet food to the mouth. The axis between wet and dry, used in this way allows of a correspondence between intimacy and distance, thus linking this aspect of the food system to a dimension of the social system.

The implications of this research are more than meets the eye. For one, it uncovers a basic English system that underlies regional variations. It will be possible to depart from this basis to a study of Glasgow food and predict why it is equally difficult to insert new fruit and vegetables into that diet. In our examples, fresh fruit had no place in the system whatever, unless it could be smothered in cream and so become like a trifle. For a middle class dietician to appear on television and tell the great British public that its mothers can cope with rising prices by simply serving an ungarnished apple instead of pudding is very insensitive. To serve stew instead of Sunday joint or Christmas bird is likewise unreal. To change our food habits we must understand them much better.

One piece of understanding that we can offer to a symposium on bread concerns the steady rise in importance of the biscuit. Miss Marr suggests that the biscuit has kept its place better than bread because it is a luxury food, expensive and so free of the fate of necessities. But cake is a luxury in the same sense, and even more expensive, yet cake has succumbed to the trend. Are biscuits expensive? Certainly there are a vast quantity of very cheap biscuits. I shall be much obliged to anyone who can guide me through the literature comparing quality and prices of biscuits in England, France and Germany. My superficial impression is that the British biscuit is relatively cheap. Its behaviour as a technical luxury (i.e. as a 'good' with a high income elasticity) is due to the fact that in a non-technical sense it is a special kind of necessity. In the sense that brandy is necessary to round off the sequence of wines in a good French meal, so the biscuit is the necessary conclusion to the sequence of cereals in the food system I have described. As the hat to the coat, as the rhyme-end to a line of verse, the biscuit is a summing and completion. It is also the nearest thing to a stop signal saying that eating must come to an end.

REFERENCES

Aron, J-P. (1973). *Le mangeur du Dix-neuvième siecle.*

Aylward, F. (1970). *Chemistry and Industry in the 1990s*, Society of the Chemical Industry, London, 75.

Douglas, M. (1966). *Purity and Danger*, Penguin, London.

Douglas, M. (1972a). 'Self-evidence, the Henry Myers Lecture 1972', *Proc. Roy. Anthropol. Inst.*, 27–43.

Douglas, M. (1972b). 'Deciphering a meal', *Daedalus, J. Amer. Acad. Arts Sci.*, Myth, Symbol and Culture, Winter 1972.

Elliston, Allen D. (1968). *British Tastes*, Hutchinson, London.

Firth, R. (1960). *Social Change in Tikopia*, Allen and Unwin, London.

National Food Survey Committee (1973). 'Household Food Consumption and Expenditure', 1970 and 1971, HMSO, London.

Marr, Jean W. (1973). 'Some trends in food consumption in Great Britain 1955–1971', *Health Trends*, **5**, 37–39.

Marr, Jean W. and Berry, W. T. C. (1974). 'Income, secular change and family food consumption levels: a review of the National Food Survey 1955–1971', *Nutrition*, **XXVIII** (1), 39–52.

Nicod, M. (1974). 'A Method of Eliciting the Social Meaning of Food', Report to Department of Health and Social Security. Unpublished M.Phil. Thesis, London.

Prais, S. J. and Houthakker, H. S. (1971). *The Analysis of Family Budgets*, OUP.

Tambiah, S. J. (1969). 'Animals are good to think and to prohibit', *Ethnology*, **VIII** (4), 425–459.

DISCUSSION

Chairman: Thank you very much, Professor Douglas. I thought it would be fascinating having an anthropologist talking about bread, and it has proved so. I have enjoyed it very much and I am sure everyone else has. In opening the discussion I think we should start by trying to answer the two questions Professor Douglas posed early in her talk. First, what are the physiological reasons, or what is known about these, for taste? Secondly, why do human beings overeat and why do we not have a stop signal as do other animals? Who will deal with the first? Professor Yudkin?

J. Yudkin (Emeritus Professor of Nutrition, University of London): I can try the second question, but not the first because I don't think we know anything really very much about taste. When we start discussing taste in human beings, we have to explain why different animal species eat very different sorts of food, presumably because to them these foods taste well. We are nowhere near knowing the answers.

As for the reasons why we overeat, I think the answer is largely that we are now able to make more and more palatable foods and we are able to make foods more and more palatable. In non-food production species—all species other than man, and man himself before he went into the business of agriculture and food production—palatability is a guide to the selection and to the sorts of food as well as being an adequate stimulus for eating or for stopping eating. Now that we have a whole series of new foods we eat because they are palatable even though our needs are satisfied. I think that is the answer. May I now speak more generally?

I want to say how important it is that nutritionists should realise that their nutrition is not complete until they have some sort of communication with people, like Professor Douglas, in anthropology and other social sciences. It is a tremendous failing of nutritionists to tend to work on their own and think in terms of biochemistry and physiology and not enough in terms of social sciences. But I hope also that Professor Douglas will begin to work more closely with conventional nutritionists. I think that what she has been talking about is the reason why people eat food, and she touched on palatability, economics and convenience, and she dwelt, of course, mostly on cultural food determinants. The nutritionist is concerned with what happens when people eat food, the benefits they derive, and increasingly nowadays, we are also more and more concerned with the disbenefits, why we eat too much and why we get coronary thrombosis and so on. But we need to know why the reasons for eating foods, and the choice of particular foods and of structured meals, provide benefit and adequate nutrition.

K. Blaxter (Rowett Research Institute, Aberdeen): May I ask Professor Douglas why there has been a decline in the consumption of bread, and also why throughout the ages there has been this aspiration towards whiter bread? Is there not some component missing from the story regarding the movement from social class to social class, and is aspiration to eat a different diet, that in the upper social class, responsible? One should also ask why the upper social classes adopted the use of highly refined flours in their bread and why their consumption of bread grains declined.

M. Douglas: I thought I had answered the question why the proportion of bread is declining, as bread has shared the fate of all staples with rising income. Thus with rising income over time in a given community, people have more scope for spending, which becomes more diversified and the necessities take a fixed smaller part. I should like to have dealt with the other point—the question of white bread and refinement of presentation—and I am very tempted to see a trend in bread consumption, though I haven't the evidence for it. The reason I do not have the evidence is that the trend I want to see is a universal one, and the answer would be equally so. If one assumes that a meal, except breakfast, would be a celebration, or part of a social celebration or ceremony, then I should like to see if I can detect a tendency to more complex, intricate and lengthy processing towards the ceremonial end of the scale. So the trend I should like to discuss would be one towards greater differentiation of foods, so that the move to white bread would only be part of a general possibility of celebrating in ways which would always include more processing at the more ceremonial end. The top end of the social distribution is the end which sets the tone for the movement towards greater processing; incomes are higher, there is more money to spend on food and more entertaining and official representation.

F. Fidanza (Institute of Nutrition and Food Science, Perugia): I am very interested in this paper and have several points to raise. How do you obviate the decrease in physical activity in some communities leading to a decrease in the consumption of cereals and in bread and pasta, which is similarly affected by the fashion for slimming? I suppose you have been applying your system model to a non-nutritionally educated population group: what will happen if you use a nutritionally educated community? Presumably it would be different, while I expect your meal ceremony thesis can only be applied to your country. We are doing some quite active work in Italy on nutrition education and have conducted a survey including a psychological and sociological approach. It is necessary to know the food motivation.

M. Douglas: Please don't emphasise the psychological part of nutritional education, as psychology aims to tell you things we all have in common, doesn't it? I am saying that taste in food and palatability is socially determined. These discriminations are provided by the characteristics of your social situation and these must be understood. I think your thoughts on the effect of nutritional education are very interesting as this can obviously lead to new trends. I don't really know what to say about slimming, but I think it follows from the aesthetics of food and the aesthetics of the human body, which don't necessarily coincide. I have thought about the matter of cereals with fats and the amount of physical activity. Perhaps we can talk about it afterwards: you know that people can exhibit very extensive physical energy without any cereal intake. You know that the Eskimos never eat any cereals and they are very active. I thought that the fact that we were just taking our energy out of our diet in a greater proportion of fat than carbohydrate was part of the answer to your question.

R. A. McCance (Cambridge, UK): I am sorry to say I have rather a naughty mind and I wanted to ask two questions and make a comment on what you said. I enjoyed the paper very much indeed, that is beside the point, but in the first place you have told us a lot about biscuits and you have several times said 'Breakfast is not a meal'. I am sorry to say to nutritionists it is a meal, so we have perhaps to think of things a little differently. The second point is this: you did talk a great deal about biscuits and about staples, but could I ask the anthropologist what she has to say about cheese?

M. Douglas: I think the point about breakfast is fair comment. We are very vulnerable in this bit of research to questions of that kind because of the very small sample. One cannot call it a sample as it was a pilot survey, and I should like to obtain the funds for a proper national survey with this kind of approach in mind to test some of these ideas. There are so many things to deal with. I don't really feel I should apologise for the fact that our people didn't eat much breakfast. If they had eaten a lot or very little but in a regular form we should have had to include it by our own rules on which we set up our survey. I left out the cheese because where it comes into our system is in meal B which shifts from a potato staple to a cereal staple in the weekday or Sunday tea. It came in with the bread in the second meal of the system, with butter, and it took the place of meat or eggs, which would have been the corresponding position in the hot-potato-wet part of the system. I had to cut it out for the sake of brevity.

Chairman: Ladies and gentlemen: I think we must stop here. Once more I think we must thank Professor Douglas for her excellent talk and also for the delightful and informative way in which she has dealt with the questions. This has insured a valuable and interesting discussion.

Origins of Wheat

RALPH RILEY

Plant Breeding Institute, Cambridge, UK

We are assembled at this symposium as technicians who are in one way or another involved in improving the use of wheat either by farmers, by industrial processors—millers or bakers—or by the 1000 million or so people of the world for whom wheat is a staple of the diet. In attempting to assess the contemporary status of the wheat crop and to contemplate its future, we need guidance from the past. We need to know the course of the evolution of the crop itself and of the systems in which it was employed by man. From my personal viewpoint, as a plant breeder/geneticist, I need to know as much as possible of the genetic structure of the species and this becomes much more comprehensible from an understanding of the sequence by which the structure evolved.

But this may be too narrow and specialist a view of the crop. For there were more profound consequences of its adoption, along with a few other cereal species, as the principal support for human societies. Societies built on grain-production farming differed from those which relied on the cultivation of vegetatively propagated crops, such as roots, or on pastoral systems, in that forward planning and the timeliness of farming operations became paramount. As a result measurements of space and time were required—so the grain farmers sowed the seeds that ultimately grew into the 'measuring' societies with science-based technologies in which we live today. These effects of grain cultivation on the development of reasoning societies do not, of course, apply only to wheat, but also to the associated crops of the Near East—barley and pulses—and in addition to maize in the Western Hemisphere and to rice in the East. However, it is with wheat that I am concerned today, so I will leave the broader issues and turn specifically to this crop.

SPECIES AND SUBSPECIES OF WHEAT

Bread wheat—scientifically *Triticum aestivum* ssp. *vulgare*—is the most widely cultivated form of the crop currently. *T. aestivum* is a hexaploid with 42 chromosomes and is part of a polyploid series in which there are 14-chromosome diploids and 28-chromosome tetraploids. I will go on to discuss the diversity of forms in this polyploid series.

27

The *diploids* are the most primitive wheats with the most limited range in morphology and physiology. There are two well-established species, *T. boeoticum* and *T. monococcum*, which are often called 'einkorn'. The former is wild growing in natural habitats in western Asia Minor and from southern Turkey across Iraq to western Iran. Elsewhere in the Near East it grows as a weed in arable fields and in disturbed habitats. *T. monococcum* is the cultivated form now little used in agriculture. The difference between *T. boeoticum* and *T. monococcum* lies principally in that the former is adapted to the free dispersal of its seeds because of the brittleness of the rachis of the ear which causes the spikelets to separate. The separated spikelets become inserted into the ground because of the toughness of the point of the rachis segment that remains attached to the spikelet (Zohary, 1969). By contrast *T. monococcum* has a tough rachis and no seed dispersal mechanism and so is adapted only to agricultural harvesting.

At the *tetraploid* level there is wide morphological and genetic diversity in two species, *T. turgidum* and *T. timopheevi*. Both species contain wild and cultivated forms. The wild form in *T. turgidum* is designated subspecies (ssp.) *dicoccoides*. While in *T. timopheevi* it is designated ssp. *araraticum*. The wild forms, like *T. boeoticum*, have brittle rachises and are adapted to native habitats, but they are larger and more robust plants, generally with two or more grains per spikelet. Ssp. *araraticum* is found in natural habitats in southern Turkey and presumably in adjacent areas of Iraq (Zohary, 1969) whereas ssp. *dicoccoides* is found in the same region and also in northern Israel, southern Syria and Lebanon. Ssp. *dicoccoides* and *dicoccum* are often called 'emmers'.

The cultivated tetraploids most closely related to the wild-growing forms are *T. turgidum* ssp. *dicoccum* and *T. timopheevi* ssp. *timopheevi*, which is grown in a single area of the Republic of Georgia. All the forms I have mentioned thus far have grains closely invested by the palea and lemma and do not thresh freely. By contrast the remaining forms of cultivated tetraploid wheat are free-threshing and include such types as ssp. *durum* (the macaroni wheat), ssp. *turgidum* (Rivet wheat), ssp. *polonicum*, ssp. *carthlicum* and ssp. *orientale*. Some of these were widely cultivated in the past and of course ssp. *durum* is still important in regions with mild winters and hot dry summers, being valued for the production of pasta semolinas.

There are two species at the *hexaploid* level, namely *T. aestivum* and *T. zhukovskyi*. Hexaploids are all cultivated and it is unlikely that any has ever existed as a wild-growing or weedy form. *T. aestivum* ssp. *vulgare* is the bread wheat of commerce and compared with this all the other subspecies are of relatively trivial significance. Ssp. *vulgare* has, of course, a tough rachis and free-threshing grain. The only other subspecies with these characters are ssp. *compactum*—the club wheat cultivated in

India and in North America for its pastry flours—and ssp. *sphaerococcum* —the little club wheat of India. The remaining hexaploids, ssp. *spelta*, *macha* and *vavilovii*, have invested grain and in some forms considerable rachis brittleness. Ssp. *spelta* is still cultivated in southern Iran and in restricted areas in the Ardennes and in Switzerland, where it is used as a fodder grain. *T. zhukovskyi* has close affinities with the tetraploid *T. timopheevi* and may well have originated from it quite recently following hybridisation with *T. monococcum*.

These diploid, tetraploid and hexaploid forms of *Triticum* are close relatives of the genera *Secale* (rye), *Aegilops* (goat grass), *Agropyron* (wheat grass) and *Haynaldia*. Some authorities believe that the appropriate taxonomic treatment would be to lump the genera *Triticum* and *Aegilops* in order to comply with the rules of nomenclature. The general arguments for and against such taxonomic modifications are well stated by Morris and Sears (1967). My own view is more pragmatic—in that I prefer to continue to use the two names, since they exist for the convenience of the users and to ensure clear communication there is no benefit to be gained by the change. (Incidentally I notice that in the Proceedings of the 4th International Wheat Genetics Symposium (1973), of the papers in which it is mentioned the name *'Aegilops'* is used in twenty-five and *'Triticum'* in seven, so at this point in time I am with the majority.)

THE GENOMES

The relationships between species at different ploidy levels in *Triticum* was revealed by classical genome analytical methods (for refs *see* Riley, 1965). For this purpose the genome is defined as the haploid set of chromosomes of distinctive diploid species or gained at each advance in the level of ploidy. In wheat a genome contains 7 chromosomes. The relationships can be set out as follows where a genome is indicated by a capital letter:

Diploid	*T. monococcum*	$(2n = 14)$	AA
Tetraploid	*T. turgidum*	$(2n = 4x = 28)$	AABB
Hexaploid	*T. aestivum*	$(2n = 6x = 42)$	AABBDD

From this it will be seen that *T. turgidum* contains the full set of chromosomes of *T. monococcum*, and *T. aestivum* the full set of *T. turgidum* (and therefore the full set of *T. monococcum*). These relationships are revealed because at meiosis in the 21-chromosome hybrid between *T. monococcum* and *T. turgidum* 14 chromosomes pair to form 7 bivalents while 7 remain as unpaired univalents. Knowledge of the meiotic behaviour of the chromosomes of *T. turgidum* in other situations shows that the 7 bivalents are formed between 7 chromosomes of *T. turgidum* and 7 of *T. monococcum*, so indicating close homology. Analogous evidence reveals the presence of the A and B genomes in *T. aestivum*.

By genome analysis (Riley and Chapman, 1960) and by the production of synthetic *T. aestivum* ssp. *spelta* (McFadden and Sears, 1946) and synthetic *T. aestivum* ssp. *vulgare* (Kerber, 1964 and Kerber and Dyck, 1969), the D genome of *T. aestivum* has been shown to be derived from the 14-chromosome diploid species *Aegilops squarrosa*. The strength of the evidence that *Ae. squarrosa* is the donor of the D genome now seems unassailable. I will turn later to a consideration of the circumstances in which *Ae. squarrosa* could have hybridised with *T. turgidum* and of the form of *T. aestivum* that might have originated following chromosome doubling in the sterile 21-chromosome hybrid.

Much more uncertainty surrounds the source of the B genome that was associated with the A genome in the origin of *T. turgidum*. The debates have been prolonged, commencing when McFadden and Sears (1946) proposed that the B genome might have been contributed by *Agropyron triticeum* (= *Eremopyron triticeum*). Subsequently, on the grounds of gross plant morphology (Sarkar and Stebbins, 1956), and of chromosome structure (Riley *et al.*, 1958), it was suggested that the likely donor was *Ae. speltoides*. However, Sears (1956a) had opposed this view, on morphological grounds, suggesting instead *Ae. bicornis*. More recently the debate has been revived (Kimber and Athwal, 1973; Kimber, 1973) because of evidence from meiotic chromosome pairing which has been interpreted to imply that the affinity between the chromosomes of *T. aestivum* and *Ae. speltoides* is inadequate for the latter to be the source of the B genome. My conclusion is that the question is still open and that we must await detailed exploration of diploid relatives of wheat and the use of new techniques before a more conclusive position is attained. Irrespective of its precise source (and it must be recognised that the exact donor may no longer be extant) it seems clear that the B genome was contributed by one, or a combination, of the species closely related genetically to *T. monococcum* and *Ae. squarrosa*.

GENETIC STRUCTURE

Because of the combination in *T. aestivum* of the full chromosome complements of three species that were closely related genetically many genetic activities in the hexaploid wheat are triplicated. The general evidence of this was first established by Sears (1954, 1956b, 1966) who showed that the full set of 21 homologous pairs of chromosomes could be classified in three classes, each of 7 pairs, representing the genomes derived from different diploid parents. It could also be classified into 7 so-called homoeologous groups, each of 3 pairs (Table I). Homoeologous chromosomes are genetically corresponding chromosomes of different genomes. While the absence of any single pair causes gross abnormalities of physiology and development, when 1 pair is absent but a homoeologue is in excess dosage—being present four times instead of twice—there are few developmental anomalies. So increased dosage of one homoeologue can compensate genetically the absence of another homoeologous chromosome. It is assumed that homoeologous chromosomes were derived in evolution from the same chromosome of the prototype diploid species from which the three progenitor species of *T. aestivum* evolved.

TABLE I

CLASSIFICATION OF THE CHROMOSOME PAIRS OF *T. aestivum*
SSP. *vulgare* INTO GENOMES AND HOMOEOLOGOUS GROUPS

Homoeologous groups	Genomes A	B	D
1	1A	1B	1D
2	2A	2B	2D
3	3A	3B	3D
4	4A	4B	4D
5	5A	5B	5D
6	6A	6B	6D
7	7A	7B	7D

This duplication or triplication of genetic activities buffers hexaploid wheat against many genetic irregularities. Moreover, since a gene, controlling a particular activity, can be present at each of 3 homoeologous loci and since at each locus allelic variation can occur (and possibly there may not be allelic identity at homoeologous loci), a wide range of genetic conditions is possible. So, by natural evolution and by the breeders' intervention, the genotype can be finely tuned to adjust the plant to specific needs. An example of the triplication of genetic activities is seen in the loci *R1*, *R2* and *R3*, which determine red grain colour and are located on the homoeologous chromosomes 3D, 3A and 3B respectively (Metzger and Silbaugh, 1970; Kimber, 1971). A white grained variety, like Holdfast, has the genotype *r1 r1 r2 r2 r3 r3* while varieties, with the fullest red colour like Koga II or Thatcher have the genotype *R1 R1 R2 R2 R3 R3* (McIntosh, 1973). Genotypes with only one or two dominants homozygous have intermediate levels of intensity of 'redness'.

There are thus close genetic affinities between homoeologous chromosomes yet at meiosis, in normal plants of *T. aestivum*, chromosome pairing is confined to fully homologous chromosomes and there is no pairing of homoeologues. This is revealed by the simple Mendelian disomic inheritance from wheat hybrids. The absence of homoeologous pairing is mostly attributable to the activity of a single locus, designated *Ph*, on the long arm of chromosome 5B (for refs *see* Riley, 1965; Morris and Sears, 1967; Mello-Sampayo and Canas, 1973; Riley *et al.*, 1973). In the absence of the *Ph*, allele homoeologues will synapse with each other and wheat ceases to behave like a classical bivalent-forming allopolyploid and behaves more like an autopolyploid or a segmental allopolyploid. The presence of this genetic inhibition of chromosome pairing between homoeologues has been of crucial significance in the evolution of the polyploid wheats. Regular bivalent-forming meiotic chromosome behaviour is associated with high fertility and genetic stability, which are of crucial importance in crops of which the economic product is the seed. In addition the system of meiosis found in wheat allows homoeologous chromosomes to maintain their genetic and structural integrity and so to evolve along separate channels—only being balanced relative to each other by selection in terms of interactions at the level of gene products.

ARCHAEOLOGICAL AND ECOLOGICAL EVIDENCE

I would now like to consider evidence of the origins of wheat that can be derived from archaeological research. Table II shows the discoveries that have been made of wheat species in excavations in the Near East that are dated earlier than 5000 BC. It will be seen that there is only one site, Tell Mureybat—dated 8050–7542 BC, at which *T. boeoticum* (wild einkorn) was found in the absence of *T. monococcum* (einkorn). Also there is no instance in which *T. turgidum* ssp. *dicoccoides* (wild emmer) has been discovered in the absence of *T. turgidum* ssp. *dicoccum* (emmer). Moreover only at Tell Mureybat was einkorn found in the absence of emmer—so apparently both diploid and tetraploid forms of wheat were adopted for agricultural use simultaneously. It also seems that the establishment of settled sites and the change from a 'hunter-gatherer' to an 'agricultural' economy must have been closely associated in time with the emergence of wheats with tough rachises that were better adjusted to use in farming than the wild-growing forms from which they were derived.

Of course we can only speculate at the nature of the processes by which wheat were taken into cultivation about 10 000 years ago. However, Zohary (1969) is clearly correct when he points out that when all the grain collected is used for food the stage of development is that of collecting or gathering. When part of the grain is intentionally saved for seed, and is planted, then the stage is that of farming and the plant species are being domesticated. At the gathering stage plants with tougher rachises would have a greater probability of being collected by man while those with brittle rachises would have a greater probability of contributing to the next generation. This might constitute positive selection against tough rachises. Under cultivation the tough rachis forms would also be selected as part of the intentionally saved seed so the proportion of the population with tough rachises, being favoured by selection, would increase.

Recently views about the origins of agriculture in the Near East have changed (Flannery, 1969). A major stimulus to this was the report that natural stands of wild wheats can still be found in southern Turkey, Iraq

TABLE II
DISCOVERIES OF WHEAT IN THE NEAR EAST ON THE EXCAVATION OF SITES DATED PRIOR TO 5000 BC (AFTER RENFREW, 1969)

Dates (BC)	Region	Site	Wild Einkorn	Einkorn	Wild Emmer	Emmer	Bread wheat
7 500–6 750	Iran and Iraq	Ali Kosh	×	×	—	×	—
6 750–6 000		Ali Kosh	—	—	—	×	—
5 500–5 000		Tepe Sabz (Sabz)	—	—	—	—	×
6 200–5 500		Tepe Guran	—	—	—	—	—
5 800–5 600		Tell es-Sawwan	—	×	—	×	×
8 050–7 542		Tell Mureybat	×	—	—	—	—
c. 7 000		Tell Ramad	—	×	—	×	C
c. 7 000	Palestine	Jericho, P. P. Neo.	—	×	—	×	—
c. 7 000		Beidha, P. P. Neo. B.	—	—	—	×	—
c. 6 750	Zagros	Jarmo	×	×	×	×	—
c. 5 500		Matarrah	—	—	—	×	—
c. 5 750	Syria	Amuq A.	—	—	—	×	—
c. 5 750		Mersin, E. Neo.	—	—	—	—	—
5 850–5 600	Anatolia	Catal Hüyük, VI–II	—	×	—	×	×
c. 7 000		Aceramic Hacilar	×	—	—	×	—
5 800–5 000		Ceramic Hacilar	—	×	—	×	×
c. 5 250		Can Hasan, L. Neo.	—	—	—	W	—
c. 6 100	Greece	Knossos, Stratum X	—	—	—	×	×
c. 6–5 000		Aceramic Ghediki	—	×	—	×	—
c. 6–5 000		Aceramic Sesklo	—	—	—	×	—
c. 6–5 000		Aceramic Argissa	—	×	—	×	—
c. 6–5 000		Aceramic Achilleion	—	—	—	×	—
c. 6 200		Nea Nikomedeia	—	—	—	W	—
c. 5 000	Bulgaria	Karanovo I	—	×	—	×	—
c. 5 000		Azmaska Moghila, E. Neo.	—	×	—	×	—

W = Wheat unspecified.   C = Club wheat.

and northern Palestine over many thousands of hectares (Harlan and Zohary, 1966). Subsequently Harlan (1967) showed that in 1 h, using a flint knife, he could harvest 1 kg of clean grain from these stands in which growth was very nearly as dense as in a cultivated field. This suggested that a family of experienced gatherers 'without even working very hard' could in a period of 3 weeks gather more grain than they could possibly consume in a year. Of course this implies that there would be no incentive to cultivate in those areas in which the wild progenitors of wheat were most abundant. It has been suggested that settled sites such as that at Tell Mureybat might have been based on such a gathering economy exploiting wild-growing cereals (van Loon, 1966) and might not have depended on cultivation.

This has led to the view that it was only when population pressure became excessive, in the areas with natural stands of wild cereals, that man was driven into less favourable habitats and there forced into the practice of cultivation that had been unnecessary in the areas from which he had migrated (Flannery, 1969). Early dry land farming was probably started between 8000 and 7500 BC. Subsequently, as expansion took place into even less favourable areas, irrigation became necessary; its earliest uses probably occurring between 5500 and 5000 BC.

During this time the tetraploid forms of wheat diversified but it is not clear that any free-threshing tetraploids, such as the ssp. *durum*, *turgidum* or *carthlicum* were present before 5000 BC. But curiously wheats that have been identified as bread wheat—that is *T. aestivum* ssp. *vulgare*— have been found at sites dating from 6100 BC at Knossos and between 5800 and 5000 BC in Iran and Iraq and in Anatolia.

It is very difficult to account for the origin of bread wheats from the hybridisation of *T. turgidum*, ssp. *dicoccum* and *Ae. squarrosa*, since the synthetic hexaploid derived from this hybrid most closely resembles *T. aestivum* ssp. *spelta*. But ssp. *spelta* is not found at all, even at later levels, in some locations where bread wheat has been found. Where bread wheat is found very early, and where ssp. *spelta* does occur in the archaeological record, as in central Europe, ssp. *spelta* post-dates the first occurrence of ssp. *vulgare* by about 1000 years (Renfrew, 1969).

As I pointed out earlier, *Ae. squarrosa* which combined with *T. turgidum* in the formation of *T. aestivum*, does not occur in nature much to the west of the Caspian Sea from where it extends eastwards into central Asia. *Ae. squarrosa* is also, however, an aggressive weed in arable cultivation and in this role extends from central Turkey to Afghanistan. Indeed in some samples of wheat sold as chicken feed at Chalus on the southern shore of the Caspian Sea there was one spikelet of *Ae. squarrosa* to every four grains of wheat (Kihara and Tanaka, 1958). It seems reasonable to presume that *Ae. squarrosa* must have been a weed in wheat crops before 6000 BC, when the crops concerned would have consisted of some form of *T. turgidum*. If so, hybridisation could well have taken place in conditions of cultivation—that is bread wheat might have been derived from a hybrid between the crop and its weed. This also implies that the hexaploid wheat could not have emerged until cultivation had spread to the areas in which *Ae. squarrosa* was endemic.

GENETICS versus ARCHAEOLOGY

However, to describe the equivocal nature of the evidence on the form of *T. turgidum* that gave rise to hexaploid wheat, it is necessary to discuss the genetic basis of the differences between the subspecies of *T. aestivum*. Three genetic loci are involved determining the syndrome of characters that distinguish ssp. *vulgare* from ssp. *spelta*, *compactum* and *sphaerococcum*. Ssp. *spelta* is homozygous recessive *q q* while *vulgare* is *Q Q*. Ssp. *compactum* is homozygous dominant *C C* while ssp. *vulgare* is *c c*. Ssp. *sphaerococcum* is homozygous recessive, *s1 s1* while ssp. *vulgare* is *S1 S1*. The *Q* locus is on chromosome 5A, the *C* locus on 2D and the *S1* locus on 3D. Putting together the conditions at all three loci the subspecies are genetically:

	Chromosome/locus		
	5A	2D	3D
vulgare	*Q Q*	*c c*	*S1 S1*
spelta	*q q*	*c c*	*S1 S1*
compactum	*Q Q*	*C C*	*S1 S1*
sphaerococcum	*Q Q*	*c c*	*s1 s1*

It is the *Q* locus which creates the problem in explaining the origin of *T. aestivum*, since *T. turgidum* ssp. *carthlicum* is the only tetraploid homozygous for the dominant *Q* allele which is present in *T. aestivum* ssp. *vulgare*. If, as suggested by the archaeological evidence, *ssp. vulgare* were the original hexaploid from which all other subspecies arose by mutation, then it must be presumed that it was derived from a tetraploid carrying the *Q* allele, that is like ssp. *carthlicum*. But there is no evidence of a *Q*-bearing form of *T. turgidum* existing prior to the origin of ssp. *vulgare*. Indeed it has even been suggested that the *Q* allele of ssp. *carthlicum* might have been introgressed into *T. turgidum* from *T. aestivum* (Morris and Sears, 1967).

This issue is further complicated by the suggestion of Muramatsu (1963), following dosage studies, that the *Q* allele could have been derived from *q* by a numerical repetition of the *q* segment within the locus. If this interpretation of the status of the *Q* allele is correct it means that, while it could be derived from *q*, the reciprocal charge could not occur unless preceded by the origin of *Q* by a repeat mechanism.

There are few ways by which the archaeological and cytogenetic evidence can be reconciled—the former implying that ssp. *vulgare* was the first hexaploid and the latter that it must have been ssp. *spelta*. Two possibilities exist, however. The tetraploid parent of the first hexaploid may have been a rare mutant in the *T. turgidum* population that happened to carry the *Q* allele, and ssp. *spelta* may have arisen independently from a subsequent hybridisation between a *q*-carrying form of *T. turgidum* and *Ae. squarrosa*. Alternatively some of the early archaeological finds attributed to *T. aestivum* ssp. *vulgare* might have been from a tetraploid form corresponding to ssp. *carthlicum*, which gave rise to *T. aestivum* ssp. *vulgare* but which has left no extant derivations at the tetraploid level. It must be confessed that neither of these suggestions is very plausible but the reconciliation of the evidence forces strained explanations.

In addition it must be admitted that the origin of *T. aestivum* spp. *vulgare* and ssp. *spelta* by separate hybridisation events appears less likely because, although interchanges of segments between genetically unrelated chromosomes have occurred quite often in wheat, some forms of ssp. *vulgare* and ssp. *spelta* have chromosome complements with identical structures (Riley *et al.*, 1967). This is not entirely incompatible with the idea of their polyphyletic origin but makes it slightly less probable. Finally in support of the notion that ssp. *spelta* was derived from ssp. *vulgare* are the observations that so-called 'speltoid' forms arise in ssp. *vulgare* by mutation (and without the loss of chromosome 5A which can give a similar phenotype). By contrast I know of no example of a form resembling ssp. *vulgare* arising from ssp. *spelta* by mutation.

ADAPTATION AND THE D GENOME

Zohary (1969) has emphasised the morphological diversity of *Ae. squarrosa* and the extraordinarily wide range of habitats to which it has developed adaptation. In its natural distributional centre in northern Iran, Turkey, Syria and over into Soviet central Asia and Afghanistan, it is adapted to conditions ranging from dry steppes to desert margins and to the temperate and wet forests on the southern coast of the Caspian Sea. While the tetraploid emmers are adapted to the mild wet winters and hot dry summers of the Mediterranean margins, *Ae. squarrosa* is adjusted to the severe conditions of the steppes of middle Asia. Moreover as an aggressive and successful weed in cereal crops and as an occupant of disturbed habitats it extends well beyond the region of its natural distribution.

The consequence for wheat of the acquisition of the D genome from *Ae. squarrosa* was a great extension of the range of climates in which the crop could be cultivated. Whereas tetraploid forms of wheat are adapted to the Mediterranean-type climates referred to earlier, the addition of the genes of *Ae. squarrosa* apparently resulted in hexaploid wheat being capable of adaptation to extreme mid-continental conditions as well as to the cool, damp and temperate, oceanic conditions of north-west Europe. Moreover, because of the weedy potentialities of *Ae. squarrosa* it may be presumed that hexaploid wheat was well adapted to agriculture from the outset.

GENETICS AND WHEAT TECHNOLOGY

I have referred earlier to the triplication, on all the chromosomes of homoeologous group 3, of the genetic loci with alleles causing red or white coloration of the grain. Such effects of the hexaploid status of bread wheat are of course of considerable importance to milling and baking technology. In the case of the red alleles (*R1, R2* and *R3*) their importance lies in the association of resistance to sprouting with red coloration of the grain—this being the reason why all varieties grown in Britain since Holdfast (introduced 1935) have had red grain. Other technologically important characters are similarly controlled by loci that are apparently homoeologous. For example Nishikawa and Nobuhara (1971) discovered that twelve major brands representing isoenzymes of α-amylase could be displayed by isoelectric focusing of extracts of germinated seeds of the variety Chinese Spring. Specific brands were eliminated in the absence of one arm of each of the chromosomes of homoeologous group 6 and of homoeologous group 7. Thus six genes determining variants of the α-amylase molecule were recognised as follows:

	Genome		
	A	B	D
Homoeologous group 6	*Amy-6A*	*Amy-6B*	*Amy-6D*
Homoeologous group 7	*Amy-7A*	*Amy-7B*	*Amy-7D*

Removal of chromosome arms did not affect any of the other six of the twelve bands. This means either that the isoenzymes concerned are coded for by genes on chromosome arms for which no deletion stock was available or that they are determined by genes that are precisely duplicated on different (possibly homoeologous) chromosomes. In addition, of course, some bands may represent dimers or polymers formed between the products of different structural genes.

However, from this example it will be realised that the *Amy-6* group of loci and the *Amy-7* group of loci, were probably derived from two loci of the prototype diploid which gave rise to the three diploid species that combined in the formation of hexaploid wheat. The α-amylase enzyme system is of great importance to millers and bakers in Britain but its inheritance and genetic determination are of considerable complexity.

The lesson that the breeder learns from this is that there can be little benefit in attempting to modify structural genes with the aim of reducing the adverse effects of the enzyme in grain technology. Alternatively benefit could be obtained by genetic modification of the regulator genes—possibly related to genes responsible for gibberellic acid production—which de-repress the structural genes at the initiation of germination.

This example of studies on an enzyme shows how knowledge of the genetic structure and evolution of the crop provides guidance to the breeder and technologist. In a further example from work in biochemical genetics my colleague Dr R. B. Flavell is beginning to provide important information for breeders. The work is based on DNA–RNA molecular hybridisation and is aimed at determining the numbers of genes coding from ribosomal RNA (rRNA) in different genotypes of *T. aestivum* ssp. *vulgare*. Such fundamental studies are of great practical significance since ribosomes are responsible for protein production and while the evidence is not yet to hand it is a reasonable speculation that the availability of ribosome may constitute a limit to protein production. Chromosomes 1A, 1B, 5D and 6B carry nucleolar organisers and the associated genes that code for rRNA production. Such genes were thus—as would be expected—introduced from every diploid parent but they are present in three homoeologous groups. Wheat varieties have different numbers of rRNA genes and indeed among the genotypes studied the widest difference was between ssp. *spelta* and ssp. *vulgare* cv. Holdfast; the content of the former being 2·2 × higher. Homologous nucleolar organising loci also differ in the number of genes they carry—chromosome 1A contributing more genes for example to ssp. *spelta* than it does to the variety Chinese Spring (Flavell and Smith, 1974).

It would appear that, since the origin of polyploid wheat, the numbers of ribosomal genes at the nucleolar organising loci have diverged in different lines of descent. In speculating about this I would suppose that the total number of rRNA genes in the original hexaploid wheat was in excess of the requirement for ribosomal production and that this genetic redundancy—unsupported by selection—allowed drift to occur in the number of genes. If, however, we discover that a higher number of rRNA genes provides economic advantage in protein production then the capabilities exist for the construction of more favourable genotypes.

T. aestivum ssp. *vulgare* is designated 'bread' wheat to indicate that it uniquely has the property, on milling, of producing flour which can be baked into a raised loaf. No doubt we shall hear more about the visco-elastic nature of dough that confers this characteristic elsewhere in this symposium. For my purpose it is sufficient to indicate that it is generally contended that these desirable rheological features of the dough are principally determined by the category of proteins called 'gluten' that can be separated from flour when the starch is removed under running water. Gluten has two simple fractions: the alcohol soluble gliadins and the alcohol insoluble glutenins.

From the emergence of unique dough characteristics at the hexaploid level in wheat it might be expected that they arose as a result of the presence of the D genome contributed by *Ae. squarrosa*. The earliest work that I know of in which this expectation was explored was that of Yamashita *et al.* (1957). They showed that the flour of *Ae. squarrosa* had a high content of dry gluten (27·1–27·3%) compared with *T. monococcum* (9·3%). A good loaf could be made from *Ae. squarrosa*.

Subsequent work, on the determination of the chromosomes implicated in the inheritance of milling and baking characteristics, has been somewhat equivocal. Welsh and Hehn (1964) reported that chromosome 1D controlled the good baking quality of the variety Itana in comparison with Kharkov. But 1D was reported to reduce quality in Cheyenne by Morris *et al.* (1966) and in Timstein by Welsh *et al.* (1968). Finally the great significance of chromosome 1D has been emphasised by Orth and Bushuk (1973) who point out that it codes for four subunits of glutenin that can be recognised electrophoretically. These authors suggest that two of the subunits may be of considerable importance in breadmaking quality.

Chromosome 5D seems to play a very important role affecting dough strength and loaf volume and flour yield in Cheyenne (Morris *et al.*, 1966; Mattern *et al.*, 1973). Flour yield in Hope (Welsh and Hehn, 1964) and protein content in Atlas 66 (Morris *et al.*, 1973) are also increased by the activity of 5D. In relation to the effect of 5D in increasing protein content in Atlas 66 it may be recollected that this chromosome has a role in ribosome production.

From this it will be seen that there are some clear D genome activities promoting quality, but Morris *et al.* (1966) also report that B genome chromosomes are important in Cheyenne. A case for the determination of breadmaking quality by the D genome has been partially established. However, we should bear in mind the possibility that these characteristics of the endosperm may arise from additive, or interactive, effects of genes in the D genome possibly with others in the B genome. Certainly Wrigley and Shepherd (1973), in a detailed investigation by two-dimensional electrophoresis of the chromosomes coding for gliadin proteins, found them to be determined only by homoeologous groups 1 and 6. However, chromosomes in these groups in all three genomes were found to be implicated. From this point of view the present array of gliadin polypeptides in ssp. *vulgare* appears as a simple addition of those present in parental diploids.

I hope from what I have said about the genetic control of quality components you will appreciate that we are at the opening of a new phase of investigation. In this it will be possible to bring together knowledge of the origin of wheat, and of its genetic architecture, with biochemistry in a way which should give access to problems in wheat quality that have previously been intractable. The solution of these problems will have practical benefits for wheat technology.

CONCLUSION

In conclusion may I remind you of the unpromising beginnings of our contemporary wheat crops. In the relatively short space of 10 000 or so years we have advanced from *T. monococcum* and *T. turgidum* ssp. *dicoccum* to varieties of *T. aestivum* ssp. *vulgare* capable of returning yields in favourable environments of more than 8·5 tonne/ha. During its evolution the crop has provided a mainstay for the development of Near Eastern, European and some Asian civilisations. The origins of the crop have had a significance far beyond our concerns as mere specialist technologists. It is important that we recognise the symbiotic relationship of man and the crop. For most of the past 10 000 years they have evolved together and become co-adapted. Man has selected the crop but the crop has also selected man. For many years there was adaptation in the human population to use the crop. The situation is now changing—man is now adapting to many other kinds of environmental support—the use of crops is of less importance. But let us recognise the extent to which our present attributes as individuals and as societies have emerged as co-adaptations to our crops. In contemplating the origins of wheat we are considering our own origins.

REFERENCES

Flannery, K. V. (1969). 'Origins and ecological effects of early domestication in Iran and the Near East', in *The Domestication and Exploitation of Plants and Animals* (Ed. P. J. Ucko and G. W. Dimbleby), Gerard Duckworth & Co., London, p. 73.

Flavell, R. B. and Smith, D. B. (1974). 'Variation in nuclear organiser *r*RNA gene multiplicity in wheat and rye', *Chromosoma* (in press).

Harlan, J. R. (1967). 'A wild wheat harvest in Turkey', *Archaeology*, **20**, 197.

Harlan, J. R. and Zohary, D. (1966). 'Distribution of wild wheats and barley', *Science*, **153**, 1075.

Kerber, E. R. (1964). 'Wheat: reconstruction of the tetraploid component (AABB) of hexaploids', *Science*, **143**, 253.

Kerber, E. R. and Dyck, P. L. (1969). 'Inheritance in hexaploid wheat of leaf rust resistance and other characters derived from *Aegilops squarrosa*', *Canad. J. Genetics Cytol.*, **11**, 639.

Kihara, H. and Tanaka, M. (1958). 'Morphological and physiological variation among *Aegilops squarrosa* strains collected in Palestine, Afghanistan and Iran', *Preslia*, **30**, 241.

Kimber, G. (1971). 'The inheritance of grain colour in wheat', *Z. Pflanzenzuchtg.*, **66**, 151.

Kimber, G. (1973). 'The relationships of the S genome diploids to polyploid wheats', *Proc. 4th Intern. Wheat Genetics Symposium*, p. 81.

Kimber, G. and Athwal, R. S. (1973). 'A reassessment of the cause of evolution of wheat', *Proc. Nat. Acad. Sci. USA*, **69**, 912.

Mattern, P. J., Morris, R., Schmidt, J. W. and Johnson, V. A. (1973). 'Locations of genes for kernel properties in the wheat variety "Cheyenne" using chromosome substitution lines', *Proc. 4th Intern. Wheat Genetics Symposium*, p. 703.

McFadden, E. S. and Sears, E. R. (1946). 'The origin of *Triticum spelta* and its free-threshing hexaploid relatives', *J. Heredity*, **37**, 81 and 107.

McIntosh, R. A. (1973). 'A catalogue of gene symbols for wheat', *Proc. 4th Intern. Wheat Genetics Symposium*, p. 893.

Mello-Sampayo and Canas, A. P. (1973). 'Suppressors of meiotic chromosome pairing in common wheat', *Proc. 4th Intern. Wheat Genetics Symposium*, p. 709.

Metzger, R. J. and Silbaugh, B. A. (1970). 'Location of genes for seed colour in hexaploid wheat, *Triticum aestivum* L.', *Crop Science*, **10**, 495.

Morris, R., Schmidt, J. W., Mattern, P. J. and Johnson, V. A. (1966). 'Chromosomal location of genes for flour quality in the wheat variety "Cheyenne" using substitution lines', *Crop Science*, **6**, 119.

Morris, R., Schmidt, J. W., Mattern, P. J. and Johnson, V. A. (1973). 'Chromosomal location of genes for high protein in the wheat cultivar Atlas 66', *Proc. 4th Intern. Wheat Genetics Symposium*, p. 715.

Morris, R. and Sears, E. R. (1967). 'The cytogenetics of wheat and its relatives', in *Wheat and Wheat Improvement* (Ed. K. S. Quisenberry and L. P. Reitz), American Society of Agronomy Inc., Madison USA, p. 19.

Muramatsu, M. (1963). 'Dosage effects of the *spelta* gene *q* of hexaploid wheat', *Genetics*, **48**, 469.

Nishikawa, K. and Nobuhara, M. (1971). 'Genetic studies of alpha-amylase isoenzymes in wheat. 1. Location of genes and variation in tetra- and hexaploid wheat', *Japan. J. Genetics*, **46**, 345.

Orth, R. A. and Bushuk, W. (1973). 'Studies of glutenin. VI. Chromosomal location of genes coding for sub-units of glutenin on common wheat', *Cereal Chemistry*, **51**, 118.

Renfrew, J. M. (1969). 'The archaeological evidence in the domestication of plants: methods and problems', in *The Domestication and Exploitation of Plants and Animals* (Ed. P. J. Ucko and G. W. Dimbleby), Gerard Duckworth & Co., London, p. 149.

Riley, R. (1965). 'Cytogenetics and the evolution of wheat', in *Essays on Crop Plant Evolution* (Ed. J. B. Hutchinson), Cambridge University Press, p. 103.

Riley, R. and Chapman, V. (1960). 'The D-genome of hexaploid wheat', *Wheat Information Service*, **11**, 18.

Riley, R., Chapman, V. and Willer, T. E. (1973). 'The determination of meiotic chromosome pairing', *Proc. 4th Intern. Wheat Genetics Symposium*, p. 731.

Riley, R., Coucoli, H. and Chapman, V. (1967). 'Chromosomal interchanges and the phylogeny of wheat', *Heredity*, **22**, 233.

Riley, R., Unrau, J. and Chapman, V. (1958). 'Evidence of the origin of the B genome of wheat', *J. Heredity*, **49**, 91.

Sarkar, P. and Stebbins, G. L. (1956). 'Morphological evidence concerning the origin of the B genome in wheat', *Amer. J. Botany*, **43**, 297.

Sears, E. R. (1954). 'The aneuploids of common wheat', Research Bulletin Missouri Agricultural Experiment Station, 572.

Sears, E. R. (1956a). 'The B genome of *Triticum*', *Wheat Information Service*, **4**, 8.

Sears, E. R. (1956b). 'The systematics, cytology and genetics of wheat', *Handbuch der Pflanzenzucht*, **2**, 164.

Sears, E. R. (1966). 'Nullisomic-tetrasomic combinations in hexaploid wheat', in *Chromosome Manipulation and Plant Genetics* (Ed. R. Riley and K. R. Lewis), Oliver & Boyd, Edinburgh and London, p. 29.

van Loon, M. (1966). 'Mureybat: an early village in inland Syria', *Archaeology*, **19**, 215.

Welsh, J. R. and Hehn, E. R. (1964). 'The effect of chromosome 1D on hexaploid wheat flour quality', *Crop Science*, **4**, 320.

Welsh, J. R., Watson, C. A. and Green, C. W. (1968). 'Chromosomal control of flour properties in three substitution sets of common wheat (*Triticum aestivum* L.)', *Crop Science*, **6**, 81.

Wrigley, C. W. and Shepherd, K. W. (1973). 'Electrofocusing of grain proteins from wheat genotypes', *Ann. N.Y. Acad. Sci.*, 154.

Yamashita, K., Tanaka, M. and Koyama, M. (1957). 'Studies on the flour quality in *Triticum* and *Aegilops*', Report of the Kihara Institute for Biological Research, **8**, 20.

Zohary, D. (1969). 'The progenitors of wheat and barley in relation to domestication and agricultural dispersal in the Old World', in *The Domestication and Exploitation of Plants and Animals* (Ed. P. J. Ucko and G. W. Dimbleby), Gerard Duckworth & Co., London, p. 47.

DISCUSSION

Chairman: Thank you very much, Professor Riley. We might deal first with the topics of the new refined genetic analysis and the processing characters of wheat. We have reached a stage of sophistication in genetic analysis and of detailed knowledge of the basis of wheat processing that were unthought of by the early breeders concerned with wheat quality, and in fact by those in more recent times. Genome analysis, the genetic significance of individual chromosomes and their manipulation have provided the basis for much greater precision in breeding techniques, matched in significance by the utilisation of more exact selection criteria and methods for grain quality and processing attributes. I should like to ask Dr Johnson if he has any comments to complement what Dr Riley has said.

V. A. Johnson (Nebraska University, USA): Not really very much. I was going to make some mention of these matters in my presentation tomorrow. I think Dr Riley has pointed out the key things concerning the Nebraska work, so I prefer not to comment.

A. Spicer (Lord Rank Research Centre, High Wycombe, Bucks): May we have some comment from Professor Riley on this question of quality *versus* yield? This is a problem affecting farmer and user. Also, whether in exploiting genetic engineering we are still faced with biological limitations? Will improvements inevitably affect them?

R. Riley: It is true to say that in this country we have been troubled by an inverse relationship between yield and quality in so far as the latter is determined by the protein content of the crop. Some people believe that over a range of varieties although yields may differ greatly, the actual amount of nitrogen harvested does not change. This is strictly not true: some genotypes appear to deviate, like Atlas 66, Nap Hal and April Bearded, as well as genotypes we have in our breeding programme. There is thus not a rigid set of relationships, and some escape is surely possible.

E. Kodicek (Strangeways Research Laboratory, Cambridge, UK): I would like to ask if there is any work done on differences in the prenol content, quantitatively or qualitatively, which could be responsible for the lack of certain proteins. It would be most interesting if particularly glyco-protein synthesis, in which prenols appear to be concerned, is affected.

R. Riley: I do not have a very satisfactory answer. The work is really at its beginning and we are starting to take out the chromosomes to look at some of the biochemical processes involved. The work is rapidly developing and not very sophisticated in relation to biochemistry and genotype.

S. K. Majumder (Technical Food Technological Research Institute, Mysore, India): What is the present status of work and interest in high lysine in wheat, and also in genetic breeders?

R. Riley: The Nebraska workers have conducted an enormous survey on 12 000 wheat genotypes in relation to high lysine content. Maybe this is too low! Diversity in lysine content was detected, but I think with no dramatic distinction as in maize or barley. Wheat showed a normal distribution with little indication of the kind of variation that can be easily manipulated.

There continues to be major commitments in several laboratories to the development of Triticales, the longest probably are CIMMYT in Mexico and the University of Manitoba while we at Cambridge and others have small programmes. There is still much work to do and major problems to solve.

Chairman: What about the technological problems of using and processing Triticale grain?

R. Riley: There may be improved amino acid balance with a good deal higher lysine content. I understand that Soviet scientists feel they can make reasonable bread from Triticale grain.

A. Neuberger (Lister Institute, London): I wondered whether, in the situation of so many protein polypeptides being characteristic of any one particular strain of wheat, and which must lead to a unique phenomenon of iso-proteins produced, they have been actually isolated. If they could be isolated, and regional patterns defined, and also if they differed very much, one might be able to do much more purposeful genetic engineering than at present. I also wondered whether there is information I have not seen which would give the sequence of the various polypeptides which have been indicated.

R. Riley: You are defining a very real problem not yet launched upon thoroughly, and though numbers of people in various laboratories are beginning, we do not yet have an answer. Clearly, once you can exploit genetic variation in this way, and isolate polypeptide fractions of distinct genetic origin one would be in a better position than hitherto.

M. A. Cookson (R.H.M. Bakeries Ltd, London): Could I return to the subject of yield versus breadmaking quality? Maris Huntsman is, as far as we have seen, positively detrimental in its breadmaking quality. Could Professor Riley comment on the danger of breeding varieties for yield and with such adverse effects?

R. Riley: The situation in the UK has changed materially from that pertaining during the long period involved in breeding this variety, as it was then much less apparent that there would be a need to be more dependent on home-grown wheat for breadmaking. In the changed circumstances of the need for greater self-sufficiency it is clearly a disadvantage to provide wheats like this. There is, of course, the matter of economics and price but our policy is to try and produce wheats with the maximum yield and the highest quality. I am confident you will see this change in the varieties of this country in the next few years.

F. Pushman (Cambridge, Plant Breeding Institute, UK): I would like to refer to the previous point that the number of recognised wheat proteins is becoming larger and larger. I think that cereal chemists must look further and in more detail to try and define quality before geneticists can really pin it down to a particular group or combination of chromosomes.

V. A. Johnson: I have difficulty in accepting the idea that increases in productivity in wheat must of necessity be associated with inferior or depressed quality, except in regard to the general relationship, not very fixed, that increased productivity may result in a somewhat depressed protein content. Our experiences during the last 25 years makes it totally unacceptable to ascribe increased productivity to a depression of other factors of quality.

Any plant variety is a compromise and you have to decide where to make your compromise. At the time of the production of Maris Huntsman, the important thing was to increase yield in this country, and it would be entirely irresponsible for us to abandon this notion now. But there is always a lag in advancing yield in relation to other characters, and we seek to incorporate quality into the increasingly higher standards of yield attained.

D. Hollingsworth (British Nutrition Foundation, London): Is the protein the only characteristic of quality that people are interested in, or are there factors relating to, for example, the structure of starch?

R. Riley: As implied by Fiona Pushman in an earlier comment, I think this is absolutely the situation. Quality is extremely complex: it relates to the capacity of the grain to give the maximum amount of flour, to the nature of the flour determined by both the nature of the protein and other processing properties. The inheritance is very complex, and thus extremely difficult to handle by the breeder.

J. Edelman (R.H.M. Research Ltd, High Wycombe, Bucks): Did I understand you to say that the relationship between the nucleolar organising part of the chromosome and the ribosomes is related to the amount of protein found in the grain, and therefore has an effect on quality? If you look at the high protein wheats, do they have larger—or more—nucleoli?

R. Riley: We have only just begun to explore this situation having recognised last year that there are differences between genotypes of the species in their numbers of ribosomal genes. Previously it had been generally assumed that the number was constant for any plant or animal species. I am hesitant about talking of 'protein' content because the results are so recent, but we have observed, at least in plant green tissue, that with more ribosomal genes there appears to be more protein. We can as yet make no statement on grain protein. If there is a limitation to the production of protein in the grain it may be associated with the ribosomal content.

J. Edelman: Would this be a tool? If increased volume or numbers of nucleoli are expressed in the somatic cells, would this be a way of screening very early on for high protein wheats? Is there any indication of this? Or, does this only express itself in nuclei in the developing grain?

R. Riley: This is what we are examining at the moment, and we are hopeful it will provide the means of both manipulating genotype and describing ways by which one can increase grain protein content. Atlas 66 owes a good deal of its high protein content to chromosome 5D which also carries a nucleolar organiser. We are trying to take that particular chromosome and put it into adapted genotypes.

The Structure and Biochemistry of the Wheat Grain

K. KINGSWOOD

Cereal Processing Department,
The Lord Rank Research Centre,
High Wycombe, Bucks, UK

The title that I have been given for this paper is broad enough to more than occupy the whole week of this seminar.

Pomeranz, as the latest editor of the Cereals Chemist's Bible—or at least, New Testament—*Wheat Chemistry and Technology,* manages to restrict the subject to a mere 280 pages with only 1378 references.

Some guidance as to what aspect to choose from this mountain of information is given by the title of the symposium—Bread. Since in addition the paper is being given on the day devoted to 'Fundamentals' we can combine both of these qualifications with the original title, and safely restrict most of this paper to consideration of some of those aspects of wheat structure of importance in wheat processing, which tends to be the modern name for milling.

Exploitation of the food reserves of the cereal seed has been absolutely basic to the ascent of civilisation. The protein and starch reserves of the endosperm could be utilised by animals in much the same way as the plant embryo achieves their solubilisation, by simply chewing the whole grain, or consuming a gruel. However, as soon as the peculiar ability of the wheat protein reserves to form a coherent hydrated network was noted, the story of gluten quality must have begun and the Cereal Chemist was in business.

In our relatively recent past, at least for most uses, it has been the practice to separate the endosperm from the bran and embryo. This is not a modern practice which began when roller milling was adapted to replace stone milling.

The processor therefore has long had an interest in the amount of bran free endosperm that he could extract from the grain and I would like to consider some of the factors controlling this quantity, i.e. the extraction rate.

Before discussing the endosperm itself, it is interesting to look at the morphology of the wheat grain with respect to the ratio of crease to grain. The volume occupied by the crease has been calculated to range from 0·7 to 1·9% of the total grain volume and its relative size affects the milling process in terms of ability to extract flour and its potential for providing a hospice for fungal growth at grain maturity. This latter problem is especially relevant to wheat grown in the UK climate.

Cross-sections (Fig. 1) show how great a variation occurs. All but the last grain are of varieties available for incorporation into UK bread grists.

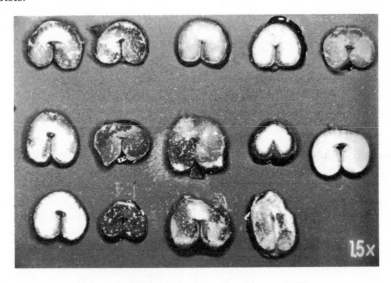

FIG. 1. (Original photograph reduced by one-half.)

There is some interest being shown in breeding for the elimination of the crease, as in the last grain. This is a sample of Triticum Spherococcum and a crease can be seen as a thin line across the grain. Some cultivars of spherical grains with only a residual crease have been developed. If these ever became a commercial possibility they would have a considerable impact on the present milling process.

It would appear from dissection studies that the quantity of endosperm or potential flour present, varies between 80 and 84% of the whole grain weight. Hinton (1947) found this range by dissection of English wheats, although for an Australian wheat he obtained a figure of 86%. This figure relates to the starchy endosperm content. Although the aleurone is part of the endosperm botanically, it usually remains with the bran in a modern milling process. Other methods of calculation from volumes of sections (Petrenko, 1968) and chemical determinations of starch contents (Greer, 1950) give figures ranging from 80 to 86% starchy endosperm. More recently Stenvert and Moss (1974) have published figures based on a neutral detergent fibre method which gives estimates of endosperm content falling into the range of 80–84%. However, the yield of flour obtained in practice is not necessarily predicted by the amount of endosperm present.

Farrand and Hinton (1974) publish some of the dissection work carried out by Hinton which illustrates this point. The endosperm content of two different varieties of English wheat, Cappelle and Maris Widgeon, were determined by dissection of representative samples and mean endosperm contents of 84·3% obtained from the Maris Widgeon and 83·9% from the Cappelle. When test milled on the shortened system of the Laboratory Buhler mill, a yield of 75% flour was obtained from the Maris Widgeon compared with 69·7% from Cappelle. There is, therefore, an important difference in processing quality between these two wheats with respect to the ease with which the endosperm can be separated from the bran and embryo.

This quality difference has important interactions with what determines the final quality of the flour. It appears to be related to at least three facets of endosperm structure, namely, the apparent hardness, the total protein content and possibly the composition of the endosperm cell walls.

Hardness, in this sense, relates to the way in which the endosperm fractures during the milling process. A hard wheat gives regularly shaped free flowing particles which sieve or dress easily so that good separation of bran and endosperm takes place before hard grinding or reduction occurs.

Soft wheats on the other hand produce irregular 'fluffy' particles with a large amount of free starch. This hardness characteristic shows little variation between harvests. Records for English wheats over very different seasonal conditions indicate that the hardness factor is little influenced by changes in environment, in contrast to most other attributes of the grain. The final flours from hard and soft wheats differ in bulk density and also in the amount of starch 'damaged' by passage through the mill.

The damaged starch content is of great importance to subsequent processing as it is one of the main factors controlling the water absorption of the flour. It should be remembered that figures quoted for starch damage are almost invariably based on reducing sugar produced after a standard enzyme treatment and they make no comment as to the distribution of damage among a granule population.

There is a critical level of starch damage required for successful bread production. This is related to the α-amylase and protein content of the flour (Farrand, 1969).

That hardness is not another modern quality obsession, following the advent of the roller mill, is indicated by milling data published by Moritz and Jones (1950) using a Roman domestic stone mill or quern. With hard wheats they obtained flour yields of 71%, whereas with soft, where it was

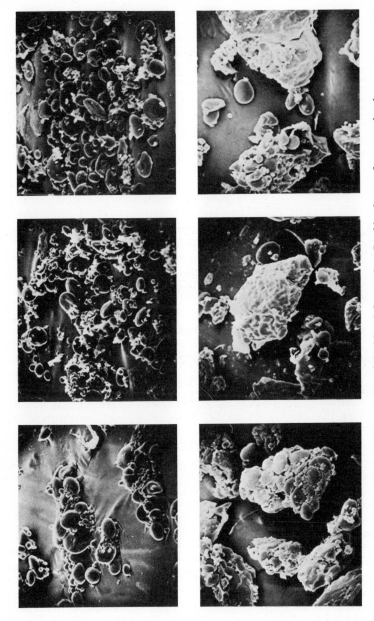

FIG. 2.　Upper: first, second and third break flours —Joss Cambier. Lower: first, second and third break flours—Cardinal.

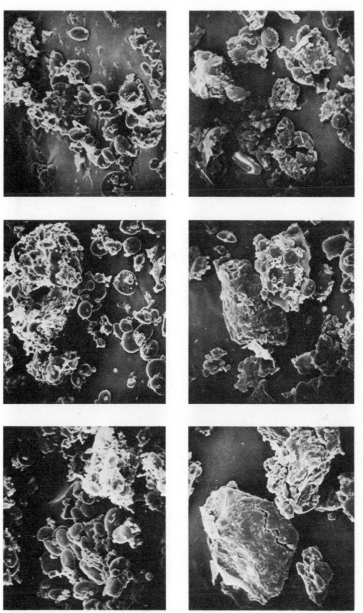

FIG. 3. Upper: first, second and third reduction flours—Joss Cambier. Lower: first, second and third reduction flours—Cardinal.

impossible to regrind the middlings, they obtained only 54% yield. As a further diversion the importance of fine grinding and its consequent starch damage on maintaining water absorption and therefore yield of bread, also predates the roller mill. Cobbet (1831) mentions this as a well-established practice in a treatise on corn.

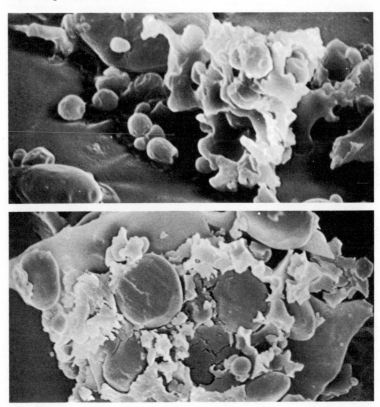

FIG. 4. Upper: portion of third break flours—Joss Cambier. Lower: portion of second reduction flour—Cardinal.

The difference in starch damage between normally milled hard and soft wheats appears related to the degree of attachment between the starch granule and the protein matrix. It is extremely difficult to mechanically damage a free starch granule. A hard wheat endosperm is held to split initially along the plane of the cell walls and then with increasing pressure, across the cell. This latter cleavage appears to simultaneously split the starch granule. In contrast, on splitting open the cells of a soft endosperm, the granules are readily released from their protein matrix.

Figure 2 shows SEM photographs from a soft wheat—Joss Cambier—and a hard wheat—Cardinal—and are taken from the flour streams of a Laboratory Buhler mill.

The overall view of the three break flours shows this difference very clearly.

Similarly for the reduction flours (Fig. 3), in the case of hard wheat, starch does not appear in any quantity until late in the reduction stage.

Figure 4 shows fragments of the protein matrix. In the soft wheat the granules have readily separated from the protein, whereas in the hard wheat they have been retained and split open in the process. This difference in texture which is of such fundamental importance to the processor has not been fully explained biochemically.

Barlow *et al.* (1973) obtained near isogenic lines of cultivars differing only in their relative hardness, and determined, using a penetrometer technique, the hardness of both the protein matrix and the individual starch granules. These were found to be identical between hard and soft cultivars. In addition it was shown that the glutenin/gliadin/albumin ratios were virtually identical between the near isogenic lines and gel electrophoresis revealed no qualitative difference between the gliadin components. It was suggested that there might be differences in a postulated cementing layer between the granule and the storage protein. Using a fluorescent antibody staining technique it was shown that there is a specific water soluble protein area around each starch granule. In a further paper Simmonds *et al.* (1973) extracted protein material from the surface of free starch granules obtained by pin milling. Good correlation was obtained between the hardness of the wheat and the amount of water soluble material extractable from the granule, the hard wheats giving the highest amount of extractables.

However, since some storage protein was still attached to the hard starch granules and some gliadin dissolved under these extraction conditions, their findings appear to be a partial restatement rather than an explanation for the difference between hard and soft wheats.

It was shown, however, that the protein associated with the granule surface possessed both β-amylase and proteolytic activity which might explain the easier release of starch from hard wheat semolinas after the material has been moistened and then dried, i.e. allowing some proteolysis and therefore weakening of the starch protein bond to take place.

The interaction between tempering or conditioning moisture and endosperm structure has been reported by Wolf *et al.* (1952). The optimum moisture for separation of the endosperm and bran was considerably higher than that for the release of free protein. They found that at lower moisture levels there was a greater tendency for the endosperm to split along the starch protein interface. The differential effects of moisture treatment on the endosperm structure is an area requiring further study, especially when the requirements for air classification procedures are considered.

Figure 5 shows the fractured endosperm surface of the same two wheats —Joss Cambier and Cardinal. It can be seen that air spaces are present in the soft variety which probably form during maturation and drying of the kernel. The consequent shrinkage produces different effects in the two wheats which possibly (Hoseney and Seib, 1973) explains the difference

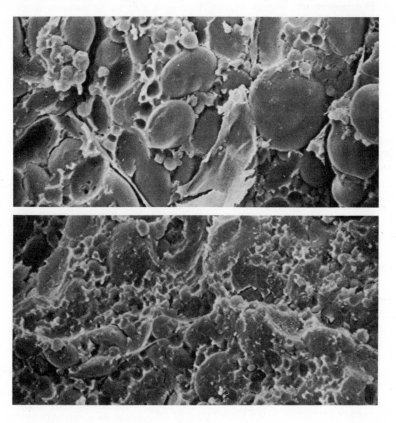

FIG. 5. Upper: fractured endosperm—Joss Cambier. Lower: fractured endosperm—Cardinal.

in appearance between vitreous and mealy wheats. Air spaces in the latter will cause diffraction of light whereas the homogeneous hard grain will appear translucent, i.e. vitreous. Wheats exhibiting the starch release and milling pattern of a hard wheat are, however, not invariably vitreous, nor are soft wheats always mealy and this appearance factor is possibly influenced by speed of maturation as well as any inherent differences in endosperm strength. Presumably the traditional preference for vitreous wheats for breadmaking reflects the greater probability that they will be hard and have a higher protein content. SEM studies (Seckinger and Wolf, 1970) show differences in the ultrastructure of the protein particles from Soft and Hard Wheats, hard wheat particles being considerably more compact.

Returning to the topic of ease of separation of the endosperm from the bran, the possibility of differences in structure of the endosperm cell walls has been considered.

Larkin *et al.* (1952) has reported studies on the endosperm cell walls of American wheats of differing milling quality. Hydrolysis of the clean endosperm wall material showed that between 70 and 95% of the hemicellulose was accounted for by xylose and arabinose. Quantitative differences in this ratio did not correlate with milling differences in terms of flour release.

Cross-sections of these grains were also treated with dilute sulphuric acid and it was found that degradation occurred mainly in the endosperm cells nearest the aleurone layer. The thickness of the cell walls near the aleurone were found to be inversely proportional to the milling quality of the wheats. However, these determinations were made over a somewhat restricted range of mainly soft low yielding cultivars.

Mares and Stone (1973) have examined cleaned preparations of endosperm cell walls and have shown them to contain approximately 15% protein, 64% arabinoxylan with about 6% of β-glucan and 6% β-glucomanan. Endosperm cell wall preparations from Insignia, Wren and Olympic wheats were all of similar composition in terms of the above components. However, these three varieties would also be classed soft or semi-soft milling wheats. It would be interesting to know if a qualitative difference in cell wall composition exists between recognised soft and hard milling wheats. If no differences are found then possibly the initial endosperm fragmentation of hard wheats, along the plane cell walls, is due to the adhesion of the cell protein content, to the cell walls. Kent and Evers (1966) have reported that the reducibility of the sub-aleurone endosperm on pin milling is lower than that of the inner endosperm. Since the inner endosperm cells have a much higher starch content this suggests that differences in endosperm hardness must be associated with the whole endosperm cell rather than simple differences in starch and protein adhesion.

I would now like to refer to the distribution within the endosperm of the major components—starch and protein. It is this distribution and its interaction with structure/hardness that determines the efficiency of processing, whether it be by conventional milling, air classification or a wet separation process. I think it is pertinent to mention briefly, the way in which the endosperm develops. This has been described in papers by Evers (1970) and Hoshikawa (1961).

Endosperm tissue in the developing grain is recognisable 2 days after fertilisation and the volume of the endosperm mass increases for approximately a further 14 days. During this time cell division occurs mainly in the cells adjacent to the nucellar epidermis so that the first formed cells are pushed away from the periphery and into the endosperm space. Some radial divisions also occur but it is true to say that the bulk of the inner endosperm cells are the first formed material. After 16 days cell division ceases and the outer cell layer differentiates into the characteristic thick-walled aleurone cells. Owing to the folding of the grain the cheek areas are bounded on both sides by what was meristematic tissue so that there is a progression of cells from the outside towards the centre in terms of both age and size. Kent and Jones (1952) give volumes of 0.217×10^{-6} ml for the outer, 0.547×10^{-6} ml for the middle and 1.310×10^{-6} ml for the inner endosperm tissue cells.

At cell division, sites for starch granule development—the amyloplasts—can be seen and starch granules observed 4 days after fertilisation. These granules continue to develop, the oldest and largest ending up in the centre of the endosperm. This first type of starch granule is lenticular in

TABLE I

ENGLISH WINTER WHEATS

Time	Days	Events	Endosperm development	Weather
May		Late 'N' Application Boosts protein		↑
June	1	Anthesis		Rain
	3		Endosperm cell division	+ve cor-
	7		Type 'A' granules appear	relation with
	13		Protein bodies appear	protein
July	17		Endosperm cell division ends	
	18		Type 'B' granules appear	↓
		Senescence Protein transfer to grain?	↑ Endosperm cell growth ↓	
August	40		Cell growth ends ↑	↑ Sunshine
			Maturation? Enzyme fall off. Protein loss? ↓	
	55	Harvest Ripe Delayed Harvest		+ve cor- relation with
September		Yield/Qual. Loss		flour yield ↓

shape showing an equatorial groove and usually only one or two granules arise at each amyloplast. After 14 days smaller granules, mainly spherical but deformed by contact, arise in the spaces between the large granules. These B or type 2 granules appear to arise only after the A or type 1 granules have attained maximum development and are therefore found mainly in the inner endosperm. It has been suggested that the trigger for B starch deposition is the attainment of maximum A granule size possible within the cell volume and further starch accumulation can take place only by filling in the intergranular spaces. Evers (1973) has reported micro sieving tests on endosperm tissue of a soft wheat variety which indicated that these small granules account for approximately 30% by weight of the total starch content.

It has been suggested that these two types of granule have differing functional properties. If their relative ratios will be one determinant of flour quality.

Protein bodies are observable at approximately 13 days after fertilisation and protein deposits can be observed by about day 16. Deposition of starch and protein ceases approximately 35 days after fertilisation.

As a digression I have tried to relate these events to the crop. Table I is intended to indicate an area for discussion rather than be an accurate presentation. The data relating yield and weather has been published by Farrand (1972).

It seems that there is a need for what might be described as a 'unified field' theory to relate the plant physiologists' data, the growing conditions and treatments, to the quality of grain arriving at the mill gate.

Evers (1970) using the cell size data of Kent has calculated the protein content per endosperm cell and deduced that the amount of protein in each endosperm cell is approximately the same independent of its age. From this he suggests that the well-known gradient which exists in protein concentration from the sub-aleurone cells to the inner endosperm is a result of dilution of a fixed protein level by starch deposition.

The implications of this gradient of protein content are demonstrated by the work of Farrand and Hinton (1974) who dissected the endosperm into four morphologically different areas. In this work, they dissected the endosperm of high and low protein samples of a semi-hard wheat and a soft wheat into four divisions. Nitrogen contents shown in Table II increase markedly from inner to outer endosperm.

When nitrogen levels are plotted against the log of the proportion of endosperm in each division, a linear relationship is obtained, the gradient of which is proportional to the protein content rather than the hardness of the wheat.

This paper goes on to relate the dissection data to the protein distribution encountered on normal milling with its many differing flour streams and shows, by a somewhat complex mathematical transformation, that a similar functional relationship can be used to express the Hand dissection, Buhler test milling and Commercial milling data. From this it is suggested that the mill flour streams may be grouped to represent their origin within the endosperm and therefore reflect the gradients of 'quality' which exist therein. Since 25% of the starchy endosperm protein is contained within the 11% volume that the sub-aleurone represents, location of this flour within the mill is of great importance.

TABLE II

NITROGEN CONTENT OF DISSECTION FRACTIONS

Maris Widgeon	Sample 1 High protein %N	Sample 2 Low protein %N
Endosperm 1	5·04	3·55
Endosperm 2	3·15	2·15
Endosperm 3	1·83	1·38
Endosperm 4	1·41	1·01
Endosperm Total	2·08	1·52
Cappelle-Desprez	*High protein* %N	*Low protein* %N
Endosperm 1	5·10	2·70
Endosperm 2	3·03	1·93
Endosperm 3	1·80	1·29
Endosperm 4	1·37	0·91
Endosperm Total	2·04	1·25

The figures quoted by Farrand are based on kjeldahl nitrogen determinations and make no comment on the quality of the storage protein. However, although the 'quality' of flour from these different endosperm sites varies, there is little evidence to suggest any differences in the gluten quality *per se*, arising from different areas of the same grain. Kent and Evers (1969) showed that the ratio of glutenin–gliadin storage protein to water soluble protein varies from the sub-aleurone to the inner endosperm. Thus the normal total kjeldahl nitrogen determination on flours as an indication of flour quality throughout the milling process, will give misleading results if it is interpreted as a measure of the potential gluten content of that flour.

McDermott and Pace (1960) showed that the lysine and arginine contents of the endosperm of wheats were inversely proportional to their total protein content. This is consistent with the previous reference since lysine is associated with the functional water soluble fraction of the total protein, which is subsequently diluted by the storage protein.

That the quality of the gluten complex does not differ between the inner and outer endosperm is supported by some rheological work using a micro mixer (Kingswood, 1973). It was found that the variation in consistency of gluten washed from a range of break and reduction flours could be adequately accounted for in terms of the efficiency with which the storage protein could be extracted rather than from any intrinsic differences between gluten properties. This variation in ease of separation is particularly relevant to the requirements of wet gluten/starch separation processes. The wheat requirements for this process differ markedly from those for conventional milling.

Such differences as are apparent in the flours from different parts of the endosperm, may in part be due to differences in enzyme concentration throughout the endosperm. Engle and Heins (1947) showed that protease in mature wheats is restricted to the aleurone and sub-aleurone tissues, the rest of the endosperm being free of activity. However, the whole endosperm showed some autolytic activity. Little work has been reported on the protease reacting specifically with its own protein rather than an extraneous substrate. Bushuk et al. (1971) have reported that weak glutens have significantly higher proteolytic activity and this is an area needing further investigation, especially with respect to some of the new English high yielding wheats, e.g. Maris Huntsman. Engle (1947) has also reported that β-amylase is restricted to the outer endosperm tissue. Simmonds et al. (1973), however, found sufficient β-amylase activity in the water soluble fraction from starch granules isolated from hard wheat to account for all of the β-amylase activity, indicating that this enzyme is spread throughout the endosperm.

α-Amylase activity in contrast is restricted to the aleurone and scutellum of mature wheats. Even at relatively high levels of α-amylase activity in the whole grain, there is initially very little activity within the inner endosperm so that the level of α-amylase is reduced considerably on milling (Booth, 1973). This is especially true if the cultivar is both free milling, i.e. the endosperm separates easily from the aleurone, and hard, i.e. there is little back contamination in the subsequent sieving operation.

I suppose it is not possible to conclude without commenting on gluten quality in general, although I know that people far more knowledgeable will be discussing this topic during the week.

Studies by reconstitution of extracted protein fractions—especially gliadin—have so far not produced a clear-cut formula for breadmaking quality. It appears essential for glutenin, the elastic component, and gliadin, the viscous component, to be present for breadmaking but no specific gliadin component has been isolated which is clearly more able to restore quality to reconstituted glutens. It has been proposed that, assuming a wheat is sound, i.e. not heat damaged or showing excessive enzymatic activity, then all glutens can be brought to the same physical state. This is really saying that a baker, given a free hand in terms of chemical additives and baking processes could produce satisfactory bread from any gluten 'quality' providing there was sufficient 'quantity'.

While this might be true it is of little comfort to the operator of a modern breadmaking plant who must keep all factors as constant as possible. It is certainly true that some wheat varieties are more tolerant of a range of test baking conditions than others and where there are only a few wheat varieties in a grist and in a situation where protein is expensive, it is in the baker's interest to isolate these more tolerant varieties.

Quality with respect to the protein complex is best defined—and I quote Barmore (1948) as—'That property or combination of properties that make it possible to produce bold well rounded loaves'. I would suggest that even if these are not quite the shape of loaf required by the plant baker, it is this property which will give the most tolerance to small changes in the milling and baking process, so that research into gluten quality continues to be relevant.

Wrigley (1972) has suggested that more attention be given to the glutenin component of the storage protein which has been somewhat neglected, because of its lower solubility, in favour of gliadin. Several workers, Wrigley (1972) and Hoseney et al. (1970) have highlighted the importance of the remnants of cellular inclusion, i.e. amyloplast and protein body membranes within the gluten. If these mainly lipo protein membranes survive in the mature grain they are likely to have marked effects on gluten rheology. They will also be unevenly distributed throughout the endosperm giving a further milling quality gradient.

In summary the following endosperm gradients have been suggested:
Protein content
Ratio of storage/total protein
Starch content
Starch 'quality'
Hardness
Enzyme levels
Cellular inclusions

The overall amount of flour of acceptable quality extracted from a mature grain will depend primarily on the ease of separation between the aleurone and sub-aleurone cells and upon the grain hardness. Fulfilment of both of these conditions, however, does not in itself ensure good baking quality.

If it is accepted that the milling process achieves a separation of endosperm in terms of its morphological origin, then it is important to obtain more information on these within grain gradients. A more precise specification for the type of endosperm required can then be given to the plant breeder. With respect to 'baking quality', however, this specification will probably be written in terms of what to avoid rather than what to include.

REFERENCES

Barlow, K. K., Buttrose, S. M., Simmonds, D. H. and Vesk, M. (1973). 'The nature of the starch protein interface in wheat endosperm', *Cereal Chem.*, **50** (4), 443–454.
Barmore, M. A. (1948). 'Wheat protein', *Bakers Dig.*, **22**, 10–14.
Booth, M. R. (1973). Private Communication.
Bushuk, W., Hwang, P. and Wrigley, C. W. (1971). 'Proteolytic activity of maturing grain', *Cereal Chem.*, **48**, 637.
Cobbett, W. (1831). *A Treatise on Cobbett's Corn.*
Engle, C. (1947). 'The distribution of enzymes in resting cereals', *Biochim. Biophys. Acta*, **1**, 42–49.
Engle, C. and Heins, J., (1947). 'The distribution of enzymes in resting cereals', *Biochim. Biophys. Acta*, **1**, 190–196.
Evers, A. D. (1970). 'Development of the endosperm of wheat', *Annals of Botany*, **34**, 136, June.
Evers, A. D. (1973). 'The size distribution among starch granules in wheat endosperm', *Die Stärke*, **9**.
Farrand, E. A. (1969). 'Starch damage and alpha amylase as bases for mathematical models relation to flour water-absorption', *Cereal Chem.*, **46**, No. 2, 103–116.
Farrand, E. A. (1972). 'Potential milling and baking value of home grown wheat', *J. Nat. Inst. Agric. Bot.*, **12**, 464–470.
Farrand, E. A. and Hinton, J. J. C. (1974). 'Study of relationships between wheat protein contents of two U.K. varieties and derived flour protein contents on varying extraction rates. II Studies by hand dissection of individual grains', *Cereal Chem.*, **51**, 561–574.
Greer, E. N. (1950). 'The milling and baking properties of home-grown winter wheat 1947–1949', *J. Nat. Inst. Agric. Bot.*, **5**, 459.
Hinton, J. J. C. (1947). 'The distribution of vitamin B1 and nitrogen in the wheat grain', *Proc. Roy. Soc. (London)*, **B134**, 418.
Hoseney, R. C., Finney, K. F. and Pomeranz, Y. (1970). 'Functional (breadmaking) of wheat flours and biochemical properties of wheat flour components', *Cereal Chem.*, **47**, 135–140.
Hoseney, R. C. and Seib, P. A. (1973). 'Structural differences in hard and soft wheat', *Bakers Dig.*, Dec., p. 26.
Hoshikawa, K. (1961). 'Studies on the maturation of wheat', *Nihon sakumotsu gakkai kiji*, **29** (4), 415–420.
Kent, N. L. and Evers, A. (1966). 'Endosperm reduction in hard red spring wheat', *The North Western Miller*, Dec.
Kent, N. L. and Evers, A. D. (1969). 'Variation in protein composition within the endosperm of hard wheat', *Cereal Chem.*, **46**, 293.
Kent, N. L. and Jones, C. R. (1952). 'The cellular structure of wheat flour', *Cereal Chem.*, **29**, 383–398.

Kingswood, K. and Farrant, E. A. (1973). 'An investigation of the relationship between gluten and flour properties of Buhler mill fractions', Ref. paper at Annual Conference of the A.A.C.C., St. Louis.

Larkin, R. A., et al. (1952). 'Relation of endosperm cell wall thickness to the milling quality of seven Pacific Northwest wheats', Cereal Chem., 29, 407–413.

Mares, D. J. and Stone, B. A. (1973). 'Chemical composition and ultrastructure of the cell walls', Aust. J. Biol. Sci., 26, No. 4, 793–812.

McDermott, E. E. and Pace, J. (1960). 'Comparisons of the amino acid composition of the protein in flour and endosperm from different types of wheat', J. Sci. Fd & Agric., 11, Feb., 109–115.

Moritz, L. A. and Jones, C. R. (1950). 'Experiments in grinding wheat on a Romano/British quern', Milling, 114, 594.

Petrenko, T. P. (1968). 'The technological importance of the structure of the wheat grain', Izv. vysch. uchet. zav. Pishchevaya. Tekhnologyja, (4), 18–22.

Seckinger, H. L. and Wolf, M. J. (1970). 'Electron microscope study of endosperm protein from hard and soft wheats', Cereal Chem., 47, 236–243.

Simmonds, D. H., Barlow, K. K. and Wrigley, C. W. (1973). 'The biochemical basis of grain hardness in wheat', Cereal Chem., 50 (5), 553–562.

Stenvert, N. L. and Moss, R. (1974). 'The separation and technological significance of the outer layers of the wheat grain', J. Sci. Fd & Agric., 25 (6), 629–636.

Wolf, M. J. et al. (1952). 'Studies of water insoluble hemicelluloses of the endosperm cell walls in relation to milling quality of seven Pacific Northwest wheats', Cereal Chem., 29, 399–406.

Wrigley, C. W. (1972). 'The biochemistry of the wheat protein complex and its genetic control', Cereal Sci. Today, 17, No. 12, Dec., 370–375.

DISCUSSION

Chairman: Mr Kingswood's talk has stressed the relationships between the anatomical structure of the wheat grain and its chemical composition and subsequent processing. First, I should like to invite Dr Munck to comment on some aspects of structure and hardness in relation to amino acid composition.

L. Munck (Carlsberg Research Laboratory, Copenhagen): Wheat is polyploid and its genetic manipulation is thereby complex. Barley is diploid and simply inherited changes in chemical composition are more easily recognised, e.g. genes for changed amylose–amylopectin ratio or for changed amino acid profile in the endosperm. The gene controlling high-lysine content in Hiproly barley (Munck, Karlsson, Hagberg and Eggum, *Science*, **168**, 985–7, 1970) is closely linked with the genetic character for hard endosperm. Amino acid analyses show no difference in amino acid composition between hard and soft high-lysine selections in barley (Table D1). However, the significant negative correlation existing between lysine (g/16 g N) and crude protein in soft barley is completely absent in the hard type. This evidence suggests an interaction between endosperm texture and the lysine to crude protein ratio (see Munck, *Hereditas*, **72**, 1–128, 1972).

TABLE D1

CORRELATION COEFFICIENTS (r) BETWEEN SOME AMINO ACIDS (g/16 g N)
AND PROTEIN % IN HARD ($n = 15$) AND SOFT ($n = 17$) HIGH LYSINE BARLEY

	Amino acids in:		r Amino acid g/16 g N—protein	
	Hard	Soft		
	g/16 g N	g/16 g N	Hard	Soft
Lys.	3·99±0·17	4·07±0·15	0·0	−0·8
Arg.	4·77±0·16	4·80±0·12	0·3	−0·7
Glu.	21·85±0·88	21·77±1·19	−0·4	0·7
Protein (N×6·25)	14·74±1·46	13·82±1·43		

Chairman: Mr Kingswood also projected a slide relating the deposition of chemical components within the wheat grain to the growth and maturity of the grain. In England, this process covers about 55 days from fertilisation to harvest. Would any one wish to comment, either from a biochemical or processing viewpoint?

R. Riley (Plant Breeding Institute, Cambridge, UK): It is now possible to apply nitrogen fertiliser rather late in the cycle of development of the wheat plant, either as urea or nitrate, and so influence the amount of protein deposited in the grain. Various experiments are in progress in the UK, but in Germany wheat growers in the Rhineland have already adopted this technique of late-nitrogen application. Can anyone say what consequences this change may have for the processor?

E. G. Heyne (Kansas University, USA): First, I should like to make the point that the timetable of development for hard wheats in North America is much shorter, on average about 30 days. When late-nitrogen is applied during the formation of the inflorescence, the extra protein laid down in the grain has good physical properties for breadmaking. If the nitrogen is applied later in grain development, then the extra protein has a poorer processing quality. We have raised protein content from 9 to 16% in hard wheats, but only nitrogen applied before flowering produces an increase in yield, and so very late N-treatment is uneconomic for the farmer.

A. Spicer (Lord Rank Research Centre, High Wycombe, Bucks): I think the experiments in Germany, and the one we are undertaking here, give the nitrogen in two parts; the first increases yield, the second increases protein levels. If these applications are made with minimum mechanical damage to the crop, say by aircraft spraying, then we should be able to secure good yields and increase quality protein levels by 1–2%.

Chairman: Can we now move to a more general discussion of the paper. Are there other aspects of Mr Kingswood's presentation upon which members of the symposium would wish to comment?

A. Spicer: May I ask one question based on innocence? One of Mr Kingswood's slides illustrated the gradient of protein distribution in the grain: he also discussed grain morphology, especially the importance of the crease, and its relationship to the milling process. Can he visualise the development of an economical milling process leading to a good quality and high-protein flour, which would not result in excessive losses of protein in the bran faction?

K. Kingswood: As people will know, that question is not as innocent as it sounds! If one could develop using *Triticum spherococcum*, a rather round wheat grain (as in rice), then one could devise a process that could take advantage of the gradient. Until that time the ease of fracture between the endosperm and the sub-aleurone and aleurone itself will remain the dominant factor.

A. Neuberger (Lister Institute, London): Is there any possibility that heavy nitrogen applications to the wheat crop may lead to an induced sulphur deficiency?

G. A. H. Elton (Ministry of Agriculture, Fisheries and Food, London): The sulphur content of wheat is fairly low, but I believe an inverse relationship exists between the cysteine content of protein and the total level of protein. It resembles the inverse relationship between lysine and protein levels cited for barley by Dr Munck. Therefore, the more the protein content is raised, the lower the proportions of S-containing amino acids and lysine in protein become. However, there is still a real need for the user of the wheat to specify more definitely what chemical and biochemical characters he wants in the product. Only then can the breeder achieve the goals expected of him.

K. Kingswood: I suggested at the end of my paper that it will never be possible to isolate one or two factors that determine quality, and say, to the breeders 'this is what we wish to have'. It is probably easier to say what we must not have—and this is where the Maris Huntsman story is relevant.

J. Mesdag (Foundation for Agricultural Plant Breeding, Wageningen, Netherlands): Have the U K millers determined what type of hardness they prefer? In the Netherlands, millers are uncertain on this point. If industry could give a firm indication of their needs, it would be rather simple for breeders to attain the required degree of hardness.

K. Kingswood: Hardness is not clearly specified other than in general terms, soft, semi-hard and hard. Our millers would probably pay a premium for wheats classed as semi-hard or hard. Milling extremely hard wheats causes unacceptable levels of starch granule damage, whereas soft wheats generally give too highly coloured flours. The ideal would probably be something slightly harder than Maris Widgeon.

F. Pushman (Cambridge): I should like to return to the question of spraying urea-N on the crop. We can increase protein content substantially, but there appears to be a decrease in flour extraction.

A. Salem (University of Alexandria, Egypt): We have very similar findings in Egypt. Although urea spraying at the heading stage increased protein content, starch production was reduced and flour yield and baking quality were lower.

G. N. Irvine (Canadian Grain Commission, Winnipeg, Canada): We have discussed enhanced protein content, hardness, the desirability of whiteness in flour, and how to recover during milling the sub-aleurone protein. It has been our experience in Canada that we get a much better recovery of protein in the flour from the harder wheats. If you develop harder wheats in Britain, I wonder whether this would not result in a higher percentage of the protein being recovered in the flour. The milling process is important. Some years ago I was in mills in the UK where it was not possible to produce a 15% protein flour in more than 5% yield from a 13·5% protein grist. Yet in North America we regularly produce from hard wheats substantial quantities of a 17% protein flour from a 13·5% protein grist.

Chairman: We must now conclude this interesting discussion that has ranged from fundamental considerations of the wheat plant's physiological response to fertiliser-N applications to technological considerations of how enhanced protein levels are best handled during the milling process. Clearly, we must strive to ensure that both the quality and quantity of grain protein is increased in ways leading to better baking flours.

The Crop, the Environment and the Genotype

F. G. H. LUPTON AND FIONA M. PUSHMAN
Plant Breeding Institute, Cambridge, UK

The yield and grain quality of a wheat crop depend on the interaction between the variety and the environment in which it is grown. Environmental factors which may limit productivity comprise first, daylength, temperature and light intensity, over which the farmer has little control; and secondly, those such as soil type, drought or attack by disease, the effects of which he may be able to mitigate by adjustment in his methods of husbandry or by a suitable choice of varieties. Genetic variation is, however, available in both groups of factors and must be considered by the breeder in the selection of new varieties.

DAYLENGTH

The length of day is an aspect of the environment which shows no seasonal change in a given locality and to which many wheat varieties are very sensitive. Consideration of daylength sensitivity must be combined with the requirement of the crop to be exposed to low temperatures at early stages of its development, that is to its vernalisation requirement. These characters are associated with winter hardiness in autumn sown wheats and are also known in spring wheats, where two aspects should be considered: first, the crop must be grown in an environment in which it will enter the reproductive phase in a reasonable length of time, and secondly, the environment must be such as to avoid an excessively rapid development of the crop so that there is not sufficient time for the ears and other reproductive organs to develop properly. This problem is well illustrated by the work of Bingham (1972). He compared five Mexican wheat varieties and the European variety Kolibri, grown under 12 h and 18 h daylengths either with no vernalisation treatment or following 14 days' exposure to a low temperature of 3 °C (Table I). When grown without vernalisation and with 12 h daylength the Mexican varieties were slow to develop but all eared satisfactorily after a maximum of 100 days; but the west European variety Kolibri had not eared after 130 days. In an 18 h daylength all varieties eared much more quickly and two of the Mexican varieties, Yecora and Inia, eared after 34 and 33 days respectively, that is much too quickly to develop satisfactory ears; the other varieties took rather longer to ear in this environment but the ears were adequately large. The effect of vernalisation was most marked on the variety Saric which eared after 43 days instead of after 58 days in the unvernalised environment; under these conditions there was not sufficient time for Saric to form ears which could give a reasonable grain yield.

TABLE I

THE EFFECT OF VERNALISATION AND PHOTOPERIOD ON DAYS TO EARING IN THREE SPRING WHEAT VARIETIES

	12 h day		18 h day	
	No. vernalisation	*14 days vernalisation at 3 °C*	*No. vernalisation*	*14 days vernalisation at 3 °C*
Yecora	77	77	34	33
Inia	70	67	33	33
Saric	100	87	58	43
Pitic	89	86	55	47
Siete Cerros	98	96	44	42
Kolibri	>130	>130	51	49

Bingham's experiments were carried out under controlled environment but were confirmed later by an experiment carried out in the field where it was found that satisfactory ears were formed by Pitic and Siete Cerros. These varieties have been widely used in breeding programmes in this country whereas Yecora, Saric and Inia are much less satisfactory and form very small ears of very low yielding capacity. These results are perhaps a little surprising in the case of Saric but it is evident that the temperature in the spring or early summer in Britain is sufficiently low to meet the vernalisation requirement of Saric and to cause it to ear much more rapidly than would have been expected under Mexican conditions. This example illustrates how the daylength neutrality of the Mexican wheats, though important in low latitude countries, creates problems when these varieties are grown in conditions of very widely differing daylength.

SENSITIVITY TO LOW TEMPERATURES

Daylength sensitivity and vernalisation requirement are frequently very closely related to winter hardiness. In this context it is useful to distinguish between cold resistance and the capacity of the crop to survive waterlogged conditions during the winter months. The latter is often associated with tolerance to snow mould, *Fusarium nivale*, which may attack crops while under snow cover, and is best tested under natural conditions in the field.

Cold resistance may be estimated by growing plants under exposed conditions in which there is no snow cover and recording the percentage of survival. Alternatively, it may be estimated as described by Jenkins and Roffey (1974), by growing crops in a controlled environment, in which they are exposed to very low temperature, and then measuring the electrical conductivity of the leaves. It is found that cold exposure will destroy the cell structure and increase the conductivity of the leaves of susceptible varieties whereas resistant varieties survive with very little change in electrical conductivity. Complications may arise, however, because varieties develop hardiness as the winter progresses and may be badly damaged by a sudden cold spell in early winter, but would survive a similar or colder spell after a reasonable level of hardiness had been acquired.

LIGHT INTENSITY

The yield of a wheat crop is obviously dependent to a large extent on its photosynthetic capacity and this is determined by the intensity and duration of the light energy falling on it. The efficiency with which the energy is used, however, is extremely low. Thorne (1971) calculated that a wheat crop normally only uses about 0·5% of the radiant energy which falls upon it, although this figure could be increased to between 2 and 2·5% if only the period of grain development is considered. These figures should be compared with the theoretical maximum efficiency of about 8% quoted by Niciporovic (1954) leaving a considerable scope for improvement, although there are many reasons why the gap cannot be narrowed completely. The first is, that wheat, which uses the C_3 pathway for photosynthesis, is easily saturated with light energy in comparison with such crops as maize and sugar cane which use the C_4 pathway (Stoy, 1965).

Lupton (1972) demonstrated differences in rates of photosynthesis between one of the new short-strawed wheats which have been developed at Cambridge and the taller variety Cappelle-Desprez. For this purpose the crop was considered to comprise a series of inverted cones (Fig. 1) each cone representing a zone of photosynthetic tissue such as the ears, flag leaves or flag leaf sheaths. Measurements of the light intensity incident on the crop, made each minute throughout the period during which the grain was filling, could thus be used to give an estimate of the light intensity at each zone in the crop and thus of its rate of photosynthesis. These measurements were combined with estimates of the translocation of photosynthate from the leaves and ears to the grain of the crops concerned, obtained using radiocarbon as a tracer, to give an estimate of crop yield, thus demonstrating the physiological basis of the yield difference between the two varieties compared (Table II).

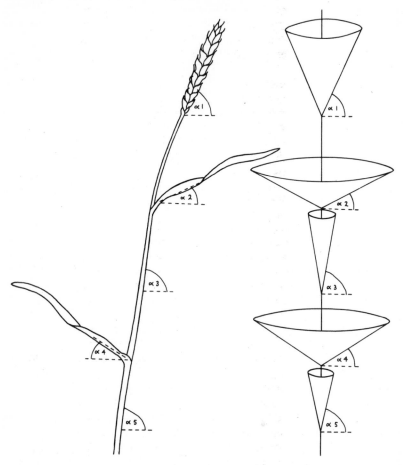

FIG. 1. Diagrammatic representation of canopy structure in wheat.

It was also possible to use the inverted cone model to work out the effect of different crop structures on yield. This showed that there was almost no effect on crop yield if all the leaves instead of being at an angle of approximately 70° had in fact been vertical. If, however, the leaves had been horizontal, so that the flag leaves largely shaded all those below them, there was a 10% loss in total yield capacity. This therefore gives an indication of an important physiological character which the plant breeder can use in selection and shows how consideration of the structure of the crop can enable him to select for improved yielding capacity.

The situation may, however, be complicated by compensations which take place within the crop. This is illustrated by the work of my colleagues, Austin *et al.* (1974), who studied the photosynthetic behaviour of a wheat crop under field conditions by covering a small portion of the crop

TABLE II

CONTRIBUTIONS OF PHOTOSYNTHETIC ORGANS TO GRAIN YIELD ($g m^{-2}$)

	TL365a/25 (semi dwarf)	Cappelle-Desprez
Ears		
Direct sunlight	21	24
Indirect light	48	38
Flag leaves		
Direct sunlight	30	28
Indirect light	105	101
Flag leaf sheaths		
Direct sunlight	8	7
Indirect light	70	62
Second leaves and sheaths		
Direct light	1	1
Indirect light	9	7
Total	292	268

with a transparent cuvette, through which air was rapidly pumped. The CO_2 content of the air was monitored before and after passing across the experimental portion of the crop, enabling them to follow the pattern of photosynthesis through the day and at different times during the growing season. The contributions of different parts of the canopy were estimated from time to time using radiocarbon as a tracer. A comparison of the rates of photosynthesis of two wheat varieties showed that the net carbon dioxide fixation of a selection with erect leaves was significantly greater than that of a closely related selection with drooping leaves. The increased photosynthesis was largely contributed by the lower leaves of the erect leaved selection, which senesced more slowly. There was, however, no yield difference in this case between the two selections as the deficit in photosynthate was made up by translocation of reserves from the stems and peduncles of the selection with drooping leaves.

THE CONTRIBUTION OF AWNS TO
PHOTOSYNTHESIS

Crops with awns are frequently found in hot dry climates, but are less commonly grown in maritime countries. This is probably because the leaves of crops grown in very hot environments tend to die relatively early in the development of the crop, so that the awns become important as photosynthetic organs. They may also have a valuable function in increasing transpiration, particularly in irrigated crops, when air temperatures are high and relative humidity low. In these circumstances, over half the radiant energy incident on the crop may be dissipated as latent heat, thus reducing the temperature of the chloroplasts to a level more suitable for photosynthesis (Bingham, 1973).

Evans and Rawson (1970) compared the rates of photosynthesis of an awned and an awnless wheat under hot dry conditions in Australia. They found that the rate of ear photosynthesis of the awned variety was double that of the awnless variety and that the awned ears contributed 30% of the total grain carbohydrate, in comparison with 20% from the awnless ears. Similar results were found by Birecka and Dakic-Wlodkovska (1963) working with spring wheat in Poland and by McDonough and Gauch (1959) working with durum wheat in Maryland, USA. In view of these findings it is remarkable that the majority of the wheats cultivated in Australia are awnless.

A research student at the Plant Breeding Institute, L. B. Olugbemi, has been studying the importance of awns under temperate conditions at Cambridge. He has shown that although awns make a positive contribution to photosynthesis under these conditions, this is compensated by a lower photosynthetic activity by leaves and other green organs, so that there is no net gain in yield.

IMPORTANCE OF 'SOURCE' AND 'SINK' IN
DETERMINING YIELD

The compensation of photosynthetic activity between the leaves and the ears under temperate conditions draws attention to another important feature of crop physiology. This is the interaction between the source of carbohydrate and capacity of the plant to utilise it, in other words to the interaction of 'source' and 'sink' in determining crop yield. In a recent growth analysis experiment (Lupton et al., 1974) we were able to show that approximately 40% of the variation in yield between a range of hybrids between short and taller wheat varieties could be explained in terms of differences between these hybrids in relation to leaf area duration, tiller number and flag leaf size. If, however, at the same time we also considered the rate of growth of the ear primordia, we were able to explain approximately 90% of the variation between the selections, thus showing that any physiological analysis of yield must consider both the capacity of the plant to photosynthesise and its capacity to utilise the available photosynthate.

EFFECTS OF DISEASE

The balance between source and sink in carbohydrate metabolism may be disturbed by the effects of disease attack, particularly by the attack of diseases which influence the photosynthetic capacity of the leaves. This is well illustrated by the work of Siddiqui and Manners (1971) who investigated the effect of yellow rust (*Puccinia striiformis*) on the development of wheat. They found that the photosynthetic capacity of plants inoculated with yellow rust fell to approximately a quarter of the rate in uninoculated control plants during the month after inoculation. This was accompanied by a marked reduction in the rate of growth of the roots which had ceased to grow a month after inoculation (Fig. 2). In addition

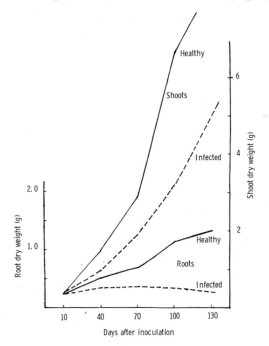

FIG. 2. Effect of rust on shoot and root growth of wheat (after Siddiqui and Manners, 1971).

to reducing the capacity of the leaves to carry out photosynthesis the developing mycelium and spores of the rust form a new sink, utilising carbohydrate that might otherwise have been used in filling the grain or for other useful plant growth. This can be particularly important when rust attack hits the ear of a growing wheat crop and may result in the production of poorly filled grain.

EFFECTS OF DROUGHT

Water supply is the principal factor limiting crop productivity in many parts of the world and much of the recent advance in crop productivity, particularly that due to the spread of the wheats from Mexico in the CIMMYT programme has been due to the availability of irrigation schemes in the areas to which they have been introduced. The breeding of drought tolerant varieties may be considered under two headings. First, selection for varieties which pass through their growth stages relatively rapidly and so avoid the worst effects of drought, and secondly, selection of those which are best able to tolerate conditions of limited water supply.

One of the most important factors which must be considered in breeding for true drought resistance is concerned with the development of the root-ing system. This must fully exploit the environment in which the crop is grown so as to utilise all the water which is available, but at the same time should not be excessively extravagant in water utilisation in the early stages of crop growth, which would leave a relatively small amount for the critical stage of grain formation. Thus it may be desirable to select for a rooting system which develops slowly but which will still be fully de-veloped and capable of utilising residual water at the end of the growing season (Passioura, 1972). This situation may be compared and contrasted with one which would be most suited to the western European conditions where water supply is unlikely to be limiting and in which the most rapidly developing root system would probably be the most desirable. In some work at Cambridge (Lupton et al., 1974) for example, we have compared the rooting systems of semi-dwarf and taller winter wheat varieties, and found that the semi-dwarf varieties have root systems which are as fully extensive as those of the taller varieties with which they have been com-pared. Furthermore, the root systems of the semi-dwarf varieties are more extensive and more efficient in utilisation of available fertiliser at greater depths, thus demonstrating that the reduced aerial system of these wheats is not associated with a reduced rooting system. We have also been carrying out experiments on water utilisation, comparing a range of spring wheats with the use of a neutron probe. This has demonstrated that under conditions of water stress certain varieties, notably the Mexican variety Pitic, is more extravagant in its water utilisation and uses up the reserves of water available in the soil more rapidly than the varieties with which it is being compared (Fig. 3).

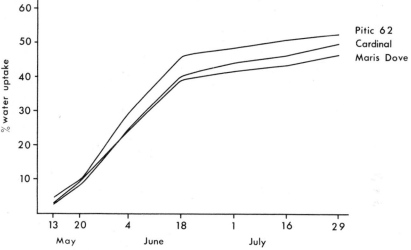

FIG. 3. Water uptake of 3 wheat varieties growing in a droughted environment.

THE EFFECT OF THE ENVIRONMENT ON GRAIN QUALITY

The final grain quality of a wheat crop reflects the extent to which its potential quality has been modified by the environment in which it was grown. This is clearly shown by the wide differences in the quality of wheats grown in the Winter Wheat Performance Nursery Trials throughout the world (Stroike and Johnson, 1972). Such variation also occurs between samples from closer geographic locations and may arise annually in a region subject to variable climatic conditions.

Any factor influencing the yield of a variety will, *ipso facto*, affect its quality because of the negative correlation between total grain yield and protein content. Thus the baking quality of wheat from a high yielding district, such as Western Europe, is not as good as that from Canada and the hard red spring wheat area of the USA, where yield is limited by water supply and a relatively short growing season.

The climatic conditions at harvest further influence grain quality. Hot dry weather throughout the summer ensures that the grain is harvested in good condition although premature ripening or échaudage may cause serious problems in hotter climates. Bad harvest weather may also cause premature germination of the grain, resulting in the problems of dough stickiness associated with high α-amylase activity. Adverse harvesting conditions may also result in wheat with a high microbiological flora and poor flour colour and the problems of quality may be exacerbated if insufficient care is taken in grain drying.

Thus within the western European environment, the quality of British grain is less consistent than that from France or Germany because the weather at harvest is less reliable and because the yields are somewhat higher and the protein content correspondingly lower.

Despite its profound effect on protein content, the environment has relatively little effect on the electrophoretic patterns of wheat albumin, globulin and gliadin proteins (Lee and Ronalds, 1967). Although biochemical analysis of wheat proteins has become highly sophisticated it has not yet been possible to correlate stable protein characteristics with the final quality of wheat without discrepancies and inconsistencies.

The environment may thus be an additional complication in breeding varieties with improved quality, but there is considerable potential for improvement which will be considered in a later section.

BUILDING OF A CROP IDEOTYPE

The physiological considerations discussed can be used to construct an ideotype most suited to the varied environments in which the crop may be grown; in considering this ideotype it is important to remember that the individual plant must always be considered as part of the community within which it grows, and, to use the concept of Donald (1968), that it must be strongly competitive with other species while at the same time offering a minimum of competition to members of its own species. The breeder should not be deterred because it is possible to suggest many models of contrasting design but apparently equal potential. He must declare his preference and work towards its realisation, without allowing subsidiary considerations to deflect him from achieving this purpose.

The ideotype must clearly be adapted to the daylength in which the crop is to be grown and must also be adapted to such conditions of cold exposure as will give adequate winter hardiness and vernalisation. It must also carry sufficient resistance to drought or to environmental effects such as diseases or pests to which the crop will be exposed. The crop should have short straw, strong enough to withstand lodging at levels of fertility in which it is likely to be grown but at the same time not so short as to suffer a major risk of weed competition; short straw also has advantages in terms of competition between the ear and the stem for carbohydrate supply.

The ideotype should have leaves with a high photosynthetic activity and long leaf area duration; it should have an erect leaf habit enabling the light to penetrate well into the crop and at the same time exposing a large proportion of the leaves to light of a suitable photosynthetic intensity. The ears should also remain green for as long as possible and have a high photosynthetic activity, although the value of awns depends to some extent on whether the crop is being grown for a hot dry climate or for maritime conditions.

A uniculm habit is probably to be avoided but crops should be selected for economy of tillering, that is for a growth habit in which a large proportion of the tillers survive to form ears at harvest. Although the greater part of the carbohydrate in the grain is derived from photosynthate translocated directly to it from the flag leaves and from the ear itself, a considerable gain in yield may be achieved by temporary storage of carbohydrates in the internodes, such carbohydrate being subsequently translocated to the grain. Such sequestration of carbohydrate may take place during the period of grain formation when the young grains are too small to utilise all available carbohydrate or may take place at an earlier stage of development, building up reserves in the stem before anthesis which can subsequently be translocated to the developing grain. This may be specially valuable in hot dry climates where temperature and water supply may limit photosynthesis during the period of grain formation. This critical period should be synchronised with the longest days or with other factors such as water supply which may limit growth of the developing grain. In temperate zones this may involve a more rapid development of the crop to the stage of ear formation and anthesis, but this should not be achieved at the expense of the development of large ears with an adequate capacity to store carbohydrate. It may, however, be achieved by the elimination of one or more internodes in the developing stem so that formation of the ear starts slightly earlier in the ontogeny of the crop.

The root system should be adapted to the most efficient utilisation of water and nutrients available in the soil. In crops designed for maritime climates the root system should exploit the soil zone as quickly as possible and should be sufficiently extensive to make full use of available water supply and nutrients. Crops for dry areas may need to have root systems which conserve the water supply so as to leave adequate available water during the critical period of growth. In both cases it should be remembered that root growth can only take place by utilising carbohydrate sequestrated from other parts of the crop.

ADJUSTING THE PHENOTYPE TO FIT THE IDEOTYPE

Wheat is a self-pollinating annual crop so that the varieties in common cultivation consist of near homozygous true breeding lines. In recent years attempts have been made to develop F_1 hybrid wheats; such wheats would be derived from carefully chosen parents selected to show a high degree of hybrid vigour in the F_1 generation. There are, however, considerable technical difficulties in the production of such wheats. These are mainly concerned with developing male-sterile lines and fertility restoring lines suitable for crossing together in F_1 hybrid wheat production. The consideration of this problem is, however, out of the scope of the present paper.

Because normal bread wheats are true breeding homozygous lines, variability for production of new varieties must be based on crosses between varieties chosen to show the various characters which it is aimed to combine. If possible a simple inter-varietal cross may be used but if several characters from different parents are being combined more complex programmes may be required; it may also be necessary to use back-crosses when it is desired to introduce simple characters such as disease resistance from one parent to another. Subsequent selection is based on a pedigree system in which the best plants are selected in successive years and their progenies grown for more detailed selection. In the earliest generations, when selection is on a single plant basis, only qualitative characters can be considered, but when sufficient grain is available for replicated tests it is possible to test quantitative characteristics such as grain quality and yielding capacity. In the system which is used at the Cambridge Plant Breeding Institute, yield trials and pedigree selection are maintained in parallel; it is thus possible to start the early stages of multiplication of a new variety while the equivalent selections are being grown in a yield trial and the best lines for further multiplication chosen.

Selection for physiological characters is difficult in a programme of this sort and can only be carried out for easily recognised characteristics such as tillering capacity, or high degree of tiller survival, for leaf angle and duration, for straw height or for such characters as winter habit or time of coming into ear. Improvement in more complex characters is based largely on an original choice of parents showing complementary assets followed by detailed examination of progeny at a more advanced generation. The results obtained have, however, been very satisfactory as wheat yields in Britain have gone up by approximately 1% per annum for the last 40 years. Similar results have been obtained in other parts of the world. The results of the Mexican programme are of course well known and highly successful programmes have been conducted in many other countries. In others, particularly where maintenance of grain quantity has been a prime consideration, the improvement in yielding potential has been less marked but a round figure of 1% increase in yield per annum may be taken as a world average.

PROBLEMS OF BREEDING FOR DISEASE RESISTANCE

Selection for disease resistance has always been an important part of wheat breeding programmes. Until recently breeders have used simply inherited major genes in order to introduce resistance to most diseases, particularly the foliar diseases caused by the rust fungi and by powdery mildew. Such major gene resistance was relatively easy to use, tests were done on seedlings in a glasshouse and only those seedlings showing hypersensitive resistance were retained. It was found, however, that the fungi were very quick to adapt themselves and produce races capable of attacking varieties carrying such major gene resistance; the breeder has been compelled therefore to research for new sources of resistance and in particular for non-race-specific resistance which may be expected to have greater durability. In this search he has been looking for varieties which although slightly susceptible to disease never appear to be badly attacked, in the hope that such resistance will be long lived. Experience with stripe rust in Britain has, however, pointed to the difficulties of this type of work. The variety Joss Cambier, for example, was quoted as showing horizontal resistance of this type but a new strain of rust developed some 3 years ago which is now strongly aggressive on this variety.

It is essential therefore for the breeder to study more closely the mechanism by which rust resistance is expressed in the hope of finding a better form of resistance to use. An example of this was noted by my colleague G. E. Russell who examined the field resistance of the variety Maris Widgeon. This variety is derived from a cross between the varieties Cappelle-Desprez and Holdfast; when inoculated with yellow rust, Holdfast shows a relatively small number of spore infections per unit area of leaf while in the case of Cappelle-Desprez there is a long time interval between initial infection and the development of the first spores of the next generation. Maris Widgeon has inherited the two characters and therefore shows a level of field resistance considerably better than that of either of its parents.

An alternative approach is suggested by my colleagues Johnson and Law (1973). Moderate levels of field resistance to yellow rust are shown by a number of varieties of winter wheat, but the inheritance is complex and difficult to handle by conventional methods (Lupton and Johnson, 1970). Johnson and Law have, however, shown that the resistance of one of these varieties, Bersee, is mainly determined by genetic factors carried on a single chromosome, and that this resistance can be transferred to a susceptible variety by substitution of this chromosome into its genotype. This demonstration of the possibilities of breeding for disease resistance by using cytological techniques is very encouraging to the plant breeder, as it enables him to handle a complex character with confidence even though many closely linked genetic factors may be involved.

Meanwhile systematic fungicides have been developed so that it is possible for the farmer to protect his crop if a new strain of fungus should appear during the growing season and it is likely that the development of these new fungicides will introduce a new era in which the plant breeder will combine with the chemical manufacturer to ensure the success of the farmer's crop. As an alternative it may be necessary for the farmer to grow mixtures of varieties of very similar phenotype but carrying different factors for disease resistance. The growing of such crops may limit the spread of the disease and thereby enable him to obtain a satisfactory crop in most years without the risk of a new race spreading to cause serious economic loss.

Experience with stripe rust in Britain is similar to that with other fungi in other parts of the world, but mention should be made of the *Septoria* diseases, *Septoria tritici* and *Septoria nodorum* which have caused serious loss in wheat yields in many countries in recent years. It has been claimed that the spread of these diseases has been synchronised with the introduction of wheats derived from the Japanese variety Norin 10 which has been the basis of the short-strawed Mexican varieties and that their spread has been associated with the microclimate engendered by growing a short-strawed variety in which air circulation near the ground was limited. Although this is undoubtedly a contributory factor, a wide range of susceptibility has been found both between short varieties and between taller strawed varieties and we have now developed at Cambridge a number of semi-dwarf wheats which show a reasonable level of resistance to these diseases. Knowledge of the epidemiology and mechanism of infection of the *Septoria* diseases is at present very limited but further experience is being gained which may ease the task of the plant breeder.

Mention should also be made of the soil-borne diseases caused by eyespot *Cercosporella herpotrichoides*, by take-all *Ophiobolus graminis*, and by the *Fusarium* species. The importance of these diseases has increased in recent years following the use of extensive rotations and the introduction of minimal cultivation systems. Satisfactory resistance to eyespot has been known for some years and a new and more effective source has recently been introduced from the species *Aegilops ventricosa*. Resistance to take-all and to the *Fusarium* species is not known although active work to search for suitable sources of resistance is now being carried out.

BREEDING FOR IMPROVED GRAIN QUALITY

Grain quality is the summation of several milling, baking and physical dough characters which may be conveniently considered as separate breeding characters. Because the components of quality are differently influenced by the environment, a knowledge of the heritability of each, of their interdependence, and of the extent to which they can be modified is essential. The aspects of grain quality over which the breeder has most control are first, those concerned with the production of α-amylase in the grain at harvest time; secondly, those concerned with milling quality and flour yield; and, thirdly, those determining baking quality of the flour.

α-Amylase may be produced in the grain endogenously or as a result of premature germination resulting from a short period of grain dormancy. The endogenous production of α-amylase was first demonstrated by Bingham (1968). He estimated the α-amylase production of six wheat varieties growing under field conditions at Cambridge, during a season marked by hot dry weather in early August followed by wet conditions as grain maturity was reached in late August and September. Three of the varieties he compared, Atle, Cappelle-Desprez and Rothwell Perdix, were very resistant to premature germination and had a low α-amylase content throughout the experiment. Two varieties, Holdfast and Minister both with white grain, had a very short period of grain dormancy and consequently showed a high percentage germination associated with high α-amylase production in late August. The sixth variety, Professeur Marchal had a long period of dormancy and was therefore resistant to premature germination, but showed nevertheless a high α-amylase activity throughout the period of grain ripening, even during the hot dry weather in early August.

This variety thus produces α-amylase endogenously and, as Bingham also demonstrated, will do so when grown under rain free conditions in the glasshouse. Bingham also showed that this character is strongly heritable, and apparently mainly determined by recessive genetic factors. The character has unfortunately been inherited by a number of high yielding derivatives of Professeur Marchal—notably the varieties Maris Nimrod and Maris Huntsman—but there is no reason why this defect should not be eliminated in future selections.

A low level of grain dormancy is commonly seen in white grained varieties, and it has been suggested by Wellington (1956) that the longer dormancy of red grained wheats may be pleiotropically associated with the red pigment. Grain colour is simply inherited, but a range of levels of resistance to premature germination is shown by red grained varieties and the inheritance of the character is complex.

Flour yield is determined partly by factors influencing grain filling and partly by the texture of the endosperm. Grain filling is clearly much influenced by the environment in which the crop is grown, but is also under genetic control and therefore subject to improvement by the plant breeder. Endosperm texture, on the other hand, is independent of the environment and can readily be combined with high yield. Adequate small scale tests have been developed which can be used to assess this character in the early stages of a breeding programme (Bell and Bingham, 1957; Shuey and Gilles, 1973). Essentially, these tests are concerned with assessing the ease with which the endosperm can be separated from the bran. Very wide and strongly heritable varietal differences are found in this character. Although quantitative estimates of the flour, bran and offal proportions are necessary for fine distinctions between varieties, preliminary selection can be based on eye judgement of the quantity of flour adhering to the bran of grain milled under standardised conditions. At the Plant Breeding Institute, we use the first break of a Brabender stone mill for this purpose, and can assess milling quality using half the product of a single plant, the other half being retained for sowing if the quality is satisfactory.

There are considerable problems in combining high yielding capacity with satisfactory baking quality because of the negative correlation between grain protein content and grain yield. This partly arises because plant breeders have concentrated on improving the yield of carbohydrate without at the same time seeking to improve the yield of protein. As a result, the yield of protein per hectare has hardly changed in the past 20 years while the yield of carbohydrate has increased by some 25%. The protein percentage of modern varieties grown under conditions comparable to those used 25 years ago is thus about 25% less than that of the original varieties. It should, however, be remembered that because of their shorter and stronger straw, modern varieties are usually grown at higher levels of fertility than those previously used, so that the fall in protein percentage has largely been prevented by changes in husbandry.

A study of the yield–protein relationship within the USDA World Wheat Collection has shown that certain varieties, such as Atlas 66, April Bearded and Nap Hal have a 2–3% higher protein content than might have been expected from their yielding capacities (Middleton et al., 1954). This advantage was maintained in a range of environments (Johnson et al., 1972), and the varieties have therefore been used in breeding programmes from which high protein lines have been selected. But the yields of these lines are much less than those expected by European farmers and further breeding programmes have been initiated to incorporate the high protein genes in wheats adapted to European conditions.

In areas where wheat is the major source of dietary protein, the nutritional balance of the protein is a major aspect of quality. The possibility that high protein lines derived from Atlas 66 might have an inferior amino acid balance was therefore investigated because of the negative correlation frequently found between lysine per unit of protein and total protein content. It was, however, shown that there was no such correlation at high protein levels and that the amino acid balance of high protein Atlas

66 derivatives was similar to that of other wheats and therefore nutritionally superior to lower protein derivatives (Mattern *et al.*, 1968).

There are many tests available by which various aspects of flour quality may be evaluated but the breeder requires relatively simple tests which will enable him to predict the baking quality from a small sample. This is more difficult because flour protein, particle size, enzyme activity, starch damage, water absorption, mixing requirement, mixing tolerance and oxidation requirement all influence the volume and crust and crumb characteristics of the loaf. Breeding stations thus vary in the type of quality testing used: some make early selection on a micro-baking test which integrates all the characteristics; others prefer to use two or three tests assessing the important baking properties from which inference as to other important characters can be drawn. The range of quality tests performed also depends on the relative importance of quality and yield in the particular breeding programme.

TABLE III

QUALITY CHARACTERISTICS OF WHEAT VARIETIES, CAMBRIDGE, 1972

	Yield tonne/ha	Flour extraction (%)	Protein (%)	α-amylase Farrand units	Water absorption gal/sack	Loaf volume ml	Loaf score
Maris Hobbit	6·02	56·3	10·9	16·4	15·1	1 286	47
Maris Huntsman	5·44	68·1	12·1	45·7	14·8	1 228	43
Maris Freeman	4·89	69·5	13·0	18·2	15·3	1 379	63
Cappelle-Desprez	4·78	54·7	12·7	15·3	14·5	1 395	65
West-Desprez	4·67	57·2	13·3	13·1	15·1	1 353	63
Maris Widgeon	4·39	71·0	13·6	18·3	15·0	1 416	74

Characterisation of the wheat proteins, in particular the gluten fraction, is regarded as a primary factor in the assessment of flour potential. Use of physical dough testing machines, such as the farinograph, mixograph and extensograph, allows the flour to be defined in terms of the mixing characteristics, extensibility and resistance to extension of its doughs. These tests are widely used commercially and although models exist for small samples, the amount of flour necessary for a test precludes their use with very early generation material. Thus breeders often use rapid tests such as the Zeleny sedimentation test and the Pelshenke wheat-meal fermentation time test for early generation quality selection. Although these methods may be less precisely related to baking quality than other tests, they provide a valuable division of types and later selections can be evaluated more fully.

At the Plant Breeding Institute, selection in early generations is based on lines combining hard milling, low α-amylase and long Pelshenke time with good agronomic characteristics. Subsequent assessment is by a baking test using the Chorleywood mechanical dough development method, a method most widely used in the British baking industry.

The difference in some of the quality attributes of six wheats commonly grown in Britain is shown in Table I I I. A consideration of the complexities of wheat quality and the interrelationship of the various physical and chemical characteristics is too large a subject for this discussion and will be considered in more detail by other speakers. However, it is of vital importance that wheat breeders, cereal chemists and processors are aware of the problems and progress within each others' fields.

CONCLUSION

The wheat crop, and more specifically the loaf of bread, is thus a highly complex product resulting from the interaction of a wide range of environmental factors. Many of these, such as sensitivity to daylength or to extremes of temperature, are beyond the control of the farmer, and limit the range of environments in which a variety can be grown. There remains, however, a wide range of characters over which the farmer and the breeder have considerable influence as is shown by the improved productivity which has been achieved in the last 20 or 30 years.

It has been suggested that we may now be approaching a yield plateau above which further advances cannot be made, but we consider this to be an unduly pessimistic view. The potential yield of the wheat crop clearly falls short of its maximum as its photosynthetic rate falls short of Niciporovic's theoretical limit of 8% utilisation of incident solar energy, and recent advances in crop physiology point to ways in which this gap may be narrowed.

The achievement of the theoretical maximum may also be prevented due to losses caused by diseases or insect pests. Such losses are likely to be more serious as levels of fertility are increased and cultivation becomes more intensive, but advances in plant pathology show how these hazards may be overcome, possibly by the combined efforts of the breeder and the agricultural chemist.

There remains the more difficult problem of combining high yields with good grain quality, and here we feel that the chief contribution of the breeder will be to produce varieties which lack the main faults, such as the high α-amylase content or soft milling properties, of some modern varieties. Such varieties should also have desirable agronomic features such as short stiff straw which enable the farmers to apply the nitrogenous fertilisers necessary to obtain satisfactory baking quality in the grain.

REFERENCES

Austin, R. B., Ford, M. A. and Edrich, J. A. (1974). *Photosynthesis, translocation and grain filling in wheat*, Report, Plant Breeding Institute, 1973, pp. 169–170.

Bell, G. D. H. and Bingham, J. (1957). 'Grain quality: a genetic and plant breeding character. I. Wheat', *Agric. Rev.*, **3**, 10–22.

Bingham, J. (1968). 'Zur genetischen und planzenzüchterischen Betrachtung der Weizenqualität', *Getreide und Mehl*, **18**, 61–66.

Bingham, J. (1972). 'Physiological objectives in breeding for grain yield in wheat', in *The Way Ahead in Plant Breeding*, Proceedings of the Sixth Congress of Eucarpia, Cambridge, 1971 (Ed. F. G. H. Lupton, G. Jenkins and R. Johnson), 15–29.

Bingham, J. (1973). 'Physiological objectives in breeding for high grain yields under irrigated and rainfed conditions', FAO Information Bulletin, *Cereal Improvement and Production*, **10** (3), 7–17.

Birecka, H. and Dakic-Wlodkovska, L. (1963). 'Photosynthesis, translocation and accumulation of assimilates in cereals during grain development III. Spring wheat —photosynthesis and the daily accumulation of photosynthates in the grain', *Acta Societ. Botanica Polonica*, **32**, 631–650.

Donald, C. M. (1968). 'The breeding of crop ideotypes', *Euphytica*, **17**, 385–403.

Evans, L. T. and Rawson, H. M. (1970). 'Photosynthesis and respiration by the flag leaf and components of the ear during grain development in wheat', *Aust. J. Biol. Sci.*, **23**, 245–254.

Jenkins, G. and Roffey, A. P. (1974). 'A method for estimating the cold hardiness of cereals by measuring electrical conductance after freezing', *J. Agric. Sci., Cambridge*, **83**, 87–92.

Johnson, R. and Law, C. N. (1973). 'Cytogenetic studies on the resistance of the wheat variety Bersee to *Puccinia striiformis*', *Cereal Rusts Bulletin*, **1**, 38–43.

Johnson, V. A., Mattern, P. J. and Schmidt, J. W. (1972). 'Wheat protein improvement', in *Rice Breeding*, International Rice Research Institute, Los Banos, Philippines, 407–418.

Lee, J. W. and Ronalds, J. A. (1967). 'Effect of environment on wheat gliadin', *Nature, Lond.*, **213**, 845–846.

Lupton, F. G. H. (1972). 'Further experiments on photosynthesis and translocation in wheat', *Ann. Appl. Biol.*, **71**, 69–79.

Lupton, F. G. H. and Johnson, R. (1970). 'Breeding for mature plant resistance to yellow rust in wheat', *Ann. Appl. Biol.*, **66**, 137–143.

Lupton, F. G. H., Oliver, R. H., Ellis, F. B., Barnes, B. T., Howse, K. R., Welbank, P. J. and Taylor, P. J. (1974). 'Root and shoot growth of semi-dwarf and taller winter wheats', *Ann. Appl. Biol.*, **77**, 129–144.

Lupton, F. G. H., Oliver, R. H. and Ruckenbauer, P. (1974). 'An analysis of the factors determining yield in crosses between semi-dwarf and taller wheat varieties', *J. Agric. Sci., Cambridge*, **82**, 483–496.

Mattern, P. J., Salem, A., Johnson, V. A. and Schmidt, J. W. (1968). 'Amino acid composition of selected high protein wheats', *Cereal Chem.*, **45**, 437–444.

McDonough, W. T. and Gauch, H. G. (1959). 'Contribution of the awn to the development of bearded wheat', University of Maryland Agricultural Experimental Station Bulletin, **A103**, 1–16.

Middleton, G. K., Bode, C. E. and Bayles, B. B. (1954). 'A comparison of the quantity and quality of protein of certain varieties of soft wheat'. *Agronomy J.*, **46**, 500–502.

Niciporovic, A. A. (1954). 'Photosynthesis and the theory of obtaining high crop yields', Translation in *Field Crop Abstracts*, **13**, 169–175.

Passioura, J. B. (1972). 'The effect of root geometry on the yield of wheat growing on stored water', *Aust. J. Agric. Res.*, **23**, 745–752.

Shuey, W. C. and Gilles, K. A. (1973). 'Milling evaluation of Hard Red Spring wheats in relation to wheat protein, wheat ash, bran pentose, flour pentose and starch on bran to milling results', *Cereal Chem.*, **50**, 37–43.

Siddiqui, M. Q. and Manners, J. G. (1971). 'Some effects of general yellow rust (*Puccinia striiformis*) infection on [14]carbon assimilation, translocation and growth in a spring wheat', *J. Exper. Botany*, **22**, 792–799.

Stoy, V. (1965). 'Photosynthesis, respiration and carbohydrate accumulation in spring wheat in relation to yield', *Physiologia Plantarum*, Suppl. IV, 1–125.

Stroike, J. E. and Johnson, V. A. (1972). 'Winter wheat cultivar performance in an international array of environments', University of Nebraska Research Bulletin 251.

Thorne, G. N. (1971). 'Physiological factors determining the yield of arable crops', in *Potential Crop Production* (Ed. P. F. Wareing and J. P. Cooper), Heinemann, London, pp. 143–158.

Wellington, P. S. (1956). 'Studies on the germination of cereals. 2. Factors determining the germination behaviour of wheat grains during maturation', *Ann. Botany*, **20**, 481–500.

DISCUSSION

Chairman: Dr Lupton, you have given us a wealth of topics upon which to base our discussion. Your last slide of loaves baked from flours of different wheat varieties was intriguing—I almost wanted to taste them!

K. Blaxter (Rowett Research Institute, Aberdeen): Is it possible to make a good loaf out of Huntsman?

F. Pushman (Plant Breeding Institute, Cambridge, UK): Although the protein level of Huntsman can be increased by nitrogen treatments, and a higher protein flour obtained, the detrimental factor is the high α-amylase level producing a loaf with a very sticky crumb. There are also inherent problems concerning the protein type that cannot be compensated for by husbandry methods.

K. Blaxter: I find it difficult to reconcile the last remark with Mr Kingswood's statement that the only thing that really mattered was total protein since baking technology could deal with single wheats.

N. Chamberlain (Flour Milling and Baking Research Association, Chorleywood): I think Mr Kingswood made two qualifications. First, that the grain should be sound, and second that it must have low amylase activity. Huntsman certainly does not fulfil the second requirement.

P. W. Russell Eggitt (Spillers Ltd, Cambridge): I should like to confirm that Maris Huntsman could not be included in British breadmaking grists in any substantial amount. The majority of British bread is sliced and wrapped—bread containing substantial amounts of Huntsman flour just would not slice. May I add that baking quality means different things in different countries. French and British bakers arranging breads in an order of merit based on their crumb characteristics would put them in precisely the same order but in the reverse direction. The Frenchman wants his holes!

Sir David Cuthbertson (Glasgow University): I was interested in Dr Lupton's comments regarding nitrogen fertilisation, yield, grain size and protein content. Is he arguing that smaller grains have higher protein contents?

F. Lupton: I have no specific answer. Many of the higher-yielding new varieties do have larger grains, especially winter wheats. But some of the successful spring wheats yield well because they have more grains, rather than larger ones.

V. A. Johnson (Nebraska University, USA): Within a genotype we have been unable to demonstrate a significant effect of grain size upon protein content.

J. Mesdag (Foundation for Agricultural Plant Breeding, Wageningen, Netherlands): Dr Lupton said that he could not find much difference in yield of protein per hectare between older and newer varieties. Breeders in Europe have never sought this quality, and have looked only for total yield—isn't that the right way?

F. Lupton: This is fair comment. Breeding has been for total yield, presumably primarily for carbohydrate. It is unlikely that large differences occur between varieties in the efficiency with which they take up nitrogen from the soil, and so different grain protein contents probably reflect the better utilisation and transport of nitrogen already within the plant. I feel there is a limit to improvement in this direction, and the plant breeder can perhaps best contribute by strengthening the straw so that the plant can fully respond to increased applications of nitrogen.

Chairman: I see Dr Edelman ready to comment and I presume he will take us back to ideas of photosynthetic efficiency raised early in Dr Lupton's paper.

J. Edelman (R.H.M. Ltd, High Wycombe, Bucks): At a recent seminar, we discussed dry matter yield in UK crops. These probably yielded not more than 5 tons per acre, and 4 tons may be more realistic. Are the breeders of wheat straining after 3 or 4 tons and beyond? You mentioned that wheat is a C_3 plant, whereas high yielding grasses, like maize, are C_4 plants. (C_4 plants can fix CO_2 more effectively at very low concentrations.) Can we get C_4-type fixation into wheat by breeding from its relatives? Or should we strive to artificially increase CO_2 concentrations around the growing wheat plant? Some experiments indicate the latter course to be disappointing, so is there some other limiting factor holding down yields?

F. Lupton: First, I should say that we have now got well above the 3 ton limit as far as yield is concerned. The key to a further advancement in yield probably rests in the plant's ability to utilise carbohydrate, and not in its production. In the new short strawed varieties, the ear proves to be a better sink having more grains per spikelet, and yields tend to be higher. From a very young stage in winter wheats (March) the ear primordia of the newer high-yielding varieties tend to be larger than those of tall varieties.

F. Aylward (Reading University): Do your figures of percentage photosynthetic efficiency refer to material laid down in the grain, or to the total crop?

F. Lupton: The flag leaf is the major photosynthetic organ in the wheat plant at the time of grain development. During rapid grain growth, 60–80% of the carbon fixed by the flag leaf is transported to the ear and eventually found in the grain.

F. Aylward (Reading University): I understand that the amounts of protein and other constituents may vary from grain to grain in the same ear. Has any extended work been done in this direction?

V. A. Johnson: It is certainly true that the position of the grain on the ear has an effect on protein content, with the first-formed grains near the centre of the ear having an advantage in protein over the last ones formed.

A. Salem (Egypt): Is the utilisation of nitrogen for protein production genetically controlled?

V. A. Johnson: Can I respond with regard to nitrate reductase? One of our high protein selections has been shown to have elevated levels of nitrate reductase activity. Nitrate reduction may be an important rate-limiting step in protein synthesis in wheat.

Chairman: Can we turn to other aspects of Dr Lupton's paper? Would anyone like to comment on the effects of disease on yield or upon breeding for disease resistance?

V. A. Johnson: I believe that the implications of disease and resistance to disease go far beyond considerations of yield. I suspect that environments fostering foliar diseases have a depressing effect upon protein content: we have some evidence to suspect this.

Chairman: Dr Lupton, you took us through a typical breeding programme where the fifth year was the first in which you could test for yield. Aren't you now trying to speed up the process?

F. Lupton: Yes, in two ways. We can get two generations in the first year by growing plants in a glasshouse over winter. For the spring crops, that have no vernalisation requirement, we grow alternate generations in the northern and southern hemispheres within the course of a single year.

Chairman: We have had a most interesting and wide-ranging discussion this afternoon. I come to the end of the session realising that when you take a mixed bunch of people from very many countries and with different food habits, you are certainly not going to get a uniform view. It is certainly clear that 'quality' means different things to different people: even with 'bread' there are opposing viewpoints.

Session II

QUALITY ASPECTS

The Nutritive Value of Wheat Proteins

K. J. CARPENTER
Department of Applied Biology,
Cambridge University, Cambridge, UK

SAFETY

The first consideration in the evaluation of any protein source must be its safety. Certainly, wheat is a staple food in areas of the world where the average expectation of life is high, and we can conclude that for the average man there is nothing about wheat protein that will prevent him living to a healthy old age (cf. Aykroyd and Doughty, 1970).

Coeliac disease

However, this is not true for the whole population and it is now accepted that for a small minority wheat products are toxic, damaging the mucosa of the upper small intestine and producing the group of symptoms characteristic of coeliac disease (Dicke *et al.*, 1953). The susceptibility is genetically transmitted with an estimated incidence of 25 000 people in the UK (i.e. 1 in 2000), with a higher proportion (approximately 1 in 400) in those of Celtic stock (Creamer, 1974).

There appears to be no alternative for the sufferer but a life-time avoidance of any foods containing products of wheat, oats, barley or rye (Hamilton and McNeill, 1972). These cereals have in common the possession of a gluten fraction. Within that fraction toxicity has been narrowed down to the gliadins (review by Patey, 1974). Among the hypotheses to explain the disorder is an immunological response to specific proteins; antibodies to gliadins are found in the serum of most sufferers (review by Kasarda *et al.*, 1971).

It is not known exactly which is the toxic protein fraction. *If* we did know and *if* it could be bred out of wheat at some cost in average yield, or inactivated by a procedure giving a small decrease in loaf volume, it would be a difficult moral problem to know how to balance 'the *slightly* greater happiness of the greatest number' against the severe difficulties of a small minority. An individual's judgement might well depend on whether he personally had a friend or relative who was a sufferer.

Possible reactions with 'improvers'

The flour milling industry has, of course, provided the classic example of a food protein being made toxic (though fortunately not to man) by a chemical treatment thought at the time only to have an effect on the physical behaviour of proteins. It is now known that 'Agene' (nitrogen trichloride), for 25 years or so the commonly used 'improver' of bread flours in the U K and elsewhere, reacted with a proportion of the methionine units in the wheat flour protein, converting them to methionine sulphoximine (Bentley et al., 1950). This, on liberation in the digestive tract is a potent nerve poison, and explains the toxicity of heavily 'agenised' flour, to dogs, cats and ferrets (Mellanby, 1946; Bentley et al., 1950; Newell et al., 1947). There is no evidence that it is toxic to man or rats. With monkeys no more than abnormal brain waves have been observed (Newell et al., 1947). If it had turned out that it had a chronic toxicity for man with effects on the brain centres, what an unimaginable tragedy would have occurred.

Probably it is this near shave and the more recent thalidomide tragedy which have really brought home to those with responsibilities for food safety the implications and possible effects of their decisions. In trying to find the moral of the 'Agene' story, a worrying aspect is that testing *was* done by responsible people in a way that, in the light of the knowledge available at the time, seemed to give complete reassurance (cf. Kent-Jones and Amos, 1957). We know more today, but tomorrow people will know more again and be able to pass judgement on the holes then apparent in our present knowledge.

Each successive food toxicity problem has confirmed the apparent capriciousness of species differences for different toxins. For the aflatoxins, rats and pigs are sensitive and mice and sheep highly resistant by comparison (review by Kraybill, 1969). The nitrosamines, on the other hand, are actually *more* toxic to sheep than to rats and pigs (Sakshaug et al., 1965). The discovery of nitrosamine formation as a result of preserving fish with nitrite, prior to drying them for animal feeding, was discovered *after* a series of unexpected deaths of animals. Again, those responsible for developing the process had seemingly taken all reasonable precautions of biological testing and control, *but* (1) the reaction occurring had been quite unexpected, (2) the species used for testing, chicks, rats and pigs, were all relatively resistant and (3) finally the factory hands had not exactly followed their instructions (Koppang and Helgebostad, 1966).

The protein molecule with its variety of reactive amino acid side groups is such a potential site of unexpected reactions with added chemicals that we cannot be too careful in checking that none of these units is converted into a molecule that could have some subtle but ghastly effect. We know that chlorine dioxide has passed all of a series of tests by which the action of agene could have been detected (Newell et al., 1949), but it seems pertinent to remember the adage about generals always trying to re-fight the last war.

There is a psychological difficulty in an official body continuing to sponsor investigation of a process once it has officially approved it, as if it threw doubt on its own decision. But surely, as scientists, we know that all our decisions are based only on the best evidence available at the time, and that we ought to continue investigation regardless.

INTRODUCTION TO NUTRITIONAL STUDIES

There are many hundreds of papers in the literature on the protein value of wheat. I will try to summarise the main findings so as to leave some time to consider their practical implications, some of which are highly controversial.

It is impossible to avoid the matter of extraction rates of flour entirely because one must specify what material was used in particular experiments, but I will try to leave discussion of this aspect to Dr Widdowson, whose paper comes later in the symposium.

One other introductory point. The nutritionist concerned with the 'protein' content of a mixed diet, often including ingredients whose characteristics are incompletely known, is forced to rely on kjeldahl nitrogen analyses, and to make an estimate of 'crude protein' from the conventional constant '$N \times 6.25$'. Since he must be consistent when making calculations with single ingredients and with mixtures, he cannot adopt the cereal chemist's factor of $N \times 5.7$ for wheat products. One has, therefore, to check that protein and amino acid values from different sources are calculated on the same basis. Amino acid analysis values in the present paper are expressed as '$g/16 \, g \, N$', which is equivalent to '$g/100 \, g$ crude protein $(N \times 6.25)$'.

ANIMAL TESTS OF PROTEIN QUALITY

'Most of what we know, or think we know, about human nutrition has been obtained from experimental observations upon laboratory animals. Nutritional experiments upon human subjects are difficult to carry out . . .' (Bricker et al., 1945). And, of these animal experiments, most have been with young rats—they are small (but not too small), omnivorous, docile, rapidly growing and they do not attract sympathy from the public.

For an assay specifically of *protein* quality, all other nutrients (i.e. energy, vitamins and minerals) must be supplied at luxus levels in the diet. Most procedures employ only one level of test material, usually to provide 9–10% crude protein in the diet; this is still not quite sufficient for maximum growth even if the protein is of good quality. Then, in most tests, the rats are allowed to eat as much as they wish for an experimental period that may vary from 1 to 8 weeks. The response of the rats is most simply measured by changes in body weight. One can measure specifically 'protein growth' using whole carcass analysis; alternatively, nitrogen retention can be estimated by a balance between dietary intake and the nitrogen content of excreta. Finally, instead of measuring response as the change from day zero, one can keep control rats on a protein-free diet and take their condition at the end of the experimental period as the base line. 'Net protein utilisation' (NPU), calculated on this basis, has a theoretical upper limit of 100%.

The pros and cons of different measurements have been the subject of much debate. This and the special nomenclature have been reviewed elsewhere (Bender and Doell, 1957; Allison, 1968; National Research Council, 1963; Eggum, 1970). Just what these differences can mean in practice is seen in the results set out in Table IV below, in connection with an apparent improvement in the nutritional value of wheat by soaking. Clearly, care is needed in the design of such assay experiments. Nevertheless, it has been the universal finding, even for NPU, that the value of wheat flour as the sole source of protein for the growing rat is no more than 40–50% that of the best animal protein sources. And with a more sophisticated procedure using several levels of dietary protein and measuring slope-ratios for incremental growths, the 'relative nutritive value' (RNV) of white flour is only 25% that of the standard, the milk protein lactalbumin (Miladi et al., 1972). The low value was obtained despite the protein being highly digestible.

TABLE I

THE UTILISABLE PROTEIN CONTENT (NdP Cal %[a]) OF A
NUMBER OF STAPLES
(Miller and Payne, 1969)

Sago	0·3	Rice	4·9
Cassava	0·9	Sorghum	4·9
Plantain	1·6	Millet	5·3
Yam	4·6	Potato	5·9
Maize	4·7	Wheat	5·9

[a] Net dietary protein calories as % of total calories (cf. requirement for adult man = 4·0%).

Although the quality of wheat protein has usually been found to be rather lower than that of the other main 'staple' energy sources used by man, the *quantity* of protein present is rather higher. When therefore one takes a measure of 'quantity × quality', the final net protein value is equal to that of potatoes and the other cereal staples, and, of course, much superior to cassava and plaintains (Table I).

AMINO ACIDS

It is easy to criticise the relevance of simple rat experiments. They compare performance at sub-optimal levels of protein, whereas in man we are only concerned with the formulation of optimal diets, and they use only one protein source whereas all practical human diets include mixtures of several protein sources. However, they have led to an understanding of the relation between the amino acid composition of proteins and their nutritional value. Block and Mitchell (1946) took the amino acid composition of whole egg protein as a provisional 'ideal' and then calculated the level of each essential amino acid in a test protein as a percentage of the level of the same amino acid in egg. The lowest of these percentages was termed the 'chemical score' of the protein source as a whole. Compilation

TABLE II

AVERAGE GAIN IN WEIGHT PER DAY, AND PER G OF CRUDE PROTEIN CONSUMED BY THE RATS RECEIVING DIFFERENT SOURCES OF PROTEIN

(Ericson, 1960)

Diet no.	Protein source	Average gain in weight (g/day)	Average gain in weight per g crude protein consumed (per)
1	Basal bread[a] diet	1·36	1·57
2	Basal bread[a] diet + 0·4% L-lysine-HCl	4·27	2·91
3	Basal bread[a] diet + 0·4% L-lysine-HCl + 0·2% DL-threonine	5·78	3·36
4	Spray dried skim milk (33·2%)	4·60	3·22
5	Egg albumin (14·6%)	4·10	3·58
	(Pooled SE of means)	(±0·24)	(±0·08)

[a] Bread made from 70% extraction flour. Glycine added to diets 1 and 2 to make amino acid supplements iso-nitrogenous with diet 3. All diets contained approximately 12·5% crude protein.

of data for a range of test materials showed a significant correlation between NPU and chemical score. Also the amino acid 'scored' as being most deficient was also, in almost every case, the only one which improved the test material's NPU value for rats when added as a supplement to the diet. These findings have stimulated work so as to determine the requirements of man and other species for individual amino acids more exactly.

There is still considerable debate as to what are the amino acid requirements of man, but with present methods of amino acid analysis it is possible to predict fairly well how far particular mixtures of protein sources will meet the requirements of a particular diet for animals. Further, where biological performance has been less than was predicted from chemical analysis, the partial 'unavailability' of an amino acid has been brought to light, and in some instances this has been shown to be due to processing damage which could be avoided by a change in method of manufacture.

In common with most other cereals the chemical score of all types of wheat flour makes lysine the most limiting amino acid, and this is confirmed in tests with rats (Tables II and III). Although lysine is the only single amino acid supplement which gives a response in rat experiments, with wheat it only brings it up to the point where the next amino acid, threonine, becomes limiting. In contrast, most 'high protein' foods, whether the vegetable grain legumes or meat and milk have adequate lysine, but are limiting in the sulphur-containing amino acids.

TABLE III

THE VALUE OF WHEAT PRODUCTS AS SOLE PROTEIN SOURCES
FOR RAT GROWTH
(Miladi et al., 1972)

| | Protein content (%) | Am. acids, g/16 g N | | | Rat results | | |
		Lys.	Met. + Cys.	Threo-nine-	N. dig. (%)	Relative nutr. value (%)	Utilisable protein (%)
White flour	14·4	1·9	4·6	2·6	99	24(62)[a]	3·5
Whole wheat	16·7	2·5	4·3	2·8	91	39(63)	6·5
Middlings	19·7	4·2	4·1	3·3	84	57(69)	11·2
Bran	17·2	4·1	4·0	3·3	69	51(59)	8·8
Germ	25·2	4·9	3·8	3·5	92	79(80)	19·9

[a] Values in brackets obtained with added lysine.

Wheat endosperm contains a mixture of many proteins and over 100 years ago chemists were differentiating wheat gluten into what they called 'vegetable casein' and 'vegetable gelatin' (cf. Bailey, 1944). Fractionating the crude gluten of approximately 1·3% lysine content into alcohol-soluble and insoluble fractions respectively gives gliadins containing approximately 0·6% lysine and glutenins with approximately 2·0%. The remaining saline-soluble proteins, many of them functioning as enzymes, are of much higher lysine content, from 3 to 15%, but are present only at very low levels (review by Kasarda et al., 1971). Whitehouse (1973) has discussed how these values differ from those for the protein fractions of other cereals.

Surprisingly, in view of the contrasting analyses of individual proteins, commercial samples of wheat have shown only small differences in lysine content (g/16 g N), e.g. 2·4–3·0 for hard wheats of high protein content and 2·7–3·1 for soft wheats of lower protein content. It has, however, been demonstrated that wheats giving higher lysine values can be found, even in high protein samples (e.g. Johnson et al., 1968) and Professor Johnson will be discussing his recent work later in the symposium.

'ASSAY' EXPERIMENTS WITH HUMANS

Human tissues have a closely similar amino acid composition to those of the rat, and the same amino acids are nutritionally essential for each species (Allison, 1968). However, there is an important species difference in the slower rate of human growth, so that at all ages children use very little protein for growth as compared with maintenance (metabolic and endogenous loss of nitrogen; sweat and skin losses). In the young rat used for assays the need for growth predominates, and in work with the adult rat, the pattern of amino acid requirements for maintenance shows a much reduced need for lysine. Whether or not man also has a lower lysine requirement for his 'maintenance' needs is a crucial point that is not yet settled (cf. Hegsted, 1969; Said and Hegsted, 1969). Whole egg protein, the original 'standard' (Block and Mitchell, 1946) contains 7% lysine, whilst some work suggests that human adults require no more than 2·2% in their dietary protein (review by FAO/WHO, 1973). In any case, the main conclusions from rat work need direct confirmation with man.

The first finding is that wheat proteins are well digested (i.e. c. 90%) even by infants (Bressani et al., 1960; Graham et al., 1969) and schoolchildren (Daniel et al., 1968). Although there has been a general finding (cf. review by Hegsted et al., 1954) that in man the apparent digestibility coefficient of high-extraction products is somewhat lower, McCance and Widdowson (1947) have argued that the increased faecal nitrogen is largely from bacteria and cell walls—an effect always obtained with a more fibrous diet.

Where experimental assay conditions have been organised so that protein alone was limiting in the diet, and wheat the sole source of protein, both infants (Bressani et al., 1960; Graham et al., 1969) and pre-school children (Pereira et al., 1969) have shown improved nitrogen retention and growth as a result of supplementation with lysine. There are results with schoolchildren which indicate also that threonine is the second limiting amino acid (Daniel et al., 1968). However, this and other experiments with children that are based on nitrogen balance data over a period of a few days (e.g. Panemangalore et al., 1962) give values for 'nitrogen retention/day' that are, on the better diets, so much greater than one would expect from longer term growth studies that it is difficult to interpret their real meaning.

Scrimshaw *et al.* (1973) have presented evidence that for adult men lysine is the first limiting amino acid in wheat gluten fed as the sole source of protein (at a level of 0·73 g/kg live weight/day). Net protein utilisation was some 8% units higher with added lysine, and nitrogen balance almost obtained when calorie intake was also high.

Rice *et al.* (1970) have reported an experiment in which young men received 0·7 or 1·0 g protein per kg body weight per day, all from white bread, and their nitrogen balance recorded. They conclude that lysine supplementation gave a significant positive response, but it is difficult to understand their reasoning as the change-over was from 'wheat + glycine' to 'wheat + lysine', and the nitrogen balance improved to almost the same degree when the preliminary diet was continued unchanged.

Bolourchi *et al.* (1968), using a longer experimental period of 50 days, obtained an apparently sustained positive nitrogen balance with unsupplemented white wheat flour fed to young men at a level of 1·0 g crude protein/kg/day. Bricker *et al.* (1945) had obtained a similar result with women students, and the white flour protein apparently had some 58% of the value of milk protein in meeting maintenance needs.

PROCESSING

Wheat is always eaten cooked. The general impression from the literature is that none of the common methods causes serious damage to the protein. Immediately after harvest, wheat may be artificially dried. However, it seems that there is no significant nutritional damage to the protein even with conditions much more severe than those that can be tolerated as regards baking quality (Milner and Woodforde, 1965). Nor is there evidence that bleaching and 'improving' treatments have had a measurable effect on the protein quality of the flour (e.g. Chamberlain *et al.*, 1966).

Bread and other baked products have given values indicating in most cases a fall of approximately 15% in protein value for rats (Sabiston and Kennedy, 1957; Kennedy and Sabiston, 1960; Clarke and Kennedy, 1962), but this has not always been found (e.g. Calhoun *et al.*, 1960). When damage occurs it appears to be mainly in the crust (Morgan, 1931; Hutchinson *et al.*, 1960) and is probably explained by the Maillard reaction between free lysine groups and reducing sugars (Clegg and Davies, 1958; Carpenter, 1973). A similar fall in value has been reported for 'puris', i.e. whole-wheat dough fried in fat (Shyamala and Kennedy, 1962). Some damage also occurs to milk protein or synthetic lysine when added to the bread ingredients, but it is not sufficient to nullify their effect (e.g. Sabiston and Kennedy, 1957; Hedayat *et al.*, 1968).

On the other hand one set of experiments led to the impression that making 'chapatis' by heating a soft dough (water 3:flour 1) gave an actual improvement in PER and thus in protein value. However, this effect of high-moisture treatment of wheat, noticed in a number of laboratories (e.g. Beaudoin *et al.*, 1951), has another explanation.

TABLE IV

THE COMPARATIVE PROTEIN VALUE OF RAW AND STEEPED WHEAT FOR GROWING RATS, AS CALCULATED IN DIFFERENT WAYS

(Milner and Carpenter, 1969)

	N-free diet	Wheat diets[a] Raw	Wheat diets[a] Steeped and dried
1 Weight gain/rat/day, g	−0·64	0·71	1·08 (+53%)**
2 Protein eaten/day, g	——	0·57	0·67
3 Weight gain/g protein eaten (protein efficiency ratio, PER)	——	1·25	1·62 (+30%)**
4 Net weight gain/day, g (i.e. in excess of 'N-free' controls)	——	1·35	1·72
5 Net weight gain/g protein eaten (net protein ratio, NPR)	——	2·43	2·63 (+8%)*
6 Protein % in rat carcases at end of experiment	18·2	17·4	17·1
7 Net protein gain by rats/g protein eaten (net protein utilisation, NPU)	——	0·369	0·378(+2½%)NS

[a] Wheat contributing 10% crude protein.
* Significantly different at the 1% level.
** Significantly different at the 0·1% level.

Table IV summarises the results of an experiment in which weanling rats were fed for 10 days on a diet containing 10% crude protein from either whole ground American hard winter wheat, or the same wheat pre-soaked in tap water at 80 °C for 70 min, drained and freeze-dried (Milner and Carpenter, 1969). The rats receiving the steeped wheat gained weight 50% faster and even protein efficiency ratio (PER), i.e. 'weight gain/g protein eaten' was 30% greater than for the control wheat. On the other hand, once one allows for the 'maintenance' requirement of the rats, by using control rats that have received a protein-free diet as the baseline, the difference is much reduced. And then with a further correction for the protein content of the rat carcases, i.e. by calculating 'net protein utilisation' (NPU), the difference becomes so small as to be non-significant.

Thus an apparently dramatic effect of steeping wheat on the quality of the proteins seems on further scrutiny to be an artefact. The real effect is on the palatability of the wheat. Rats usually show an almost constant intake of metabolisable energy in relation to their metabolic size, i.e. (body weight)$^{0.7-0.88}$ (Hegsted and Haffenreffer, 1949; Carpenter, 1953) but intake is apparently depressed on diets containing a high level of raw wheat, presumably because their mouths get stuck up with the gluey proteins. This does mean, of course, that we must have reservations about all simple 'weight gain' rat experiments in which uncooked wheat serves as the control. There are also special difficulties in using growth assays to assess the availability of individual amino acids in cereals (cf. Harper, 1963; Carpenter, 1973).

Although raw wheat has detectable trypsin inhibitor activity (Shyamala *et al.*, 1961) the level seems too low to have any practical effect in animal feeding tests.

PRACTICAL MIXED DIETS

Up to now we have been concerned with wheat as the sole source of protein in a diet. In practice, human diets (post-weaning) always contain a mixture of protein sources. In the most affluent countries 75% of the protein comes from non-cereal foods, and even in the poorest of the wheat-eating areas, 35% of the protein comes from other sources, mostly as animal protein (cf. West, 1969).

Both animal and pulse (i.e. pea and bean) proteins are generally quite rich in lysine and threonine, but somewhat deficient in the sulphur-containing amino acids. Because of this there can be a mutual supplementation between these and wheat, as is illustrated in Fig. 1. The results of Bricker *et al.* (1945) for a wheat–soya mixture are consistent with this. It has been estimated that it is the sulphur amino acids, rather than lysine, that are first limiting in the mixed proteins of most human diets (Miller and Payne, 1969). This is also, in general, the case with practical poultry diets (cf. review by Biely, 1973), though lysine is a common cost-limiting factor in the formulation of balanced pig diets. Calculations have been made of the likely commercial value of high-lysine cereals in a variety of situations (Carpenter, 1970).

There have been a number of investigations as to whether increasing the lysine content of wheat would have a beneficial effect in a practical situation where wheat played an important role. King *et al.* (1963) carried out such a trial with Haitian schoolchildren who were believed to have a particularly poor basal diet. For the children over the whole age range from 4 to 10 years, the mean daily protein intake was estimated to be 37 g protein and 1600 cal. At one school the children received a wheat bun contributing 13 g protein and 400 cal on every school day for 9 months;

at another they had a similar bun with an additional 500 mg lysine; and a third school had neither. The buns apparently had no effect on gain in height, though they were associated with greater weight gain—particularly the lysine-supplemented buns. A generally similar trial was carried out in Iran (Hedayat *et al.*, 1973). Here a school lunch based on wheat products was associated with greater height and weight gain, but the lysine supplementation was associated with a *smaller* height increase (Table V).

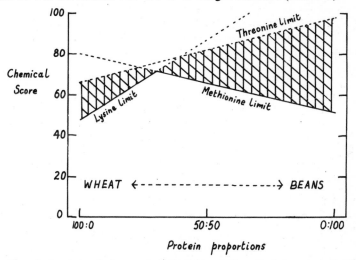

FIG. 1. The calculated chemical score of whole wheat and *Phaseolus* bean proteins in differing proportions. The shaded area on the left represents the improvement possible from added lysine and that on the right the improvement from added methionine (cf. Carpenter, 1970).

Such experiments, with no measure of home food consumption, and the assumption that one school or one village is equivalent to another, are obviously difficult to interpret. In addition, there are problems, including seasonal factors that complicate experimentation in peasant communities (cf. Young, 1971). From the two experiments just quoted the only positive conclusions are that the extra food (contributing both protein and energy) which was provided at school had an effect on their weight gain; presumably their consumption at home was not cut down at any rate to the full extent of the supplement. One cannot conclude that the supplementation of wheat with lysine was useful.

The experiment of Pereira *et al.* (1969), already quoted was considered as an 'assay' rather than as one carried out with a 'practical' diet, as the fat content of the children's diet was increased by the addition of 41 g peanut oil per day. This had the effect of reducing the '*P*' value of the diet (i.e. percentage of energy contributed by protein) from 12 to 9. This reduction of protein level provided an 'assay diet' but it was no longer characteristic of poor S. Asian diets that are very low in fat.

Doraiswamy *et al.* (1962) used an Indian orphanage diet of more normal type containing only 10 g total fat per day. Their finding was that children receiving a supplement of groundnut flour, contributing 22 g protein per day, gained in 6 months an extra 1 cm in height and 0·6 kg in weight more than controls receiving an equi-caloric supplement of sugar. The basal diet contributed 37 g protein per day; all was vegetable, 10 g from pulses and vegetables and the remainder from cereals, mostly wheat. The diets all contained only 1300 cal/day, which was 70% of the calculated standard energy requirements of the children.

TABLE V

THE GROWTH OF POOR CHILDREN RECEIVING A SCHOOL LUNCH
OF WHEAT PRODUCTS WITH OR WITHOUT SUPPLEMENTARY LYSINE

	Controls (no meal)	Unfortified wheat	Wheat + lysine
1. *Gain in height (cm)*			
Haiti[a]	3·76	3·70	3·78
Iran[b]	2·7	3·1	2·8
2. *Gain in weight (kg)*			
Haiti	2·32	2·77	3·45
Iran	0·12	1·21	0·97

	Age of children	Period of trial
[a] King *et al.* (1963)	4–18 yr	9 months
[b] Hedayat *et al.* (1973)	6–11 yr	7 months

The classic European experiment (Widdowson and McCance, 1954) was done with children in post-war Germany when the ordinary animal protein foods (meat, fish and milk) were in very short supply. At the orphanages used for this work the daily rations provided only one-quarter of the 42 g/day of animal protein consumed by British children in the 1930s. For 12–18 months these children of an average age of 9–10 years were given vitamin and calcium supplements and the opportunity to eat as much bread (made from flour of 12–13% crude protein content) as they wished; they consumed 41 g wheat protein per day, together with less than 9 g animal protein and 11·5 g other plant proteins (from green vegetables, potato and some pulses). Some of the results are summarised in Table VI. In short, they grew well and showed a good health record; matched groups of children who received supplements of milk did no better.

TABLE VI
GROWTH OF DUISBERG ORPHANAGE CHILDREN WITH
UNRESTRICTED BREAD AND DIFFERENT MILK RATIONS
(Widdowson and McCance, 1954)

	Low	*High*
Protein intake, g/day:		
85% extr. bread	41·0	34·6
Other vegetable foods	11·5	11·5
Animal foods	8·8	26·5
Total	61·4	72·6
% of dietary energy from protein	11·7	13·9
Total energy, kcal/kg/day	66·6	67·0
Mean results over 6 months		
Gain in height (cm)	2·9	2·9
Gain in weight (kg)	2·5	2·5
(Calculated daily gain of		
crude proteins (g)	(2·2)	

TABLE VII
PROTEIN INTAKES IN THE HIGH-WHEAT ORPHANAGE
EXPERIMENTS COMPARED WITH THE CALCULATED
REQUIREMENTS OF CHILDREN FOR 'IDEAL' PROTEIN
(FAO/WHO, 1973)
(Widdowson and McCance, 1954)

	Orphanage	
	Duisberg	*Vohwinkel*
Protein intake/day (g)	61·4	51·0
(% from wheat)	(67)	(49)
Mean weight of children (kg)	30·5	30·1
N intake (mg/kg/day)	322	271
Weight gain/day (g)	13·7	13·4
FAO/WHO calculations:		
N gain (mg/kg/day)	13·9	13·8
Obligatory N loss	73	73
Theoretical min. N need	87	87
Efficiency required of		
dietary N	27%	32%

This result was quite unexpected at the time but we must remember the slow rate of growth of children as compared with animals. Calculation of protein and amino acid intakes show that the diet calculated meets requirements with a fair margin of safety (FAO/WHO, 1973). The mixed dietary protein needed to be utilised with no more than 27% efficiency and, at a second orphanage where 70% extraction flour was used and only 8·8% of the energy was in the form of protein, with 32% efficiency (Table VII). Thus, although the experiment continues to be of the greatest interest from many points of view we cannot use it to put a particular value on wheat protein as such. It confirms the general experience that protein deficiency is not to be expected in wheat-eating societies where individuals are able to satisfy their energy requirements.

PRACTICAL IMPLICATIONS

We have seen that the quality of wheat protein as measured in standard tests, is rather lower than that of other cereals, and that this is explained primarily by the low lysine content of the endosperm proteins. Naturally this has led to considerable debate as to whether or not wheat should be fortified with synthetic lysine, particularly shipments being sent as aid from the USA to India.

Industrial chemists and technologists have been enthusiastic for its use (e.g. Altschul, 1971; Jansen, 1974). Nutritionists and field workers have been sceptical in view of the recognised overall shortfall of food production in the developing countries, coupled with a lack of concentrated weaning foods. Neither of these problems is corrected by a technological 'package' from the West (cf. Hegsted, 1968; McLaren, 1974). It is now increasingly recognised that a much deeper understanding of these cultures is required in order to help them to solve their problems (cf. Payne, 1973; Whitehead, 1973).

Turning to the plant breeder's objectives, it is certainly true that improving the protein content of wheat, and maintaining the same proportion of lysine or even raising it, increases the value per ton. The only danger is that plant breeders should feel that, on nutritional grounds, this objective should have priority over others, such as disease resistance, that increase yield without affecting quality. In fact it is the general opinion of nutritionists that the priority problem is the production of *more* food, and that this will by itself allow a general improvement in dietary standards in the areas where cereal grain is the staple, provided also that social conditions in the impoverished countries allow its distribution to those in greatest need.

SUMMARY

1. There is no evidence that wheat protein is a harmful food ingredient for man except for a small minority who suffer from coeliac disease as a result of eating gluten. Nor is there evidence that chemical treatment of wheat proteins with the presently used bleaches and 'improvers' induces toxicity, though investigation must continue.

2. The mixed proteins of the endosperm of wheat give a relatively low value in rat growth experiments, approximately one-half or less than that of the best animal proteins.

3. This is explained by their lysine content being only some 40% of the ideal. The value of lysine-supplemented proteins is then limited by threonine present at 65% of the ideal level. The mixed proteins of whole wheat are somewhat higher in lysine content and give values some 20–60% greater than endosperm proteins in rat experiments.

4. Amongst the common staples, wheat flour is similar in its net protein value (quantity × quality) to rice, maize and potatoes, and much superior to cassava and plaintains. None of the common procedures for cooking wheat products appears to cause a significant degree of damage to the proteins.

5. In natural, mixed diets the amino acid limitations of cereal proteins are compensated for to a considerable extent by the high-lysine proteins of legumes, meat and milk.

6. Man is a particularly slow growing species and children do not need to have such a high proportion of protein (and of individual amino acids) in their diets as do laboratory animals and productive pigs and poultry.

7. Wherever wheat-eating communities have the resources to satisfy their food energy needs they also appear to satisfy their protein requirements with a fair margin of safety. This is so even when low-extraction rate flours are used.

8. Where wheat-eating communities are impoverished, diets appear to be at least as deficient in energy as in essential amino acids, and *more food* even of the same type may correct both deficiencies. This may still leave a problem for pre-school children that needs special measures for providing low-bulk sources of both energy and protein.

9. It appears therefore that the 'nutrition-improving' value of increases in the overall yield of wheat without change in its proportions should be recognised as having at least as wide an application as improvements in the yield of protein and lysine content alone.

REFERENCES

Allison, J. B. (1968). 'The nutritive value of dietary proteins', in *Mammalian Protein Metabolism*, Vol. 2, Academic Press, New York and London, p. 41.

Altschul, A. M. (1971). 'Amino acid fortification of foods', in *Amino Acid Fortification of Protein Foods* (Ed. N. S. Scrimshaw and A. M. Altschul), The MIT Press, Cambridge, Mass., p. 521.

Aykroyd, W. R. and Doughty, J. (1970). *Wheat in Human Nutrition*, FAO Nutritional Studies No. 23.

Bailey, C. H. (1944). *The Constituents of Wheat and Wheat Products*, Reinhold, New York.

Beaudoin, R., Mayer, J. and Stare, F. J. (1951). 'Improvement of the protein quality of wheat', *Proc. Soc. Exptl Biol. Med.*, **78**, 450.

Bender, A. E. and Doell, B. H. (1957). 'Biological evaluation of proteins: a new aspect', *Brit. J. Nutr.*, **11**, 140.

Bentley, H. R., McDermott, E. E., Moran, T., Pace, J. and Whitehead, J. K. (1950). 'Action of nitrogen trichloride on certain proteins. I. Isolation and identification of the toxic factor', *Proc. Roy. Soc. B.*, **137**, 402.

Biely, J. (1973). *The Nutritive Value of Wheat in Poultry Rations*, The Canadian Wheat Board, Winnipeg.

Block, R. J. and Mitchell, H. H. (1946). 'The correlation of the amino acid composition of proteins with their nutritive value', *Nutr. Abstr. Rev.*, **16**, 249.

Bolourchi, S., Friedmann, C. M. and Mickelsen, O. (1968). 'Wheat flour as a source of protein for adult human subjects', *Amer. J. Clin. Nutr.*, **21**, 827.

Bressani, R., Wilson, D. L., Behar, M. and Scrimshaw, N. S. (1960). 'Supplementation of cereal protein with amino acids. III. Effect of amino acid supplementation of wheat flour as measured by nitrogen retention of young children', *J. Nutr.*, **70**, 176.

Bricker, M., Mitchell, H. H. and Kinsman, G. M. (1945). 'The protein requirements of adult human subjects in terms of the protein contained in individual foods and food combinations', *J. Nutr.*, **30**, 269.

Calhoun, W. K., Hepburn, F. N. and Bradley, W. B. (1960). 'The availability of lysine in wheat, flour, bread and gluten', *J. Nutr.*, **70**, 337.

Carpenter, K. J. (1953). 'The concept of an "appetite quotient" for the interpretation of ad libitum feeding experiments', *J. Nutr.*, **51**, 435.

Carpenter, K. J. (1970). 'Nutritional considerations in attempts to change the chemical composition of crops', *Proc. Nutr. Soc.*, **29**, 3.

Carpenter, K. J. (1973). 'Damage to lysine in food processing. Its measurement and its significance', *Nutr. Abstr. Rev.*, **43**, 423.

Chamberlain, N., Collins, T., Elton, G. A. H., Hollingsworth, D. F., Lisle, D. B. and Payne, P. R. (1966). 'Studies on the composition of food. 2. Comparison of the nutrient content of bread made conventionally and by the Chorleywood bread process', *Brit. J. Nutr.*, **20**, 747.

Clarke, J. A. K. and Kennedy, B. M. (1962). 'Availability of lysine in wholewheat bread and in selected breakfast cereals', *J. Food Sci.*, **27**, 609.

Clegg, K. M. and Davies, N. (1958). ' "Available lysine" in wheat, flour and bread', *Proc. Nutr. Soc.*, **17**, x.

Creamer, B. (1974). 'Adult coeliac disease', *Nursing Mirror*, June 14, 47.
Daniel, V. A., Doraiswamy, T. R., Rao, S. V., Swaminathan, M. and Parpia, H. A. B. (1968). 'The effect of supplementing a poor wheat diet with L-lysine and DL-threonine on the digestibility coefficient, biological value and net utilisation of proteins and nitrogen retention in children', *J. Nutr. Dietet.*, **5**, 134.
Dicke, W. K., Weijers, H. A. and Kamer, J. H. van de. (1953). 'Coeliac disease. 2. The presence in wheat of a factor having deleterious effect in cases of coeliac disease', *Acta Paediat. Uppsala*, **42**, 34.
Doraiswamy, T. R., Joseph, K., Panemangalore, M., Sankaran, A. N., Rajagopalan, R., Swaminathan, M., Srinivasan, A. and Subramanian, V. (1962). 'Effect of supplementary high-protein food on the growth and nutritional status of school children, subsisting on a Indian diet based on wheat', *Food Sci. Mysore.*, **11**, 211.
Eggum, B. O. (1970). 'Current methods of nutritional protein evaluation', in *Improving Plant Protein by Nuclear Techniques*, International Atomic Energy Agency, Vienna, p. 289.
Ericson, L. E. (1960). 'Studies on the possibility of improving the nutritive value of Swedish white bread. II. The effect of supplementation with lysine, threonine, methionine and tryptophan', *Acta Physiol. Scand.*, **48**, 295.
FAO/WHO (1973). 'Energy and protein requirements', *FAO Nutrition Meetings Report Series* No. 52, FAO, Rome.
Graham, G. G., Placko, R. P., Acevedo, G., Morales, E. and Cordano, A. (1969). 'Lysine enrichment of wheat flour: evaluation in infants', *Amer. J. Clin. Nutr.*, **22**, 1459.
Hamilton, J. R. and McNeill, L. K. (1972). 'Childhood coeliac disease: response of treated patients to a small uniform daily dose of wheat gluten', *J. Paediatrics.*, **81**, 885.
Harper, A. E. (1963). 'The nutritive value of cereal proteins with special reference to the availability of amino acids', *Proc. 5th Intern. Congr. Biochem.*, **8**, 82.
Hedayat, H., Sarkissian, N., Lankarini, S. and Donoso, G. (1968). 'The enrichment of whole wheat flour and Iranian bread with lysine and vitamins', *Acta Biochimica Iranica*, **5**, 16.
Hedayat, H., Shahbazi, H., Payan, R., Azar, M., Bavendi, M. and Donoso, G. (1973). 'The effect of lysine fortification of Iranian bread on the nutritional status of school children', *Acta Paediatr. Scand.*, **62**, 297.
Hegsted, D. M. (1968). 'Amino acid fortification and the protein problem', *Amer. J. Clin. Nutr.*, **21**, 688.
Hegsted, D. M. (1969). 'Nutritional value of cereal proteins in relation to human needs', in *Protein-Enriched Cereal Foods for World Needs* (Ed. M. Milner), Amer. Assoc. Cereal Chem., St. Paul, Minn., p. 38.
Hegsted, D. M. and Haffenreffer, V. K. (1949). 'Calorie intakes in relation to the quantity and quality of protein in the diet', *Amer. J. Physiol.*, **157**, 141.
Hegsted, D. M., Trulson, M. F. and Stare, F. J. (1954). 'Role of wheat products in human nutrition', *Physiol. Rev.*, **34**, 221.
Hutchinson, J. B., Moran, T. and Pace, J. (1960). 'The quality of the protein in germ and milk breads as shown by the growth of weanling rats: the significance of the lysine content', *J. Sci. Fd Agric.*, **11**, 576.
Jansen, G. R. (1974). 'The amino acid fortification of cereals', in *New Protein Foods. 1A. Technology* (Ed. A. M. Altschul), Academic Press, New York, p. 39.

Johnson, V. A., Mattern, P. J., Whited, D. A. and Schmidt, J. W. (1968). 'Breeding for high protein content and quality in wheat', in *New Approaches to Breeding for Improved Plant Protein*, International Atomic Energy Authority, Vienna, p. 29.

Kasarda, D. D., Nimmo, C. C. and Kohler, G. O. (1971). 'Proteins and the amino acid composition of wheat flours', in *Wheat Chemistry & Technology*, 2nd ed. (Ed. Y. Pomeranz), Amer. Assoc. Cereal Chem., St. Paul, Minn., p. 227.

Kennedy, B. M. and Sabiston, A. R. (1960). 'Quality of the protein in selected baked wheat products', *Cereal Chem.*, **37**, 535.

Kent-Jones, D. W. and Amos, A. J. (1957). *Modern Cereal Chemistry*, 5th ed., Northern Publ. Co., Liverpool, p. 20.

King, K. W., Sebrell, W. H., Severinghaus, E. L. and Storvick, W. O. (1963). 'Lysine fortification of wheat bread fed to Haitian school children', *Amer. J. Clin. Nutr.*, **12**, 36.

Koppang, N. and Helgebostad, A. (1966). 'Toxic hepatosis in fur animals', III. *Nord. Ved.-Med.*, **18**, 216.

Kraybill, H. F. (1969). 'The toxicology and epidemiology of mycotoxins', *Trop. Geograph. Med.*, **21**, 1.

McCance, R. A. and Widdowson, E. M. (1947). 'The digestibility of English and Canadian wheats with special reference to the digestibility of wheat protein by man', *J. Hyg. Cambridge*, **45**, 59.

McLaren, D. S. (1974). 'The great protein fiasco', *Lancet*, 93.

Mcrae, T. F., Hutchinson, J. C. D., Irwin, J. O., Bacon, J. S. D. and McDougall, E. I. (1942). 'Comparative digestibility of wholemeal and white breads and the effect of the degree of fineness of grinding on the former', *J. Hyg. Cambridge*, **42**, 423.

Mellanby, E. (1946). 'Diet and canine hysteria. Experimental production by treated flour', *Brit. Med. J.*, **2**, 885.

Miladi, S., Hegsted, D. M., Saunders, R. M. and Kohler, G. O. (1972). 'The relative nutritive value, amino acid content and digestibility of the proteins of wheat mill fractions', *Cereal Chem.*, **49**, 119.

Miller, D. S. and Payne, P. R. (1969). 'Assessment of protein requirements by nitrogen balance', *Proc. Nutr. Soc.*, **28**, 225.

Milner, C. K. and Carpenter, K. J. (1969). 'Effect of wet heat-processing on the nutritive value of whole-wheat protein', *Cereal Chem.*, **46**, 425.

Milner, C. K. and Woodforde, J. (1965). 'The effect of heat in drying on the nutritive value of wheat for animal feed', *J. Sci. Fd Agric.*, **16**, 369.

Morgan, A. F. (1931). 'The effect of heat upon the biological value of cereal proteins and of casein', *J. Biol. Chem.*, **90**, 771.

National Research Council (1963). 'Evaluation of protein quality', Washington Publ. No. 1100, N.R.C.

Newell, G. W., Erickson, T. C., Gilson, W. E., Gershoff, S. N. and Elvehjem, C. A. (1947). 'The role of "agenized"-flour in the production of running fits', *J. Amer. Med. Assoc.*, **135**, 760.

Newell, G. W., Gershoff, S. N., Suckle, H. M., Gilson, W. E., Erickson, T. C. and Elvehjem, C. A. (1949). 'Feeding tests with chlorine dioxide-treated flour', *Cereal Chem.*, **26**, 160.

Panemangalore, M., Parthasarathi, H. N., Joseph, K., Rao, M. N., Indiramma, K., Rajagopalan, R., Swaminathan, M., Srinivasan, A. and Subramanian, V. (1962).

Effect of supplementary high protein food on the retention of nitrogen, calcium and phosphorus in children subsisting on a poor wheat diet', *Food Sci. Mysore*, **11**, 214.

Patey, A. L. (1974). 'Gliadin: the protein mixture toxic to coeliac patients', *Lancet*, April 20th, 722.

Payne, P. R. (1973). 'Some observations on the use of protein foods in nutrition', in *Proteins in Human Nutrition* (Ed. J. W. G. Porter and B. A. Rolls), Academic Press, London, p. 119.

Pereira, S. M., Begum, A., Jesudian, G. and Sundararaj, R. (1969). 'Lysine-supplemented wheat and growth of pre-school children', *Amer. J. Clin. Nutr.*, **22**, 606.

Rice, H. L., Shuman, A. C., Matthias, R. H. and Flodin, N. W. (1970). 'Nitrogen balance responses of young men to lysine supplementation of bread', *J. Nutr.*, **100**, 847.

Sabiston, A. R. and Kennedy, B. M. (1957). 'Effect of baking on the nutritive value of proteins in wheat bread with and without supplements of non-fat dry milk and of lysine', *Cereal Chem.*, **34**, 94.

Said, A. K. and Hegsted, D. M. (1969). 'Evaluation of dietary protein quality in adult rats', *J. Nutr.*, **99**, 474.

Sakshaug, J., Sögnen, E., Hansen, M. A. and Koppang, N. (1965). 'Dimethylnitrosamine: its hepatoxic effect in sheep and its occurrence in toxic batches of herring meal', *Nature, Lond.*, **206**, 1261.

Scrimshaw, N. S., Taylor, Y. and Young, V. R. (1973). 'Lysine supplementation of wheat gluten at adequate and restricted energy intakes in young men', *Amer. J. Clin. Nutr.*, **26**, 965.

Shyamala, G., Kennedy, B. M. and Lyman, R. L. (1961). 'Trypsin inhibitor in whole wheat flour', *Nature, Lond.*, **192**, 300.

Shyamala, G. and Kennedy, B. M. (1962). 'Protein value of chapatis and puris', *J. Amer. Diet. Assoc.*, **41**, 115.

West, Q. M. (1969). 'The quantitative role of cereals as suppliers of dietary protein', in *Protein-Enriched Cereal Foods for World Needs* (Ed. M. Milner), Amer. Assoc. Cereal Chem., St. Paul, Minn., p. 2.

Whitehead, R. G. (1973). 'The protein needs of malnourished children', in *Proteins in Human Nutrition* (Ed. J. W. G. Porter and B. A. Rolls), Academic Press, London, p. 103.

Whitehouse, R. N. H. (1973). 'The potential of cereal grain crops for protein production', in *The Biological Efficiency of Protein Production* (Ed. J. W. G. Jones), Cambridge University Press, London.

Widdowson, E. M. and McCance, R. A. (1954). 'Studies on the nutritive value of bread and on the effect of variations in the extraction rate of flour on the growth of undernourished children', *Med. Res. Council Spec. Rept. Ser.*, No. 287, HMSO, London.

Young, H. B. (1971). 'Measurement of possible effects of improved nutrition on growth and performance in Tunisian children', in *Amino Acid Fortification of Protein Foods* (Ed. N. S. Scrimshaw and A. M. Altschul), The MIT Press, Cambridge, Mass., p. 395.

Young, V. R. and Scrimshaw, N. S. (1971). 'Clinical studies in the United States on the amino acid fortification of protein foods', in *Amino Acid Fortification of Protein Foods* (Ed. N. S. Scrimshaw and A. M. Altschul), The MIT Press, Cambridge, Mass., p. 248.

DISCUSSION

F. Fidanza (Institute of Nutrition and Food Science, Perugia): As the chemical score cannot be considered a very good method for protein evaluation, and also the biological one, as you have shown, is not really very good for grading the protein quality, we have a separate method for protein quality evaluation that is a combination of the two. Comparing with eggs, as reference, we can have an index for essential amino acids, in raw and cooked foods. For bread, this index, taking 100 for egg, is 67 for the dough just before cooking and is 52 for bread from Perugia with crust, not like the bread we have here. If the bread is cut in slices and then put back in the oven, the value is down to 49. So we have about 25% lower protein value due to baking.

Chairman: The literature says that methods of digestion seem to be very inefficient compared with *in vivo*. The whole combination of the human or the animal's guts seems extremely efficient at digesting protein compared with anything we can do in a test tube. So that I would be just a little sceptical as to whether the reduction you find in a glass vessel is fully going to be seen in a biological material. But I certainly agree with you on that, anybody who has worked with toasted materials shows a lower quality; but of course, for most of us, I am sure that a little bit of damage to our protein doesn't matter.

F. Aylward (Reading University): As far as the Iran experiment is concerned, anyone who has travelled round the villages of Iran knows that bread is eaten with considerable quantities of cheese, even among the poor families. It should be stressed that there is always some sort of supplement; the bread and cheese or equivalent being something that is not just confined to western Europe, but is typical of many parts, certainly of western Asia. I think one could have forecast beforehand that cheese was going to balance out any possible effects of low lysine.

I have one query about Dr Carpenter's abstract, where he talks about the importance of improving the level of the total quantity of food, namely that the protein would look after itself. Well, as far as bread is concerned it seems that there is very considerable variation in the protein level of wheat in the different areas of the world. This raises the question of the basis of calculations, as to what figure is being used. I believe one wants to maintain or increase the level of cereal production at an adequate protein level; the question of what is adequate being an area of debate.

K. J. Carpenter: I agree with all that; I had already, actually, slightly qualified the last point in my abstract and it will appear in publication slightly modified, because I agree with you that that should have been made clear. Thank you.

A. Spicer (The Lord Rank Research Centre, High Wycombe, Bucks): All your slides have referred to schoolchildren from the age of one onwards. I don't remember now whether you participated in the conference we had a couple of years ago discussing the protein requirements of the expectant mother, in which we particularly stressed not only the quantitative, but also the qualitative requirements, that are vital for these two sections of the community. Bacon Chow and other workers in this field have clearly shown that unless critical protein requirements are met no subsequent improvements in the feeding programme can undo the harm that has been done to the new born.

K. J. Carpenter: I think that the nutrition of the expectant mother is not really a problem if one works out the relatively small demands of the foetus in comparison with her total intake of food, especially if we compare it with other species. But with the question of infants, I did try to make the point that infant nutrition is a special subject, and needs special treatment, special kind of education, special ways of feeding. It is a separate problem from what one does about supplementing the diets of the bulk of the population, which are 90% of the food being eaten by adults and schoolchildren.

S. Majumder (Central Food Technological Research Institute, Mysore, India): In India generally, rice as well as wheat have become an important part of the daily diet throughout the country. Since rice protein is better in quality than wheat protein, the experiments seem to have shown that the protein deficiency may not be related to the cereal intake alone. The opinion now held is that the protein requirement appears to be lower than what it was believed to be a year ago. Recently P. A. G. has mentioned that 0·5 g/kg seems to be an adequate protein requirement. In our Institute recently diet surveys were carried out in the rural areas; the traditional diets have shown that there is no deficiency from the calculated amount of protein requirement, provided the person is able to buy, that is, if the purchasing capacity of the person is there, the food is not deficient. But the results show that infection of the intestine has been largely responsible for insufficient response to the adequate diet. If the infection is controlled the results with a poor rice diet seem to be quite good with regard to intake and our biological pattern.

K. J. Carpenter: My last paragraph reads 'In fact, it is the general opinion of nutritionists that the priority problem is the production of *more* food, and that this will by itself allow a general improvement in dietary standards in the areas where cereal grain is the staple, provided also that social conditions in the impoverished countries allow its distribution to those in greater need'. So that was the point I meant to make. Thank you for mentioning it.

The other point about rice being roughly equivalent to wheat — well of course, this did rather tie up with the slide I was showing, that net protein value was about the same because rice has less protein but higher quality than wheat.

A. Albanese (Nutrition Reports International, New York): Some years ago, when I was involved very much in this problem of amino-acid requirements in infants and what could be done about the improvement of various foods, we developed a procedure for determining the effect of various proteins on amino-acid levels. We gave specific proteins in given amounts to children, and adults later on, and found out what was the effect on the so-called amino-acid pattern of the blood. What we found basically was this: that when we fed cereal grain foods which were known to be low in lysine, we found that the levels of lysine in the blood did decrease. When they drank milk, the level of lysine in the blood increased; then when we added lysine to the cereal or the bread, we had an increase in lysine level in the blood. The point of this is, that the amino-acid balance in the blood is more important and more easily traced than the nitrogen balance, which is an overall figure, and as Dr Carpenter said, not significant.

I wish to relate this with what was said by Professor Spicer regarding the long term effects of the so-called sub-optimum conditions which prevailed in the amino-acid level and other nutrients in the blood. I do feel that it is important that we consider these newer approaches to the nutritional level situation rather than these gross methods, which we now know to be rather inaccurate.

K. J. Carpenter: This does raise an extremely interesting point, but of course, you must remember that Dr Albanese is talking about what I was calling an assay type of experiment with one protein fed by itself, but supposing we go to the Widdowson–McCance orphanage experiments, which were carried on for 18 months, with children on these different diets, and where they were growing and remaining as healthy by all clinical tests. Supposing we had free amino-acid analyses of blood and found the lysine lower in some groups than others, which I imagine we would, in the sense that those which had a high amount of milk probably had more lysine in their blood, and if they had had even more milk they would have had even more lysine. I would be very sceptical in saying 'Because the lysine levels were different, the children must have been in different health'. I think one must go the other way round and say 'Is there any evidence that the children are in different health' and, if there is, that tells us that these differences in lysine levels are very good predictions.

E. Kodicek (Strangeways Research Laboratory, Cambridge): In one of your slides you showed the interaction between mixed food, mainly the lysine deficient wheat and beans—a most interesting slide, the nutritionist should be able to devise a practical nutritional index, which would be the safe relation of a staple food in which there is a limiting substance. In a mixed diet, where the other diet compensates completely the index would be one. One should be able to work out this particular index to give indication for the agronomist, geneticist and so forth, how far it is important to aim at improving a staple food or not, and it would apply not only for lysine, but for iron, for nicotinic acid or for any other foods; it would be a staple index which would give some indication to those who are not particularly in nutrition, what the nutritionists feel.

K. J. Carpenter: The animal nutritionist is faced with this sort of practical problem all the time; for thinking up economic diets he doesn't use biological values at all; he takes the level of the three or four amino acids most likely to be limiting, regards these as important nutrients; he perhaps doesn't bother about total protein at all and simply makes sure his diets contain enough of each of these amino-acids.

Milling and Baking Quality

G. N. IRVINE
Grain Research Laboratory,
Canadian Grain Commission,
Winnipeg, Manitoba, Canada

When I was invited to speak on this subject at this symposium on 'Bread', I felt that it was something which I should be able to do justice to. I have worked for 29 years in a laboratory which has been committed to research in this area for over 60 years. I have also been privileged to travel pretty well all over the world observing milling and baking practices at first hand. But when I got down to the 'nitty-gritty', I began to realise that perhaps I knew far too much about the subject. For every definitive statement I could make, I was also aware of half a dozen qualifications that had to be made. Quality is very much in the mind of the consumer of a product and what is one man's meat is another man's poison. So I decided to go back to 'square one' and examine the concepts of milling and baking quality as they have evolved historically to see what basic factors emerged, what factors had evolved along the way and what factors are broadly relevant today. What has emerged is not a scientific paper but I hope it will put the subject matter in reasonable perspective for those in the audience who are not specialists in the area: for me to talk on this subject for the experts who are in attendance here would be like trying to teach my great grandmother to suck eggs!

If all the wheat grown in the world were exactly the same we would have no concept of what constituted either milling or baking quality. Thousands of years ago as man first began to use the wheat plant to sustain his life this was essentially true in the microcosm of each primitive settlement: wheat was wheat, period. But over time, as nature practised her eccentricities, one year's harvest might be remembered as better than another year's; perhaps drier, freer from fungal diseases, less shrunken, or for any number of other reasons. Also it eventually became necessary to store the harvest for gradual consumption until the next harvest was gathered; depending on storage conditions, and again on the whims of Mother Nature, the wheat would deteriorate and become infested to a greater or lesser extent. Newly harvested grain would be generally preferred to eleven-month-old grain and so we see the emergence of *condition* or *soundness* as probably the first criterion of wheat quality to be recognised.

This criterion is still very much with us today although it is generally taken for granted, because of the various grading systems under which most wheat moves in international commerce today. Here then were the beginnings of the concept of good quality being 'consistent with what is known and expected'.

As urbanisation developed with advancing civilisation, and intercourse developed between towns, areas and regions, so too did trade develop. Doubtlessly there would be from time to time surpluses of wheat in some areas and deficits in others. Regional differences in processing wheat for human consumption would become apparent as well as regional variations in the type of wheat grown. No longer would wheat simply be wheat. Within a small region the local wheat would be best, as it fitted the quality generalisation 'consistent with what is known and expected' and wheat from outside the region might well be considered poorer because it was different. Differences in *colour* and in *hardness* or *vitreousness* would become quality factors, as they would affect the grinding characteristics and the colour of the meal produced. These elements are still with us.

With the growth of the complex, cosmopolitan, city states and the development of a wealthy leisure class, we had the development of wheat milling and bread baking as industries. The milled product was sieved to remove coarse bran particles and so the *colour* of the flour and bread crumb became quality criteria in the marketing of flour and bread respectively. Since time immemorial white has been the symbol of purity and has been preferred. Here also we would have had the concern of both the miller and the baker for yield: the miller, for more flour from a given amount of wheat; the baker, for more loaves from a given amount of flour. Somewhere along the line the concept of *bushel weight* must have developed. Where wheat was bought on a basis of volume, the miller would soon learn that certain types of wheat produced more flour from a given volume than others. We are still saddled with bushel weight as a criterion of milling quality today but since we long ago started to merchandise wheat on a weight basis rather than a volume basis, the original notion of the importance of bushel weight as a factor of milling quality has disappeared.

It seems probable that baking quality criteria were for hundreds of years based largely on the fact that wheats from certain origins were considered to be better than others, but all that the baker could haggle with the miller about would be the colour of the flour and its speckiness, the yield of bread and that most mysterious of all complaints which bakers still make to millers, that the flour doesn't work properly.

The beginnings of modern criteria of milling and baking quality can probably be traced to the Austro–Hungarian empire around the middle of the last century. The wheats grown on the Hungarian plain were fairly closely related to some of our hard wheats of today and the Hungarian millers developed a great expertise in milling these on sophisticated stone mills, and later, on roller mills which they had a large hand in developing. The bakers in Vienna developed a great expertise in using these flours in the concoction of a wide variety of gastronomic delights in the form of breads, rolls and cakes. The renown of this Austro–Hungarian combination spread throughout Europe and to America as well, and Hungarian flour was considered the best in the world.

Shortly after this great flowering, three important events occurred within a short time period. These were:

(1) The development of the principles of plant breeding based on Mendel's work.
(2) The development of the roller milling process and the improvement of the millings purifier.
(3) The exploitation of the great wheat producing areas of the United States, Canada, Australia and Argentina.

At a time of great social change in Europe, with populations rapidly increasing, with industrialisation moving people rapidly from the country to the cities, the basis was developing for the international wheat trade which built up rapidly until the outset of the First World War. The Great Plains area of the USA and Canada was suited to the Hard Winter and Hard Spring wheats and the domestic and European milling industries, with the changeover to roller milling, were now ready to make the most of these wheats, which had previously been held in low regard by millers in most countries. The hard wheats of North America, Argentina and yes, at that time, of Australia too, were enthusiastically received by European millers and so too, of course, were the hard wheats from Russia. Now *gluten quality* and *gluten quantity* were added to the list of quality criteria, along with *vitreousness, yield of patent flour*, and *flour ash content*. By now the early cereal chemists were at work in the flour milling industry and began to more clearly define what constituted milling and baking quality. Now, through the development of the new science of plant breeding, we had the means to modify the quality of the wheats being grown in the wheat exporting countries, and in the wheat deficient countries as well. Rapid advances were made in the first years of the present century and probably the most spectacular success occurred in Canada, where Dr Charles Saunders, following in his father's footsteps as a wheat breeder, produced Marquis wheat in 1910. This wheat solidified Canada's reputation in Europe for the highest quality milling wheat for bread flours; by the late 1920s over 80% of the spring wheat acreage in Canada and the USA was planted to this variety alone. Marquis wheat set the standard of quality in the international grain market for many years and it is still officially the standard of quality for Canadian Hard Red Spring wheat varieties.

What were the characteristics of this wheat which gave it such a lasting and worldwide reputation? First of all, it looks nice; it is dark red in colour, with short, wide kernels. It is also high in bushel weight—a factor that at one time was considered to be very important as an index of milling quality. Present-day Canadian varieties are not as attractive in appearance, nor as high in bushel weight but have superior milling quality in terms of flour yield, ash and colour. The baking quality of the flour produced from Marquis wheat was well suited to its time; it has a great deal of tolerance in a very wide variety of baking procedures; it performs well with or without improving agents such as potassium bromate; and it gives excellent support in admixture with soft or weaker wheats. Many of the Canadian wheats developed by Canadian plant breeders during the past 30 years have surpassed Marquis in one or more of our numerous quality criteria but few have surpassed it in 'all aroundness'.

While milling and baking technologies have progressed markedly during the past 50 years, and this is especially true of baking technology, the criteria of milling and baking quality have remained basically unchanged. The miller is inseparable from the baker in considering wheat quality for bread flour. While the miller has his own criteria of milling quality related to economics, his flour must have the inherent quality that will meet the needs of the baker. Thus he looks for sound, clean, relatively low moisture wheat with uniform kernels; he wants a high yield of flour of good colour from wheat which mills easily when properly conditioned; and he wants a wheat which offers him no surprises on his mill. For his customer the baker, he needs a wheat which will produce flour having a high water absorption, reasonably short mixing time or low power requirement for development, good tolerance to variations in processing, capable of producing bread of good and consistent volume and texture. And most of all he wants these properties to be uniform and consistent over time, be it days, weeks, or years.

These basic, simple criteria have remained essentially unchanged over a long period of time. But the milling technologists and the cereal chemists have, over the past 60 years, elaborated a bewildering array of parameters which must be satisfied to ensure success in achieving the desired end. Dr Charles Saunders, who developed Marquis wheat, was both a plant breeder and one of Canada's first cereal chemists. He was by training a chemist but by inclination a violinist—the combination made him a first-rate plant breeder as plant breeding is both an art and a science. At the turn of the century, when he was making the selections that would lead him to Marquis, his screening test for quality was to chew a handful of kernels from each line. Based on hardness on his teeth he selected for milling quality; the gluten, which he had in his mouth after chewing the wheat, he tested between his fingers for strength and elasticity. He knew what he was looking for. In our laboratory today we spend several months each year, using several hundred thousand dollars' worth of equipment, testing the new varieties of wheat put forward by our plant breeders.

In the old days bushel weight functioned as a one-element grading system. Any adverse effects on wheat during growing or harvesting invariably are reflected in lower bushel weights, as are admixtures of other grains or weed seeds, dirt, etc. So there was considerable merit in the importance placed on high bushel weight. The early grading systems established in countries having substantial quantities of wheat for export tended to be based on appearance (as an indication of soundness), bushel weight and origin or variety. While these grading systems have changed somewhat over the years to take more account of specific milling and baking quality criteria, they remain largely based on visible factors; only in Canada, where a standard of milling and baking quality is named in the grade specifications, have we attempted to include internal or intrinsic quality as a major grading factor. It is this intrinsic quality which can be subject to some uncertainty these days with the widespread exchange of new varieties and with the great increase in plant breeding efforts both by governments and the private sector largely aimed at increasing yield of grain. As the biochemical basis of wheat quality is still incompletely understood, we make up for our ignorance by undertaking a plethora of tests to ensure that our judgements will prove to be right when the wheat is put on the mill and the flour sent along to the bakery. In testing wheat today a good laboratory may require information on the following factors:

On wheat
    Origin or variety.
    Grade, if it is a wheat sold on grade.
    Moisture.
    Bushel weight.
    1000-kernel weight.
    Protein content.
    Falling number.
    Sedimentation value.
    Flour yield, derived from experimental milling.

None of these factors at whatever level when taken by itself gives a guarantee or assurance of either the milling quality of the wheat or the baking quality of the flour. But taken together, if all are within a favourable range the milling quality should be good and the prospect for baking quality is favourable. However, if any of the values are outside the favourable range there will still remain some doubt. In any event it will

still be essential to carry out some or all of the following tests on an
experimentally milled flour:

On flour
    Ash content.
    Colour.
    Starch damage.
    Protein content.
    Gassing power or diastatic activity.
    α-amylase or amylograph viscosity.
    Water absorption by farinograph test.
    Rheological properties by extensograph, alveograph or mixograph.
    Dough development time, usually by farinograph or mixograph.
    Baking quality, as measured by some standard baking test.

These tests are all essentially aimed at indicating the *yield* and *quality
of the bread* that can be baked from the flour. Again, all should be within
a favourable range. The decision on the limits of this favourable range
will vary somewhat from one mill to another even within the same area
of a particular country, and will depend primarily on the experience of
those assessing the results of the tests. Amongst all these tests there are
obviously two which should suffice: the experimental milling test, which
should give an indication of the yield of flour on the commercial mill, as
well as providing a flour for the other test, which is the baking test. If
the flour yield is satisfactory and the bread yield, volume, crumb colour
and texture and loaf appearance are satisfactory then these two tests
should tell you all you want to know. But most laboratories still prefer
to use 'belt and braces' and continue to add supplementary tests to aug-
ment the baking test.

Of course the reason that laboratories continue to make all these
tests is because there are often some uncertainties or surprises arising
from the two basic tests and by using a battery of tests it is usually possible
to determine where the trouble lies and to decide whether or not it can be
corrected for in the mill.

The expertise that is building up in the milling industry is making mills
less dependent on specific sources and qualities of wheat. Within certain
limits, millers have learned how to increase water absorption of their
flours and thereby give the bakers better bread yields; with modern
baking systems, especially those where dough development replaces the
traditional fermentation process, the quality of protein is somewhat less
important than formerly and the quantity of protein becomes more of a
decisive factor. One factor which is still not completely under the control
of the miller as yet, is the α-amylase level in flour. If it is too low, the miller
can readily increase it through addition of malt flour or fungal amylases;

but if it is too high he has no way of reducing it. Thus α-amylase level in wheat has become a major quality factor.

As the milling industry learns more and more how to take maximum advantage of the quality of a given wheat, and the baking industry learns to take maximum advantage of the quality of a given flour, so the margin for error for each decreases and specifications for wheat and flour become more rigid and uniformity of wheat and flour become more critical requirements. The past 15 years have seen a greatly increased demand for wheats at specific protein levels and the USA, Canada, Australia and the USSR have all taken to marketing some portion of their hard wheats with guaranteed protein levels. Canada was the last of the four to move in this direction and has carried protein segregation further than the others, applying it to our entire marketing of high grade milling wheat. Our No. 1 CW Red Spring wheat is the most closely quality controlled wheat offered on the market today. The grade ensures the basic soundness of the wheat. Our variety control ensures that all the varieties making up the grade are uniform in their milling and baking characteristics; and the protein level is controlled at the levels of 12·5, 13·5 or 14·5% at the option of the buyer. This we believe is the closest anyone has come to merchandising the ideal wheat in terms of continuing uniformity.

But this is not intended to be a sales pitch for Canadian wheat; that would be completely out of place in such a symposium. Nor is it to say that other suppliers do not offer similar qualities of wheat. The grade that I have described is the most expensive bread wheat marketed today and thus the ingenuity of the milling industry is continuously being exercised to minimise the amount of this wheat they use. In the process they have learned to make the most of other, lower priced wheats. Quality of wheat for milling and baking, as with most other commodities, cannot be divorced from price. Again, the quality which I have attempted to describe as the present ideal is not a universal standard but only applies in areas where white, yeast raised, breads or rolls are the major item in bread consumption.

At the moment the question of what constitutes milling quality *per se* is quite widely accepted by most millers in North America, Europe, Japan and other areas where white bread is the major end use product of wheat flour.

The nature of baking quality would be less readily agreed upon by bakers in these same areas as there are still considerable differences in baking methods from area to area and from bakery to bakery. We are in the midst of a revolution in baking technology whose end is not yet in sight. The first shot fired in the revolution would seem to be a paper by Swanson and Working (1926) published in Cereal Chemistry entitled 'Mechanical modification of dough to make it possible to bake bread with only the fermentation in the pan'. They were far ahead of their time, however, and there was no rush to their banner. But in retrospect, it seems apparent that Dr J. C. Baker in the USA got the message and over the next 25 years he and his collaborators published a steady series of first class papers examining all the various facets of the breadmaking process. This work culminated in 1950 with the announcement of the Baker Process for continuous bread production without the use of bulk fermentation. This was an updated, completely automated version of the Swanson and Working principle, using intensive mechanical development of the dough to accomplish the work of bulk fermentation. Within 15 years over 50% of the plant bread production in the USA was being produced on one or other of the two commercially marketed versions of Dr Baker's brainchild. Originally it was claimed that one could produce any kind of bread desired, using this process, but this has not turned out to be true. To a very large extent the baker is a captive of the process and for this reason it has not caught on to any significant extent outside the USA. However, the impact was colossal. The past 15 years have seen a great deal of work, in many parts of the world, aimed at exploiting some of the basic features of the process to produce breads more in line with those produced by the various traditional bulk fermentation processes. The Chorleywood Bread Process so widely used today in the UK has been the most widely adopted of these further developments.

The rapidity with which these two technological developments were put to use in the USA and the UK spawned a great deal of investigational work by the mills who had to produce flours for use in these systems. A great deal of the research was *ad hoc* and we still are a long way from a complete understanding of the chemical changes taking place in a bread dough during mechanical development. More systematic research in recent years, much of it in our own laboratory, is bringing us closer. We find that the amount of power required to mechanically develop a flour varies quite widely depending on the origin of the flour; also the length of time it takes a given mixer to impart the required amount of power varies amongst different flours; and, of course, both of these are highly dependent, as well, on the type of mixer being used. Thus the particular mixer used and the flour used, together have certain critical requirements that must be met for successful bread production using mechanical development. Certain reducing agents, such as the amino acid cysteine, have a marked effect on the mixer-flour interaction and this phenomenon leads to the concept of 'chemical dough development' or 'chemically accelerated dough development' as we prefer to call it.

We seem to be well on our way to being able to make a silk purse out of a sow's ear. But there is a catch. All of the various development systems require fairly high levels of oxidising improvers such as potassium iodate, potassium bromate and ascorbic acid. A number of countries prohibit the use of some of these and also additives such as cysteine. Working out the permutations and combinations of flours, systems, mixers and additives now gets to be a complicated business and more and more millers are having to develop specific flour types for specific bakers. And continuing uniformity of flour quality becomes ever more critical.

Above the clatter of the baking revolution as it evolves, one hears more and more voices saying 'but what are you doing to the taste of our bread?' There has been some retrenchment here and there but there is no question in my mind that the basic elements of the revolution are here to stay. Meanwhile the response to the question of what are the criteria of baking quality in a bread flour becomes: it depends on what you are going to do with the flour. At the present time there are more alternative ways of making bread than ever before. What we have referred to for years as *protein quality* in talking about wheat or flour is now a more flexible concept than it was. But does that help? The more sophisticated the baking industry becomes the more critical its requirements, in terms of specific flour quality and continuing uniformity. One answer, of course, is to produce flours with more tolerance so that some variability can be tolerated. But the sow's ear doesn't usually display this kind of tolerance so we are back to 'square one'.

In Canada we are holding on to all our former criteria of quality for our new wheat varieties but we have added some new ones. The new varieties must have relatively low power input requirements and relatively short mixing time requirements for development processes, but must maintain the traditional tolerance associated with our type of wheat.

Today wheat is grown in almost every part of the world. There is a very wide range of types and environments under which they are grown. In many areas wheat cultivation has been going on for many hundreds of years. Over the centuries, the form in which the wheat was consumed in various areas became ritualised and, generally speaking, it would be a form that was compatible with the characteristics of the indigenous wheat. Thus each area has its particular products and each its own criteria of quality which more often than not differ markedly from those we have been looking at.

One of the problems today is that the technology of cereal chemistry has developed overwhelmingly in North America and in Europe. The methods and the instrumentation are almost exclusively developed for the evaluation of wheats and flours for white, yeast-raised, breadmaking purposes. Sometimes when underdeveloped countries seek technical assistance through the United Nations, or other programmes, they end up with a laboratory full of nice new equipment from America or Europe which has little or no relevance to their needs and objectives.

Thus when we attempt to define what parameters make up the concept of milling and baking quality we must be very careful to make clear 'with whom we are having the pleasure' and be fully cognisant of those other 'worlds' outside of our own where these do not apply. As usual the problem comes back to semantics. We talk about milling and baking in our terms but we also use these words for what the Egyptians, the Iranians, the Indians and others do with wheat when it is really not the same thing at all.

REFERENCE

Swanson, C. O. and Working, E. B. (1926). 'Mechanical modification of dough to make it possible to bake bread with only the fermentation in the pan', *Cereal Chem.*, 3, 65–83.

DISCUSSION

Miss D. Hollingsworth (The British Nutrition Foundation, London): I would like to take up the last point of Dr Irvine's paper. There is a very vocal minority in this country which doesn't like the kind of white sliced bread which has been described. If one looks at trends in food consumption the most notable drop in consumption in this country is in large white loaves. The consumption of brown loaves is stable as is the consumption of other kinds of speciality bread. Now what research in milling and baking quality is going into the problems of producing good speciality breads of a different kind from plant bread? Have we got milling and baking quality testing programmes which are devoted to producing good speciality bread; not only the brown ones but also the ones that people are always calling for, bread with good crust for example?

G. N. Irvine: Well, this of course is the question that comes up at every meeting of this sort. Although I'm not associated with the milling or baking industries in the commercial way, I can assure you that both the milling and baking industry are only too anxious to make a buck and they'll make it from any reasonable source they can. If they were assured that 80% of the population wanted to eat bread baked from stone-milled flour, they would be making stone-milled flour for bread. The problem is that given a free choice of the wide variety of breads there are available in this market the great majority of the public chooses to eat that white sliced, wrapped pap that 'everybody' complains about.

Most of the mills in North America, the UK and Europe are producing speciality flours for any baker that wants them. Now when you insist on that nice crisp crust, you're playing right down my alley because the only way you can get that is to go back to a nice high protein Canadian flour—but I gather the trend is the other way at the moment.

G. A. H. Elton (Ministry of Agriculture, Fisheries and Food, London): There is no necessity for research to produce crusty bread, bakers are very capable of doing this at the moment. I don't think Dr Irvine made the point that the modern dough making processes apply up to the dough stage, once you've got the dough you can do what you like with it. From the same kind of dough, you can make sliced wrapped bread by baking it one way or you can make acceptable crusty bread out of the same dough by baking it for longer at a lower temperature. I'll take issue with what Norman Irvine said here; you don't need Canadian flour to make crusty bread. The French can do it, the Spanish and the Greeks can do it using their flour. The trouble is that once you make really crusty bread you've got a thermodynamically unstable situation; you've got a low moisture content crust and a high moisture crumb; you get exchange between the two and the bread goes stale very rapidly. The type of bread that is sold, as Dr Irvine said, is determined by consumer demand and if what is wanted is the wrapped sliced bread which keeps well, then that's what you'll get. There is a vocal minority, but they are not buying the majority of the bread. If a demand is there, there is no need for research; you can easily make the bread required with the present techniques.

P. W. Russell Eggitt (Spillers Ltd, Cambridge): There is one aspect of baking quality that perhaps hasn't had quite enough emphasis and that is the question of keeping properties. The French housewife will buy her bread up to twice a day and that is extremely crusty and without much Canadian wheat in it. In Britain the majority of housewives expect bread to remain fresh for five days. This is possibly where Canadian wheat does help because the stronger wheats do produce bread where the starch changes are slower and so quality lasts longer. The research we have to do is into making the breads currently produced in the U K, containing up to half European wheats or more, keep as well as those which we made when we had the benefit of larger percentages of Canadian Western Red Springs.

G. N. Irvine: There is an area for research here, to try and improve the keeping quality of the speciality breads. If we go back 20 years we were in more or less the same situation with the common white bread and we have certainly improved on its keeping quality since them.

R. Riley (Plant Breeding Institute, Cambridge): Dr Irvine made some points about bushel weight and of the significance of this as a quality criterion for the miller. Clearly there is some relationship between the flour yield and bushel weight; however, the indications are from what he said that bushel weight could perhaps be regarded of less significance. Now it is important to wheat breeders to have this guidance even though in the present circumstances in the European economic community, we may be compelled to try to increase bushel weight in order to meet the intervention standards for wheat even if this is not as relevant a criterion of quality as it used to be. I would be very interested to hear of the significance which breeders should pay to bushel weight as a real quality criterion rather than a criterion which is necessary to meet the bureaucratic demands.

G. N. Irvine: I think we are in a particularly advantageous position in our laboratory because we have access to such a wide variety of wheats. We can look at things like bushel weight and I could prove anything you want. I can get a set of samples which will establish with a statistical significance of 99% that there is a very close relationship between flour yield and bushel weight. I could also produce a set of samples which prove exactly the reverse. The point really is well illustrated by my comments on Marquis. Marquis wheat for whatever reason was chosen as much on aesthetics as by the chewing test and the feeling on the teeth, but that happened to be a very high bushel weight wheat. Marquis is our standard of quality today in Canada, all the new varieties must meet it, but we've never been able to meet that bushel weight specification, although all have been far superior in milling quality to Marquis. They get higher yields of flour, better colour and lower amylase. Cereal chemists will all agree that bushel weight is not a criterion. On the other hand if you have a given type of wheat, then the higher bushel weight wheat normally will give a better flour extraction, or at least be an easier wheat to mill and would be preferred for that reason. But as a blind criterion that the plant breeder has to meet, I would much prefer the milling test to be the judge of how well he was doing.

Cultural, Genetic and Other Factors Affecting Quality of Wheat

V. A. JOHNSON, P. J. MATTERN AND K. P. VOGEL

US Department of Agriculture, and Department of Agronomy,
University of Nebraska, Lincoln, Nebraska, USA

INTRODUCTION

The quantity and composition of the protein in the grain of wheat contribute significantly to its nutritional and processing quality. Although all quality factors are under genetic control, the production environment also exerts a strong effect. The magnitude of these environmental effects led a geneticist to say of seed protein manipulation, 'The background noise is loud, and the genetic signal is weak'. The comparatively little research on genetic improvement of seed protein before 1950 reflects in part this problem.

The Agricultural Research Service, US Department of Agriculture, in co-operation with the Nebraska Agricultural Experiment Station, has engaged in research on genetic improvement of wheat protein since 1955. The research initially was concerned with protein content of wheat grain but was broadened in 1966 to include amino acid composition of wheat protein. Major research findings from the project are discussed.

PROTEIN CONTENT OF WHEAT

Satisfactory commercial bread production in the USA requires wheat with approximately 12% protein content. Hard winter wheat produced in the southern and central plains of the USA has averaged 12% protein. Hard spring wheat produced in the northern plains of the USA and in Canada characteristically has from 1 to 3 percentage points higher protein content than the winter wheat. The protein advantage of the spring wheat probably is caused by genetic potential for higher protein and by lower productivity, on the average, than the winter wheat.

Environment strongly influences the protein content of wheat. Fixed protein levels cannot be achieved by breeding alone. Varieties with high grain-protein potential do not always produce grain with high protein

127

content. In breeding for high protein we rely in our breeding programme on relative levels of protein in comparably produced material.

A century of wheat production in the southern and central high plains where, historically, minimal or no nitrogen fertiliser has been used, has tended to lower soil fertility and the protein content of the wheat grain. Doubling of wheat yields during this period has accentuated the protein problem. Grain now produced in some localities without nitrogen fertilisation may average only 10% protein.

Inheritance of protein content

Our first evidence of major genes for high protein in US wheats came with the development in North Carolina of the 'Atlas 50', CI12534, and 'Atlas 66', CI12561, varieties of soft wheat (Middleton *et al.*, 1954). Modest protein differences among hard red winter varieties were demonstrable, but were not attributed to major genes. Field experiments in which Atlas 66 was compared with selected hard winter varieties in the southern plains produced results shown in Table I. Atlas 66 produced a higher mean grain yield than the hard wheat varieties and the protein content of its grain was significantly higher.

TABLE I

GRAIN YIELD AND PROTEIN CONTENT OF ATLAS 66, COMANCHE, AND WICHITA WHEAT VARIETIES GROWN IN FOUR TRIALS IN THE SOUTHERN PLAINS OF THE USA IN 1958

(From Haunold, A., Johnson, V. A., and Schmidt, J. W. (1962) Agron. J. 54, 121–125.)

| Variety | 4-test mean | |
	Yield	Protein[a]
	bu/a	%
Atlas 66	24·9	19·4
Comanche	21·7	17·5
Wichita	18·6	15·4
LSD$_{0.05}$	ns	0·7

[a] Dry-weight basis.

The existence of major genes for high grain protein in Atlas 66 was demonstrated in crosses of Atlas 66 with 'Comanche', CI11673, and 'Wichita', CI11952 (Johnson *et al.*, 1968). High protein is inherited as an incompletely dominant trait, which involves at least two genes with major effects. One of the genes is linked genetically with a gene for leaf rust resistance. F_5 lines homozygous for leaf rust reaction were analysed for protein content. Resistant lines were high or intermediate in protein; susceptible lines were low or intermediate in protein suggesting the presence of at least one gene for protein content that is not linked to leaf rust resistance. Ease of recovery of lines as high in protein content as the Atlas 66 parent pointed to a small number of genes.

Heritability estimates for protein content ranged from 0·58 to 0·82, depending on the method of computation. This range of values compares favourably with values for other traits in wheat in which significant breeding progress has been made and suggests that significant progress in breeding for high grain protein can be made.

Atlas 66 has poor bread wheat milling and baking properties. High protein lines from Atlas 66/Comanche had widely differing dough-mixing and breadmaking characteristics, suggesting that the high-protein trait was inherited independently from other bread wheat quality traits (Johnson et al., 1963).

TABLE II
PERFORMANCE OF ATLAS 66/CMN/LANCER, NE701132, IN NEBRASKA AND REGIONAL TRIALS, 1970–1973

| Variety | Mean grain yield | | Mean protein content[a] | |
	Bu/a	% of check variety	%	% of check variety
	1970 (x̄ of 3 trials in Nebraska)			
NE701132	60	115	14·4	123
Scout 66	52	100	11·8	100
	1972 (x̄ of 25 regional trials)			
NE701132	49	100	14·1	108
Scout 66	49	100	13·1	100
	1973 (x̄ of 24 paired nursery plots in Nebraska)			
NE701132	55	96	15·7	113
Centurk	57	100	13·3	100

[a] 14% moisture basis.

We have achieved, from Atlas 66 crosses, productive hard winter wheat lines possessing genetic potential for 2 to 3 percentage points higher protein than ordinary wheat. This is demonstrable at yield levels as high as 60 bu/a (Table II). A high protein line selected from Atlas 66/Comanche//Lancer, NE701132, is currently undergoing foundation seed increase at the Nebraska Agricultural Experiment Station for probable release as a commercial variety in 1975. Commercial mill and bakery collaborators who have evaluated NE701132 report that it has entirely satisfactory ·bread wheat milling and baking properties.

Genetic sources of high protein

Genes for high grain protein in Atlas 66 and Atlas 50 are believed to come from the South American parent variety 'Frondoso', CI12078. A high protein experimental soft wheat variety, selected at Purdue University from a cross involving Frondoso, exhibited high protein potential comparable to that of Atlas 66 in the International Winter Wheat Performance Nursery.

The Nebraska Wheat Quality Laboratory systematically screened the World Collection of common and durum wheats maintained by the US Department of Agriculture in a search for additional genetic sources of high protein and high lysine. More than 16 000 wheats were analysed. Several varieties with potential value were identified.

One of these, Nap Hal, PI176217, which produces grain with above normal protein and lysine contents, was crossed with Atlas 66 to ascertain whether its genes for high protein were different from those in Atlas 66. F_2 progeny bulks were studied in the F_3 and F_4 generations at Yuma,

TABLE III

F$_5$ SELECTIONS FROM THE CROSS NAP HAL/ATLAS 66, GROWN AT YUMA, ARIZONA IN 1973, THAT SHOW PROMISING LEVELS OF GRAIN PROTEIN

Variety	Row no.	Protein[a] (%)	Lysine/ protein (%)	Adjusted lysine/ protein (%)
Nap Hal	x̄ of 9 rows	20·0	3·1	3·3
Atlas 66	x̄ of 9 rows	19·9	2·8	3·0
Nap Hal/Atlas 66 (F_5)	15 138	24·2	2·8	3·0
Nap Hal/Atlas 66 (F_5)	14 169	23·7	2·9	3·1
Nap Hal/Atlas 66 (F_5)	15 164	23·7	2·9	3·0
Nap Hal/Atlas 66 (F_5)	11 602	23·4	3·1	3·2
Nap Hal/Atlas 66 (F_5)	11 444	23·2	3·1	3·3
Nap Hal/Atlas 66 (F_5)	12 926	22·5	3·0	3·2

[a] Dry-weight basis.

Arizona (Johnson *et al.*, 1973). Evidence of transgressive segregation for high protein was obtained in both generations. F_2 progeny bulks that were 2–4 percentage points higher in protein content than the parent varieties were identified. The protein contents of some F_5 selections made from the best of the F_2 progeny bulks are shown in Table III. Under the conditions of the Yuma tests, the grain from varieties with normal protein potential ranged from 16·0 to 17·5% protein.

We conclude that the parent varieties Atlas 66 and Nap Hal possess different genes for high grain protein content, which together produce protein levels exceeding that of either parent variety. The development of wheat varieties with genetic potential for 5 percentage points higher protein than ordinary varieties may be possible.

Kernel site of the high protein effect

Kernels of Atlas 66, Nap Hal, and selected other varieties were fractionated to separate the endosperm from the other kernel parts. The fractions were analysed separately for protein and lysine (Table IV). The high-protein effect in Atlas 66 appears to reside entirely in the endosperm.

TABLE IV
PROTEIN AND LYSINE CONTENT OF WHOLE GRAIN, ENDOSPERM, AND NON-ENDOSPERM FRACTIONS OF 4 WHEAT VARIETIES GROWN AT YUMA, ARIZONA IN 1973

Variety	Protein content[a] (%)			Lysine content (%) protein		
	Whole grain	Endosperm fraction	Non-endosperm fraction	Whole grain	Endosperm fraction	Non-endosperm fraction
Nap Hal	19·6	18·9	24·5	3·1	2·5	4·6
Atlas 66	19·4	19·3	19·8	2·8	2·5	4·4
CI13449	15·5	14·5	19·6	3·1	2·8	4·4
Centurk	15·4	15·0	19·6	3·0	2·5	4·5
$LSD_{0.05}$	1·0	0·9	1·0	ns	ns	ns

[a] Dry-weight basis.

In Nap Hal, both the endosperm and non-endosperm fractions show elevated levels of protein compared with the varieties Centurk, CI15075, and CI13449.

Preliminary data from fractionation of very high protein selections from Nap Hal/Atlas 66 show protein elevation of both the endosperm and non-endosperm fractions (Table V). Because the protein content of the endosperm is involved, much or all of the effect should be transmissible to milled white flour.

Effect of yield on grain protein content

High wheat yields often are accompanied by depressed protein content of the grain. This observation has been interpreted incorrectly by some as evidence that these two important traits are incompatible and that one could be achieved only at the expense of the other. The International Winter Wheat Performance Nursery, organised in 1969 by the Nebraska-ARS Wheat Research Team with funds from the US Agency for International Development, presented the opportunity to test the yield–protein relationship over a wide spectrum of production environments.

Yield was correlated with grain protein content in each of 9 varieties grown in 1969 at 20 International Nursery sites and in 1970 at 25 sites. Three of the varieties were known to have genes for high protein. No correlation could be demonstrated in 6 of the varieties. Low but statistically significant negative correlations of yield with protein were shown in 3 varieties. Computed thus, yield level provided no predictive value for protein.

TABLE V

PROTEIN AND LYSINE CONTENT OF WHOLE GRAIN, ENDOSPERM, AND NON-ENDOSPERM FRACTIONS OF LINES SELECTED FROM NAP HAL/ATLAS 66 AND NAP HAL/CI13449 CROSSES

| Line no. | Protein content[a] (%) | | | Lysine content (% protein) | | |
	Whole grain	Endosperm fraction	Non-endosperm fraction	Whole grain	Endosperm fraction	Non-endosperm fraction
		Nap Hal/Atlas 66				
15138	24·2	23·6	25·8	2·8	2·3	4·4
12120	23·6	23·2	26·7	2·9	2·5	4·5
10078	23·3	20·9	25·5	2·7	2·7	4·0
		Nap Hal/CI13449				
18640	16·8	15.6	24·9	3·4	3·0	4·7
16946	16·5	15·6	22·6	3·2	2·6	4·6
16691	16·1	15·3	22·6	3·3	2·6	4·5

[a] Dry-weight basis.

Yield and protein of a group of 24 varieties, tested in the International Nursery and not known to possess genes for high protein, were correlated at each of 13 international test sites. Statistically significant negative and positive correlations were detected. At Stillwater, Oklahoma where the negative correlation (-0.61) was largest, mean yield of the 24 varieties was 39 bu/a, and mean protein content was 17·3%. The largest positive correlation of $+0.65$ was at Eskisehir, Turkey where mean yield was 68 bu/a and mean protein was 12·8%. At Cambridge, England, where mean yield was 50 bu/a and protein only 12·4%, the correlation coefficient was -0.35. A relatively small part of protein variation could be accounted for by differences in grain yield, even at sites where the negative correlations were the largest.

Soil fertility and protein content
In most wheat-production situations applications of generous amounts of nitrogen fertiliser increase both grain yield and protein content. Grain yield response may occur first, and protein response may be minimal until yield response to the fertiliser reaches maximum. This is frequently true

in high-rainfall areas. In low-rainfall areas, protein response to nitrogen fertiliser may be shown more readily than yield response.

The effects of nitrogen fertiliser on protein content of rain-fed wheat grown on nitrogen-starved soils in central and western Nebraska were studied during a 3-year period (Johnson *et al.*, 1973). The responses of a high protein line from Atlas 66/Comanche, CI14016, and Lancer are compared in Table VI. Both varieties responded similarly to increments of nitrogen fertiliser with higher grain protein content and somewhat higher grain yields. Throughout the entire range, CI14016 maintained a protein advantage over Lancer of approximately 2 percentage points. The average protein content of each variety was increased more than 3 percentage points with application of 120 lb of nitrogen.

TABLE VI

AVERAGE YIELD AND PROTEIN RESPONSES OF CI14016 AND LANCER WHEAT VARIETIES TO NITROGEN FERTILISER AT SEVERAL NEBRASKA TEST SITES IN 1969 AND 1970
(From Johnson, V. A. and Lay, C. L. (1974). J. Agr. Food Chem. 22, 558–566.)

Nitrogen applied (lb/a)	Grain yield (bu/a)		Protein content (%)	
	Lancer	CI14016	Lancer	CI14016
0	38	38	10·8	12·5
20	44	41	11·2	13·3
40	47	44	11·8	14·0
60	46	45	12·6	14·9
80	46	45	13·2	15·4
100	46	45	13·6	15·8
120	45	46	14·0	16·3

These data demonstrate that high protein in wheat is not assured by genetic potential for high protein in the varieties grown. Ample soil fertility also is required. Equally important, however, is the evidence that CI14016 can be expected to produce higher protein than Lancer at any level of soil nitrogen availability.

PROTEIN QUALITY

Amino acid composition

The nutritional value of wheat protein is limited by its short supply of the essential amino acid lysine. Ordinary wheat protein seldom contains more than 3% lysine. Increase of lysine to more than 4% would be required to bring it into reasonable balance with other essential amino acids. Nearly one-half of the protein in wheat is alcohol-soluble prolamin, which is low in lysine content. Genetic improvement of lysine content probably would require reduction of the prolamin fraction.

Genetic variability for lysine
Laboratory analyses of 16 000 common and durum wheats revealed substantial variability for lysine (Vogel *et al.*, 1973). Values for the common wheats ranged from 2·2 to 4·2%, with a mean of 3·2%. Most of the values were in the 2·8–3·6% range. Identification of the genetic component of total lysine variation is complicated by the effect of protein level on lysine, shown in Fig. 1.

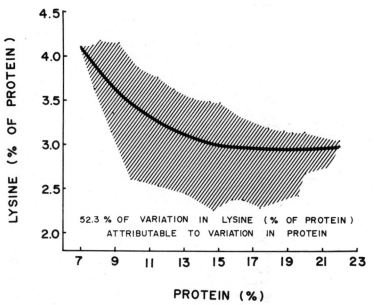

FIG. 1. Relationship of grain protein content and lysine per unit protein among 12 613 common wheats from the USDA World Collection (shaded area indicates dispersal of values about the regression line).

As the protein content of 12 613 common wheats in the World Collection increased from 7 to 22%, lysine, expressed as percent of protein, decreased from approximately 4 to 3%. The negative relationship is strongly curvilinear, being most pronounced between 7 and 15% protein and minimal above 15%. Protein variability above the 16% level has little if any demonstrable effect on lysine. A similar protein–lysine relationship exists for rice, in which protein variability above 10% has little effect on lysine content of the protein (Juliano, 1972).

Lysine, expressed as percent of grain weight, increases with protein (Fig. 2). The positive correlation indicates that the contribution of protein to lysine per grain weight more than compensates for the tendency for high protein to be associated with lower lysine content of the protein.

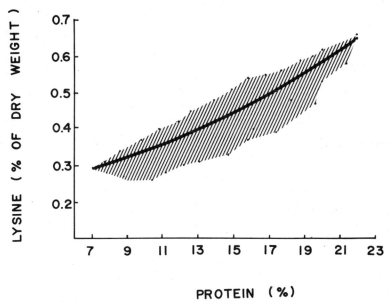

FIG. 2. Relationships of grain protein content and lysine expressed as percent of dry grain weight among 12613 common wheats from the USDA World Collection (shaded area indicates dispersal of values about the regression line).

We use the protein–lysine relationship seen in Fig. 1 to adjust lysine per protein values to a common protein level. This permits direct comparison of lysine values in varieties or lines that differ in protein content. Based upon our analysis of World Collection wheats, the third degree polynomial model provides the best fit for the regression of lysine percent of protein on percent protein (Vogel et al., 1973).

This adjustment of lysine values to minimise the effect of protein level is especially important in the analysis of populations, such as the Nap Hal/Atlas 66, in which there is suspected genetic segregation for both protein and lysine. Adjustment of the World Collection lysine data to a common 13% protein eliminated most unadjusted values that were above 3·6%. Our data suggest that the genetic component of total lysine variation in the World Collection is no greater than 0·5 percentage point. We believe, however, that this component is of sufficient magnitude to be useful in breeding programmes.

Inheritance of lysine

A semi-dwarf experimental wheat developed at Washington State University, CI13449, produced the highest adjusted lysine per unit protein value of any common wheat among 13 000 analysed by our laboratory to date. Nap Hal, because of high protein content combined with above-normal adjusted lysine value, also was of special interest.

Nap Hal was crossed with CI13449, and F_2 progeny bulks from the cross were analysed in the F_3 and F_4 generations for protein and lysine. The mean adjusted lysine content was 3·23% for Nap Hal and 3·35% for CI13449. Eleven percent of the F_2 progeny bulk rows produced adjusted lysine values that were outside of the variability limits of the parents. Twenty-two rows among 437 had adjusted lysine values that exceeded 3·5%. This apparent transgressive segregation for lysine indicates that the parent varieties have different genes and the opportunity for progress in breeding for improved lysine level in wheat.

TABLE VII

F_4 SELECTIONS FROM THE CROSS NAP HAL/CI13449 GROWN AT YUMA, ARIZONA THAT SHOW PROMISING COMBINED HIGH LEVELS OF PROTEIN AND LYSINE IN THEIR GRAIN

Variety	Row no	Protein[a] (%)	Lysine/ protein (%)	Adjusted lysine/ protein (%)
Nap Hal	x̄ of 26 rows	17·5	3·2	3·4
CI13449	x̄ of 2 rows	15·5	3·1	3·3
Nap Hal/CI13449 (F_4)	16 900	19·4	3·4	3·6
Nap Hal/CI13449 (F_4)	16 927	17·8	3·4	3·6
Nap Hal/CI13449 (F_4)	16 921	17·7	3·4	3·6
Nap Hal/CI13449 (F_4)	18 640	16·8	3·4	3·6
Nap Hal/CI13449 (F_4)	17 330	16·2	3·6	3·8
Nap Hal/CI13449 (F_4)	16 442	15·3	3·5	3·7

[a] Dry-weight basis.

Protein and lysine values for promising selections from the best F_2 progeny bulk rows are shown in Table VII. Lines were recovered that combined high protein with adjusted lysine values higher than that of the Nap Hal parent.

Kernel site of the high lysine effect

Whole kernel lysine contents of Nap Hal and C I13449 were 0·3 percentage points higher than that of Atlas 66 (Table IV). The endosperm fraction of Nap Hal was not different in lysine content from that of Atlas 66 but its non-endosperm fraction was higher. In contrast, the endosperm fraction of C I13449 was higher in lysine than the endosperms of other varieties analysed. Statistically significant differences for lysine could not be demonstrated among the parent varieties, probably because of the small number of rows analysed.

Seed from high protein and high lysine selections from Nap Hal/C I13449 and Nap Hal/Atlas 66 also was fractionated. Data for representative selections appear in Table V. The endosperm and non-endosperm fractions of most selections of Nap Hal/C I13449 were equal or intermediate in lysine to the parent varieties.

Chromosomal location of genes affecting quality

We are using the monosomic and chromosome substitution methods to determine the chromosomes of Atlas 66 possessing genes that contribute to high protein in wheat. The monosomic studies, while inconclusive, suggested that chromosomes 5A, 5B and 5D of Atlas 66 are involved (Morris et al., 1973). Chromosome 5D appears to be responsible for the association of high protein and leaf rust resistance.

Group 5 chromosomes of Atlas 66 were substituted into Chinese Spring, C I14108. Chromosome 5D was implicated in the high protein effect. The contributions of 5A and 5B could not be clearly identified.

Flour milled from the hard red winter variety Cheyenne, C I8885, has strong gluten that requires long dough mixing time. These Cheyenne quality characteristics are partially dominant and involve a low number of genes (Heyne and Finney, 1965). When each of the 21 chromosomes of Cheyenne were singly substituted for the corresponding chromosomes in Chinese Spring, chromosomes 4B, 7B and 5D could be demonstrated to contribute to the strong gluten qualities of Cheyenne (Morris et al., 1973). Subsequent studies of substituted lines identified chromosomes 7B and 5D as carrying major genes contributing to the milling properties of Cheyenne.

SUMMARY

Wheat quality is strongly influenced by genetic as well as by environmental factors. The large effect of environment may mask genetic effects.

High protein genes from Atlas 66 have been transferred to productive hard red winter wheats that have acceptable processing quality. The Atlas 66 genes provide genetic potential for 2–3 percentage points more protein than ordinary wheat.

Potentially useful genetic variation for protein quantity and quality in wheat has been identified. Hybridisation of Nap Hal, PI176217, a high protein–high lysine strain from the USDA World Collection, with Atlas 66, CI12561, produced strong evidence of transgressive segregation for high protein. Recovery of selections that are significantly higher in grain protein content than either parent variety suggests that different genes are responsible for high protein in the parent varieties.

The high grain protein effect in Atlas 66 resides entirely in the endosperm kernel fraction. In Nap Hal the high protein effect is detectable in both the endosperm and non-endosperm fractions.

Protein variation among varieties grown in an International Winter Wheat Nursery was not consistently associated with yield differences. In Nebraska, a high protein and a normal protein variety responded to nitrogen fertilisation with increased protein content. At all levels of nitrogen application, the high protein variety maintained 2 percentage points protein advantage over the normal variety.

Only modest genetic variation in lysine content of wheat has been identified. Lysine tends to be negatively correlated with protein content below 15%. Some evidence of transgressive segregation for high lysine was obtained in a cross of two varieties with above-normal lysine content. In one parent variety, the effect was in the endosperm fraction of the grain and, in the other, was in the non-endosperm fraction.

Chromosomes 5A, 5B and 5D appear to possess genes that contribute to high protein in Atlas 66. Chromosomes 4B, 7B and 5D contribute to the strong gluten properties and 7B and 5D to the milling properties of the Cheyenne, CI8885, variety.

REFERENCES

Heyne, E. G. and Finney, K. F. (1965). 'F$_2$ progeny test for studying agronomic and quality characteristics in hard red winter wheats', *Crop Sci.*, **5**, 129.

Johnson, V. A., Dreier, A. F. and Grabouski, P. H. (1973). 'Yield and protein responses to nitrogen fertilizer of two winter wheat varieties differing in inherent protein content of their grain', *Agron. J.*, **65**, 259–263.

Johnson, V. A., Mattern, P. J., Schmidt, J. W. and Stroike, J. E. (1973). 'Genetic advances in wheat protein quantity and composition', *Proc. 4th Int. Wheat Gen. Symp.*, Columbia, Mo., 1973, 547–556.

Johnson, V. A., Schmidt, J. W. and Mattern, P. J. (1968). 'Cereal breeding for better protein impact', *Economic Botany*, **22**, 16–25.

Johnson, V. A., Schmidt, J. W., Mattern, P. J. and Haunold, A. (1963). 'Agronomic and quality characteristics of high protein F$_2$-derived families from a soft red winter-hard red winter wheat cross', *Crop Sci.*, **3**, 7–10.

Juliano, B. O. (1972). *Rice Breeding*, The International Rice Research Institute, Los Banos, Philippines, 389–405.

Mattern, P. J., Morris, R., Schmidt, J. W. and Johnson, V. A. (1973). 'Locations of genes for kernel properties in the wheat variety "Cheyenne" using chromosome substitution lines', *Proc. 4th Int. Wheat Gen. Symp.*, Columbia, Mo., 1973, 703–707.

Middleton, C. K., Bode, C. E. and Bayles, B. B. (1954). 'A comparison of the quantity and quality of protein in certain varieties of soft wheat', *Agron. J*, **46**, 500–502.

Morris, R., Schmidt, J. W., Mattern, P. J. and Johnson, V. A. (1966). 'Chromosomal location of genes for flour quality in the wheat variety "Cheyenne" using substitution lines', *Crop. Sci.*, **6**, 119–122.

Morris, R., Schmidt, J. W., Mattern, P. J. and Johnson, V. A. (1973). 'Chromosomal locations of genes for high protein in the wheat cultivar Atlas 66', *Proc. 4th Int. Wheat Gen. Symp.*, Columbia, Mo., 1973, 715–718.

Vogel, K. P., Johnson, V. A. and Mattern, P. J. (1973). 'Results of systematic analyses for protein and lysine composition of common wheats (*Triticum aestivum* L.) in the USDA World Collection', *Nebr. Res. Bul.*, **258**, 27 pages.

DISCUSSION

A. Albanese (Nutrition Reports International, New York): Some years ago we were involved in the effect of fortifying bread with lysine. We showed that bread contained 5 or 6% of the protein as lysine, and that the lysine–tryptophan ratio needed to be about 6, in other words one gramme of tryptophan for 6 grammes of lysine. In the analysis of your various wheats, did you measure tryptophan content?

V. A. Johnson: Yes, we do measure tryptophan content and generally it is reasonably high. We have done complete amino acid profiles on a number of these wheats and generally what we have found is that the somewhat elevated lysine does not seem to be associated with any depression of the other essential amino acids.

L. Munck (Carlsberg Research Laboratory, Copenhagen): From our work in barley and maize we find the gene background has a very big influence on the expression of the high lysine yield. For instance I can transfer the high protein gene into a genetic background, where it does not express itself and yet I know it's there, because I have genetic markers. Thus I can completely wipe off the expression of the high protein gene. When you have all these other genomes, then I think it is decidedly bad for you to move the genetic background (the old battering system to force this change in the essential amino acids). I agree with you that the protein content is extremely variable and the genetical implication is small but significant. Your graph of adjusted lysine in protein suggests its heritability in wheat is extremely high, and would be analogous to the situation we have found in barley. However, the difference you get is quite small and therefore it takes a lot of time to show up. Finally, I do think that the high lysine in wheat has a potential. Of course, in countries like India the baking quality needs are quite different from those in other countries. It also has implications if one wants to use winter wheat for feed in this country.

V. A. Johnson: The AID supported research, that has been in progress for several years at the University of Nebraska, has as its principal thrust to somehow make wheat more nutritious in those areas of the world where great masses of people rely very heavily upon wheat as a dietary mainstay. I would hope, Dr Munck, that we may find sometime that the genetic background may have some effect upon the expression of the elevated lysine trait in wheat.

K. Blaxter (Rowett Research Institute, Aberdeen): You have said that the relationship between yield and protein content varies from station to station, and that for some reason in the UK this relationship is a negative one, whereas in other parts of the world it is on occasion positive. Can you suggest why this should be so?

V. A. Johnson: I really wish that I could provide definitive information on this. I can only draw on some of the things that I think I know about wheat production in England and the kind of environment that leads to very high yields. Yesterday I commented that the environment at Yuma, Arizona is an area where there is virtually no cloud at any time during the growing season. If ever I've seen a place where wheat grows and diseases of all kinds are totally absent, it would be in this place. I suspect that the rains, the heavy precipitation which you have in England here involves a very rapid leaching of nitrogen downwards. I suspect that the great amount of time in which you have cloud cover and low light intensity may all work against the accumulation of protein in the seed. Interestingly, one of the highest yields we have ever obtained was at Kabul, Afghanistan in the International Nursery. The protein content of that wheat with those very high yields ranged from 16 to $18\frac{1}{2}\%$.

Wheat Starch (Structural Aspects)

R. ANGOLD

The Lord Rank Research Centre,
High Wycombe, Bucks, UK

The wheat starch granule is an enigmatic structure. Chemically, starch is well defined: It consists of two major components, amylose which is a straight chain polymer of D-glucose, linked by 1 : 4 α-glycosidic bonding. The other component of wheat starch is also an α 1 : 4 linked glucan. This is amylopectin. However, amylopectin also contains α 1 : 6 bonds, which, for wheat starch, occur on average once in 23 glucose units. Both of these molecules are big, and a number of workers have attempted to determine the degree of polymerisation. There is a range of values in the literature, but the concensus seems to be, for wheat, a value of the order of molecular weight of 140 000 for amylose, and around four million for amylopectin (Potter and Hassid, 1948). That, briefly is the chemical structure of starch. I shall return to these molecules later.

The starch granule contains more than amylose and amylopectin. During its development in the endosperm, other materials find their way into the granule. Fat and other lipids are present, and nitrogenous and phosphorus compounds are closely associated with the starch fraction of wheat flour. The lipid content appears to be about 1%. This fraction is more readily removed by hydrophilic than hydrophobic fat solvents.

How are the component molecules put together to make the starch granule?

Wheat starch is a carbohydrate derived from photosynthetic activity. The leaves of the wheat plant, and the glumes on the developing spike containing the wheat grain, are engaged in the solar energy driven process of combining carbon dioxide and water to provide us with the objects which we blame for increasing our waistlines. The production lines for carbohydrate are the granal lamellae of the chloroplast. The chloroplast is a beautiful structure; elegantly assembled, and its importance to man-kind—or the existence of life as we know it—cannot be overstressed. It is the key to the production of bread. Chloroplasts around the world are still combining more energy than our so-called energy starved world can use at present.

Antonin van Leeuwenhoek, the father of the microscope, was the first to look at starch with this instrument. Since his studies (in 1719) to the

1920s, the wavelength of light has been the limiting factor in the micro-scopic study of the starch granule. In the mid-1920s de Broglie pointed out that a stream of electrons could be likened to a wave-system, and that the effective wavelength was very short indeed, several orders of magnitude shorter than the effective wavelength of a stream of photons or particles of light.

FIG. 1. A large (A type) starch granule surrounded by the smaller, B-type granules. The scars formed as a result of the compression of the B-type granules against the larger granule during the later stages of development in the amyloplast are clearly visible. (Magnification × 5000.)

By the early 1930s the electron microscope was born. Ruska had built an instrument in which a beam of electrons was focused by a series of magnetic lenses. Its resolution was worse than the light microscopes of a century before, but it had been done. We now take the electron micro-scope for granted.

The restriction which has made the electron microscope less useful than might be expected is the necessity to put the specimen into a vacuum (electrons bounce off air molecules) and to make the specimen extremely thin (a few millionths of an inch thick). Thus, starch examined under the electron microscope is examined in a vacuum, and has to be sliced extremely thinly. By the 1960s, however, a 20th-century electron microscope was being conceived. This owes its origins to John Logie Baird, and it scans the specimen like a TV camera, collecting the electrons which bounce off the surface, enabling the examination of three-dimensional objects. The resolution of these instruments is not as good, however, as the transmission instrument. Nevertheless, this instrument resulted in a burst of microscopic examinations of entire starch granules.

Before the availability of scanning instruments, and, nowadays, to obtain high-resolution images, the transmission electron microscope was, and is, used. Various techniques are used to obtain views of the surfaces of objects. Replicas made in vacuo, and shadowed, are used, and also the technique of freeze-etching (Moor *et al.*, 1961). The resolution of these techniques is about 20 Å, compared with some 200 Å for most scanning electron microscopes.

Figure 1 is a scanning electron micrograph of wheat starch. There are two distinct populations of granule sizes. The larger are the A-type granules, and the smaller the B-type. The scars on the larger, A-type granule are the results of compression—a group of the smaller, B-type granules will have formed there. Figure 2, by courtesy of Dr A. D. Evers

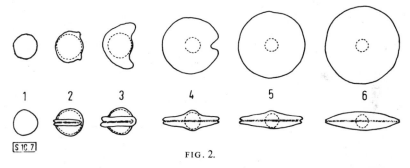

FIG. 2.

of the Flour Milling and Baking R.A. at Chorleywood, is a beautiful demonstration of the way in which the starch granule forms. He has shown, in these images, a story which is fascinating (Evers, 1971). The diagram shows the developmental sequence of the A-type granule within the amyloplast. The nucleus at 1 is progressively surrounded by starch deposits which build up preferentially in the equatorial plane. Growth arises from one side of the granule so that the nucleus of the granule during the earlier stages of development is surrounded by lip-like structures which eventually fuse (4, 5), further starch is added over the entire surface of the granule, thus reducing the depth of the groove in the mature starch granule. Figure 3 shows the granules 4 days, 10 days, 12 days,

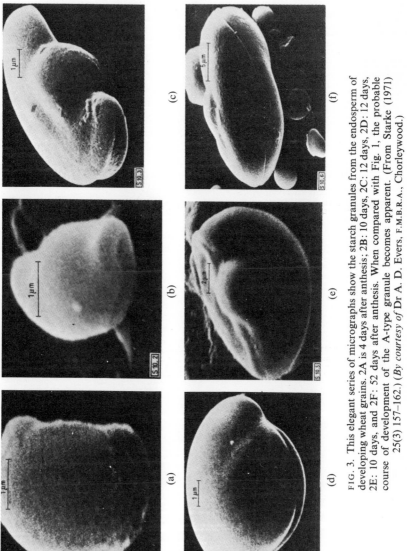

FIG. 3. This elegant series of micrographs show the starch granules from the endosperm of developing wheat grains. 2A is 4 days after anthesis; 2B: 10 days, 2C: 12 days, 2D: 12 days, 2E: 10 days, and 2F: 52 days after anthesis. When compared with Fig. 1, the probable course of development of the A-type granule becomes apparent. (From Starke (1971) 25(3) 157–162.) (*By courtesy of* Dr A. D. Evers, F.M.B.R.A., Chorleywood.)

12 days (new angle), 10 days and 52 days after anthesis. This slide, too, is from Dr Evers' work, and I am indebted to him. Figure 4 shows starch from milled wheat, the mature endosperm content, still displaying this lenticular shape and the equatorial furrow.

Thus, we have lenticular shaped A-starch granules, and the smaller but more numerous B-starch granules which grow in diverticula of the amyloplast membranes, and whose shape is determined by the constraints of the neighbouring granules.

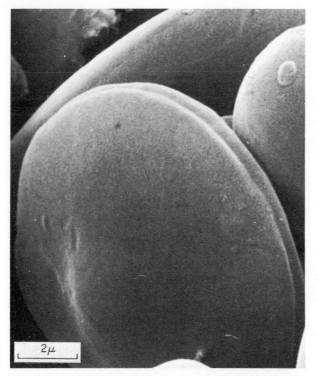

FIG. 4. Mature starch granules from 'Snowdown' flour. The lenticular shape of the A-type granule, and the peripheral groove, are clearly illustrated. (Magnification × 8000.)

How are the molecules of amylose and amylopectin, the main constituents of the granule, put together to form the granule? It has long been known that starch exhibits a lamellation when seen under the light microscope. Although this is most clearly shown in starches like potato starch, it can also be seen in cereals. Thus, the granule must contain layers, or shells, of varying refractive index. Ultrathin sections, examined under the electron microscope (Fig. 5) do not show this layering: a disappointing observation, but not surprising since differences in electron density do not always result from differences in refractive index. The dark areas are artefacts; they have been shown by Gallant and Guilbot (1971) to be a result of using water as a flotation medium during ultrathin sectioning. The use of butanol gives sections free of these wrinkles, which are caused by water absorption.

FIG. 5. Ultrathin section of a granule from 'Snowdown' flour. The dark areas radiating from the centre are an artefact caused by water uptake in the section. No other structure is visible in the granule. (Magnification × 18 000.)

If starch granules are exposed to amylases, or are taken from germinating wheat seeds it becomes apparent that the enzymes can distinguish layers within the granule. Figure 6 is of starch from an 8 day germinated wheat grain. This is a scanning electron micrograph and clearly shows the layering of the starch granule. It has fractured across at the groove, itself a plane of weakness to enzyme attack. Structurally, however, starch granules do not vary in strength across these layers. A fractured granule of wheat starch shows no evidence of the layering. Even potato starch, clearly lamellated under the light microscope, does not show such lamellation when fractured and observed under a scanning electron microscope. At least the potato starch granule shows some radial order; the wheat starch granule only shows conchoidal fracture planes, and if freeze-etching is used in an attempt to look at the grain at high magnification, all that one sees is a micro-conchoidal fracture (Fig. 7). This is disappointing—the granulation shown by the surface is about 20 Å or 2 nm. This is of the order of size of the amylose chains; but no pattern emerges.

Light microscopy of starch granules tells us more than that they are layered. Under crossed polars, it is evident that the starch granule has a radial crystalline structure. Biot recorded this first in 1844, and Meyer

FIG. 7. Starch from the endosperm of a wheat grain which has been allowed to germinate for 8 days. The granule has fractured around the groove, and we are looking at the inner face of one half. The enzymes within the germinating grain can distinguish, and thus emphasise, the concentric shells within the starch granule. A mechanical fracture of the starch granule does not reveal this. (Magnification × 7400.)

FIG. 6. Mechanically fractured starch granule. The only structures visible are the fracture planes at the end of the conchoidal fracture. Concentric shells, if shown, would be at right angles to these fracture planes. (Magnification × 40 000.)

used these observations in 1881 to base his ideas of radial arrangements of trichites, grown by opposition of lamellae. We don't seem to have got very much further than this in the subsequent three-quarters of the 20th century. X-ray diffraction studies have confirmed the radial orientation of the crystallinity of the starch, and attacks on the starch granule with the sharp instruments of enzymes rather than the blunt instruments of freeze-etching, thin sectioning, and, perhaps the worst, simply knocking the granules about until they break, has shown that the granule is made up of concentric shells of material. The crease, shown by Evers to extend through the granule, shows as an area susceptible to enzyme attack (Fig. 8).

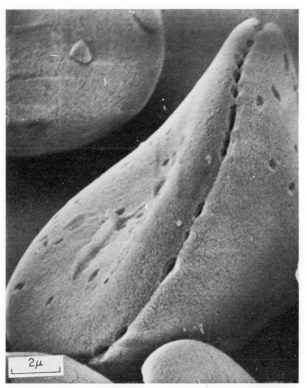

FIG. 8. Starch granule from the endosperm of wheat which has been germinated for 8 days. The main area of attack by the enzymes has been along the groove. Pits are also evident over the rest of the surface of the granule, but the density is much lower. (Magnification × 6900.)

So how do we fit amylose, a molecule some 7000 Å long, and amylopectin, a molecule which could be a triangular pyramid 1000 Å high, together to reproduce the starch granule?

Figure 9 is drawn from the work of Frey-Wyssling and Muhlethäler (1965). It is a hypothetical crystal of amylose, with all the chains parallel. Alternatively, crystalline areas could result from folded amylose chains. The triangle shown for amylopectin is a simplification; a symbol. The crystallinity exhibited by amylose suggests that many of the chains are parallel: thus it is unlikely that amylose is a spherical molecule, with the glucan chains in all directions in space. The branching every 20 or so glucose units may give a pyramidal structure with the majority of chains running parallel.

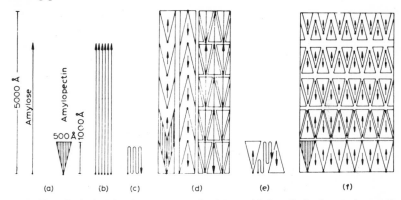

FIG. 9 Hypothetical molecular structures of a 0·5μm wide lamella in the starch granule; (a) individual amylose ($n = 1100$) and amylopectin ($n = 5 \times 10^5$) molecules; • indicates aldehydic pole, arrows → point to the non-aldehydic ends of the molecular chains; (b) crystallised amylose; (c) folded amylose chain; (d) overlapping molecules of amylopectin in anti-parallel array or shifted in such a way as to permit insertion of amylose chains; (e) amylose chain shortened to the length of amylopectin by folding; (f) anti-parallel orientation of amylopectin, accounting for the radially decreasing optical density within the lamella.

Frey-Wyssling and Muhlethäler believe that the granule is constructed from anti-parallel stacked pyramids of amylopectin and that the interstices are filled with folded amylose chains. This is highly plausible until one remembers that a fundamental characteristic of starch is its ability to bind iodine. This, according to Rundle et al. (1944) is dependent on the relative size of the molecules of iodine and the helix of amylose. That is difficult to account for in terms of a folded linear molecule. I can only quote Frey-Wyssling, 'At present, it is not possible to picture the bimolecular structure of the starch in a manner free from contradictions'.

There are many theories of starch granule structure. That outlined above is more plausible than most, but none is satisfactory. A much fuller knowledge of the molecular structure of amylose and amylopectin is needed before we can begin to theorise with any confidence about the structure of the granule itself.

It is the gelatinisation of the starch granule which gives it its important characteristics as far as the food industry is concerned. The hydrogen bonding holding our hypothetical antiparallel stacks renders the granule insoluble in cold water, even though the molecules themselves are hydroxylated and hydrophilic. There is enough water, about 10%, in the wheat starch granule to form a starch monohydrate, and this is probably water of constitution, for its removal changes the X-ray diffraction pattern. However, at around 60 °C, or a little above, enough energy is available to break the hydrogen bonding, and any water bridges present. Water floods into the granule, causing it to swell and lose its birefringence. When an excess of water is available, the granule continues to take up water and to expand until, in the case of wheat starch, its volume has increased 20-fold. The granule, however, retains its integrity, and the viscosity of a starch paste is a result of the retention of this integrity. The swelling of the granule is also influenced by the non-starch components. I have already mentioned that the starch granule contains about 1% of lipid. The removal of this lipid results in a more rapid swelling of the granule, although it does not much reduce the temperature at which the granule begins to gelatinise.

The gelatinisation of the granule will be influenced, too, by solutes present in the water, which 'compete' for the water, and, for most substances used in foodstuffs, reduce the rate of gelatinisation. Similarly, a shortage of water will restrict the rate of gelatinisation, and raise the temperature at which gelatinisation commences. These factors become important in baking, for they influence the development of the texture of a baked product. Starch is not just an inert filler. In the breadmaking process, the starch dilutes the gluten, improving the rheology and furnishes a surface suitable for strong adhesion of the gluten. As it gelatinises and swells, it becomes flexible. In the restricted water content of the baking loaf it does not swell totally and disrupt but provides flexibility for the gas cell wall, permitting it to stretch as the loaf expands. During baking, the starch continues to dehydrate the gluten, causing the gluten film to set and give the loaf its firm texture.

Figures 10–12 show scanning electron micrographs of the gas cell structure of bread. These are from a set taken of stale bread. Figure 12 shows that areas of the starch granules showing through the gluten matrix are decorated. The staling of bread is not a drying process. It has been known for more than a century that staling can occur without loss of moisture (Boussingault, 1852) and that, when the original moisture is retained, the heating of the leaf above 60 °C reverses the staling. Starch pastes also show a tendency to increasing firmness with ageing. This is thought to be a result of an increase in crystallinity (Katz et al., 1930–1939), the realignment of the linear portions of the amylopectin and the amylose molecules and the reformation of hydrogen bonds. If a loaf is

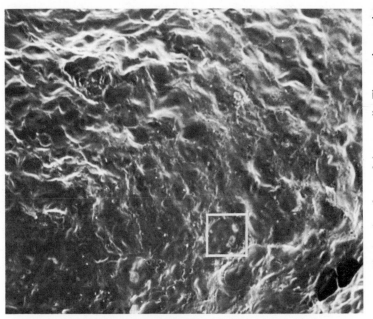

FIG. 11. The interior of one of the gas cells. The starch granules are invested with a film of gluten. The square denotes the area of Fig. 12. (Magnification × 400.)

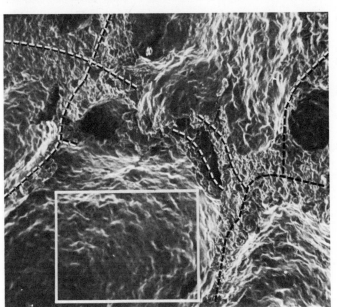

FIG. 10. Low magnification view of a number of gas cells in a stale loaf. The smooth surfaces are the inner faces of the gas cells, and the rougher zones, with dotted lines marking their centres, are the walls between adjacent gas cells, which have been fractured during the preparation of the sample. The square denotes the area of Fig. 11. (Magnification × 150.)

baked with cross-linked starch, the freshly baked loaf has the characteristics of a stale loaf.

We can see that, although the structure of the granule is an enigma, that
structure has a profound influence on the behaviour of starch. Its physical
properties profoundly influence the behaviour of what are, apparently,
fairly simple molecules.

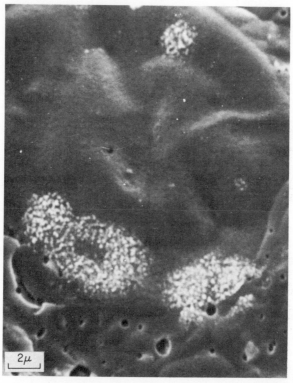

FIG. 12. One starch granule, enveloped in gluten, from the inner surface of the gas cell of
stale bread. The 'decorated' areas are only seen in stale bread. Here, the bread is 7 days old.
(Magnification ×4000.)

The gelatinisation of the starch granule to give a structure which is 20
times greater in volume without a loss of its essential integrity has led
to speculation as to whether there is a membrane at the surface of the
granule, holding it together. There are several observations which tend
to refute this. The exposure of wheat starch to amylases producing holes
in the surface, and therefore, any membrane, still results in an apparently

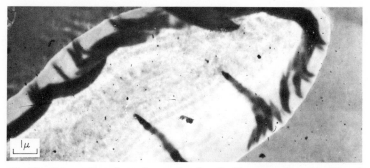

FIG. 13. Ultrathin section of starch granule after Soxhlet extraction with chloroform–methanol for 6 h. The artefacts noted in the legend to Fig. 5 are still evident. The dark line at the periphery of the granule, however, is gone. In addition to this, there is now a suggestion of the concentric shells within the granule. (Magnification × 6420.)

normal pattern of gelatinisation. Also during gelatinisation, short lengths of amylose are lost to the surrounding water.

A lipid membrane would not permit the passage of such hydrophilic molecules. However, there is certainly a differentiated region at the surface of the granule. This is hardly surprising. The enzymes which have been engaged in the synthesis of the starch granule must be at the periphery at the completion of the synthesis and there have been amyloplast membranes surrounding the granule. Figure 5 shows a dark line at the surface of the granule. This stains with electron stains normally associated with lipids, and is removed by vigorous treatment with lipid solvents (Fig. 13). Also shown up by this treatment is a trace of lamellation within the granule, suggesting that small quantities of lipid may be left behind within the granule during its synthesis.

If one looks at the surface of the granule at high resolution by freeze-etching (Fig. 14), the lipids appear as regions of continuous plate, each

FIG. 14. Starch granule surface. Sheets of material are investing the granule. The thickness of these sheets is between 50 Å and 70 Å. There may be more than one thickness of these sheets. (Magnification × 42 000.)

of these steps represents an additional layer of molecules, so there is not enough to cover the granule after a 4- or 5-fold surface expansion during gelatinisation. Solvent extraction removes this layer from the granule surface (Fig. 15) and renders it hydrophilic, as shown by the microcrystals of ice which are adhering to it after this treatment. The behaviour of the granule would be profoundly influenced by the presence of lipids at the

FIG. 15. Starch granule surface. This has been solvent extracted for the removal of lipid. Like Fig. 14, this is a freeze-etching, and the removal of lipid has rendered the surface hydrophilic, resulting in the formation of ice crystals on the surface during the preparation of the specimen (arrowed). (Magnification × 18 600.)

granule surface. Such an area may explain why the granule is not simply taken apart from the outside by amylases. The characteristic pitting shown by the amylose-treated granules would be a result of the inaccessibility of surface starch complexed with lipid.

A transmission electron micrograph shows that the granule is, indeed, taken apart from the interior (Fig. 16). Figure 17 shows starch granules, and the crumb structure, in bread found in a tomb at Thebes and dating from about 1500 BC. Thus, these starch granules have existed for nearly 3500 years, and they are still quite recognisable. It is also noticeable that in this bread, the starch is not so intimately incorporated into the gluten film. The bread is not so developed.

Thus, the starch granule is a complex object. It is a structure which is, as yet, not fully understood. It is assembled from amylose (about 30%) and amylopectin (about 70%) with around 1% lipid and small amounts of phosphorus. The behaviour of the granule has a profound affect on the structure of bread, and other baked goods.

REFERENCES

Biot, J. B. (1844). *Compt. Rend.*, **18**, 759.
Boussingault, J. B. (1852). 'Experiences ayant pur but de determinen la cause du transportation du pain tendre in pain rassis', *Ann. Chim. Phys.*, **36**, 490.

FIG. 16. Ultrathin section through a starch granule from 8 day germinated wheat. The erosion of the interior of the granule is evident, and the layering has been revealed. No swelling artefacts are evident, since the section was cut on to butanol. (Magnification × 3900.)

FIG. 17. Starch granule within the crumb of bread found in a tomb in Thebes. This bread dates from 1500 BC. The gas cells do not have an investing lining of gluten.
(Magnification × 1860.)

Evers, A. D. (1971). 'Scanning electron microscopy of wheat starch. III. Granule development in the endosperm', *Starke*, **23** (5), 157–162.

Frey-Wyssling, A. and Muhlethäler, K. (1965). *Ultrastructural Plant Cytology*, Elsevier, Amsterdam.

Gallant, D. and Guilbot, A. (1971). 'Artefacts au cours de la préparation de coupes de grains d'amidon. Etude par microscopie photonique et electronique', *Starke*, **23** (7), 244–250.

Katz, J. R. *et al.* (1930–39). 'The physical chemistry of starch and breadmaking', *Z. Physik. Chem.* (*Leipzig*), A150–184.

Leeuwenhoek, A. van. (1719). 'Opera Omnia, sen Arcana Naturae', *Delphis*, 1719.

Meyer, A. (1881). 'Veber die Strüktur der Stärkekörner', *Bot. Z.*, **39**, 841–857.

Moor, H., Muhlethäler, K., Waldner, H. and Frey-Wyssling, A. (1961). 'A new freezing ultramicrotome', *J. Biophys. Biochem. Cytol.*, **10**, 1–13.

Potter, A. L. and Hassid, W. Z. (1948). 'Starch. II. Molecular weights of amyloses and amylopectins from starches of various plant origins', *J. Am. Chem. Soc.*, **70**, 3774.

Rundle, R. E., Foster, J. F. and Baldwin, R. R. (1944). 'On the nature of the starch-iodine complex', *J. Am. Chem. Soc.*, **66** (12), 2116–2120.

DISCUSSION

Chairman: Thank you very much, Dr Angold.

Before we get on to discussion, Professor Jakubczyk would like to show a few slides.

T. Jakubczyk (Warsaw Agricultural University): I would like to present pictures taken on the scanning electron microscope of wheat and rye starch showing both the big and the small granules. When glucoamylase acts on wheat starch, the surface is eroded generally and not into deep pits. However, wheat starch fractured during the milling process shows more intensive enzyme penetration on the exposed surfaces. When we look at the starch in the crumb of model bread made out of starch, the gelatinised granules can be seen deformed. When bread is made after the addition of glucoamylase, we can see both the effect of gelatinisation and of the glucoamylase on the starch granules during the baking process. The surface of the granule is eroded. It should be borne in mind that there might be some artefact because we have added the enzyme to starch, or because we have prepared the bread from starch alone. In the preparation of bread from whole flour, there are many more components than the starch and many more enzymes than the glucoamylase, and the pictures might well be different.

Chairman: Thank you very much indeed for that presentation. We have seen some very fascinating scanning electron micrographs of starch granules. How does one reconcile these pictures with the microstructure of starch?

I am going to take the Chairman's privilege of showing a few slides, for it would be very unrealistic to think that in this particular field matters are tied up completely.

I want to start by endorsing what Dr Angold said about the role of the starch granule in baked goods being rather more important than has been hitherto accepted.

Wheat protein baked into a pseudo loaf does not resemble bread, but when wheat starch alone is mixed under suitable conditions with the yeast and salt and baked, the structure does resemble a loaf. This illustrates that the starch granule is more important in determining the structural and textural characteristics of the loaf than it is usually given credit for.

To understand the granule you have to start with the botanical source, i.e. rye or barley, and isolate the starch yourself. The reason for this is shown by the scanning electron micrograph of a commercial wheat starch. The starch granules are not free but are in a rather unpleasant mass of proteinaceous material.

A fundamental study of starch necessitates fractionation to disorganise the structure, dispersion of this and then by adding a polar organic molecule you can form an insoluble amylose complex, whilst in the supernatant liquor there is a solution of amylopectin.

Unfortunately this is not the end of the story. The so-called 'amylose' component is *not* a linear material; it is a mixture of molecules which are linear and those which have some degree of branching: not the short-chain branching associated with the amylopectin component, but long-chain branching. When we come to the size of these molecules, the undegraded amylose has a molecular weight of 1–2 000 000. The amylopectin is a branched material, although we don't understand the exact fine structure. I have a hypothesis that it is two-dimensional branching, rather than three-dimensional branching: if we want an analogy, it is more like a leaf than a tree.

Intermediate material which is neither amylose nor amylopectin is present in all starches. This can vary from 5 to 35% or more. If we take some of the maize starches, we have something like 35% of material which is not amylose or amylopectin. Even in wheat starch we have 5–10% of such material.

I think that starch material exists as a range of molecules, from essentially linear ones through various degrees of branching up to a very highly branched system. I think it is only lack of experimental methods that do not enable us to sort out this branched material.

There is no such thing as starch, e.g. wheat starch, with a fixed characteristic. The characteristics of any starch depends entirely on the time at which you happened to have isolated it. In the early stages of growth, the starch product bears no resemblance to the material at maturity. A large number of changes take place as the plant matures: there is an increase in starch content with increase of maturity, the granules increase in size; there are changes in iodine binding capacity, usually indicating a dramatic increase in the amount of amylose present; the gelatinisation temperature changes; and, if you fractionate the material, the properties of the starch components also vary.

This makes it impossible to draw up a picture of the starch granule because it is not a static biosynthetic entity. Unfortunately, we have no idea at the moment of what factors control these things.

The granular structure is crystalline in the sense that it shows an X-ray diffraction pattern. It is birefringent because it shows effects under the polarising microscope. These do illustrate different degrees of structural order, and the problem, as Dr Angold said himself here, is: what do they mean?

I hope these slides show that we have a lot of factors to take into account—most of which unfortunately we cannot give any answer to—and the problem is trying to reconcile the few facts we have with the vast amount of information that is coming along.

A. Salem (Alexandria University): Is the branching in amylose of α-1–3 or α-1–6 type?

Chairman: The enzyme pullulanase, which is specific for the α-1–6 bonds, will remove the barriers that exist to β-amylase itself. These α-1–6-branch points occur to the extent of one branch point per several thousand glucose units.

A. Salem: Mature starch granules cannot be attacked by α-amylase unless they are damaged through milling or pre-gelatinisation. Does this fact suggest that the starch granule is surrounded by amylopectin type material?

R. Angold: This does not appear to be the case in the material we have been looking at.

F. Lynen (Max-Planck Institute, Munich): The fact that β-amylase can attack the starch granule suggests that the amylopectin surrounds the starch granule more than amylose?

R. Angold: It certainly could.

M. S. Mohamed (Alexandria University): Looking at the structure on these slides, do you know the location of starch synthesis?

R. Angold: I know little of the chemical and biochemical behaviour at the surface of the granule during development, but believe that it is formed by surface accretion and not by intussusception.

F. Lynen: Do you know the location of the enzyme involved?

R. Angold: This knowledge would tell us a great deal about the structure of the granule, but I do not think anybody has done it at the necessary resolution.

J. Edelman (RHM Research Ltd, High Wycombe, Bucks): I am not an expert on starch, but I do know that the original work that was done to isolate potato starch synthetase used the trick of the whole starch granule being part of the synthetic process—up to that time it was, of course, amylase phosphorylase or starch phosphorylase that was considered to be the synthetic agent.

F. Lynen: Would the use of autoradiography show where the enzymes are located?

R. Angold: I think the resolution that one would get in any autoradiographic technique would not be sufficient, because I suspect they are pretty intimately mixed.

P. W. Russell Eggitt (Spillers Ltd, Cambridge): Using the electron microscope, my colleagues have tried a technique of compressing the starch grains and watching what happens in motion. Would this show up anything on the inside that you cannot see from still pictures? Also, is Hess right from his work on air classification and protein shifting, to say the starch granules in wheat had a very, very thin film of adhesive protein on the surface.

R. Angold: Starch granules between glass slides under the light microscope tend to fracture in a radial fashion. But I would love to have a go under an electron microscope. The phosphorus content of the starch tends to come away with the lipid, which suggests that there may be phospholipid present.

H. Matsumato (Osaka Women's University): Gluten film has small pin holes. Do you think every gas cell has a similar pressure inside the dough?

R. Angold: In these bread samples, one is looking at a series of exposed surfaces rather than the total volume of the loaf, but nearly every gas cell was inter-connected with other gas cells by these pin holes.

J. Edelman: The interesting thing about the wheat plant, and virtually all cereal plants, is that they do not make any starch until the last few weeks.

K. Tolboe (Jutland Technological Institute): How old were the rye breads when they were examined? Could the effects be retrogradation?

T. Jacubczyk: No, because the bread was no more than two or three days old, and the rye bread was fresh.

R. Angold: Those regions do not show in fresh bread; they start to appear after six or seven days and after a couple of weeks you could find a lot of it.

A. Salem: Is starch recrystallised during staling in a different manner to that of the native starch?

R. Angold: Yes.

A. Salem: Retrogradation is irreversible, but staling is reversible; how do you explain that?

Chairman: Retrogradation by definition is irreversible. If a solution of amylose retrogrades, the only way you will get it back into dispersion is to put it into a pressure cooker with 10 M alkali. The simple answer to the question is that the changes that are taking place in the starch are due to changes in the amylopectin crystallisation.

G. A. H. Elton (Ministry of Agriculture, Fisheries and Food, London): What was the local temperature of starch granules under an electron microscope?

R. Angold: Probably terrifyingly high.

G. A. H. Elton: Is it above the normal gelatinisation temperature?

R. Angold: Yes, the immediate surface temperature may rise rather sharply, but nobody really knows how much. Also, the surface coating of gold conducts heat away and in the vacuum there is no water for gelatinisation.

F. Pushman (Plant Breeding Institute, Cambridge): Is there any comment about the role of the small starch granules?

R. Angold: The chemical composition of the A- and the B-starch granules is not vastly dissimilar. They are more resistant to enzymic attack. They are more numerous, but they provide a rather smaller fraction of the total volume; the weight could form about 30% of the total starch.

Chairman: I think they are more important than has been anticipated in the past, because there are so many of them.

T. Jacubczyk: In my opinion, the role of small granules and their effect on baking lies in the temperature of gelatinisation and the susceptibility to enzyme action.

M. S. Mohamed: This fat or protein film around the granules: has there been any attempt to use any enzymes before taking electron micrographs?

R. Angold: Yes, we have; lipases and amylases together have a synergistic effect on the breakdown of the starch granule.

Chairman: Ladies and gentlemen, I feel that at this stage we should bring this discussion to an end. Before closing, I would, on your behalf, like to thank Dr Angold for his stimulating lecture and the discussion provoked, and ask you to show your appreciation in the usual manner.

Session III

YIELD FACTORS

Limitations to Productivity by Diseases and Pests in the Field—North America

D. J. SAMBORSKI

Canadian Department of Agriculture,
Winnipeg, Manitoba, Canada

Wheat production in North America has increased steadily in this century through expansion of the cultivated areas and increased yields per acre (Table I). Considering the huge acreage involved, a small percentage loss in production is translated into millions of bushels of wheat. Although adverse weather conditions such as drought, excessive spring moisture, hail and frost are major factors in reducing production, my intent is to deal only with the effects of diseases and insect pests. Data to document these effects are scarce in North America as yield loss surveys, when they are carried out, usually cover a limited area and often a specific disease in that area. Further, in Canada, insect surveys, such as the grasshopper survey, are done to forecast outbreaks and plan control operations and not to measure losses. In spite of these limitations, it is believed that the loss estimates that have been made are reasonably accurate.

TABLE I

AVERAGE WHEAT ACREAGES AND YIELDS PER ACRE IN NORTH AMERICA DURING 1955–59 AND 1962–64[a]

Country	Acreage (1000 acres)		Yield (bu/acre)	
	1955–59	*1962–64*	*1955–59*	*1962–64*
Canada	22 730	28 023	20·4	22·4
United States	49 128	45 946	22·3	25·5
Mexico	2 214	1 911	20·2	33·7
Total North America	74 160	75 970	21·6	24·6

[a] Quisenberry and Reitz, 1967.

Before dealing with diseases and pests, I should like to illustrate fluctuations in production that are not caused by inclement weather or diseases and insect pests. In 1969, approximately 25 million acres were planted to wheat in Canada; in 1970, the acreage fell to 12·5 million acres (Table II). A huge surplus of wheat taxed storage facilities and farmers were encouraged to reduce production. Indeed, in 1970, we fulfilled the perversion of making one blade of grass grow where two grew before. Such a decrease in production represents a real loss to the world's supply of food although it may have a local economic justification.

The cultivation of wheat in western Canada began in 1812 in the Red River Valley. As early as 1818, the crops were destroyed by grasshoppers (Buller, 1919; Riegert, 1968), and grasshoppers have remained a threat ever since. In 1974, the potential area expected to require control for grasshoppers was 400 000 acres in Manitoba, 5 million acres in Saskatchewan, and 1 million acres in Alberta. Other insects, including cutworms, wireworms, and wheat stem sawfly, present in native range grasses also found wheat to be a suitable food (McGinnis and Kasting, 1967).

TABLE II

WHEAT ACREAGES, YIELDS PER ACRE, AND PRODUCTION OF
WHEAT IN CANADA DURING 1968–73[a]

Year	Area (1 000 acres)	Yield/acre	Production (1 000 bushels)
1968	29 422	22·1	649 844
1969	24 967	27·4	684 276
1970	12 484	26·6	331 519
1971	19 228	27·2	523 693
1972	21 349	25·0	533 288
1973	24 760	25·4	628 738

[a] Statistics Canada.

In 1938, over 20% of the wheat crop in Saskatchewan was destroyed by grasshoppers and 3·4% by sawfly giving a loss in excess of 34 million bushels. Damage by sawfly to wheat in Saskatchewan in 1943 was estimated at 20 million bushels. During the period 1926–58, it is estimated that grasshoppers and sawfly caused a total loss of 400 million bushels of wheat in Saskatchewan (McGinnis and Kasting, 1967). Most of the arable land of the prairies can be infested with grasshoppers but since 1931, forecasts of outbreaks have usually enabled the stockpiling of sufficient insecticide to protect most of the crop and have warned farmers of the necessity of control. Considerable control of wheat stem sawfly can be obtained with resistant varieties that have been available since 1946. Although cutworms and wireworms have occasionally severely damaged wheat, no reliable estimates of yield losses in Canada are available. Wireworms can be controlled by seed treatment with insecticide but in Saskatchewan the average annual losses to wireworms in the period 1954–64 were estimated at 10 million bushels of wheat.

The only comprehensive compilation of yield losses in the USA is found in the US Department of Agriculture Handbook No. 291 (1965). The values given, although estimates, were made by qualified and experienced workers and, at least for wheat, appear realistic. Insect pests were estimated to have caused annual losses of 6% or 74·5 million bushels of wheat during the period 1951–60 (Table III). The wheat stem sawfly, *Cephus cinctus* Nort. occurs from Kansas to Canada, but in the USA it is most injurious

TABLE III

ESTIMATED AVERAGE ANNUAL LOSSES IN YIELD
OF WHEAT CAUSED BY SPECIFIC INSECT PESTS
DURING THE PERIOD 1951–60[a]

Insect	Loss (%)
Greenbug	1·4
Hessian fly	1·2
Wheat stem fly	1·0
Cutworms	0·9
Armyworms	0·6
Brown wheat mite	0·5
Grasshoppers	0·4
Total	6·0

[a] United States Department of Agriculture, 1965.

to wheat in North Dakota and Montana. Since 1945, resistant varieties have reduced damage from this sawfly and from the Hessian fly, *Mayetiola destructor* Say. In 1969, a US Department of Agriculture survey showed that 24 wheat varieties resistant to the Hessian fly were grown on over 8·5 million acres in 34 states. The same survey showed that 7 varieties resistant to the wheat stem sawfly were grown on 1·5 million acres in 7 states. However, losses from insect pests are still severe, and in 1972 it was estimated that insects were responsible for the loss of over 100 million bushels of wheat (Cooperative Economic Insect Report, 1973). In addition, the cereal leaf beetle, *Oulema melanopus* L., an immigrant from Europe, is potentially destructive to wheat.

The English grain aphid, *Macrosiphum granarium*, is the only serious insect pest in Mexico and is generally controlled with insecticides (Borlaug, 1968).

Historically, the bunt species have been the most destructive of the wheat smuts in North America. In Canada, yield reductions from bunt of 30–40% were common at the turn of the century (Green *et al.*, 1968), while it is estimated that one-quarter to one-half of the wheat crop in Kansas was sometime destroyed by bunt around 1890 (Fischer and Holton, 1957). With the widespread use of seed treatment chemicals and, more recently, resistant varieties, bunt is no longer a serious problem except in the Pacific Northwest where soil contamination by windborne spores of dwarf smut during harvest may cause devastating losses in localised areas.

Leaf rust and common root rot are currently the most damaging diseases on the Canadian Prairies. Losses from root rot occur throughout the wheat growing area and have been estimated at 5·7% for the period 1969–71 (Ledingham et al., 1973). Estimated losses of wheat in Manitoba for this same period from leaf rust, miscellaneous leaf spots, virus diseases, and bacterial diseases, range from 5 to 8% of the potential production (Hagborg et al., 1972). This value is probably generally applicable to wheat grown in western Canada in the absence of severe epidemics of stem rust and suggests that diseases reduce production by at least 75 million bushels of wheat when a crop in excess of 600 million bushels is produced.

The average annual loss of wheat in the USA from all wheat diseases for the period 1951–60 was estimated at 174 million bushels or 14% of the potential yield (US Department of Agriculture, 1965). These losses were due principally to a series of epidemics, including the rust epidemics in the early 1950s, wheat streak mosaic virus outbreaks in the hard red winter wheat areas, especially in 1954 and 1959, epidemics caused by Septoria, principally in the mid-western and eastern soft winter wheat area, and bunt and stripe rust epidemics in the Pacific Northwest. The predominant role of stem rust and leaf rust is well illustrated in Table IV.

The stem rust epidemic of 1916 reduced wheat yields in Canada by 100 million bushels (Buller, 1919) and in the USA by 182 million bushels (Quisenberry and Reitz, 1967). Other epidemics in the 1930s took a huge toll of the wheat crop. Spring wheat varieties resistant to stem rust were generally grown by 1939 and there were no important losses from stem rust in the period 1939–51. In 1952, a significant increase occurred in race 15B of stem rust which could attack the previously resistant varieties.

The rust epidemics that occurred from 1953 to 1955 are well documented and illustrate the great potential for damage to the wheat crop with severe epidemics of stem rust (Peturson, 1958). In 1953, about 5 million acres of wheat were grown in the rust area of Canada. About one-half of this crop was seeded early and escaped damage. The remainder was seeded at least 2 weeks later and suffered yield reductions estimated at 25% or 45 million bushels (Peturson, 1958).

Spring in 1954 was cold and wet and seeding was generally delayed 2–3 weeks in most areas in the Prairie Provinces. Heavy spore showers arrived several weeks earlier than usual and covered an area of 11 million acres. This most severe epidemic in Canadian history caused a loss estimated at 150 million bushels of wheat (Peturson, 1958). The spring of 1955 gave indications of another catastrophic epidemic but very dry conditions in mid-summer and a considerable acreage of the resistant variety Selkirk prevented another epidemic and a loss of only 9·5 million bushels of wheat was estimated for 1955 (Peturson, 1958). Heavy losses also occurred in the US spring wheat area and in 1953 and 1954, 75–80% of the durum crop and 35% of the bread wheat crop was destroyed by stem rust and leaf rust (Reitz, 1972).

There has been no significant damage from stem rust to hard red spring wheat in North America since 1955. Selkirk is still resistant although it has been displaced on a considerable acreage by new resistant varieties. However, winter wheat was severely damaged by stem rust in the 1960s in Nebraska, Iowa and South Dakota. Leaf rust still damages wheat in

TABLE IV

ESTIMATED AVERAGE ANNUAL LOSSES CAUSED BY VARIOUS WHEAT DISEASES FOR THE PERIOD 1951–60[a]

Disease	Loss (%)
Stem rust	4·0
Leaf rust	2·5
Root rots	1·0
Septoria leaf and glume blotch	1·0
Wheat streak mosaic	1·0
Cercosporella foot rot	0·8
Loose smut	0·6
Scab	0·5
Soilborne mosaics	0·5
Common bunt	0·4
Powdery mildew	0·4
Take-all	0·2
Bacterial diseases	0·1
Dwarf bunt	0·1
Leaf and head blights	0·1
Miscellaneous virus diseases	0·1
Snow moulds	0·1
Stripe rust	0·1
Others	0·5
Total	14·0

[a] United States Department of Agriculture, 1965.

Canada and the USA. Yield reductions of 5–10% commonly occur in Manitoba and eastern Saskatchewan; a loss of 6–10 million bushels in Canada was estimated for 1973. The Cereal Rust Laboratory, St Paul, Minnesota, estimated losses from leaf rust at 21·6 million bushels in 1972 and 62·1 million bushels in 1973, largely in the hard red winter wheat crop.

Although stripe rust is not as widespread in North America as stem rust or leaf rust, it caused the most severe epidemics in the history of the Pacific Northwest in 1960 and 1961; losses were estimated at 12·5 million and 25 million bushels respectively. In Mexico, conditions are very favourable for damaging rust infections but rusts have been kept in check with resistant varieties (Borlaug, 1968).

A considerable portion of the wheat acreage in the USA is subject to damaging infections of *Septoria tritici* and *Septoria nodorum*. Reports in the Wheat Newsletter indicate that losses in affected areas of 14–20% are not uncommon. Similarly, frequent and heavy losses from wheat streak mosaic virus occur throughout the winter wheat acreage in the Great Plains regions of North America. In 1963–64, 18% of the potential yield of winter wheat in Alberta was lost because of streak mosaic (Atkinson and Grant, 1967), and in 1958, streak mosaic reduced yields of wheat by 20% in Kansas (US Department of Agriculture, 1965). Resistant sources are available for use in breeding programmes (Larson and Atkinson, 1973).

It is clear that diseases and insect pests cause annual losses in excess of 300 million bushels of wheat in North America, even in the absence of severe epidemics of stem rust. It is more difficult to determine how much of this loss can be prevented. A number of diseases and insect pests can be controlled by plant breeding and diseases such as stem rust present a clear case for resistant varieties. However, breeding is not usually carried out for resistance *per se*. It is yield that is to be improved, not disease resistance. The important factor is the relationship between any particular resistance and higher yield (Baker, 1974). Further, the control of some diseases and insect pests with resistant varieties requires a very considerable breeding effort. According to Borlaug (1968), although rust has been kept under control in Mexico the turnover in varieties has been heavy; variability in the pathogens has made it necessary to release new varieties every 4–5 years. The use of long-lived resistance to diseases such as the rusts would permit greater attention to other factors affecting yield of wheat.

ACKNOWLEDGEMENTS

I am grateful for the assistance given me by Mr W. Romanow and Dr N. D. Holmes, Agriculture Canada, and Dr K. Lebsock, Dr L. P. Reitz and Dr R. A. Kilpatrick, US Department of Agriculture.

REFERENCES

Atkinson, T. G. and Grant, M. N. (1967). 'An evaluation of streak mosaic losses in winter wheat', *Phytopathology*, **57**, 188–192.

Baker, R. J. (1974). 'Application of genetic principles to crop improvement', *Annual Wheat Newsletter*, **XX**, 4–8.

Borlaug, N. E. (1968). 'Wheat breeding and its impact on world food', in *Proc. 3rd Intern. Wheat Genet. Symp.* (Canberra), Australia.

Buller, A. H. R. (1919). *Essays on Wheat*, The Macmillan Company, New York.
Cooperative Economic Insect Report (1973). 23: 773–800, United States Department of Agriculture.
Fischer, G. W. and Holton, C. S. (1957). *Biology and Control of the Smut Fungi*, Ronald Press Co., New York.
Green, G. J., Nielsen, J. J., Cherewick, W. J. and Samborski, D. J. (1968). *The Experimental Approach in Assessing Disease Losses in Cereals; Rusts and Smuts*, Can. Plant Dis. Surv., **48**, 61–63.
Hagborg, W. A. F., Chiko, A. W., Fleischmann, G., Gill, C. C., Green, G. J., Martens, J. W., Nielsen, J. J. and Samborski, D. J. (1972). *Losses from Cereal Diseases in Manitoba in 1971*, Can. Plant Dis. Surv., **52**, 113–118.
Larson, R. I. and Atkinson, T. G. (1973). 'Wheat *Agropyron* chromosome substitution lines as sources of resistance to wheat streak mosaic virus and its vector, *Aceria tulipae*', in *Proc. 4th Intern. Wheat Genet. Symp.* (Columbia, Missouri) USA.
Ledingham, R. J., Atkinson, T. G., Horricks, J. S., Mills, J. T., Piening, L. J. and Tinline, R. D. (1973). *Wheat Losses Due to Common Root Rot in the Prairie Provinces of Canada*, 1969–71, Can. Plant Dis. Surv., **53**, 113–122.
McGinnis, A. J. and Kasting, R. (1967). 'Wheat production and insects', in *Canadian Centennial Wheat Symposium* (Ed. K. F. Nielsen), Modern Press, Saskatoon, p. 371.
Peturson, B. (1958). 'Wheat rust epidemics in Western Canada in 1953, 1954 and 1955', *Can. J. Plant Sci.*, **38**, 16–28.
Quisenberry, K. S. and Reitz, L. P. (Eds.) (1967). 'Wheat and wheat improvement', *Agronomy*, **13**, American Society of Agronomy, Madison, Wisconsin, USA.
Reitz, L. P. (1972). 'The worst diseases of crops—wheat', *Crops and Soils*, November, 14–17.
Riegert, P. W. (1968). *A History of Grasshopper Abundance Surveys and Forecasts of Outbreaks in Saskatchewan*, Mem. 52, Entomol. Soc. Can., 99 pp.
Statistics Canada. Field Crop Reporting Series No. 20, 1969–1973.
United States Department of Agriculture (1965). 'Losses in agriculture', US Dep. Agr., *Agr. Handbook* 291, 120 p.

DISCUSSION

Chairman: Thank you very much, Dr Samborski, for your very interesting paper, which is now open for discussion.

F. Lupton (Plant Breeding Institute, Cambridge): I was intrigued by what Dr Samborski said about physiological races succeeding one another in a manner which is extraordinarily similar to some of the work here in Britain. Is any research going on into the physiological mechanism, apart from major gene resistance due to hypersensitivity, which might perhaps lead to a better understanding of long-term resistance, particularly in relationship to his leaf rust work?

D. J. Samborski: Well I don't believe that anyone is working on the physiological aspects of non-hypersensitive resistance at the present time. The trouble is that the hypersensitive type of resistance is very easy to use in breeding programmes and the other type we are not very familiar with. I think that that is the type of resistance that we will have to use in the future, and learn how to work with it and of course, if possible, learn something about its physiological characteristics. But of course we don't know anything about physiological mechanisms of hypersensitive resistance— and we have been working on that for many, many years.

R. Riley (Plant Breeding Institute, Cambridge): The puzzling thing is that you in North America, who have been able to control stem rust pretty well for the last 20 years, using major gene resistance, have been less effective with the leaf rust control while we in western Europe have totally failed to control stripe rust with major genes. This is a very difficult situation to understand but I wonder what your view is on the different levels of success that you have had with the two rusts with which you are principally concerned in Canada and the USA?

D. J. Samborski: The resistance that we have against stem rust was first released in Selkirk and in the newer varieties is really very complex; there are a considerable number of genes for resistance, both of the seedling and of the adult plant type. But for leaf rust every variety that we have released has only had one gene for resistance. We are bombarded with astronomical numbers of spores which come in and leaf rusts can very quickly develop virulence when your wheat plant is protected with only one gene.

J. Mesdag (Foundation for Agricultural Plant Breeding, Wageningen, Netherlands): I well remember in the old literature about disease resistance there were attempts to use morphological resistance against rusts, etc. I think this stopped when the major type of resistance was introduced. My question is, whether you will use, or are already using, or going to use, this type of resistance?

D. J. Samborski: No, we are not using it. We are presently using purely hypersensitive resistance.

J. M. Hirst (Rothamsted Experimental Station): Can you tell me whether there is any work and hope of success for breeding for resistance against dwarf bunt?

D. J. Samborski: No. I couldn't tell you. You see we don't have dwarf bunt in Canada at all. Dr Heyne I think might have something.

E. G. Heyne (Kansas State): Dwarf bunt is primarily a problem in the Pacific Northwest and they do have genes for resistance but they are getting physiological breakdown. Several introductions from Turkey have been used extensively in that area and they do give protection in some of the new things that are coming out. I think it is P.1.17,83,83. So they do have some major gene protection against dwarf bunt but they also have the rust problem too.

Chairman: Well thank you very much, Dr Samborski.

Limitations to Productivity by Diseases and Pests in the Field—Europe

F. JOAN MOORE

Chief Scientists' Group,
Ministry of Agriculture, Fisheries and Food,
London, UK

INTRODUCTION

In attempting to put into perspective the limitations which diseases and pests may impose on increased productivity of wheat crops, it is useful to assess the contributions that have been allotted to various factors which were responsible for the substantial increase in the UK national average yields over the past 30 years. From 1947 to 1964 there was an increase from 19 to 31 cwt/acre and since then there has been a further increase to a mean 34 cwt/acre for the three seasons 1970–72. For the earlier period it has been suggested that the introduction of new, higher yielding varieties contributed 4 cwt, their interactions with fertiliser usage 5 cwt and pest, disease and weed control 3 cwt (Elliott, 1962; Strickland, 1967). The only chemical control measures for diseases and pests used during this time were seed treatments, and it was estimated that for the period 1960–64 about 98% of the wheat acreage was treated with fungicide, 46% was also treated with insecticide for the control of wireworms and 15% for wheat bulb fly. It is also of significance that during this era new short-strawed varieties were introduced and widely grown; first, Bersee and from 1953 the outstandingly popular and time-honoured variety Cappelle-Desprez, which was grown on over 70% of the winter wheat acreage for the period 1957–68 and although now outclassed in yield by many newer varieties still occupies over a quarter of the acreage. This variety has undoubtedly also made a major contribution to the control of two diseases—yellow rust and eyespot.

Records providing qualitative observations on the incidence of diseases and pests have been collected by the Ministry of Agriculture, Fisheries and Food on a national scale in England and Wales since 1919; since 1950 attempts have been made to obtain quantitative data on their effects on yield and to establish relationships between recordable levels of severity and crop loss. More recently systematic surveys to record the seasonal

171

incidence and severity have also been made. All such records are necessarily historical and environmental changes, especially those brought about by changed agricultural practices, including the introduction of new varieties and availability of new pesticides, are likely to alter apparent long-term patterns. The weather, which markedly affects the seasonal development of most diseases and pests as well as the growth and yield of wheat crops, may also have long-term effects. Climatic conditions undoubtedly have a major influence on the relative occurrence and prevalence of the various diseases and pests in different countries in Europe. It is of interest to record that the European Cereal Atlas Foundation is preparing a third volume on the prevalence of diseases and pests and it is hoped to present information on the climatic influences.

Disease and pest attack can affect all three main components of yield. Early attacks on seeds, seedlings and young plants can affect the numbers of plants and ears produced per acre; later attacks affect the number of grains produced per ear; and attacks affecting active leaf and stem tissues during grain filling stages affect the weight of individual seeds resulting in shrivelled grain. At the earlier stages of growth plants have significant powers of recovery and compensation; for instance in trials attempting to simulate slug damage in the field, thinning seedlings by 25% resulted in a final yield of 96% of the control (Jessop, 1969). In an experiment in which wheat plants were defoliated, so that they had one, two, three or four leaves only throughout the growing period, plants with only three leaves gave 90% of the yield of control plants (Large and Doling, 1962).

DISEASES

The quantitative and qualitative information collected over the years provides a useful basis for selecting the six major diseases that have limited productivity. These are: the seed-borne bunt (*Tilletia caries*), the two foot rots—eyespot (*Cercosporella herpotrichoides*) and take-all (*Gaeumannomyces graminis*) and the three foliar diseases yellow rust (*Puccinia striiformis*), mildew (*Erysiphe graminis*) and septoria (*Septoria* spp.).

Bunt has undoubtedly been a despoiler of grain stocks since time immemorial. The fascinating story of the identification of the fungus responsible and methods of control has been told by Large (1940). It was in France that it was discovered that the black dust which filled the internal tissues of grain could contaminate healthy seed to reproduce the 'disease' in a subsequent crop with no other symptoms on the growing crop. The spores imparted an unpleasant fishy smell to contaminated grain. Thanks to some of our great agricultural reformers of the 19th century, who made special efforts to watch for possible innovations from Europe, an effective copper steep seed treatment was introduced into this country and by 1856 was being widely used here well before it was common in France or Germany. In the 1930s a further advance was introduced from Germany where organomercury dusts had proved effective and much easier to apply: routine seed treatment with mercury compounds was quickly adopted and by 1942 about 70% of seed wheat was treated. Today 99% of seed wheat handled by seed merchants is treated with organomercury compounds and 85% is with dry powder formulations (Sly, 1972). Fortunately for us in the UK a second species of bunt, known on the Continent as Dwarf Bunt, has not been recorded here; it is both seed and soil-borne and consequently is only partially controlled by seed treatment.

Both foot rots have also been known for ages. The early agriculturalists were familiar with farms of 'straggling' and lodging symptoms characteristic of eyespot. Its occurrence in France in the early 1900s is well documented. But it was not until the fungus responsible was identified—in Oregon—that the disease could be specifically recorded. It was first reported in England in 1935 at Rothamsted and surveys in the 1940s showed that it was common throughout the country. The fungus attacks the base of the culm and so weakens it that it tends to break and the crop to lodge. The main features of its epidemiology were determined at Rothamsted where the unique field experimental facilities covering conventional four- and six-course rotations and long-term near-continuous cereal cropping were to provide valuable data when close cereal cropping became agricultural practice in the 1960s and 1970s (Glynne and Salt, 1958). A feature of the disease was its increased severity with increased number of cereal crops: a break of at least 3 years was necessary to reduce inoculum to insignificant levels. With the introduction of Cappelle-Desprez in 1953 it was noted that not only did the stiff short straw resist lodging but that the variety was also more resistant to infection. For instance, in one experiment the variety Yeoman suffered a yield loss of 21% whereas Cappelle lost only 3%. This resistance has since been successfully exploited by plant breeders (Macer, 1964). Today of the eight varieties on the Recommended List of the National Institute of Agricultural Botany seven have a resistance figure similar to Cappelle. If this resistance can be sustained, this disease too can hopefully be kept well under control.

The second foot rot, take-all, attacks the roots and crown and when severe causes 'whiteheads' in which little or no grain is produced. Detailed experimental work over many years has again been done at Rothamsted and a useful relationship between levels of infection and yield loss has been established (Slope and Etheridge, 1971). Take-all is also a disease of increasing importance in close cropping sequences (Glynne, 1965). However, experience has also shown that it reaches a peak severity after about 3–5 years and then 'declines' and subsequent yields, provided adequate nitrogen applications are given, can be reasonable though they never equal those obtained in the first year after several years in break crops. Barley is also susceptible but does not normally suffer so severely. Some present experimental and observational work is aimed to determine whether by growing successive barley crops to induce 'decline' it would then be possible to introduce wheat without the risk of serious attacks after a few years of continuous cropping. Take-all was considered to be the main factor limiting close cereal cropping, especially of winter wheat: that it is still a major threat to yield when two or three continuous crops are grown on arable farms has been shown recently by a survey made in the East Midlands (Rosser and Chadburn, 1968). There is also evidence that the severe attacks are often associated with poor drainage and possibly other adverse cultivation conditions.

The three foliar diseases, mildew, yellow rust and septoria, are all endemic diseases affecting the foliage and ears. They develop on successive leaves up the plant and when weather conditions are favourable can spread epidemically: mildew and yellow rust spores are air-borne and infection can spread rapidly and widely: septoria is splash dispersed and outbreaks are therefore more localised. All three diseases usually affect yield by affecting the weight of grain. Mildew was one of the first diseases for which disease severity/yield loss relationship was established: trials at eight centres over 4 years, using lime-sulphur to control infection, showed that yield loss was equal to $2 \times$ the square root of the percentage mildew recorded at growth stage 10·5 (Large and Doling, 1963; Large, 1954). During the years of these trials the mean loss in yield was about 1 cwt/acre for 3 years and was negligible in the fourth.

Of the three rust diseases occurring in Great Britain—yellow rust, black rust (*Puccinia graminis*) and brown rust (*Puccinia recondita*)—yellow rust favoured by relatively cold, damp conditions, is the most important. Black rust has caused some late epidemics in the past, especially on late-maturing spring wheats. Investigations in the 1960s into the origins of such epidemics showed that the initial inoculum was coming from the Continent (Ogilvie and Thorpe, 1961). In the southern warmer countries black rust is the most important. Brown rust is also more damaging in some European countries than it is in Britain. Rust workers in Europe have good liaison and the European and Mediterranean Rust Conferences held every 4–5 years provide a useful forum for exchange of information.

Yellow rust has long been recognised as one of the most conspicuous and damaging diseases and, following attempts in the USA to breed for black stem rust resistance, Biffen at Cambridge started in the early 1900s to breed for resistance to yellow rust: the variety Little Jess, still remarkably resistant, was introduced in 1910 and Yeoman some years later. His work has been followed up ever since by the Plant Breeding Station at Cambridge (Macer, 1972) and with other introductions from the Continent there has been a changing scene of wheat varieties and races of the yellow rust fungus which, together with favourable weather conditions for a series of 'yellow rust years', has resulted in the loss of the most affected varieties from cultivation. In recent years severe rust attacks have occurred approximately once every 5 years. In Table I these years together with the varieties affected are listed.

There were several interesting features to the yellow rust epidemic on Joss Cambier in 1971–72: a new variant of a well-established race of the rust was responsible and a postal survey showed that for the first time commercial applications of fungicides had been used for rust control— on about 9% of the acreage and almost all on Joss Cambier (Walker and

TABLE I

YELLOW RUST YEARS WITH VARIETIES MOST SEVERELY AFFECTED AND THE PREVALENT RACE

Year	Variety	Yellow rust race
1943	Wilma	Race 6
1949	Jubilegem	Race 8
1952	Nord Desprez	Race 2
1957	Heines VII	Race 8b
1961	Viking	
	Jufy 1 (Spring Wheat)	Races 2X and 8X
1966	Rothwell Perdix	Race 60
	Opal (Spring Wheat)	Race 3/55
1972	Joss Cambier	Race 3/55 variant

Roberts, 1974). In a trial in 1972 on the effectiveness of fungicides, repeated applications of an experimental rust fungicide gave very good control: yields on untreated control plots were 34% below those on the treated ones. A disease/yield loss relationship was established for levels of infection on the flag leaf at growth stage 11·1 (Mundy, 1973).

Another yield loss/disease severity relationship, similar to that for mildew, has been established for yellow rust: the loss equals 3 × the square root of infection at growth stage 10.5.3 (Doling and Doodson, 1968).

The third foliar disease, septoria, has been known in this country for many years but it is only recently that its national importance has been appreciated. It has been recognised as a damaging disease on the Continent for many years and much information on its epidemiology, yield loss potential, and possibilities for control by breeding has come from work in Switzerland (Brönnimann, 1968).

During the 4 years 1970–73 a national survey to assess the relative prevalence and severity of leaf diseases on winter wheat crops has been done by plant pathologists in the Agricultural Development and Advisory Service and estimates made of the losses attributed to the various diseases using some of the published yield/loss relationships and other experimental data (King, 1973). A summary of the results is given in Table II.

TABLE II

NATIONAL LEVELS OF LEAF DISEASES AT GROWTH STAGE
11·1 AND ESTIMATED LOSSES
(From King, 1973)

Disease/year	1970	1971	1972	1973
Septoria				
% infection on leaf 2	5	19	33	18
% loss	2	3	8	3
Mildew				
% infection on leaf 2	7	4	2	3
% loss	2	4	3	5
Yellow Rust				
% infection on leaf 1	tr.	1	2	tr.
% infection on leaf 2	tr.	2	4	tr.
% loss	neg.	4	8	3

These surveys have established the importance of septoria here. It is a seed-borne disease, also carried over on stubble and causes blotching and death of leaves and discoloration of glumes. Using many applications of fungicides to give effective control of the main species involved, *Septoria nodorum*, up to 30% increases in yield have been recorded (Jenkins and Morgan, 1969). It is especially severe in western districts but is also more prevalent than had been suspected elsewhere in the country.

Similar surveys, on the considerably smaller acreage of wheat, have been made in Scotland and the prevalence of septoria there recorded: in 1970 leaf 2 infection for septoria was 17·5% with mildew at 4·7% and yellow rust at 0·1% (Richardson, 1971). In these Scottish surveys attempts are also being made to determine factors other than disease which may be responsible for yield losses and additional data on seedling and ear counts and ear sample yield estimates are also being collected.

PESTS

Estimates made in 1965 of the national losses due to the four major pests of cereals, assuming that no control measures had been applied suggested that wireworms and slugs could each have been responsible for an average equivalent of 2% acreage loss, wheat bulb fly for 1% and cereal cyst eelworm for 0·5% (Strickland, 1965).

Wireworms (*Agriotes* spp.) can be a major cause of seedling death especially after old grass or a long lay and on heavy soils: severe damage over a whole crop is now rare. Seed treatment with an insecticide has been commonly used as a control measure since the 1950s and at present about 50% of the seed handled by merchants is treated (Sly, 1972).

Slugs (*Agriolimax reticulatus*) hollow out grain below soil level and so reduce plant populations: damage can be sufficiently severe to warrant redrilling. A country-wide survey in 1966–67 showed that about 24 000 acres were redrilled because of slug damage: the number of crops affected was greater in eastern districts and on heavy soils. About 11 000 acres were treated with chemicals for slug control (Hunter, 1969).

Wheat bulb fly (*Leptohylemyia coarctata*) larvae hatching from eggs laid in late summer on bare soil in fallow land or root crops can severely damage the central shoots of young wheat plants in early spring. They are especially troublesome in the eastern half of England. A tentative yield/ loss relationship has been established (Bardner *et al.*, 1970). Wheat bulb fly is also prevalent in central and northern Europe. Seed treatments are available as control measures and 16% of the winter wheat seed is so treated (Sly, 1972). There is, however, some evidence that the treatment process is not as efficient as it needs to be (Lord *et al.*, 1971).

In recent years saddle gall midge (*Haplodiplosis equestris*), a pest associated with close cereal cropping and heavy land, has apparently increased and spread in western Europe since the mid-1950s. A survey to determine its incidence in this country was made in the mid-1960s; it showed that the pest was widely distributed throughout the main cereal growing areas but at a low level and was consequently of little national economic importance. However, in recent years some severe attacks have been reported and potentially dangerous levels of infestation have been detected in several widely scattered areas (Golightly and Woodville, 1974).

Several species of aphid occur on cereals and as on the Continent, where infestations of 20–30 aphids per ear have been reported to cause 10% loss and prolonged attacks with up to 150 aphids/ear to give 30% loss (Kolbe and Linke, 1974) more attention is now being given to assessing their importance (George, 1974). Aphids can cause direct losses by feeding and also as vectors of virus diseases, especially barley yellow dwarf.

So much for the historical evidence brought as up-to-date as the data allows. Undoubtedly all the diseases and pests mentioned will still be with us in the future but their relative importance will change and possibly some of the many others not mentioned may well come to the fore. Activities of plant breeders will influence the relative importance and hopefully they will find some way of introducing more durable resistance than they have in the past; especially for foliage diseases. Changing agronomic practices are also likely to play a role: minimum cultivation techniques may well create new disease and pest problems and such possible effects need to be monitored. But perhaps of most significance in the immediate future will be the impact of fungicides for the control of foliar and other diseases. It will be necessary for us to assess the needs and benefits, to ensure that optimum rates and timing of applications are determined and that possible residue risks are investigated. Perhaps our aim should be to achieve the high yields of wheat in close rotations on the most suitable land, comparable with those obtained after a rotational break which does so much to keep populations of diseases and pests at minimum risk levels.

REFERENCES

Bardner, R., Maskell, F. E. and Ross, G. J. S. (1970). 'Measurements of infestations of wheat bulb fly *Leptohylemyia coarctata* (Fall.) and their relationship with yield', *Plant Pathology*, **19**, 82–87.

Brönnimann, A. (1968). 'Zur kenntnis von *Septoria nodorum* dem Erreger der Spelzenbraune und einer Blattdurre des Weizens', *Phytopathologische Zeitschrift*, **61**, 8–146.

Doling, D. A. and Doodson, J. K. (1968). 'The effect of yellow rust on the yield of spring and winter wheat', *Trans. Brit. Mycological Society*, **51**, 427–434.

Elliott, C. S. (1962). 'The importance of variety testing in relation to crop production', *J. Nat. Inst. Agric. Botany*, **9**, 199–206.

George, K. S. (1974). 'Damage assessment aspects of cereal aphid attack in autumn- and spring-sown cereals', *Ann. Appl. Biology*, **77**, 67–74.

Glynne, M. D. (1965). 'Crop sequence in relation to soil-borne pathogens', in *Ecology of Soil-borne Plant Pathogens* (Ed. K. F. Baker and W. C. Snyder), University of California Press.

Glynne, M. D. and Salt, G. A. (1958). 'Eyespot of wheat and barley', *Report Rothamsted Experimental Station for* 1957, 231–241.

Golightly, W. H. and Woodville, H. C. (1974). 'Studies of recent outbreaks of saddle gall midge', *Ann. Appl. Biology*, **77**, 97–101.

Hunter, P. J. (1969). 'An estimate of slug damage to wheat and potatoes in England and Wales', *National Agricultural Advisory Service, Quarterly Review*, No. 85, 31–36.

Jenkins, J. E. E. and Morgan, W. (1969). 'The effects of Septoria diseases on the yield of winter wheat', *Plant Pathology*, **18**, 152–156.

Jessop, N. H. (1969). 'The effects of simulated slug damage on yield of winter wheat', *Plant Pathology*, **18**, 172–175.

King, J. E. (1973). 'Cereal foliar disease surveys', *Proc. 7th British Insecticide and Fungicide Conference*, **3**, 771–780.

Kolbe, W. and Linke, W. (1974). 'Studies of cereal aphids; their occurrence, effect on yield in relation to density levels and their control', *Ann. Appl. Biology*, **77**, 85–87.

Large, E. C. (1940). *The Advance of the Fungi*, Cape, London.

Large, E. C. (1954). 'Growth stages in cereals. Illustration of the Feekes scale', *Plant Pathology*, **3**, 128–129.

Large, E. C. and Doling, D. A. (1962). 'The measurement of cereal mildew and its effect on yield', *Plant Pathology*, **11**, 47–57.

Large, E. C. and Doling, D. A. (1963). 'Effect of mildew on yield of winter wheat', *Plant Pathology*, **12**, 128–130.

Lord, K. A., Jeffs, K. A. and Tuppen, R. J. (1971). 'Retention and distribution of dry powder and liquid formulations of insecticides and fungicides on commercially dressed cereal seed', *Pesticide Science*, **2**, 49–55.

Macer, R. C. F. (1964). 'Developments in cereal pathology', *Annual Report Plant Breeding Institute Cambridge for 1962–63*, 5–33.

Macer, R. C. F. (1972). 'The resistance of cereals to yellow rust and its exploitation by plant breeding', *Proc. Roy. Soc. London*, B, **181**, 281–301.

Mundy, E. J. (1973). 'The effect of yellow rust and its control on the yield of Joss Cambier winter wheat', *Plant Pathology*, **22**, 171–176.

Ogilvie, L. and Thorpe, I. G. (1961). 'New light on epidemics of black stem rust of wheat', *Science Progress*, **49**, 209–227.

Richardson, M. J. (1971). 'Yield losses in wheat and barley, 1970', *Scottish Agriculture*, **50**, 72–77.

Rosser, W. R. and Chadburn, B. L. (1968). 'Cereal diseases and their effects on intensive wheat cropping in the East midland region 1963–65', *Plant Pathology*, **17**, 51–60.

Slope, D. B. and Etheridge, J. (1971). 'Grain yield and incidence of take-all (*Ophiobolus graminis* Sacc.) in wheat grown in different crop sequences', *Ann. Appl. Biology*, **67**, 13–22.

Sly, J. M. A. (1972). 'Cereal seed dressing', *Pesticide Usage. Survey Report* 2, Ministry of Agriculture, Fisheries and Food, 13 pp.

Strickland, A. H. (1965). 'Pest control and productivity in British agriculture', *J. Roy. Soc. Arts*, **113**, 62–81.

Strickland, A. H. (1967). 'Some problems in the economic integration of crop loss control', *Proc. 4th British Insecticide and Fungicide Conference*, 1967, **2**, 478–491.

Walker, A. G. and Roberts, E. T. (1974). 'The wheat yellow rust (*Puccinia striiformis*) epidemic 1971–72', *Science Arm Annual Report 1972*, Ministry of Agriculture, Fisheries and Food, 159–162.

DISCUSSION

D. J. Samborski (Canadian Department of Agriculture, Winnipeg, Canada): You mentioned that the aphids were vectors of virus diseases. Are virus diseases much of a problem here? Is it serious to the wheat not only in Britain but on the Continent too?

F. J. Moore: It is prevalent as I mentioned before. One of the difficulties is to find out how damaging it is. In England it looks as if it is prevalent and in some years damaging, particularly in the south-west. In a lot of the work that has been done on insecticide control of aphids on the Continent, the two possible components have not been separated out.

W. V. Single (New South Wales Dept. of Agriculture, Tamworth, NSW): We have a contamination problem, Dr Moore, and have had to stop using organomercury compounds for seed treating. Will you comment on the amount of work that is going on here to replace the dangerous chemicals with more acceptable ones for seed treatment.

F. J. Moore: There is a lot of work going on by the chemical firms for possible replacements for organomercury. We have found nothing as effective and until we do there is really no move to replace the relatively small amount of mercury we are using on our wheat and barley seed. With the insecticide I am on slightly less sure ground. There is a lot of work going on, but once again nothing so effective as the *organochlorines* has come up.

K. Blaxter (Rowett Research Institute, Aberdeen): In Dr Samborski's paper, he indicated that the magic figure of about 10% seems to be a reasonable figure to put on losses by pests and diseases except in those years like 1955 when there was an epidemic. Now from your figures, where you quote Richardson, my quick calculation using the 1973 figures, suggests that 44% is the difference between the top line of those data and the bottom line of the established yield. To what do you ascribe this very large difference? Is this entirely disease, or what other factors are involved? Can you, following your first slide, begin to subdivide the extent of this failure to reach the potential of the crop?

F. J. Moore: In that last slide I was trying to point out that somebody has looked at the difference between the two extremes. The national yield is known. The theoretical yield was obtained from a study of a number of crops and from observations of the seedlings earlier in the year. That is why I said that from our point of view we need to look into this whole subject; I feel certain there is a pest component and almost certainly a root disease component. Now root diseases are very much more difficult to sample. The leaf diseases are widespread and a sample of fewer plants will give you a representative degree of infection, particularly if you are seeking a national picture. But with root diseases you get pockets in the crop and it is very difficult to devise a practicable sampling method which gives you a good estimate. Richardson has tackled this to some extent but he realises that his data are quite inadequate. He has merely pinpointed that root diseases and diseases such as eyespot are there. There are all sorts of suggestions as to what the various factors might be, but there is no real evidence so far. It is not all plant pathology nor all entomology by any means. This area requires our combined efforts to try and get the maximum information. But the interesting thing on this 10% to my mind are the figures of 30% for the potential loss the disease can cause and 3% for a national average over a number of years that it does cause. Then we have an in-between value of 10% for 'average severe' incidence. As I said earlier we get figures in certain years of this order. For example with *Septoria* we nearly got there with 8%. Again the 10% level came up for the yellow rust year. So when you get a year where everything seems to be favourable for a disease we can get up to the 10% loss.

Pre-Harvest and Post-Harvest Losses

S. K. MAJUMDER

Infestation Control and Pesticides Discipline,
Central Food Technological Research Institute, Mysore-13, India

INTRODUCTION

In spite of intensive cultivation in many parts of the world, chronic shortage of food grains in most of the developing countries is evident. Some of these shortages of food although related to the lack of physical resources of food production are caused often by economic and socio-political factors. The traditional cultivation practices, restricted distribution, conservative dietary food habits and other inefficacies necessitate solutions that are principally socio-economic in character. Agriculture and the fisheries produce about 120% of human need for protein and food energy requirements in anticipated quantities (Schimitt, 1965). But the harvest-to-mouth losses leave only about 85% of the requirements as consumable quantities on a worldwide basis. It is also contended that if realistically only one-half of the non-food crop and potentially arable land is converted to food crop land it would increase the food output by 165% over the present status.

The food losses do not occur at a single stage, the loss in the pre-harvest period due to insects, fungi, mites, viruses, bacteria, rodents, nematodes, birds, weeds and other agencies lead to 'untaken harvest' of about 25%. The prevention of post-harvest loss during threshing, processing, distribution, storage and marketing could increase the food potential significantly (Majumder and Parpia, 1967). The estimates for harvest-to-mouth losses vary between 15 and 30% (Hall, 1969). Aggregate pre-harvest and post-harvest losses due to the depredation by the agencies such as insects, moulds and rodents are beyond comprehension (FAO, 1967) (Table I).

FIELD INFESTATION

The staple grains such as wheat, rice, maize, sorghum and the beans are highly susceptible to insect pests. The stored product insects lay their eggs on wheat in the field prior to harvest in subtropical and tropical

TABLE I

SOME ESTIMATES OF LOSSES OF DIFFERENT COUNTRIES

Country		Loss % or value	Reference
World	All crops	10%	FAO, *Grain Storage Newsletter*, 1 (2), 1959
Nigeria	Sorghum	46%	Colonial Res. Publ., 12, 40
	Cowpea	41%	
USA	Stored grain	$500 million	Metcalf, R. L., *Destructive and*
	Packed food	$150 million	*Useful Insects*, McGraw-Hill.
	All crops	$3 500 million	p. 41–43, 1962
India	All crops	25% field loss	Central Food Technological
		15% storage loss	Research Institute, 1965
		7% handling and	(Res. & Ind. Conf. 1965)
		processing	
		3% other losses	
Indonesia	Rice	15% field loss	*Int. Rice J. Yearbook*, 1957, p. 36
Germany	Harvested	DM 71·4 million	Frey, W., *Flugblatt Biol.*
			Bundesanstalt, Nr. 5, 8, 1951
Sierra	Rice	41%	Colon. Res. Studies, No. 28, 52, 1959.
Leone	Maize	14%	Roch. Rep. W. Afr. Stored Prod.
			Res. Unit No. 12, 1962
Tropical	All crops	30%	Hall, D. W., FAO Informal
Africa	(storage and		Working Bull., 24, 1964
	handling)		

parts of the world (Cotton, 1963). When the threshed grain is stored in farm storage the insects emerge as adults and cause further processes of deterioration in completing further life cycles. In most of the developing countries harvesting by hand using sickles requires low moisture content of the grains in the field itself. The mature grain is left on the cut plant in the field for further drying and the stored-product insects find an optimum moisture content on the panicles. With combine harvesting and mechanical harvesting in cold climates, the oviposition of stored-product insects in the field is not so common as the harvesting is done under high moisture conditions (Cotton, 1963). Therefore, basically clean grains without field infestation enter the silo and other sophisticated storage structures in the industrialised countries. Under the conditions of the subtropical belt and tropical areas, the field infestation is quite common but is not generally recognised as the source of infestation at the farm level. In addition to this, cross-infestation occurs from the residual populations left on the debris of the previous crop on the farm premises. The incidence of field infestation recorded in wheat is about 6% and in sorghum and pulses about 30%. Therefore, the kernels are affected prior to harvest. This insidious and latent infestation is not recognised by the tropical and subtropical farmers and is neglected in the normal regimen of crop husbandry.

The infection by storage fungi also occurs below the pericarp and bran layer. Similar to storage pests, the storage fungi are ecologically different from the fungal pathogens of the crops in the field. Both the stored-product insects and storage fungi are adapted to higher solute concentrations, in other words to high osmotic concentrations (Majumder *et al.*, 1965), whereas pathogens and pests of the crops during growth are adapted to moisture contents between 50 and 85%. The storage fungi and stored-product insects could grow on panicles with moisture content below 25%.

POST-HARVEST INFESTATION

In the harvested grain crops the infestation and infection are almost inherent from the field, and further, they obtain the load of fungi and insect population during post-harvest handling. Even in a dry grain, infestation leads to the development of high microclimate relative humidity and moisture in the infested kernel (Fig. 1). This increase in moisture and relative humidity catalyses the activities of micro-organisms and the enzymes of the seed. Commensalism between the storage fungi and stored-product insects set in. This results in thermogenesis and convection currents between the hot and cold points. These convection currents are responsible for the migration of moisture and finally for condensation when the dew point is reached.

Insect mould, moisture and mites bring about physical and biochemical changes in the kernel. The loss of carbohydrate, protein, fat and vitamins, due to their activities, though quite significant is hardly recognised. The insects carry with them both beneficial and harmful microflora. Stored-product insects have been known to transmit enteric organisms and other human pathogens to the grain. On the one hand the insects carry organisms harmful to themselves, on the other hand without the association of mycetome and symbionts, the insects cannot survive and complete the life cycle in the grain kernel. The insects attacking wheat and related grain are uricotelic in their excretory physiology. Uric acid in the crystalline form, chitin and chitosan in their exuviae and sclerites, volatile emissions from the body and also quinone, ubiquinone and similar substances elaborated by them result from infestation, as well as many toxic metabolites from their microbial associates. These excretory substances and metabolites get mingled with the food. Mites excrete guanine and most of the fungi elaborate UV fluorescent compounds and also substances designated as apparent uric acid-like products, the Benedict–Franke reaction complex. The nutritional and also toxigenic implications of these contaminants are yet to be elaborated. There is, however, no doubt that depending on the type of infestation, guanine, uric acid, chitin and the metabolites of insects add to the filth and foreign matter in the infested grains. Apart from the insect and fungi another group of pests associated with grain handling and distribution are the commensal rats. Rodent hair, faecal matter, urine and body odour are directly introduced by the rodent activities in the precincts of grain handling. Zoonoses are also carried by them. Food-borne diseases are associated with their activities.

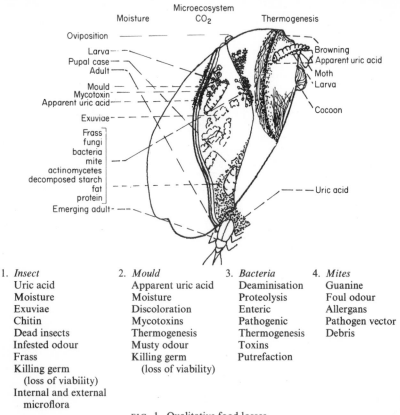

1. *Insect*	2. *Mould*	3. *Bacteria*	4. *Mites*
Uric acid	Apparent uric acid	Deaminisation	Guanine
Moisture	Moisture	Proteolysis	Foul odour
Exuviae	Discoloration	Enteric	Allergans
Chitin	Mycotoxins	Pathogenic	Pathogen vector
Dead insects	Thermogenesis	Thermogenesis	Debris
Infested odour	Musty odour	Toxins	
Frass	Killing germ	Putrefaction	
Killing germ	(loss of viability)		
(loss of viabiiity)			
Internal and external			
microflora			

FIG. 1. Qualitative food losses.

The micro-organisms are varied, e.g. *Salmonella*, *Pseudomonas*, spirochaetes, plague organisms, and may lead to serious infections. Vectors like fleas and mites transmit or disperse them to the food or directly to the human subjects. Although direct ingestion of food by rodents is quite significant, the indirect pollution of the food and related deterioration of quality are much more serious. The filth and excreta resulting from rodent infestation are the subject of food regulation, pure food law and food hygiene. Yet there is an unexplored area of research as to the microbial pollution of food-grains and their products due to birds and lizards.

It has been taken for granted in many of the developing countries that infestation is inherent and a part and parcel of food storage and handling. Sometimes allowances have been prescribed for such losses during

TABLE II

(A) LOSS AT PRE- AND POST-HARVEST STAGES[a]

	India		World		Pakistan	Africa
Pre-harvest (%)	20 (KB Lal)	15–20 Pest and disease	10 US Sci. Panel	20 (Ordish)	15–30	20 (FAO)
Post-harvest (%)	10 (post-harvest handling Comm. Preventable)	3–5 (handling) 10–15 (storage) 3–5 (processing) 4–5 (transport) 5–6 (hotels and households)	17·3 US Sci. Panel	30 (Schimitt)	18·7–30·4 (Weitz-Hettelsatter)	30 (Hall)
Total (%)	30	40–60	27·3	50	33·7–60·4	50

[a] Majumder and Parpia, 1967.

(B) ROLE OF INFESTATION CONTROL AND PROTECTION OF FOOD-GRAINS ON EXTENDING FOOD SUPPLIES FROM EXISTING LEVEL OF PRODUCTION

	Preventable losses	Addition food supply to feed	Reference
World	55 million tonnes cereals	250 million	Dobrovsky, Grain Storage Newsletter, 1 (2) 2, 1959
India	10 million tonnes cereals 3 million tonnes pulses 1·5 million tonnes Oil seeds	100 million and quality improvement	CFTRI, 1966
West Africa	30% of grains 8 million tonnes	80 million	FAO Inf. Working Bull. No. 24, 1964

storage by the organised sector of food storage and supply agencies. Several estimates of losses are available and some of those are presented in Tables I and II. Thus considering the figures for losses it becomes quite evident that the field losses range between 10 and 30% while estimates of post-harvest loss vary between 10 and 20%. However, on a conservative basis the average aggregate loss in field and in post-harvest would amount to 30% on a worldwide basis.

Schimitt (1965) mentions in his article 'Planetary Food Potential' that the potential gains through prevention of losses are very impressive. Not only would they wipe out the present food deficit but feed as many people again as there are now. Ordish (1952) estimates the 'untaken harvest' as one-fifth of the estimated production. While estimating the amount

TABLE III

EFFECT OF INSECT INFESTATION ON THE COMPOSITION
OF SOME COMMODITIES

Parvathappa, H. C. and Majumder, S. K. (unpublished data, 1967)

FFA mg KOH 100 g	Kernel damage (%)	Frass (%)	Moisture (%)	Insect count per 100 g	Uric acid (mg/100 g)
WHEAT					
Sound	10·0	3	0·1	7·4	0	5·4
Infested	47·1	86	4·0	14·4	573	30·8
RICE					
Sound	62·5	0	0	9·5	0	7·0
Infested	165·5	20	1·0	10·4	25	10·3

| | FFA | Kernel damage | Frass | Uric acid (mg/100 g) | | |
				Total uric acid	Apparent[a] uric acid	True uric acid
WHEAT						
Sound	10·0	3	0	5·4	1·8	3·6
Moderately infested	32·5	8	0·2	8·5	2·4	6·1
Highly infested	47·1	86	4·0	30·8	2·1	28·7
RICE						
Sound	62·5	0	0	7·0	6·9	0·1
Moderately infested	157·5	10	0·3	5·7	5·3	0·3
Highly infested	165·5	20	1·0	10·3	3·2	7·0

[a] Non-uric acid substances: methyl uric acid, dimethyl uric acid, ascorbic acid, resorcinol, ergothiocine, cystine, glutathione.

of protein which could be saved by disinfestation of cereal grain alone, Scrimshaw (1968) reported that 9 million tonnes of protein per annum could be made available to the world population assuming a total of cereal grain production in the world of 1000 million tonnes and average protein content of 9% and the very conservative figure of 10% for preventable losses. Thus, it can be mentioned here that, at the present stage of world food production, it is possible to project that, with the existing production, the quickest way to improve the food situation would be to launch extensive and intensive measures for preventing food losses at all stages of production, handling, storage, processing, distribution and marketing.

QUALITATIVE LOSS

Although losses have been recognised by the several authorities mentioned above, most of the estimates are based on quantitative losses or the physical loss of the constituents of grain. When a wheat seed is infested by one insect, it consumes only about 10–30% of the kernel, the rest of it is unconsumed and left behind. The moisture retention by such an infested grain

TABLE IV
EFFECT OF INSECT INFESTATION ON WHEAT FLOUR

Period of infestation (months)	Insect population per 100 g	Insect fragment (number/100 g)	Uric acid (mg/100 g)	Acceptability
0	0	0	0·1	Acceptable
1	42	370	11·2	Not acceptable
2	110	603	37·7	Not acceptable
3	299	850	68·3	Not acceptable
	Gluten (%)	Thiamine (μg/100 g)	Loaf volume (% reduction)	
0	7·4	160	–	Acceptable
1	6·8	153	7	Acceptable
2	–		19	Not acceptable
3	4·2	76	23	Not acceptabie

is higher than with sound grain, which serves as a compensating factor for the weight loss. The insect excreta, cadaver, body parts, exuviae, also remain along with the grain. These are the artefacts in the weight loss computation as these may compensate significantly. The growth of fungi in association with insects also leads to the formation of mycotoxins and related metabolites. The denaturation of protein and loss of vitamin which might occur as a result of the abnormal enzymatic activities both of the seed and also of the micro-organisms are contributors to the total loss. Thus the qualitative loss, if reckoned with, will be many times more than the physical removal of the grain constituents (Tables III and IV). The deterioration in grain quality is reflected in the taste, odour, lower baking quality, lowering of paste viscosity, loss in biological value, lower digestibility, changes in the nitrogen balance and other factors. The Protein Efficiency Ratio (PER) also appears to be affected by infestation. The selective removal of the most nutritious part of the grain by infestation of the germ and bran layers has been reported (Parvathappa et al., 1970; Venkatarao, 1960). Loaf volume of leavened bread and characteristics of unleavened bread are adversely affected even by incipient infestation (Table IV). These losses are not generally taken into account in computation of the potential losses.

PARAMETERS OF QUALITY

Several parameters have been proposed for estimating the changes in the quality of food-grains induced by the triple agencies moulds, insects and rodents. Tolerances are prescribed under the food laws of different countries. They are tentative in character and are revised from time to time depending on the improvement in the average national quality. The average quality, however, depends on the overall application of scientific measures for achieving sanitation at various stages of production, handling, distribution, processing and storage. The physical and biochemical specifications that are prescribed are directly related to the proximate composition. The tissue characteristics of the seed governs the accumulation of constituents for the nutrition, metabolism, survival and growth of the seed itself. In addition to the physical and chemical standards the contaminants, filth, pollutants and extraneous matter are also subjected to quality assessment. The body parts of insects, life-stages and their carcases, uric acid and moulds are quantitatively assessed. The indices of deterioration of fat, protein and carbohydrate are estimated. The depletion of vitamin content has also been the subject of study for determining the acceptable range, tolerance or permissible limit. These have been prescribed on the basis of survey of the samples. Indirect methods for assessment of quality have also been attempted, these refer to the estimation of carbon dioxide, reaction with tetrazolium chloride, radiographic character and petrological properties, along with the biochemical tests for free amino acid, chitin and also volatiles derived from the insect body.

The bacteriological and mycological specifications are also applied for determining quality of the grains and their products. Differential media are used for estimating the population of fungi, bacteria, actinomycetes and yeasts. The specific organisms such as *Salmonella, Escherichia coli, Aerobacter aerogenes* and also *Clostridia* are assessed. Presumptive and confirmatory tests are applied for finding out the microbial status of the sample (Table V).

The mycotoxins such as aflatoxin, citrinin, islandotoxin, fusarin, and related substances are also entering into the literature of regulatory analysis. Interesting lines of studies have emerged due to the association of different metabolites with insects, moulds, mites and other organisms. Guanine estimation for mites, true uric acid for insects, apparent uric acid (Benedict's reaction complex) for microbial degradation, chitin analysis for fragments of exocuticle, microscopic characteristics of fragments, hair and structures for various morphological groups are emerging as fascinating fields of study. The decarboxylase activity of stored wheat indicates its physiological status.

Since the grains are produced on agricultural land there is an inadvertent contamination with soils, minerals and dusts. Recent investigations have shown that the minerals and dusts which are associated with the grain sample are a guide to its origin, with special reference to its place of production, processing and handling. Studies on the crystallographic nature of the acid insoluble matter have opened up a field of study for detection of these categories of foreign matter (Table VI). The edaphic

TABLE V

SPECIES OF INTERNAL FUNGI ISOLATED FROM DIFFERENT STAGES OF
SITOPHILUS ORYZAE AND GRAINS
(Majumder, S. K., Ragunathan, A. N. and Rangaswamy, J. R., Symposium on Preservation of Wet Harvested Grain, Paris, 1973)

Grub	Pupa	Adult
Aspergillus flavus	A. flavus	A. flavus
A. ochraceus	A. restrictus	A. candidus
A. sydowi	A. terreus	A. ochraceus
A. candidus	A. chevalieri	A. chevalieri
A. restrictus	A. ochraceus	A. versicolor
A. versicolor	A. candidus	A. niger
A. niger		
A. terreus		
A. tamari		
Penicillium rugulosum		
Amblyosporium sp.		

TABLE V (*cont*)

Wheat	Rice	Sorghum
Mucor sp.	*Actinomucor repens*	*Mucor* sp.
Rhizopus oryzae	*Mucor geophilus*	*Rhizopus oryzae*
Aspergillus ochraceus	*Syncephalastrum*	*Mortiella* sp.
A. versicolor	*racemosum*	*Actinomucor* sp.
A. niger	*Asp. awamori*	*Asp. sydowi*
A. sydowi	*A. candidus*	*A. wentii*
A. flavus	*A. flavipes*	*A. tamarii*
A. candidus	*A. niger*	*A. flavus*
A. terreus	*A. sydowi*	*A. ustus*
A. ustus	*A. ustus*	*A. versicolor*
A. oryzae	*A. versicolor*	*A. niger*
A. nidulans	*A. ruber*	*A. restrictus*
A. wentii	*A. flavus var*	*A. janus*
A. flavipes	*columnaris*	*A. flavipes*
	A. terreus	*A. ochraceus*
	A. fumigatus	*A. fumigatus*
	A. glaucus group	*A. nidulans*
	A. nidulans	*A. ruber*
	A. tamari	*A. terreus*
		A. fischeri
		A. oryzae
		A. glaucus
		A. ornatus
Penicillium citrinum	*Pen. citrinum*	*Pen. corylophilum*
P. corylophilum	*P. corylophilum*	*P. tardum*
P. islandicum	*P. roseopurpurcum*	*P. islandicum*
	P. decumbens	*P. waksmanii*
	P. islandicum	
Fusarium sp.	*Fusarium* sp.	*Fusarium* sp.
Alternaria sp.		*Alternaria* sp.
Botrytis sp.	*Botrytis* sp.	*Curvularia* sp.
Amblyosporium sp.	*Trichothecium*	*Helminthosporium* sp.
Chladosporium sp.	*Nigrospora* sp.	*Verticillium* sp.
Scopulariopsis brevicaulis		*Trichothecium roseum*

and geographical factors are imprinted on a particular sample which speak of its origin and reveal them in the mineral associates of the sample. Thus the unscrupulous practice of mineral adulteration of wheat, rice and pulses can be detected. Hence a mineralogical probing might offer insight into the origin and provide possibilities for the implementation of the Prevention of Food Adulteration Act.

TABLE VI
COMPOSITION OF MINERAL AND ROCK FRAGMENTS IN GRAINS
(Venugopal, J. S., Symp. on Grain Sanitation APCS-USAID, Mysore, 1969)

Commodity	Mineral	Chemical composition	Rock type area	Mineral composition of rock
Haryana wheat	Quartz	SiO_2		
	Plagioclase feldspar	$R Si_{3-2}$ $Al_{1-2}O_8$ where $R = Ca, Na$	(Newer granites)	
	Biotite mica	$K_2(OH)_4$ $(Mg,Fe,Al)_6$ $(Si,Al)_8O_{20}$	Bihar	
Rice	Milky and smoky quartz			
	Orthoclase	KSi_3AlO_8		
	Plagioclase			
	Haematite	Fe_2O_3		
Sorghum	Quartz (smoky and milky)		Hornblende gneiss (Peninsular)	Hornblende quartz, plagioclase, biotite
	Magnetite	Fe_3O_4		
	Plagioclase		Weathered granite	Orthoclase,
	Orthoclase	$K_2(Al,Fe,Mg)_4$		quartz, biotite,
	Muscovite	$(OH)_4(Si,Al)_8$ O_{20}		muscovite and tourmaline $XY_3Al_6(OH)_4$
Green gram and Bengal gram	Quartz, Orthoclase Plagioclase, Biotite		Granites Mysore	$(BO_3)_3 Si_6 O_{18}$ where $Y = Mg$, Al, Li, Fe and $X = Na, Ca$

CONTROL MEASURES

Pre-harvest disinfestation

The science of pest control is now at the cross-roads. On the one hand a state of emergency has arisen in the struggle between the population and food supply and on the other hand the most effective tool, the pesticides, are under conservative surveillance. The conventional organic pesticides have played a very significant role in increasing the agricultural output, combating communicable diseases and increasing the comfort of man by protecting his property from the ravages of termites, weeds, birds and silver fish, reducing personal annoyance from fruit flies, ticks, mites, bed bugs, cockroaches and others, and by controlling the diseases of his animals, poultry birds, field and garden crops and protecting his timber in the forest. The subject is being reviewed with respect to their uses as our concept of ecology and environmental concern has become more quality exacting. Despite the pesticides having bestowed unparalleled wellbeing on human civilisation the chlorinated hydrocarbon pesticides are being banned in many countries due to the possibility of their being

TABLE VII

CONTROL MEASURES WHICH HAVE GIVEN BEST RESULTS
UNDER TROPICAL CONDITIONS

Pre-harvest prophylaxis to control field infestation by storage fungi	Malathion, Captan, Tricalcium phosphate
Rodent control	Burrow fumigation (with 60:40 ethylene dibromide: methyl bromide). Baiting
Sanitation of threshing yard to prevent cross-infestation with resident insect population	Ecological or habitat control
Drying to safe moisture content for inhibiting mould growth	Sun drying and mechanical drying. Fungicidal organic acid. Gaseous sterilisation
Storage in bins or rural structures	*Bacillus thuringiensis* and malathion; minifume treatment for fumigation of small bulk with ovicidal effect
Storage in bags in large quantities	Durofume process (using M B + E D B mixture and preventative insecticidal and rodent repellent spray on outer aspect of stack). Poison bait in container treated with quinine hydrochloride
Milled product	Mill disinfestation. Spot fumigation of milling machinery Entolation. Tricalcium phosphate + vitamin formulation incorporation
Processed products: pasta goods, macaroni noodles, etc.	Infra-red heat disinfestation. Serial fumigation process for in-package disinfestation

mutagenic, teratogenic and carcinogenic and in some cases they and their mimics are under restricted application. The ecological group is advocating a thorough change in the approach of pest control and protection. Instead of eradication of pests the concept of population management is gaining strong support.

In the developed countries the pest control problems are comparatively small due to long winters and short seasons for the growth of pests and disease organisms. In the developing countries situated in the tropical and subtropical belts there is less possibility for a short-cut to pest control as the life history of pests and disease organisms could occur throughout the year. Factors like diapause and hybernation do not play a positive role and therefore in the tropical and subtropical regions pest control efforts are becoming the continuous endeavour of man. The actual needs are the wide spectrum long acting selective pesticides, selective from the point of view of beneficial and harmful species. The educational and technological background of the farmers does not permit prescription of a highly sophisticated decision making process with regard to the threshold limits of population and application of the optimum methodology. Thus pest control in the field and post-harvest period should be developed according to the geographical regions and the level of understanding of the farmers with respect to the properties of the chemicals. There is a lack of appreciation of the chronic and acute toxicities, and the effect on the environment, therefore selection or choice of pesticides must be made with due consideration of these long range effects. Since the food output totally depends on the integrated approach towards pest control and conservation from the field to ultimate consumption at the various stages of agronomic practice—interculture, harvesting, crop husbandry, threshing, drying, winnowing, storage in rural structures, transportation, milling and processing, transportation of processed grains and milled materials, retail store, distribution and household store—the control measures will have to take account of every phase from production to consumption. Some of the measures which are applicable under the existing conditions in the tropical and subtropical countries are mentioned above (Table VII).

Pre-harvest prophylaxis

The field infestations of some of the stored-grain pests are quite common, particularly *Angoumois* on wheat, *Sitophilus* on sorghum and maize, *Callosobruchus* on pulses and *Sitotroga* on paddy. These pests appear in the harvested grains even before they are placed for storage. A pre-harvest prophylaxis on an extensive area will be able to disinfest the grain in the panicle or inflorescence and exert prophylactic or protective action during subsequent drying, harvesting and threshing (Majumder et al., 1961). The benefits derived out of this pre-harvest treatment are in the form of sound grains and absence of internal infestation at the time of storage. Captan, malathion, bacterial insecticide and tricalcium phosphate offer a pollution free prophylactic spray composition.

Insect-proofing

Since the grain is already free from initial infestation no fumigation process will be necessary. The farmers could adopt improved storage structures developed by research institutions in various centres of the world (Majumder, 1970; Majumder and Natarajan, 1963). The producer's stock could be protected from insect infestation by the two-pronged attack on the pre-harvest field infestation and subsequent insect-proofed containers and packages (Heiss, 1970). In grains where pre-harvest prophylaxis and introduction of insect-proofing of the rural structures and the containers, and bags, are not possible, spot fumigation can be done with fumigants like EDB, chloropicrin and ethyl formate (Pillai et al., 1970). Fumigant formulations in solid carriers or tablet form have been developed for regulated release of gaseous chemicals and safe use of these substances in rural and household conditions of pest control in stored commodities (Majumder, 1973).

Non-toxic grain protectants

Although fumigation science and technology are widely applicable even in the developing countries, the need for trained personnel, equipment for application, detectors and protective gas masks and canisters limits the practice of the technique in rural areas where 70% of the produce is stored. Therefore, attempts have been made to develop protectants which are innocuous from the human toxicity point of view.

Protection of seed or raw unprocessed grain

Activated earth, particularly kaolin, has been found to be highly insecticidal (Majumder et al., 1959). A hydrothermal acid activation process has been developed for the production of the active ingredient meta-hydrogen halloysite in the insecticidal clay. Electron microscopy, differential thermal analysis, X-ray diffraction, gas absorption, oil bleaching property, bulk density and lipophilic activity have been used for quality control in the production of this activated earth (Venugopal and Majumder, 1964). Feeding trials on rats with grains treated with activated earths have had beneficial effects on the growth of rats (Krishnamurthy et al., 1965). No acute or chronic toxicity could be observed. These insecticidal clays can be mixed with raw grains or seeds. It has been observed that in seeds it not only prevents insect attacks but also prevents the growth of saprophytic organisms, as these insecticidal clays act as dehydrating agents. The conventional pesticides of low mammalian toxicity could also be employed as protectants. Out of the pesticides, only malathion and *Bacillus thuringiensis* preparations are effective against both coleopterous and lepidopterous pests of stored grains within their tolerance limits (Godavaribai *et al.*, 1962).

Milled or processed products
Another new product which is also innocuous from the human and animal point of view but highly selectively toxic to insects is based on tricalcium phosphate. This substance affects the growth of insects by acting as a metabolic poison (Majumder and Bano, 1964, 1966; Bano and Majumder, 1965). Calcium phosphate is not required in high quantities for insect growth and metamorphosis. Histopathological studies have indicated that fat, glycogen and tissue reserves are utilised at a very fast rate when calcium phosphate is in the diet of insects. The exoskeleton of the insect becomes very hard, friable, discoloured and sometimes with nodular growth exhibiting pathological symptoms. Autolysis of tissues, supernumerary moulting and loss of weight are conspicuous symptoms of the toxicity of tricalcium phosphate to insects. With a trace of glucose and vitamins, particularly of the B-group, toxicity of tricalcium phosphate is exhibited. A dosage of 0.2% on grains and their products has been found to be sufficient to protect them from insect attack. Since the diets in many developing countries are deficient in calcium, enrichment of the human diet with this selective protectant formulation, based on calcium phosphate, glucose and vitamin, offers great promise for application during milling of wheat and other food-grains. Field trials on such metabolic inhibitors are in progress.

Yet another insecticidal product with selective effect on insects and harmless to higher animals is the bacterial insecticide from *B. thuringiensis* (Steinhaus, 1956). A submerged culture method for sporulation and production of endotoxin has been developed using d-xylose as a sporogenic sugar (Majumder and Padma, 1957). In addition, a tray culture process has been standardised for mass production of highly potent and viable spores of the organisms (Nagamma, Ragunathan and Majumder, 1972). Field trials have shown highly promising results for use on vegetable crops, oilseeds, pulses and even cereals. For controlling lepidopterous insects on wheat, paddy and other grains and their products, the spore powder even at 1–10 ppm concentrations has been found to be effective. The recent report of Smirnoff (1974) indicates that even the resistant species of insects could be rendered susceptible by formulating *B. thuringiensis* spores with the enzyme, chitinase. Our investigations point to the increase of susceptibility to *B. thuringiensis* preparation with tricalcium phosphate incorporation (Majumder, 1970). Thus, there appears to be a bright future for controlling coleopterous and lepidopterous pests of stored grains with integrated control measures.

While research on population control should be continued for achieving ecological methods of controlling insects, moulds, mites and rodents, without inflicting injury to the environment, it is not necessary to continue the approach of using pest control at various phases of production in the field and post-harvest period in isolation.

It must be appreciated that the infestation and biodeterioration are continuous processes initiated from the field and which continue until consumption. Therefore, the integrated pest control measures should be treated *as a system* and as a cycle from the seed sowing to the seed and grain utilisation. Therefore, pest control should become a part and parcel of the national approach and not just a few individuals controlling infestations when they become obvious. Attention is being paid to pest and disease control in the field during the pre-harvest period. But it is not comprehended that post-harvest protection should receive more serious attention as the harvested grain is the concentrate derived from all the hard earned inputs of seed, tillage, irrigation, interculture, fertilisers, pesticides, labour, attention, harvesting and other agronomic operations. The vast space and biomass of agriculture ultimately is represented by a small volume and mass which occupies a fraction of storage room. Any attack or depredation has larger and magnified implications on losses than in the expanse of the field.

Rural storage in the developing part of the world constitutes 60–70% of grain production. This is mostly ill-equipped and lacks technical attention. Design and development of rural receptacles, prophylactic measures, non-toxic and selective protectants, unit packaging, improved protected transportation, mill sanitation, inert atmosphere and hermetic storage and integrated pest control measures using attractant, repellent, chemosterilents, hormones, parasites, etc., are the prescriptions for abatement of loss without the problem of pollution and health hazards.

ACKNOWLEDGEMENT

The author is indebted to Dr B. L. Amla, Director of this Institute for his keen interest and valuable support in the work reviewed in this paper.

REFERENCES

Bano, A. and Majumder, S. K. (1965). 'Pathological changes induced by tricalcium phosphate in insects', *J. Invert. Pathology*, **7** (3), 384.

Cotton, R. T. (1963). 'Pest of stored grain and their products', *Burgess.*, **3**, 26, 78.

FAO, Rome (1967). *Symposium on Crop Losses*, 1–330.

Godavaribai, S., Krishnamurthy, K. and Majumder, S. K. (1962). 'Bacterial spores with malathion for controlling *Ephestia cautella*', *Pest Technology (London)*, **4** (6), 155–158.

Hall, D. W. (1969). 'Food storage in the developing countries', *J. Roy. Soc. Arts*, 'Woodstock' lecture, 562–577.

Heiss, R. (1970). *Principles of Food Packaging*, FAO, P. Keppler Verlag, VI, 255–269.

Krishnamurthy, K., Subramanyaraj Urs, T. S. and Majumder, S. K. (1965). 'Effect of insecticidal clay in the diet of albino rat on the growth and digestibility of food constituents', *Ind. J. Exptl Biology*, 3 (3), 171–173.

Majumder, S. K. (1970). 'Protecting food from deterioration during storage, handling and distribution in technologically less developed countries', *Proc. 3rd International Congress of Food Sci. and Tech.*, Washington, DC, 518–530.

Majumder, S. K. (1973). 'Some biophysical aspects of gaseous sterilisation', in *Fumigation and Gaseous Pasteurization*, APCS, 45–119.

Majumder, S. K. and Bano, A. (1964). 'Toxicity of calcium phosphate to some pests of stored grain', *Nature, Lond.*, **202**, 1359–1360.

Majumder, S. K. and Bano, A. (1966). 'Reversion of the toxicity of tricalcium phosphate to insects by trehalose', *Nature, Lond.*, **210**, 1052.

Majumder, S. K., Godavaribai, S. and Krishnamurthy, K. (1961). 'Pre-harvest prophylaxis for infestation control in stored food grains', *Nature, Lond.*, **192** (4800), 373–376.

Majumder, S. K., Narasimhan, K. S. and Parpia, H. A. B. (1965). 'Micro-ecological factors of microbial spoilage and occurrence of mycotoxins on stored grains', *Mycotoxins in Foodstuffs* (Ed. G. N. Wagan), MIT Press, Cambridge, Mass., 27–47.

Majumder, S. K., Narasimhan, K. S. and Subrahmanyan, V. (1959). 'Insecticidal effects of activated charcoal and clays', *Nature, Lond.*, **184**, 1165–1166.

Majumder, S. K. and Natarajan, C. P. (1963). 'Some aspects of the problem of bulk storage of foodgrains in India', *World Rev. Pest Control* (London), 2 (2), 25–35.

Majumder, S. K. and Padma, M. C. (1957). 'Screening of carbohydrates for sporulation of bacilli in fluid medium', *Canad. J. Microbiol.*, 3 (4), 639–642.

Majumder, S. K. and Parpia, H. A. B. (1967). 'Prevention of food losses and food potential', Proceedings—Symposium on Science and India's food problem, Indian Council of Agricultural and Research and Indian National Science Academy 1971, 388–398.

Nagamma, M. V., Ragunathan, A. N. and Majumder, S. K. (1972). 'A medium for *Bacillus thuringiensis* Berliner', *J. Appl. Bact.*, **35**, 367–370.

Ordish, G. (1952). *Untaken Harvest*, Constable, London.

Parvathappa, H. C., Ragunathan, A. N. and Majumder, S. K. (1970). 'Physical and biochemical changes in sorghum (*Sorghum vulgare*)', *Biodetn. Bull.*, 6 (3), 95–99.

Pillai, S. P., Muthu, M., Majumder, S. K., Sharangapani, M. V. and Amla, B. L. (1970). *Int. Pest Control*, 12 (1), 23–27.

Schimitt, W. R. (1965). 'Planetary food potential', *Ann. N.Y. Acad. Sci.*, **118** (17), 645–718.

Scrimshaw, N. in UN (1968). 'International action to avert the impending protein crisis', E4343/Rev. 1, New York.

Smirnoff, W. A. (1974). 'The forest must remain green', *Milieu*, 1–47.

Steinhaus, E. A. (1956). 'Microbial control—the emergence of an idea', *Hilgardia*, **26**, 107–159.

Venkatarao, S. (1960). 'Effect of insect infestation on the chemical composition and nutritive value of food grains', *Ph.D. Thesis*, Madras University.

Venugopal, J. S. and Majumder, S. K. (1964). 'Active mineral in insecticidal clays', *Proc. Symposium on Pesticides* (Ed. S. K. Majumder), 200–209.

DISCUSSION

Chairman: Thank you very much, Mr Majumder: that was a most interesting review of the problems you have to face in storage, and the very ingenious methods you have developed to overcome them. I am sure there will be a very lively discussion on the subject and the many problems involved—biological as well as technological.

I remember very well my visit to the Mysore Institute about ten years ago and how it struck me then as being full of people with very ingenious ideas. The spirit of the place seems to have remained unchanged.

This paper is now open for discussion.

H. C. Pereira (Ministry of Agriculture, Fisheries and Food, London): The large plastic sack that you showed us seems to be one of the most practical and immediately applicable methods. Do rodents chew through these, or is it possible to make them rodent-proof?

S. K. Majumder: The sacks are attacked by rodents, but we have found a repellent for rats. The problem was: how to stabilise it on the bag surface because in a few minutes it will just dissipate into the atmosphere. So we studied the best material in which it could be occluded and be slowly released; a combination of high viscosity oil, wax, with activated charcoal suspended in it has been used to trap the rat repellent. But we have only been able to do it for 120–130 days, whereas the sack will have to last for almost three years, so a single treatment is not enough for the life of the bag. But for the storage period, the peripheral aspect of the stacks of sacks could be treated every 120 days. In the slide I showed of fumigation in the warehouse; immediately the gas proof sheet is removed, the stack is treated with rat repellent and an insecticidal preparation. We use a high viscosity because the sack is woven and a low viscosity droplet could get in and contaminate the material. In order to avoid contamination we use high viscosity oil which due to larger droplets and low capillary action is not transferred from the exterior to the interior of the bag.

T. Jakubczyk (Warsaw University): Did you investigate the combination of partial dehydration and the application of organic acids like propionic or acetic acid?

S. K. Majumder: We carried out quite extended experiments on the control of microflora and the report is being printed. We screened all the organic acids and their salts, and the salts appear to be better than the organic acids themselves. The limiting moisture level of the activity of the organic acids is 16% and in the case of sodium salts we found that even beyond 15% they are not able to protect the material from attack. If the moisture content is below 15%, organic acids are quite effective; but a lower concentration of say sodium propionate is better than propionic acid. A combination of acetic acid with propionic acid, and acetic acid and sorbic acid, are what we have used. But the cost is prohibitive.

Chairman: Could I ask from where you get the spores of B. Thuringiensis and the toxin? Do you make it yourself?

S. K. Majumder: We produce them in our laboratory. both in surface culture and the submerged culture. The main problem was that the viable spores may be associated with endotoxin crystals and we were not able to produce spores in submerged culture until we found that d-xylose in the fermentation medium has a sporogenic effect. d-Xylose at 0·02% in the fermentation medium is quite effective causing considerable sporogenesis so that we could harvest a lot of spore material. But if you add arabinose or ribose instead of d-xylose, you get first balloon cells which burst and you do not get the sporogenic situation. But d-xylose is somehow able to give, not only the longest logarithmic growth phase but also maximum concentration of spores. So the hypothesis that sporogenesis is a starvation phenomenon, or the cells sporulate only in unfavourable circumstances is a little doubtful on the basis of these findings. I have a personal feeling that sporulation is only part of the life cycle in the cells, and you can commit the cells to sporulation at the maximum growth phase.

Chairman: Thank you very much, Mr Majumder.

Crop Nutrition and Soil Fertility: Some Effects on Yield and Quality of English Wheat

G. W. COOKE

Rothamsted Experimental Station, Harpenden; Herts, UK

CROP NUTRITION

Wheat, like other crops, takes from the soil six 'major' nutrients (N, P, K, Ca, Mg, S) and at least six 'micro' nutrients (B, Cu, Fe, Mn, Mo, Zn). The first group are needed on the kg/ha scale, the micronutrients in g/ha. The effects of fertilisers, and the need to use them, depend on the size of reserves of nutrients in soils and on the ability of crops to exploit these. As winter wheat is deep rooting and has a long growing season, it makes better use of nutrients in soil than many other annual crops.

In north-western Europe wheat is mostly grown on soils long used for intensive agriculture; these soils have adequate supplies of calcium, magnesium, sulphur and micronutrients and their phosphorus reserves have been built up by many years of fertilising. English wheat yields are not increased to a large extent in practice by fertilisers supplying P, Ca or Mg. Nitrogen is the nutrient most likely to be deficient in Britain where, with an annual excess of rainfall over evaporation, reserves of nitrogen in inorganic forms cannot accumulate in soil. Wheat gets enough nitrogen only from soils which have large reserves of organic nitrogen which can be mineralised, for example in land recently ploughed from pasture. On most land in continued arable cultivation nitrogen fertilisers are essential for maximum yields. After nitrogen, the nutrient most likely to be deficient for British wheat is potassium. A modern crop yielding 6–7 t/ha of grain has taken up about 120 kg/ha of K by flowering and where soil cannot supply this amount, yield will be lost. Potassium deficiency is uncommon where wheat follows heavily fertilised crops such as potatoes, but it is not uncommon where wheat follows other crops which are removed from the field and which receive little K fertiliser.

SOIL FERTILITY

Fertility can only be assessed by the yield produced since this integrates the chemical, physical and biological factors that determine whether or

201

not a soil is a good habitat for the crop. Supply of nutrients from the soil is only one aspect of fertility, physical conditions in soil that enable it to hold much water and permit good root growth are important too, as is the absence in soil of pests and disease organisms which may damage roots. The biological aspects of soil fertility often depend on previous cropping, and soils that are very similar in chemical and physical properties may produce different wheat yields if previous cropping has induced differences in the incidence of soil-borne pests and diseases.

An example where two soil fertility factors (water and nitrate), and weather, all affected the yield and protein content of wheat in the semi-arid central Great Plains of the USA was reported by Smika and Greb (1973). Their work was done because the protein contents of hard red winter wheat grown in this region sometimes decreased to less than the 11·5% minimum acceptable for breadmaking. Protein contents were negatively correlated with rain > 1·25 cm in the period from 40 to 55 days before maturity and with soil moisture reserves in the top 1·8 m; they were positively correlated with total soil nitrate to depths up to 1·8 m, and were also related to maximum air temperature for the 5 days from 15 to 20 days before maturity. When all these four factors were combined almost all of the variance in protein content was accounted for. To get maximum yield the soil had to contain 28 cm of water at seeding; at least 106 kg/ha of nitrate-N had to be available in the soil at seeding to get grain with 12% protein. Smika and Greb concluded that if N fertiliser is used to increase protein level, it must be balanced with the amount of soil water available. There was 'no apparent reason why yields even higher than found in this study (4 t/ha) cannot be obtained with protein levels > 13% when both soil water and soil nitrate can be manipulated'.

SOME RECENT RESULTS FROM ROTHAMSTED

Potassium for wheat

Evidence of the importance of potassium supply in securing large yields from British wheat was provided by Widdowson et al. (1963). They found that 200 kg/ha of K as fertiliser was needed to maintain yields of wheat grown after ryegrass which received 200 kg N/ha; the cut grass removed this quantity of K which had to be replaced. Potassium is involved in many enzyme processes in plants and also has a role in the transport of photosynthate to storage organs; perhaps this is why such large amounts are essential to good wheat yields. Although yields are often increased by K fertilisers, particularly after growing crops which exhaust soil K reserves, I am not aware of any work which shows that potassium supply affects the *quality* of wheat grain grown in normal farming.

Nitrogen, site and variety
The amounts of nitrogen which British soils supply depend on soil type, previous cropping and rainfall in the previous winter (which alters leaching of nitrate). We can increase nitrogen supply by using N-fertilisers but we cannot alter the weather. Effects of soil water reserves at seeding, so important in Smika and Greb's work, are unimportant here where unpredictable weather during spring and summer alters the effect of N on yield. Uncertain weather, and lack of information on the effect of soil type and previous cropping on *quality* make it difficult for us to produce wheat to a standard. I am therefore indebted to B. A. Stewart (British Flour Milling and Baking Research Association) and G. V. Dyke (Rothamsted) for results from a joint investigation on samples from Rothamsted and Woburn experiments. (Their figures refer to grain with 15% moisture and flour containing 14% moisture.)

The sites used at Rothamsted were (1) after beans, (2) after other wheat or barley. At Woburn the wheat followed beans. Averaging the results with four varieties, Rothamsted wheat yielded 1 t/ha more grain when grown after beans than after another cereal, and 0·8 t/ha more than wheat after beans at Woburn. Rothamsted wheat grain also gave a larger percentage of flour and the flour was of better colour, but the Woburn crops contained 11·0% protein in the flour against 10·2% at Rothamsted after beans and 10·0% after a cereal.*

The *variety* grown had large effects on yield and quality. After averaging the sites and the different rates of N tested, Maris Widgeon was outstanding in giving better percentage of flour, colour of flour, and, particularly, in percentage of protein in flour (10·9% against 9·8% protein in flour from Cappelle-Desprez). The yield of Maris Widgeon was a trifle less than the yields of Cappelle and Joss Cambier, and 0·7 t/ha less than that of Champlein.

Nitrogen fertiliser was tested at three rates (63, 126, 188 kg N/ha) all applied in spring; there was also a fourth test of the largest rate split, two-thirds of the N being given in spring and the remainder as a top dressing at flowering time. Applying 126 kg N/ha in spring gave best yields of grain and best percentage of flour; the split dressing gave slightly more grain and slightly less percentage flour; the colour of the flour became darker with increasing nitrogen, and particularly with the late dressing. Percentage protein in flour increased with increasing N fertiliser; the largest N dressing gave flour with 10·2% protein, splitting this dressing gave a further increase in protein of 0·4%. Applying 63 kg N/ha at flowering to crops which had already received 126 kg N/ha in spring, gave flour with 1% more protein, but had virtually no effect on yield of grain.

As *Maris Widgeon* was so outstanding in quality aspects, it is worth

---

* 'Protein' was calculated as %N (kjeldahl method) × 5·7.

commenting on its performance with the rates and times of N tested: yield of grain (5·5 t/ha), or percentage flour in grain (about 75% of grain yield) was little affected by the summer dressing given to the crop which had received 126 kg N/ha in spring, but protein in flour was increased from 10·7 to 11·8% while the flour was darkened from grade 2·4 to 2·9. (Elton and Greer (1971) said that for breadmaking colour grades of 2·0–3·0, and 10·5–12·5% of protein in flour, are acceptable.)

OTHER ROTHAMSTED EXPERIMENTS

I am indebted to Blanche Benzian for results with Cappelle-Desprez, summarised below, which are from the survey she is making of the effects of nitrogen on yield and %N in grain. In interpreting these data it is useful to remember Elton and Greer's (1971) statement that if all wheat in our bread is to be British grown, it must have 12% protein (or by the above convention 2·1% N); 11% protein (needed for 50% usage of home-grown

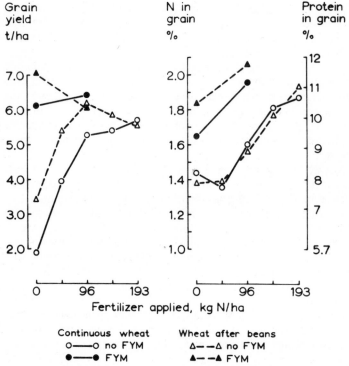

FIG. 1. Broadbalk wheat, 1969–72. Yields and N in grain at 15% moisture.

wheat in bread flour) implies 1·93% N in grain. In this section yields and %N are both for grain with 15% moisture.

Broadbalk field at Rothamsted has grown wheat continuously since 1843 (Bawden, 1969), Cappelle-Desprez has been grown only since 1968. Part of the field now has a rotation of wheat, potatoes and beans, part is still in continuous wheat. Four years' recent results are given in Fig. 1. Wheat after beans gave about 1 t/ha more than continuous wheat and needed only half as much N for the largest yield. Continuous wheat receiving 35 t/ha of farmyard manure (FYM) annually yielded better than fertiliser-grown wheat, and a little better still with FYM plus 96 kg N/ha as fertiliser. Best yield, nearly 1 t/ha more than from any fertiliser-treated wheat, came from the crop receiving FYM and grown after beans; fertiliser-N depressed the yield of this crop. 1·8% N in grain was achieved by continuous or rotation wheat receiving 143 kg N/ha, this figure was exceeded by wheat receiving FYM and grown after beans, or continuously and given extra N. Even the largest rates of N tested did not produce grain with 2·0% N. (The average used on wheat in England and Wales in 1973 was 95 kg N/ha (Church, 1974).)

Nitrogen which increases yield and %protein can come from: organic N in soil, organic manures, crop residues rich in N, or fertilisers. Figure 1 showed that bean residues which check root disease of wheat and provide extra N to increase yield had little effect on %N in grain. The crops with largest %N in grain were on the FYM plots where the available nitrogen is derived partly from mineralisation of some of the N in freshly applied manure, but also by the annual mineralisation of a small part of the extra N in the soil on this plot (there is 0·251% N in soil of the FYM plot against only 0·115% in soil of N-fertilised plots).

The intensive cereals experiment at Woburn grows wheat on a loamy sand containing very little organic matter. Figure 2 shows yields were largest in a rotation where wheat followed a ley and potatoes; they were smaller in continuous wheat and in a second wheat crop. For a maximum yield of wheat grown as the first or second crop after potatoes only 126 kg N/ha was needed, continuous wheat needed 188 kg N/ha. In spite of the large differences which rotation had on wheat yield there was little effect of previous cropping on %N in grain; grain from the continuous wheat plots had slightly larger %N at each rate of fertiliser N. Both on Broadbalk and at Woburn, crops which leave nitrogenous residues and lessen the need for fertiliser N had no effect on %N in grain. Yields at Woburn fluctuated greatly from year to year (from 3 to 5 t/ha), nitrogen content fluctuated much less; in general, %N in grain receiving 126 kg N/ha did not fall below 1·6% on average of the cropping sequences in any year from 1969 to 1973; grain grown with 188 kg/ha of N as fertiliser (or more) never contained less than 1·8% N in the 7 harvest years 1967–73. Light land such as that at Woburn has a poor reputation for growing wheat; yields in this experiment were variable and in some years were poor, but the results suggest that we should not ignore these soils if high protein in wheat is more important than yield.

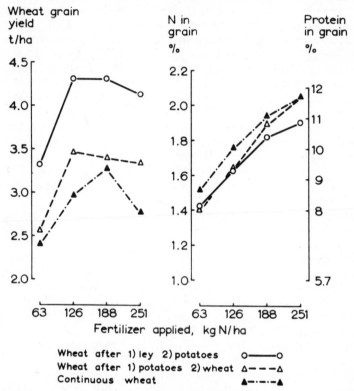

FIG. 2. Intensive cereals experiment, Woburn 1969–73. Yields and N in grain at 15% moisture.

Potatoes are regarded as a good preparation for wheat as they check cereal root diseases and leave residues from the large nitrogen dressings usually applied. The residual effects of fertilisers given to potatoes have been tested on yields of following wheat at Rothamsted (Fig. 3). When a large dressing of N (208 kg/ha) was given to 1967 potatoes, maximum yield of the 1968 wheat was achieved with only 41 kg/ha of fresh N; where potatoes received much less N (41 kg/ha) the following wheat needed 83 kg N/ha for maximum yield. Per cent N in grain was affected both by N given to the previous potatoes, and by the fresh dressings applied to wheat. After potatoes given much N the grain had 1·8% N when the wheat crop received 41 kg N/ha (the amount needed for maximum yield). With smaller dressings of N to potatoes, to achieve 1·8% N in grain needed a fresh dressing of 126 kg N/ha (considerably more than was needed for maximum yield).

Leguminous leys, and grazed grass swards leave residues of N in the soil that benefit following arable crops. The Rothamsted Ley Arable Experiments showed that less N fertiliser is needed for maximum yield of wheat grown after 3 years of lucerne than is needed for wheat grown after 3 years of arable crops. Duplicate experiments were done on two

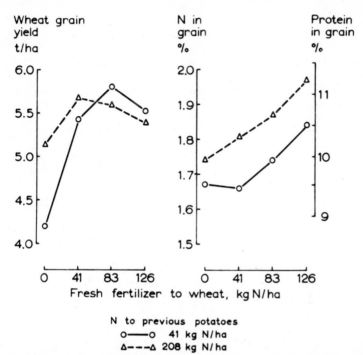

FIG. 3. Effect of nitrogen fertiliser given to previous potatoes on yield and protein content of wheat, Rothamsted 1968. Yields and N in grain at 15% moisture.

Rothamsted fields and these are average results for 3 years on the two fields. The grain from wheat grown without nitrogen fertiliser contained 1·67% N (9·5% protein) where it followed lucerne, but only 1·56% N (8·9% protein) after arable crops. Wheat which received 130 kg N/ha as fertiliser had 1·95% N (11·1% protein) in grain produced after lucerne, and only 1·78% N (10·1% protein) in grain following arable crops. The organic residues left in the soil by lucerne released nitrogen in ways that favoured its accumulation in grain. Fertiliser-nitrogen gave yields of both grain and straw in the arable rotation as large as were obtained after lucerne, but the wheat after arable crops accumulated less N. These effects of previous crops are not related to total organic matter in the soils, or to changes in gross organic matter caused by the treatments. They are related to the extra nitrogen released when lucerne leys are ploughed in. Where grass leys instead of lucerne preceded the wheat, their residues have often interfered with uptake of fertiliser-nitrogen and lessened its efficiency. Both the size and nature of these effects of crops that precede wheat vary from season to season for unknown reasons.

REFERENCES

Bawden, F. C. *et al.* (1969). 'The Broadbalk Wheat Experiment', *Rep. Rothamsted exp. Stn for 1968*, Pt 2, 7–208.

Church, B. M. (1974). 'Use of fertilisers in England and Wales, 1973', Mimeographed Report, Ministry of Agriculture, Fisheries and Food, No. SS/SAF/9 (and earlier reports).

Elton, G. A. H. and Greer, E. N. (1971). 'The use of home-grown wheat for flour milling', *ADAS Quart. Rev.*, No. 2, 85–94.

Smika, D. E. and Greb, B. W. (1973). 'Protein content of winter wheat grain as related to soil and climatic factors in the semi-arid Central Great Plains', *Agron. J.*, **65**, 433–436.

Widdowson, F. V., Penny, A. and Williams, R. J. B. (1963). 'Experiments comparing yield and residual effects on winter wheat, of 1-year clover, rye-grass and clover-rye-grass leys', *J. agric. Sci., Camb.*, **61**, 397–408.

Plant Diseases and Nutritive Value

D. A. DOLING

Crop Science Department,
The Lord Rank Research Centre,
High Wycombe, Bucks, U K

The effects of diseases on cereal yields have been studied extensively, but their effect on the nutritive value of the grain has received scant attention. The few reports available are mostly concerned with protein content: very little is known about any other constituent. Some 30 contributions on the subject appear in the world literature, coming from 9 countries and commenting on 12 diseases: these including foliar, root and ear diseases.

A severe attack of most diseases usually leads to yield decrease by reducing the accumulation of starch in the endosperm, thereby producing shrivelled grain. As most values for various components are given in percentage terms it is not surprising to find frequent references to higher percentage protein content in grain from diseased plants (e.g. Manners and Hartill, 1962; Harper, 1889; Cunningham *et al.*, 1968; Finney and Sill, 1963). This higher protein value accounted for other derived changes such as higher water absorption and loaf volume and longer mixing and sedimentation times. But there are also several unexpected results. The flour extraction was not reduced when plants were attacked by take-all disease (Cunningham *et al.*, 1968) and lower percentage protein values were recorded when plants were attacked by brown rust (Caldwell *et al.*, 1934; Keed and White, 1972) or by black rust (Headden, 1915).

The foregoing remarks demonstrate clearly that there is a very large gap in our knowledge, and the little information available is conflicting in some instances (*see also* Table I).

The few studies which give data or comment on other constituents are worthy of note here.

In a study on the effect of take-all (*Ophiobolus graminis*) on quality Cunningham *et al.* (1968) report similar flour yields, but higher protein and α-amylase content, and better quality gluten, in samples from the infected crop.

The effects of three virus diseases have received attention: barley yellow dwarf virus by Fitzgerald and Stoner (1967) and soil-borne mosaic virus and streak mosaic virus by Finney and Sill (1963). In each case the flour extraction was lower, and the ash content and protein higher in the samples from diseased plants. Higher water absorption and loaf volume could be attributed to higher protein content and not to any protein quality changes. Mixing and other physical properties of the dough were similar in samples from diseased or healthy plants.

Caldwell *et al.* (1934) studied the effects of leaf rust (*Puccinia recondita*) and unlike a number of other investigators studying other rusts, found a decrease in the protein content of grain from severely rusted plants.

TABLE I

MAIN EFFECTS OF DISEASE ON NUTRITIVE VALUE SO FAR REPORTED — SEPTEMBER 1974

Disease/causal organism	% Protein	Other comments
Yellow rust. *Puccinia striiformis*	Up	—
Black rust. *Puccinia graminis*	Up	—
	No change	Glutenin down, basic amino acids up
	Down	—
Leaf rust. *Puccinia recondita*	Down	No change of phosphorus or total ash, lower sucrose content
Glume blotch. *Septoria nodorum*	No change	—
Leaf spot. *Septoria tritici*	No change	—
Barley Yellow dwarf virus ⎫ Streak mosaic virus ⎬ Wheat mosaic virus ⎭	Down	Ash content up. Water absorption up. Mixing and physical dough properties up or no change
Take-all. *Ophiobolus graminis*	Up	Flour colour and α-amylase up
Eyespot. *Cercosporella herpotrichoides*	No change	—
Black point. *Helminthosporium sativum*	No change	—
Ergot. *Claviceps purpurea*	No change	RNA, DNA and malate down. Amino acid balance changed

They also reported slightly higher starch content and lower sucrose content, but no differences in phosphorus or total ash content. A study of the methods used by the different experimenters does not demonstrate the reasons for differences in relative protein content, but certain details referred to by some, suggest ways in which such differences could arise. In some instances the work has been done by plant pathologists, in others by food chemists. It is possible that the development of the disease epidemics differed in the various experiments, with consequent different results. Details of what happened during the collection and preparation of the grain samples for analysis are not given. It is likely that a biologist retained all the seed, shrivelled and normal; whilst it is probable that the milling technologist treated the grain by some screening procedure before he was prepared to undertake any analyses. Any future studies will require the close liaison of biologist and food technologist in order to fully understand the effects of a disease on nutritive value.

The presence of ergots in a grain sample directly affects its suitability for use in human or animal food. But this disease can also have indirect effects. Corbett *et al.* (1974) undertook detailed metabolic studies of both the fungus and the host when ergots developed in rye. They found differences in the metabolites of grains taken from infected ears as compared

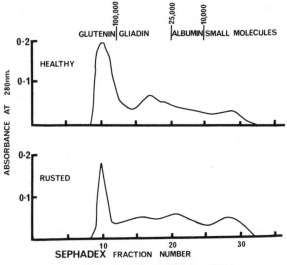

FIG. 1. (From Bushuk and Wrigley, 1971.)

with those from healthy ears. They concluded from their data that the carbohydrate, soluble sugars, and protein concentrations, were similar, but the amino acid compositions showed considerable differences. They believe these to be due to the level of alanine in infected ears being depressed by more than half during the earlier phases of grain development. Lower DNA, RNA and malate also occurred—indicative of low and retarded metabolic activity in the grains of diseased ears.

Bushuk and Wrigley (1971) also made a quantitative study. Wheat grains from plants severely rusted with both black rust (*P. graminis*) and leaf rust (*P. recondita*) in Manitoba, were compared with those from rust free plants grown in Alberta. The cultivar was Marquis. No figures for yield of grain are given but the 1000 grain weights of 8·9 (rusted) and 33·2 (healthy) suggest a very severe rust attack and an inevitable drop in yield. The percentage protein contents of the flour were similar: 12·9 and 12·8, so the inferior breadmaking quality of grain from the rusted plants, as judged by the sedimentation values and the wet gluten content were not minimised by protein differences. The ash content was over three times as much and the fibre content 10% less in the flour from the rusted sample.

The most notable differences were in the gel filtration patterns of proteins from the two samples. Healthy wheat flour contains a low molecular weight glutenin (*c.* 300 000 daltons) that is absent from rusted wheat (*see* Fig. 1). This glutenin component is synthesised during the latter stages of maturation in bread wheats and is absent in durum wheats. Its presence or absence apparently affects the breadmaking quality of the flour. The amino acid compositions of the two flours also differed. The rusted sample had higher amounts of the basic amino acids (lysine, histidine and arginine) and lower amounts of glutamic acid and proline, i.e. more water-soluble and less gluten proteins.

This very brief contribution to this symposium exposes our almost total ignorance of the significance of cereal diseases on the nutritive value of such grains as are produced.

REFERENCES

Bushuk, W. and Wrigley, C. W. (1971). 'Effect of rust infection on marquis wheat grain proteins', *Phytochemistry*, **10**, 2975–2978.

Caldwell, R. M., Kraybill, H. R., Sullivan, J. T. and Compton, L. E. (1934). 'Effect of leaf rust on yield, physical characters and composition of winter wheats', *J. Agric. Res.*, **48**, 1049–1071.

Corbett, K., Dickerson, A. G. and Mantle, P. G. (1974). 'Metabolic studies on *Claviceps purpurea* during parasitic development on rye', *J. Gen. Microbiol.*, in press.

Cunningham, P. C., Spillane, P. A., Foreman, B. T. and Conniffe, D. (1968). 'Effects of infection by *Ophiobolus graminis* on grain yields, baking characteristics of wheat and quality of malting barley', *Irish J. Agric. Res.*, **7**, 183–193.

Finney, K. F. and Sill, Jr. W. H. (1963). 'Effects of two virus diseases on milling and baking properties of wheat grain and flour and on probable nutritive value of forage wheat', *Agron. J.*, **55**, 476–478.

Fitzgerald, P. J. and Stoner, W. N. (1967). 'Barley yellow dwarf studies in wheat. 1. Yield and quality of hard red winter wheat infected with barley yellow dwarf virus', *Crop Sci.*, **7**, 337–341.

Harper, D. N. (1889). 'On the chemistry of wheat', *Minnesota Agricultural Experimental Station Bulletin*, **7**, 65–84.

Headden, W. P. (1915). 'Yellow berry in wheat—its cause and prevention', *Colorado Agricultural Experimental Station Bulletin*, **205**, 1–38.

Keed, B. R. and White, N. H. (1972). 'Quantitative effects of leaf and stem rusts on yield and quality of wheat', *Aust. J. Exptl Agric. Animal Husbandry*, **11**, 550–555.

Manners, J. G. and Hartill, W. F. T. (1962). 'Some effects of infection by yellow rust on date of ripening and on physical and chemical characteristics of the grain', *Proc. Second European Yellow Rust Conference*, Wageningen, 1960, 51–67.

DISCUSSION

V. A. Johnson (University of Nebraska, USA): A comment with regard to Dr Cooke's paper; I was amazed at the basic similarity of results from the fertiliser work you reported from Central United States and some of your own work at Rothamsted. I think while the values are different, maximum yields are certainly obtained at levels of nitrogen fertiliser long before maximum protein is achieved. Protein continues to build up.

In this connection, it seems to me that in the incorporation of genes for higher protein in wheat the real value may lie in achieving extra percentage points on protein at fertiliser levels at which yield is maximised and, therefore, the most profitable levels of fertiliser used. If the data that we have indicates that this expression of genes for higher protein occurs through a range of soil fertility levels, then this could be possible. This is a common experience.

I have a question for Dr Doling. It is not particularly surprising to me that with some diseases—particularly the leaf-infecting diseases—there can be a decrease in protein content. I should think there are two possibilities. One of them is that such diseases, particularly the rust, prematurely remove leaves as functioning organs, and surely the leaves are involved in some important way in the internal nitrogen transport system of the plant? But there is another reason, and this is that with rust, with very massive spoilation (and this spoil is largely comprised of protein) there is a very substantial direct loss of nitrogen associated with the spoilation of such diseases as rust. Does this seem reasonable to you?

D. A. Doling: Yes, I think this is so. I think the problem lies in the fact that proteins are given in terms of percentage, and not on protein per acre. If you have severely diseased crops, the protein per acre has gone down; but if the carbohydrate has gone down more, you get the anomalous situation of the percentage protein reading high. I think that a lot of the work that should be done in the future ought to be quoted in yields of protein/acre rather than percentage terms. It would clear up a lot of the problems which exist here in the literature at the moment. One could have taken a topic like this into an economic field, rather than a technical one, and thought of the whole problem in terms of the nutritive value obtained off a hectare of land. If you take it in those terms, of course, there is far less information available at the moment. But then you are quite right: the disease is reducing the total quantity of carbohydrate and nitrogen, and everything else as well.

F. Lupton (Plant Breeding Institute, Cambridge, UK): I was very interested in Dr Cooke's figure on the increased nitrogen level on grain protein level, especially at flowering time. I wonder if he could tell us whether the increased protein in fact results also in improved bread quality? The result we have obtained at Cambridge rather suggests that, although the protein content of the grain may go up with the application of nitrogen at flowering time, there is no corresponding improvement of loaf volume.

G. W. Cooke: Sorry, but I have forced the results from Mr Stewart and Mr Dart before they were ready to release them, but tests have in fact been made, and it is possible that Prof Greenwood knows whether this extra dressing of nitrogen at flowering time did improve the loaf quality. Certainly, in earlier work, loaf acceptability was increased generally by nitro-fertilisers.

R. Riley (Plant Breeding Institute, Cambridge, UK): I think what is interesting in our discussions here is that we have seen that you can obtain maximum yield in a number of ways: by growing the appropriate variety; by using an appropriate nitrogen fertiliser regime; or by keeping the crop free of disease: but whatever you do you produce a crop of lower percentage protein, and clearly it is a problem which is going to be hard to resolve. In circumstances where protein (as has been implied by Dr Cooke) becomes an important consideration and it is a difficult economic decision—whether we should aim for high protein content or the maximising of yield—I am entirely with Dr Doling in his view that we should look at the total yield of protein rather than look at it in these percentage terms as we have always historically tended to do.

F. Pushman (Plant Breeding Institute, Cambridge, UK): You have quoted figures for flour colour, but no figures for flour extraction. Were there any differences between these, or is it not yet concluded?

G. W. Cooke: Yes, I did have figures for flour extraction, but I did not think it was worth cluttering up the slides—they were around 75%. That was one factor that was not affected by nitrogen fertilisers.

G. N. Irvine (Canadian Grain Commission, Winnipeg, Canada): Dr Cooke, I would like to reassure you in connection with that figure that you put on. We found exactly the same thing from 25 years of data, that peculiar influence of temperature during the last stages of maturation. It does result in the lowering of the protein content as the temperature gets above a certain level.

G. W. Cooke: Thank you for your comments. Clearly there is room for physiology perhaps involving nutrition as well. Presumably it is the effect of temperature on the transport process.

Chairman: That brings this long session to a close, and I should like to express thanks to the speakers for their excellent contributions; and also to those who have participated in the discussion.

I should like to wind up the discussion with a professional comment. From every-thing I heard yesterday and today it seems to me quite obvious that biochemical research in future must be orientated to the intact organisms and away from sub-cellular fractions. I do not believe that we shall make much progress in this field by placing emphasis on the molecular level; and, of course, as far as the nutrition is concerned, it is quite obvious that this area particularly regarding man, has been grossly neglected and that something will have to be done about this in the near future to improve the present situation.

Session IV

EXTRACTION RATES

Extraction Rates—Milling Processing Implications

P. W. RUSSELL EGGITT and A. W. HARTLEY

Spillers Limited, Research and Technology Centre, Cambridge, UK

The shape and structure of the wheat grain are responsible for the complexity of the milling process, which seeks to obtain the maximum yield of saleable white flour with the minimum bran content.

The wheat grain consists of four main parts, as described by Heathcote *et al.* (1952):

(1) The outer coverings or the seed-coat
    (pericarp and testa)   10% approx.
(2) The aleurone layer   6% approx.
(3) The endosperm   81% approx.
(4) The germ (scutellum 1·5) (embryo 1·5)   3% approx.

The large, deep crease prevents the extraction of the theoretical maximum of well over 80% of the grain as a flour consisting solely of endosperm without significant bran or germ contamination. If this crease did not exist it would be feasible to pearl the grain and obtain a white kernel which could be ground to the required particle-size distribution. The roller milling process has been evolved to achieve the best possible separation of endosperm from the branny skins and involves tearing, scraping and grinding actions in many ways similar to those used for centuries with mill stones.

THE MILLING PROCESS

There are four main milling processes—breaking, sieving, purifying and reducing.

The opposed pairs of fluted rolls in the 'break' system run with considerable speed differential ($2\frac{1}{2}$:1) in order to tear open the grain, releasing the endosperm and scraping it off the bran as cleanly as possible. The torn stock from the first break rolls goes to the first break scalper, a nest of sieves (plansifter). The coarsest overtails from this machine pass to the second break roll, which has slightly finer flutes and the stock from this passes to the second break scalper. The coarsest overtails from the latter go to the third break roll with still finer flutes, and so on, up to four or five break passages. The overtails from the final break scalper will be bran largely scraped clean of endosperm and this is the coarse offal of the flour mill.

Simplifying matters, there are three main stocks leaving sieves of different mesh in the first break scalper in addition to the branny overtails passing to the second break rolls. The coarsest is 'semolina' consisting of chunks of clean endosperm, pieces of bran with adhering endosperm and small pieces of bran. Next there is 'middlings' which is similar to semolina in composition but finer, and finally there is some flour, the first break flour, which passes through the finest cover at the bottom of the plansifter. Every roll in a flour mill is followed by a sieve of some sort, and every roll will produce some flour.

A first objective in milling is to obtain clean semolina free from bran which can be reduced subsequently to flour. This cannot be achieved by sieving alone, hence the necessity for the third milling process—purification. A purifier consists of a slightly inclined sieve with meshes becoming coarser down the slope through which air currents are drawn in order to combine sieving with aspiration. This separates dense clean endosperm fragments from lighter particles with adhering bran and from the lightest particles of bran alone, which are lifted by the air stream. The separated stocks leaving the purifier are treated differently in the subsequent flow of the mill.

Clean semolina from the purifier passes to a pair of smooth reduction rolls running at only a small differential speed (5:4), so as to crush and grind rather than tear. The stock from the smooth rolls passes to the usual nest of sieves, yielding some flour and coarser stocks which undergo a number of passages through a cascade of smooth rolls, each followed by its own sifter. The machines at the head of the reduction system yield the most flour. Flours released lower down the system are progressively contaminated with bran powder, smaller in amount and darker in colour. Some bran passes inevitably through the purifier system to the reduction rolls which fortunately flatten the bran fragments so that they can be sieved out. It is often said that the reduction roll is the best purifier in a mill. The overtails of the final reduction sifter consist of fine bran, germ, and poor quality endosperm comprising the principal fine offal of the mill. Figure 1 shows a simplified diagram of the flour milling process after Jones (1958). For convenience machine flours are grouped into three or more streams in the mill.

Table I gives protein, ash, colour grade and fibre of machine flours in each of three mill streams which, combined in the proportions indicated, give a straight-run bread flour typical of those milled in the UK during 1974 for mechanical dough development (Chamberlain et al., 1961).

In considering the milling implications of extraction rates, it is essential

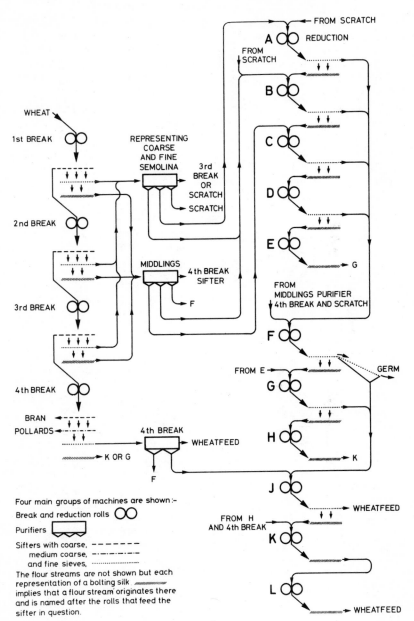

FIG. 1.

TABLE I

COMPOSITION OF MACHINE FLOURS, MILL STREAMS AND STRAIGHT RUN BREAD FLOUR

	Top stream (1st patent)	Bread flour	Middle stream	Bottom stream (low grade)
% Contribution to flour	65.0		28.0	7.0
Moisture %	13.6	13.5	14.2	13.1
Protein % (14% moisture basis)	10.4	11.0	11.5	13.4
Grade colour figure	0.4	2.7	5.0	10.5
Ash %	0.405	0.504	0.58	1.12
Fibre %	0.12	0.15	0.16	0.51

	A	B	B_2	C	D	E	F	X	1st Bk	2nd Bk	3rd Bk	BM	G	H	J	Y	4th Bk
Moisture %	14.0	14.0	13.6	13.4	13.5	12.4	13.1	14.5	14.9	15.0	14.5	14.6	12.2	12.2	11.4	14.2	13.9
Protein % (14% moisture basis)	10.25	10.85	10.2	10.9	11.0	12.0	11.1	10.9	11.5	12.65	14.2	12.25	11.9	10.75	12.2	10.35	14.45
GCF	−0.3	−0.4	0.8	0.7	1.7	4.5	5.9	5.2	4.1	3.8	5.3	4.6	8.6	8.3	9.9	7.6	10.6
Ash %	0.365	0.36	0.42	0.385	0.385	0.58	0.70	0.65	0.555	0.50	0.63	0.53	0.84	0.97	1.18	0.79	1.10
Fibre %	0.14	0.11	0.09	0.11	0.12	0.22	0.20	0.12	0.12	0.15	0.10	0.14	0.39	0.26	0.38	0.18	0.60

to see the milling system as a dynamic equilibrium; a change in one part of the mill-flow will change the pattern throughout.

EXTRACTION RATE

Care is needed in comparing extraction rates because the percentage extraction rate may be calculated in several ways. The output of flour may be expressed as a percentage of:

(1) The wheat from which it is derived (either 'dirty' as received at the silos or 'clean' as fed to the first break rolls).
(2) The mill products, flour and milling offals (either with or without 'screenings').

The extraction figure from clean wheat is lower than the figure based on products less screenings owing to small milling losses. In the UK flour yield is usually calculated commercially as a percentage of the products of the milling of clean wheat although during the period of government control rates were officially calculated with respect to 'dirty wheat', i.e. the total products, including screenings.

When only one grade of flour is being made—a 'straight-run' flour—the extraction rate can be stated with accuracy by the miller and confirmed by inspection of appropriate records. If the miller wishes to make two or more grades of flour simultaneously he may select certain of his mill streams and blend them at will. The term 'extraction rate' cannot accurately be applied to the products of this selection. The miller may, however, select mill streams in such a way as to produce a flour as nearly as possible equivalent to a flour of a known extraction rate. If a mill is set to give an overall extraction rate of, say, 76%, the whitest part of the flour from the upper mill streams could be removed as low extraction (patent) flour so that the remaining portion would be approximately equivalent to an 80% extraction flour. Methods are therefore required for assessing equivalent extraction rates.

METHODS USED IN ASSESSING EXTRACTION RATE

Ash content
Before the compulsory addition of chalk to flour, the ash determination was widely used as an index of grade in the UK and it still forms the basis for the classification of flours into types 1–5 on the Continent. Figure 2 shows the ash data of McCance *et al.* (1945) for flours milled from UK mixed grists and the similar curve produced by Mohs for

German flours. Both show that the slope changes sharply in the critical region between 70 and 80% extraction. Moreover, these curves show idealised average relationships and, in practice, there are considerable variations in the ash content of flours at any given extraction rate.

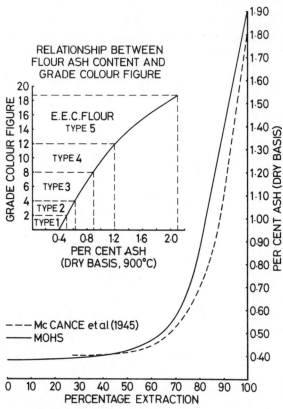

FIG. 2. Variation in flour ash content with extraction rate.

MacMasters *et al.* (1971) have shown that the aleurone layer contributes about 61% of the ash of the grain although it accounts for only 6–8% of its weight. The endosperm contributes 20% of the ash, the embryo and scutellum together 12% and the outer bran (pericarp and testa) only 7%. The amounts vary between different wheats and even between individual grains of the same wheat. Thus ash content is only a rough guide to extraction rate because it depends sharply on the amount of aleurone layer incorporated into the flour. The outer bran layers produce less ash than the endosperm.

Grade colour figure

The method for assessing the grade of a sample of flour by subjective judgement in the Pekar test has largely been supplanted by the use of the Kent-Jones and Martin, Flour Colour Grader (1950).

Kent-Jones *et al.* (1950) demonstrated a correlation between their numerical assessment of colour and the ash content. The inset in Fig. 2 shows an average relationship between ash content and grade colour figure but there is considerable scatter in the individual points as might be expected from varying distribution of aleurone layer which is high in ash content without being highly coloured. Figure 2 also illustrates the range of average values of ash content and colour grade for EEC flours types 1–5. The Flour Milling and Baking Research Association (private communication) calculated the standard deviation as ± 0.78 grade colour units when plotting grade colour against ash content for 95 type 1 flours. A flour with 0·53% ash corresponds to an average grade colour figure of 2·0 but the results imply a possible range of 0·5–3·5 units.

Thus, like ash content, the grade colour figure is not strictly proportional to extraction rate but it measures cheaply and conveniently an aspect of flour quality, directly related to market preferences. The UK miller normally aims at obtaining the maximum extraction rate without exceeding a specified maximum grade colour figure.

Fibre and carbohydrates

The fibre content of flour is useful in assessing the amount of branny material in wholemeals and brown flours. The UK Bread and Flour Regulations 1963 (SI No. 1435) state that 'wheatmeal or brown flour shall not contain less than 0·6% fibre (calculated by weight on dry matter)'. The fibre figure becomes too small for reliability in analysing flours of low extraction.

TABLE II

THE GRADE INDEX OF NICHOLLS AND FRASER

Types of flour	Grade index $\dfrac{\text{n-s carbohydrates} \times 100}{\text{starch} + \text{protein}}$
100% wholemeals	17·6, 18·1
93% brown flours	13·2–13·7
81% extraction soft flour	5·3
80% national straight-run flours:	
1952	5·5
1955	4·7
1956	4·6
72% extraction flour	4·0

Nicholls and Fraser (1958) proposed a method for calculating a grade index which involves the determination of starch, non-starch (n-s) carbohydrates and protein using methods published by Fraser *et al.* (1956). This index gives a measure of the amount of non-endosperm carbohydrates admixed with starch from the endosperm and thus the grade of the flour. Typical values are given in Table II.

SOME FACTORS AFFECTING EXTRACTION RATE

Wheat

The term 'milling quality' applied to a wheat often refers, somewhat misleadingly, to its yield of flour or 'extraction' compared with that obtained in a similar test from a reference wheat. Other factors, such as amylase content and protein quality, are assessed separately. Owing to differences in type of endosperm (flinty or floury) and in the relative quantities of endosperm and bran, flour yield depends on the type of wheat, on the variety within a type and on grain quality.

An increased usage of home-grown and European wheat in UK bread grists (to more than 50%), in response to economic constraints of EEC membership, has been made possible owing to the introduction of mechanical dough development (Chamberlain *et al.*, 1961) and more effective bread improvers during the last decade. The potential extraction of new UK varieties is thus of increasing importance. Varieties like Maris Widgeon and Bouquet can yield as much as 5% more flour than Cappelle in comparable tests. The miller must, however, give precedence to breadmaking quality in selecting his grist. Some varieties, such as Maris Huntsman and Maris Nimrod, bred for their very high yields of grain per acre, and excellent resistance to plant diseases, carry high α-amylase activity, even in the truly dormant state, so that they must be excluded or used only very sparingly in bread grists. The higher the extraction rate, the greater the problem. The fact that Maris Huntsman accounts for one-third of the wheat planted in East Anglia this year is cause for concern and suggests the need for a more rigid classification into 'milling' and 'feed' varieties.

Wheat quality is important, irrespective of variety. Grain of low bushel weight, containing thin, broken and shrivelled grains gives a low flour extraction. A fall of 1 lb in bushel weight can lead to a loss of 0·75% extraction.

Milling

Wheat is 'conditioned' by damping and resting to ensure that the endosperm is at the correct moisture for efficient reduction. Each wheat type has its optimum moisture content for milling and the various types in a grist are tempered individually and mixed shortly before grinding in order to avoid equilibration of the mixture. Butcher and Stenvert (1973) have recently shown the value of tempering hard and soft varieties of the same wheat type separately to improve extraction. The outer skins of the mixed grist are also damped shortly before entering the first break roll in order to reduce the friability of the bran, and hence the tendency to form bran powder, without allowing time for the penetration of unwanted moisture into the endosperm. Automatic moisture measurement with controlled damping is an advance of recent years.

Milling wheat dry increases break release and hence extraction rate at the expense of flour colour, but correct conditioning and adjustment of the break rolls enables the miller to produce the maximum yield of flour within a grade colour specification.

Altering the break releases by adjusting break rolls or by changing the covers on the break scalpers is the most important method of adjusting extraction rate because it controls the proportion of the grain passed to the reduction system and the proportion rejected as coarse bran. These adjustments alter the whole complex equilibrium necessitating changes in the purifier and reduction roll settings. This requires operational skill and experience rather than theoretical knowledge because each mill has its own characteristics. Adjustment of the reduction system alters the proportion of fine offal produced and hence affects extraction rate. The miller also has the option of including the lowest grade machine flour in the straight-run flour or diverting it to the offals. Extraction rate and grade colour cannot be considered in isolation. The miller is concerned with the baking quality and the yield of bread in his customers' bakeries. The reduction rolls are set to obtain the optimum flour water absorption in the bakery by controlling starch damage as discussed by Farrand (1969).

The very white, very low ash, patent flours which commanded a premium price before the Second World War are no longer in demand and this has encouraged the simplification of the milling process. High capacity, compact mills with fast running rolls and heavy feeds have been evolved. This has caused processing problems, particularly in obtaining adequate extraction at acceptable grade colour figures, which could be met only partly by design improvements in roller mills, sifters, purifiers and control systems. The most important innovation of recent years has been the introduction of flake and aggregate disrupters after certain critical reduction passages. The Entoleter is one of several machines of this type which disrupts loosely knit endosperm flaked aggregates without damaging any bran particles which may be present. These units also break down particles of endosperm previously cracked and weakened by roll grinding and generally improve subsequent sifting efficiency because of their disruptive effect. Marlow (1963) showed that the number of reduction passages could be cut from thirteen to eight while producing a flour of better grade colour at a similar extraction than the normal milling process. Modern UK compact mills have little more than 25% of the roll surface of some pre-war mills of the same capacity. Butcher and Stenvert (1972) have shown the value of the Entoleter system in improving extraction using the Buhler experimental mill.

COMMERCIAL FACTORS DETERMINING THE CHOICE OF EXTRACTION RATE

The miller is influenced in setting extraction rate by:

(1) The baking trade's assessment of the type of bread preferred by the consumer.
(2) The market demand for mill offals and their price relative to the cost of wheat in the grist.

Market preferences
The target extraction rate is determined by the maximum grade colour figure acceptable to the market and by the processing efficiency of the mill concerned.

Horder *et al.* (1954) stated 'Before the last war, the majority of the nation (estimated at not less than 95%) preferred white to brown bread'. They referred to a white bread made from lower extraction flour than would be used in white bread production today. Between the years 1939 and 1953 the extraction rate varied between 72 and 90% during the period of control by the British Government, and for several years it was held at 85% (with only a brief period of 4 months at 90% during 1946).

After decontrol of the milling industry in August 1953 the extraction rate was allowed to depart from the figure of 81% and, under the Flour Order 1953, certain specified nutrients were restored to all flours of less than 80% extraction as recommended in the Report of the Conference on the Post-War Loaf (Cmd 6701) published in 1945. At the same time National flour of 80% extraction had to be available, and under the Bread Order 1953 National bread in standard loaves had to be sold within prescribed maximum retail prices. Whiter bread was free of price control but anyone selling it by retail was obliged to have loaves of National bread available for sale. The National (80% extraction) bread was subsidised and bread from flour of lower extraction did not qualify for a subsidy.

There was considerable public interest in following the demand for white bread compared with the subsidised 80% extraction National bread and also in noting any changes in the analytical characteristics and colour of National flour. Fraser (1958) in his survey of flours sampled during

1950–56 shows how the grade colour figure for National flour gradually fell from approximately 8·0 to 3·0 with concomitant reductions in certain nutrient levels. This was ascribed to better quality wheats which were again available by 1953, and to skills gained in war-time experience which enabled British millers to produce a light-coloured flour at a much higher extraction rate than was thought to be possible in 1946.

TABLE III

CONSUMPTION OF VARIOUS KINDS OF BREAD IN THE UK[a]

Year	Total consumption oz/pers/wk	White	Per cent distribution Brown	Wholemeal	Other
1960	45·47	80·6	5·3	2·0	12·1
1961	45·17	79·9	5·3	1·9	12·9
1962	43·57	82·8	5·6	1·9	9·7
1963	43·26	85·7	6·0	1·5	6·8
1964	41·97	85·8	6·3	1·4	6·5
1965	40·60	84·5	7·0	1·7	6·8
1966	38·64	84·3	7·4	1·4	6·9
1967	40·02	84·6	7·0	1·4	7·0
1968	38·31	84·3	6·9	1·1	7·7
1969	37·74	84·8	6·4	1·5	7·3
1970	38·09	84·6	6·4	1·3	7·7
1971	35·76	83·5	8·6		7·9
1972	34·44	83·2	8·3		8·5
1973	33·42	82·5	8·3		9·2

[a] Data extracted from Annual Reports of the Food Survey Committee of the Ministry of Agriculture, Fisheries and Food, and (for 1972 and 1973) from Trade and Industry.

Amos (1956) alleged that much of this National flour was milled (or simulated) at an extraction rate well below 80%. This trend led to the setting up of the Panel on the Composition and Nutritive Value of Flour under the Chairmanship of Lord Cohen. The finding of this Panel (1956) that enriched white flour was as nutritionally acceptable as National (80% extraction) flour left the milling industry free, after October 1956, to mill to any extraction rate provided the flour conformed to standards for three specified nutrients, achieved by supplementation as necessary. There was no violent reaction by the industry to this new-found freedom, but the proportion of bread flour around 72% extraction increased in accordance with public demand for a soft white loaf with good keeping properties. The data shown in Table III indicate that since 1960 the percentage consumption of white bread has remained remarkably steady at between

80 and 90% of the total, with brown and wholemeal breads together accounting for less than 10% of total demand.

An analysis of the returns on a regional basis shows that the preference for white bread in the years 1971 and 1972 was strongest in the East and West Midlands with 86–88% and lowest in the North and Scotland with 79–81% of the total consumption. Few large-scale surveys have been made to assess public preferences using a range of breads made from flours of increasing extraction rates, but in a well-controlled study on a large heterogeneous population in Scotland it was shown by Coppock *et al.* (1952) that (1) by taste, breads prepared from 72 and 80% extraction flours were almost equally preferred, whereas breads made from 82·5 and 85% extraction flours were considerably less preferred, in that order, and (2) by appearance, bread prepared from 72% extraction flour was undoubtedly preferred to all other kinds examined.

The British preference for white bread is not new. Eastwood *et al.* (1974) have recently quoted evidence given to the Lord Mayor's Committee in Council in 1795 which shows that most of London's bread was already white by that date with an extraction rate of 72%.

Relative prices of wheat and milling offals
The price of milling offals may be regarded as a credit to set against the cost of the wheat milled (grist) when calculating the ingredient cost of the

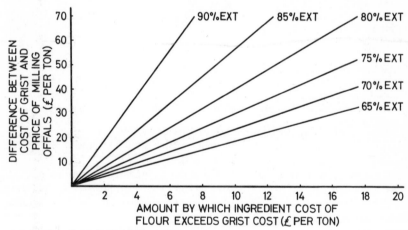

FIG. 3. The effect of price differential between wheat in the grist and milling offals on the ingredient cost of flour at various extraction rates.

flour produced. When the price commanded by offals per ton is equal to that of the grist per ton, the ingredient cost of the flour is also equal to the cost of the grist and is independent of the extraction rate. Under these conditions, or when there is little difference between the cost of the grist and the price of offals, the miller has some freedom of action. He may, within reasonable limits imposed by production capacity, running hours and other cost and market considerations, lower the extraction rate to produce a whiter and more competitive flour and increase the quantity of offals available for sale. These will also contain more starchy endosperm and possess a higher metabolisable energy in farm feeds and thus be more competitive. Under present conditions, however, when the cost of wheat is very high and substantially greater than the price realised by milling offals, the miller strives to obtain the maximum extraction rate consistent with producing flour of acceptable grade colour figure. Figure 3 shows the effect of price differential between the grist and offals on the ingredient cost of flour at various extraction rates (ignoring milling losses).

A general increase in extraction rate (and in grade colour figure) towards emergency figures of 80% would not only reduce the quantity of offals available for farm feeds but reduce their feeding value.

REFERENCES

Amos, A. J. (1956). 'The milling industry', *Food Manuf.*, **31**, 52.

Butcher, J. and Stenvert, N. L. (1972). 'An Entoleter for the Buhler laboratory mill', *Milling*, **154**, No. 7, 27.

Butcher, J. and Stenvert, N. L. (1973). 'Conditioning studies on Australian wheat. I. The effect of conditioning on milling behaviour. II. Morphology of wheat and its relationship to conditioning. R. Moss. III. The role of the rate of water penetration into the wheat grain', *J. Sci. Fd Agric.*, **24**, 1055.

Chamberlain, N., Collins, T. H. and Elton, G. A. H. (1961). 'The Chorleywood Bread Process', British Baking Industries Research Association Report No. 59.

Coppock, J. B. M., Hulse, J. H., Todd, J. P. and Urie, A. (1952). 'Some organoleptic studies on bakery products', *J. Sci. Fd Agric.*, **3**, 433.

Eastwood, M. A., Fisher, N., Greenwood, C. T. and Hutchinson, J. B. (1974). 'Perspectives on the bran hypothesis', *The Lancet*, May 25, 1029.

Farrand, E. A. (1969). 'Starch damage and alpha-amylase as bases for mathematical models relating to flour water-absorption', *Cereal Chem.*, **46**, 103.

Fraser, J. R. (1958). 'Flour Survey 1950–56', *J. Sci. Fd Agric.*, **9**, 125.

Fraser, J. R., Brandon-Bravo, M. and Holmes, D. C. (1956). 'The proximate analysis of wheat flour carbohydrates. I. Methods and scheme of analysis', *J. Sci. Fd Agric.*, **7**, 577.

Heathcote, J. G., Hinton, J. J. C. and Shaw, B. (1952). 'The distribution of nicotinic acid in wheat and maize', *Proc. Roy. Soc.*, **139**, 276.

Horder, T., Dodds, E. C. and Moran, T. (1954). *Bread. The Chemistry and Nutrition of Flour and Bread with an Introduction to their History and Technology*, Constable, London.

Jones, C. R. (1958). 'The essentials of the flour-milling process', *Proc. Nutr. Soc.*, **17**, 7.

Kent-Jones, D. W., Amos, A. J. and Martin, W. (1950). 'Experiments in the photo-electric recording of flour grade by measurements of reflecting power', *Analyst*, **75**, 133.

Kent-Jones, D. W. and Martin, W. (1950). 'A photo-electric method of determining the colour of flour as affected by grade, by measurements of reflecting power', *Analyst*, **75**, 127.

McCance, R. A., Widdowson, E. M., Moran, T., Pringle, W. J. S. and Macrae, T. A. (1945). 'The chemical composition of wheat and rye and of flours derived therefrom', *Biochem. J.*, **39**, 213.

MacMasters, M. M., Hinton, J. J. C. and Bradbury, D. (1971). 'Microscopic structure and composition of the wheat kernel', *Wheat Chemistry and Technology*, 2nd edn (Ed. Y. Pomeranz), American Assoc. Cereal Chem., St. Paul, Minn.

Marlow, A. V. (1963). 'An important step in the development of high-capacity milling', *Milling*, **140**, 558.

Nicholls, J. R. and Fraser, J. R. (1958). 'Analytical problems in the determination and control of extraction rates of flour', *Proc. Nutr. Soc.*, **17**, 43.

Report of the Panel on Composition and Nutritive Value of Flour (Cmd 9757) 1956, HMSO, London.

DISCUSSION

W. V. Single (Department of Agriculture, Tamworth, New South Wales): If breeders could reduce the crease and improve the milling configuration of some red wheat types would this present technical milling problems and should the development be encouraged?

P. W. Russell Eggitt: If completely successful, this might make some of our capital equipment superfluous and put some of us out of a job! I am not too concerned that this will happen tomorrow but the objective is laudable as it would simplify the process, although existing mills could cope with these wheats.

A. E. Salem (Alexandria University, Egypt): My experience in the USA prompts me to ask if the figures quoted for the ash contents of the first three break flours, 0·55–0·63, are not a little high?

P. W. Russell Eggitt: I think the figures reflect the softer grists we are milling today and the need to move towards higher extractions. In his paper Dr Irvine observed that British millers were reluctant to make break flour! Perhaps other millers would like to comment?

D. B. Pratt (The Pillsbury Company, Minneapolis): The extraction rate quoted by our speaker is very close to what we work to in the USA. Break release depends on the relationship of roll surface to loading and energy input. Ash is not a key issue here as the main stocks pass over the purifiers. The process must be gentle enough to avoid excessive starch damage and keep stock temperatures low enough to prevent any denaturation of the protein. There is a wide choice of where to throw these stocks.

We shall be on-stream next week with a new wet-milling process which separates the wheat into its components—solubles, protein and starch—without any dry grinding. We can end up with any combination of these and are looking for extraction rates up to 88–89%. It is a unique process which looks very favourable now but we don't know what the costs will be. Further discussion is not possible as patents are pending but the extraction rates are interesting and relevant.

P. W. Russell Eggitt: I believe the UK patent is now published. You say 89% extraction, so you make a bit of endosperm. I'd be interested in breakdown figures to compare with the conventional process.

D. B. Pratt: At present we can only base our figures on the mineral ash of the component parts. We don't know what to do with the fibre portion. It amounts to 15% and after reading some of the recent articles in the *Lancet*, maybe we ought to put it back or sell it as a fibre product.

The material, as produced, has a colour. If reconstituted at the normal protein level for a bread flour, the colour is comparable to that of a present-day bread flour. The germ is separated and is used in another product. If we combine the germ product and the endosperm we reach the 89% extraction. Using a spring wheat grist we approximate to a 0·47% ash flour, comparable to a straight-run wheat flour, but the bran has all gone.

G. Wisden (RHM Flour Mills Ltd, London): The choice between a wet or a dry milling process will depend on the economics of the operation.

I noticed that you had an overall break flour of about 28%. In today's terms I would have thought that just on the high side. Some 25–28% would be a better estimate according to the nature and the quality of the native wheat in the grist. With a hard wheat the percentage may be as low as 20%.

Returning to Dr Salem's point about the ash of the break flours, I would say they are a little high but this depends on the nature of the wheat. With good wheat I would expect an ash figure of 0·5% and not more than 0·55%.

We all know there is no correlation between colour and ash—you can get an ash figure of 0·5% with a colour figure of 3·0 or an ash figure of 0·6% with a colour figure of 2·0.

A. E. Salem: What use is made of air classification in England?

P. W. Russell Eggitt: We have been using air classification extensively in this country for nearly 20 years particularly in the manufacture of cake flours, certain speciality products like brewing flour and also for certain types of flour grading. There may be future applications in bread flours.

J. J. Groen (Leiden University, Netherlands): If bread consumption is going down all the time, who does consume your product?

P. W. Russell Eggitt: Happily the consumption is falling very slowly and it has a long way to go before it reaches the per capita level in the USA.

Chairman: Thank you all very much.

Extraction Rates—Nutritional Implications

E. M. WIDDOWSON

Department of Investigative Medicine,
University of Cambridge, Cambridge, UK

The relative value of white and brown flour has been a matter of debate for centuries. The physicians of classical Greece and Rome, as represented by Hippocrates and Galen, recognised that brown flour was laxative, and increased the bulk of the faeces, and inferred shrewdly from this that white flour was more nutritious. If, however, we look at the chemical composition of the two flours, as it is possible to do in the 20th century (Table I), we see that wholemeal flour contains more protein, more fat, more of many of the inorganic constituents and more of the B vitamins, than white flour, and it is generally believed nowadays that wholemeal flour is more nutritious than white.

TABLE I
CHEMICAL COMPOSITION OF 100% AND 70% EXTRACTION
FLOURS MADE FROM MANITOBA WHEAT (per 100 g)
(McCance et al., 1945)

	100%	*70%*
Water (g)	15	15
Protein (g)	13·6	12·8
Fat (g)	2·5	1·2
Available carbohydrate (g) (as starch)	63·0	70·0
kcal	328	341
K (mg)	312	82
Ca (mg)	27·6	12·8
Mg (mg)	141	26·9
Fe (mg)	3·8	2·2
Cu (mg)	0·60	0·18
Zn (mg)	3·73	1·16
Total P (mg)	350	97
Phytate P (mg)	242	30
Thiamine (mg)	0·40	0·28
Riboflavin (mg)	0·16	0·04
Nicotinic acid (mg)	5·0	2·0

Both points of view are in their way correct. A man will derive more energy from a given weight of white flour than he will from the same weight of wholemeal, but he will ingest more potassium, magnesium, iron and other inorganic nutrients, and more B vitamins from the same weight of wholemeal flour. The view we should adopt about which is the more nutritious depends upon which constituents of a person's diet are likely to be in short supply and which of the two flours is likely to provide these most satisfactorily.

Wholemeal flour contains two ingredients, absent or present only in small amounts in low extraction flour, that are not only not absorbed themselves, but interfere with the absorption of other nutrients in the flour, or in the diet as a whole. The first is the unavailable carbohydrate, or 'fibre' to use its popular term. This is not fibre in the chemical sense, i.e. what is left after treatment with acid and alkali. The word is used in the physiological sense to describe what is left after all the processes of digestion have gone on in the human intestine. It includes the structural polysaccharides of the outer layers of the grain, the cellulose and hemi-celluloses, and lignin, which is not strictly a carbohydrate. The ingestion of large amounts of this conglomeration produces large volumes of intestinal secretions, and the constituents of these are not all reabsorbed. The second ingredient in wholemeal flour is phytic acid, inositol hexa-phosphoric acid, mainly as its potassium and magnesium salts. This provides a means by which the seed stores phosphorus, potassium, magnesium and iron, and trace elements also, in an insoluble form. Phytic acid forms insoluble salts with calcium, iron, zinc and other metals in the wholemeal flour and also in the rest of the diet, and prevents their absorption.

NUTRIENTS IN FLOURS OF HIGH AND LOW EXTRACTION RATES AND THEIR AVAILABILITY TO THE HUMAN BODY

Protein

Table II shows the percentage of protein in flour made from low protein English and high protein Manitoba wheat at three different extraction rates. In both wheats the percentage of protein falls as the extraction rate is reduced—but the type of wheat is more important than the extraction rate in determining the amount of protein in the flour made from it.

On the other hand it is the extraction rate that determines the amount of nitrogen lost in the faeces (McCance and Widdowson, 1947). When six individuals, two men and four women, ate a diet with sufficient bread in it to provide them with 77–93% of their energy requirements and 100% of their protein intake, they excreted the same amount of nitrogen in the faeces whether the bread was made from 90% English or 90% Manitoba flour, even though their protein intake from the English flour was only about half that from the Manitoba. Similarly, when the bread was made from 80% English and 80% Manitoba flour the subjects excreted similar amounts of nitrogen, but less than from either of the 90% extraction flours. We concluded from this that the protein from wheat flour of 90 and 80% extraction is completely digested and absorbed by man, and that the

TABLE II

PERCENTAGE OF PROTEIN IN FLOUR MADE FROM
ENGLISH AND MANITOBA WHEAT AT THREE
EXTRACTION RATES
(McCance et al., 1945)

Extraction rate	English	Manitoba
100	8·9	13·6
85	8·6	13·6
70	7·9	12·8

nitrogen excreted in the faeces is entirely derived from the intestinal secretions. It was the unavailable carbohydrate in the flour containing the outer parts of the grain that stimulated the production of these additional secretions which were in turn the cause of the greater loss. However, it must be made clear that the amount of nitrogen lost in the faeces is always a small proportion of the intake, and the quantity absorbed was greater for the Manitoba than the English wheat.

In 1942 Dame Harriette Chick published a paper in the *Lancet* describing her experiments with rats (Chick, 1942). She followed the growth of rats from soon after weaning, fed on wholemeal, 85 or 75% extraction flour, the only additions being a small amount of arachis oil, a salt mixture, protein-free yeast extract to provide the B vitamins, and supplements of vitamins A and D. Table III shows that the rats eating the wholemeal flour grew better than those eating the white, with those eating the 85% extraction flour in between. The rats were allowed to eat as much food as they wished, and those having wholemeal flour ate more food. The experiment has been criticised for this reason, but the results showed clearly that the increase in weight per gram of protein eaten was greatest for the wholemeal flour. Something in the wholemeal flour made it a better food than white flour for weanling rats under the conditions of these experiments.

When we began our studies in Germany just after the war on the effect of variations in the extraction rate of flour on the growth of under-nourished children (Widdowson and McCance, 1954) we fully expected to get the same result as Dr Chick, and that children deriving 75% of their energy from wholemeal flour would grow better than those deriving 75% of their energy from white. To our surprise they did not. All grew splendidly, and those having bread made from white flour grew just as well as those having bread made from wholemeal.

Why were the results on the children different from those on the rats? It was not because the phytic acid in the wholemeal prevented the absorption of calcium, and so hindered growth, for all the flours were enriched with calcium carbonate (see later). It might have been because the children did not live entirely on bread, but had small amounts of animal protein, 8 g a day, and about 15 g from vegetables, which together made up a

TABLE III

BIOLOGICAL VALUE AND COEFFICIENT OF DIGESTIBILITY FOR RATS OF THE PROTEIN OF FLOURS OF THREE EXTRACTION RATES
(*Chick, 1942.* Average values per rat over period of 5 weeks)

Extraction rate	Dry food eaten (g)	Protein eaten (g)	Gain in weight (g)	Growth promoting value of protein[a]	Coefficient of digestibility[b]
100	317	39·9	71	1·77	83·2
85	276	34·5	57	1·67	85·4
75	246	30·9	45	1·48	87·9

[a] Growth promoting value $= \dfrac{\text{weight increase (g)}}{\text{protein eaten (g)}}$

[b] Coefficient of digestibility $= 100 \times \dfrac{\text{N ingested} - \text{N in faeces}}{\text{N ingested}}$

third of their total protein intake. We decided we must go back to rats. When we fed weanling rats with diets similar to those eaten by the German children, with two-thirds of their protein coming from flour, we found, as Dr Chick had previously found with diets in which flour was the only source of protein, that the rats having wholemeal grew better than those having the white flour diet. We then made another experiment, starting when the rats were a little older, that is 8 weeks instead of 3 weeks. These animals grew at the same rate on each kind of flour. Hutchinson *et al.* (1956, 1959) later found the reason for these conflicting results. Wholemeal flour has a higher percentage of lysine in it (0·34 g/100 g) than white flour (0·24 g/100 g). Just after they are weaned rats have a particularly high requirement for lysine, and when their white bread diet was supplemented with lysine they grew just as well as those having wholemeal. Older rats, and children, who grow more slowly than weanling rats, do not have such a high lysine requirement in relation to their energy and other amino acid requirements, and the amount in the white flour together with what they derived from the rest of the diet was sufficient for them.

Fat

Wholemeal flour contains more fat than white flour ($2 \cdot 5\%$ as compared with $1 \cdot 2\%$), but only about half the fat in wholemeal flour is digested and absorbed by man (McCance and Walsham, 1948). This poor absorption may be due to the difficulty with which the lipolytic enzymes penetrate into the cells in which the fat is situated, or with which the products of digestion escape from them.

Carbohydrate

Reference has already been made to the higher energy value of white flour. This is due to the fact that it contains more available carbohydrate in the form of starch. On the other hand wholemeal flour is the food *par excellence* rich in unavailable carbohydrate, the cellulose and hemicelluloses that make up the outer layers of the grain. Much has been written in recent years about the positive advantages of 'fibre' or unavailable carbohydrate in the diet. Fibre has been advocated for a wide variety of ills (Burkitt, 1973). It is said to protect the teeth and gums because of its cleansing and abrasive properties; prevent over-eating and obesity because the stomach feels full sooner; lessen the likelihood of diabetes because it slows down the absorption of sugars; lessen the likelihood of coronary heart disease because it prevents the reabsorption of bile acids and their breakdown products and this in turn encourages the breakdown of cholesterol, so that the concentration of cholesterol in the serum is reduced. Fibre is stated to act directly on the intestine and prevent appendicitis, diverticular disease of the colon and cancer of the large intestine. Some of these effects are probably related to the size of the unabsorbed residues or to the rate of passage of the digesta through the gut. Of the two the large amount of material reaching the large intestine is probably more important. The bulk is partly due to water which is bound by the unavailable carbohydrates, and partly to the unabsorbed carbohydrate residues themselves, with some protein and fat. There is no doubt, however, that markers such as carmine do usually pass along the whole length of the digestive tract more rapidly if a person is eating brown bread than if he is eating white. McCance *et al.* (1953) made a radiological study of the rate of passage of brown and white bread through the digestive tract and showed that the more rapid passage started in the stomach and continued to the large intestine. A person suffering from any disease that is aggravated by constipation, therefore, must benefit from a diet containing wholemeal bread. Before advocating wholemeal bread for everybody, however, its disadvantages must be set against its advantages. Whole wheat flour is not the panacea for all disease.

Inorganic constituents

The story of the interrelation of phytates with dietary calcium really begins in 1914 when the newly formed Medical Research Committee drew up a list of disabling diseases which were common in Britain at that time. Prominent among them was rickets. Mellanby was among those asked to study the disease and the problem allotted to him was 'Calcium and phosphorus balance in rickets' (Mellanby, 1934). He decided to use puppies for his investigation, for it was already known that puppies readily develop rickets. He discovered that rickets was primarily due to the deficiency of a fat soluble vitamin, but he also found that whole cereals, particularly oatmeal and wheat, had a rickets-producing effect, and the larger the amount of them eaten the more severe the disease became, provided always that the diet contained too little of the anti-rachitic vitamin (Mellanby, 1919, 1920). White wheaten flour, however, was fairly innocuous. By 1925 Mellanby had found out that the rickets-producing effect of whole cereals could be counteracted by adding calcium carbonate to the diet, and he postulated that these cereals must contain an anticalcifying toxamin (Mellanby, 1926). Now it had been known since the early years of the century that a large part of the phosphorus in whole cereals was in organic combination in the form of inositol hexaphosphoric acid, or phytic acid, and a calcium–magnesium phytate, made by Ciba Ltd was on the market under the trade name of 'Phytin'. The phosphorus in this was thought to be easily assimilated and 'Phytin' had been recommended as a tonic for children and for those suffering from tuberculosis.

When Bruce and Callow (1934) were studying the effect of low intakes of phosphorus and vitamin D on the production of rickets in rats they found, rather to their surprise, that the phosphorus in whole cereals was not so well absorbed as inorganic phosphorus. They realised that it must be the phytic acid that was not being so readily absorbed, and also that it might be precipitating calcium in the intestine and so preventing its absorption also. Mellanby at once saw the significance of this, and he and Harrison (Harrison and Mellanby, 1939) demonstrated that a diet for puppies, marginally too low in vitamin D, could be made more rachitogenic by adding sodium phytate to it.

Some months after the war started in 1939 we embarked on a long series of studies on healthy men and women to investigate their absorption and excretion of calcium, magnesium, potassium, phosphorus and iron from diets containing a great deal of bread, white bread, brown bread, white and brown bread containing added calcium carbonate or phosphate, white bread containing added sodium phytate and brown bread from which the phytate had been removed by hydrolysis with the phytase naturally present in it (McCance and Widdowson, 1942a, 1942b). Our results for calcium are summarised in Table IV. The absorption of calcium was considerably less when the diet contained much brown bread than when

TABLE IV
MEAN DAILY INTAKE, FAECAL EXCRETION AND ABSORPTION OF CALCIUM
BY HEALTHY ADULTS EATING LARGE AMOUNTS OF BREAD
(Widdowson, 1970)

Type of bread	Ca * intake (mg)	Ca excretion (mg)	Ca absorption (mg)
White	504	341	163
Brown	561	510	51
White+added Ca	1 149	892	257
Brown+added Ca	1 248	1 073	175
White+added sodium phytate	510	530	−20
Dephytinised brown	610	445	165

it contained much white bread, even though the intake was higher on the brown bread. Adding calcium either as carbonate or phosphate to the flour increased the amount of calcium absorbed. Adding sodium phytate to white flour interfered so much with the absorption of calcium that the average absorption became negative. On the other hand the removal of phytate from brown flour had just the opposite effect, for it improved calcium absorption. It was partly as a result of these studies that it was decided to fortify the war-time flour, and later white flour, with calcium carbonate, and the results also supplied the information necessary to decide on the level of fortification. Rather inconsistently commercial wholemeal flour, which contains most phytic acid, has never had to be fortified.

Interest in the interference with the absorption of calcium by phytate has been revived recently since rickets has appeared among Asian adolescents in Britain. The large amount of phytate in whole wheat flour used for making chappatis, coupled with a low intake of calcium and vitamin D, has been held to be the cause (Ford et al., 1972). Chappatis prepared in Britain, however, are not necessarily made from wholemeal flour; they are often made from white flour to which variable amounts of bran have been added. In this case the white flour would have been fortified with calcium carbonate, and the calcium intake may not be so low, or the phytate intake so high, as might be supposed.

Calcium is not the only metal that forms insoluble complexes with phytic acid. Iron is another, and in fact precipitation as ferric phytate is the most usual method for determining phytic acid chemically. In Iran unleavened wholemeal bread is the staple food of people living in the villages, and the prevalence of anaemia among them in spite of a high iron intake has been attributed to their high intake of phytic acid (Haghshenass et al., 1972).

In the early 1960s Prasad and his co-workers (Prasad et al., 1961;

Prasad *et al.*, 1963) described a syndrome of dwarfism, associated with hypogonadism, in Iran and in Egypt, and they suggested that this was due to a deficiency of zinc. Concentration of zinc in the plasma was low and there was increased uptake of Zn^{65}. When supplementary zinc as $ZnSO_4$ was given to some of these dwarfs 19–23 years old (Reinhold *et al.*, 1972), they began to grow in height and the mean increase was 10·5 cm in 6 months. There was also an increase in gonadal function and development of secondary sexual characteristics. Metabolic balance studies on adult villagers given a high zinc diet showed very high zinc retentions, which again suggested that they had previously been short of zinc.

As already mentioned the bread consumed in large quantities in the villages in Iran and also in Egypt is made from wholemeal wheat flour, without yeast, and is baked immediately, so there is no loss of phytic acid due to the action of phytase. It is believed that the high intake of phytate is responsible for the deficiency of zinc, as of iron, and this shows once more how unwise it is to advocate wholemeal flour for the prevention and cure of all ills. It may prevent some right enough, but it can certainly aggravate others.

B vitamins

There is no doubt that high extraction flour contains more of the B vitamins than white flour. Studies by Holman (1954), however, on the absorption of B vitamins by the German children previously mentioned showed that the riboflavin and nicotinic acid in wholemeal flour were less readily absorbed and utilised by the children than synthetic riboflavin and nicotinic acid added to white flour.

CONCLUSIONS

If I may now recapitulate for a moment I should like to make three points about extraction rates.

(1) Bread made from flour of high extraction may in appropriate circumstances do good by preventing various intestinal and other diseases. (2) In other circumstances it may do harm by preventing the absorption of calcium, iron and zinc. (3) Most often, perhaps, it is immaterial whether one eats wholemeal or white bread. Both breads were shown to be equally effective in promoting a high rate of growth in undernourished children. I can do no better I think than finish this paper by quoting to you the conclusion we came to in 1954: 'The greatest caution must be exercised in coming to any conclusion at all. Any conclusions that may be drawn must be restricted to the setting in which the scientific evidence was obtained. . . . Probably the most important finding concerns the high nutritive value of wheat in any of the forms customarily consumed by man.'

REFERENCES

Bruce, H. M. and Callow, R. K. (1934). 'Cereals and rickets. The role of inositol hexaphosphoric acid', *Biochem. J.*, **28**, 517.

Burkitt, D. (1973). 'Fibre—is it a dietary requirement?' in *Nutritional Problems in a Changing World* (Ed. D. Hollingsworth and M. Russell). Applied Science Publishers, London, p. 33.

Chick, H. (1942). 'Biological value of the proteins contained in wheat flours', *Lancet*, **i**, 405.

Chick, H. (1946). 'Nutritive value of proteins contained in wheat flours of different degrees of extraction', *Proc. Nutrition Soc.*, **4**, 6.

Ford, J. A., Colhoun, E. M., McIntosh, W. B. and Dunnigan, M. G. (1972). 'Biochemical response of late rickets and osteomalacia to a chupatty-free diet', *Brit. Med. J.*, **2**, 446.

Gaghshenass, M., Mahloudji, M., Reinhold, J. G. and Mohammadi, N. (1972). 'Iron deficiency anaemia in an Iranian population associated with high intakes of iron', *Amer. J. Clin. Nutrition*, **25**, 1143.

Garrison, D. C. and Mellanby, E. (1939). 'Phytic acid and the rickets-producing action of cereals', *Biochem. J.*, **33**, 1660.

Holman, W. I. M. (1954). 'Biochemical investigations into the B-vitamin metabolism of children having the experimental diet', in *Studies on the Nutritive Value of Bread and on the Effect of Variations in the Extraction Rate of Flour on the Growth of Undernourished Children*, Medical Research Council Special Report Series No. 287, HMSO, London, p. 92.

Hutchinson, J. B., Moran, T. and Pace, J. (1956). 'Nutritive value of the protein of white and wholemeal bread in relation to the growth of rats', *Proc. Roy. Soc.*, B, **145**, 270.

Hutchinson, J. B., Moran, T. and Pace, J. (1959). 'The nutritive value of bread protein as influenced by the level of protein intake, the level of supplementation with l-lysine and l-threonine, and the addition of egg and milk proteins', *Brit. J. Nutrition*, **13**, 151.

McCance, R. A., Prior, K. M. and Widdowson, E. M. (1953). 'A radiological study of the rate of passage of brown and white bread through the digestive tract of man', *Brit. J. Nutrition*, **7**, 98.

McCance, R. A. and Walsham, C. M. (1948). 'The digestibility and absorption of the calories, proteins, purines, fat and calcium in wholemeal wheaten bread', *Brit. J. Nutrition*, **2**, 26.

McCance, R. A. and Widdowson, E. M. (1942a). 'Mineral metabolism of healthy adults on white and brown bread dietaries', *J. Physiol.*, **101**, 44.

McCance, R. A. and Widdowson, E. M. (1942b), 'Mineral metabolism on dephytinized bread', *J. Physiol.*, **101**, 304.

McCance, R. A. and Widdowson, E. M. (1947). 'The digestibility of English and Canadian wheats with special reference to the digestibility of wheat protein by man', *J. Hygiene*, **45**, 59.

McCance, R. A., Widdowson, E. M., Moran, T., Pringle, W. J. S. and Macrae, T. F. (1945). 'The chemical composition of wheat and rye and of flours derived therefrom', *Biochem. J.*, **39**, 213.

Mellanby, E. (1919). 'An experimental investigation on rickets', *Lancet*, **i**, 407.

Mellanby, E. (1920). 'Accessory food factors (vitamines) in the feeding of infants', *Lancet*, **i**, 856.

Mellanby, E. (1926). 'The presence in foodstuffs of substances having specific harmful effects under certain conditions', *J. Physiol.*, **61**, XXIV P.

Mellanby, E. (1934). *Nutrition and Disease*, Oliver and Boyd, London.

Prasad, A. S., Halstead, J. A. and Nadimi, M. (1961). 'Syndrome of iron deficiency anaemia, hepatosplenomegaly, hypogonadism, dwarfism and geophagia', *Amer. J. Medicine*, **31**, 532.

Prasad, A. S., Mial, A. Jr., Farid, Z., Sandstead, H. H. Schulert, A. R. and Darby, W. J. (1963). 'Biochemical studies on dwarfism, hypogonadism, and anaemia', *Arch. Internal Medicine*, **111**, 407.

Reinhold, J. G., Amirhakimi, G. H., Ronaghy, H. A. and Halsted, J. (1972). 'The problem of zinc deficiency in the Middle East', *Proc. the First Asian Congress of Nutrition* (Ed. P. G. Talpule and K. S. Jaya Rao), Nutrition Society of India, Hyderabad, p. 631.

Widdowson, E. M. (1970). 'Interrelations of dietary calcium with phytates, phosphates and fats', in *Biological Interrelations and Nutrition*, Bibl. 'Nutritio et Dieto', No. 15, Karger, Basel, p. 38.

Widdowson, E. M. and McCance, R. A. (1954). *Studies on the Nutritive Value of Bread and on the Effect of Variations in the Extraction Rate of Flour on the Growth of Undernourished Children*, Medical Research Council Special Report Series No. 287. HMSO, London.

DISCUSSION

M. A. Cookson (RHM Bakeries Ltd, London): My congratulations to Dr Widdowson for her magnificent paper. I only wish the conclusions, if not the whole paper, could be published.

E. M. Widdowson: Thank you very much.

F. Aylward (Reading University): I also was delighted with Dr Widdowson's paper. The position in Iran is reminiscent of Britain 30 or 40 years ago. I was talking last month to various people there about rickets and about phytates, the times of fermentation, and so on. These are the things that are interesting them now.

I wish the plant geneticists and the agriculturalists and the millers could all get together and decide what Britain and other countries should try to achieve in terms of high yielding, high protein, good milling wheat.

Sir Ernst Chain (Imperial College of Science and Technology, London): I have always taken the view that it makes no difference at all, from a nutritional point of view, whether you eat white or brown bread. However, in a recent paper (*Brit. J. Nutr.*, **32**, 447, 1974), it has been demonstrated beyond doubt that in rats, fibre (from bagasse) substantially increases the excretion of bile acids, the liver enzyme cholesterol-α-hydroxylase and faecal bulk. In man (paper in press) similar results with regard to bile acid excretion and faecal bulk were obtained. If people are constipated, let them eat bran as an *addition* to their diet, and they will certainly experience relief, but I can see no reason why they should give up eating white bread if they like it. In our experience, always using bagasse as a source of fibre, the increase of the faecal bulk is due only to a minor degree of water absorption.

P. W. Russell Eggitt (Spillers Ltd, Cambridge): Professor Aylward was right. With the high usage of European wheat which we must anticipate, the percentage of protein is going to be a problem. Last year we were lucky, the average percentage of protein was 11·1%. This year it is only 10·3%.

In certain parts of Australia their wheat contains marginal amounts of protein and even half a per cent of extra protein commands a premium in their bread flours. They have for many years done a little protein 'shifting' there to bolster it up. I think similar techniques are used in France to increase the per cent of protein in their flours for baking.

R. Guinet (Ecole de Boulangerie et de Patisserie de Paris): We have used air classification in France now for about fifteen years, and this year we are fortunate to have this technique because we cannot buy wheat from North America and Canada.

E. Kodicek (Strangeways Research Laboratory, Cambridge, UK): I am sure that Dr Widdowson did not mean to suggest that all the claims about fibre have been substantiated. The ones about cholesterol have been strongly contested. I must warn this audience that fibre can never cure all the ills of this world.

We have extended Holman's findings that 87–97% of the nicotinic acid in bran is in a bound form, which is practically unavailable to man, beast, insect and bacteria. It appears to exist in a glycoside built into a glycoprotein.

F. Fidanza (Institute of Nutrition and Food Science, Perugia): A working party of the European Group of Nutritionists has recommended that we no longer use the term fibre in food tables, but give the unavailable and available carbohydrates separately, and to fractionate each of them as much as possible.

K. Blaxter (Rowett Research Institute, Aberdeen): Dr Davies of the Rowett Institute, has found that adding phytic acid to marginally zinc deficient diets can induce a zinc deficiency in the rat. This is largely due to its combining with zinc in intestinal secretions and physically removing it from the body.

Chairman: We have always appreciated this.

E. M. Widdowson: We got similar effects when we added sodium phytate to white bread.

Chairman: Would you like to make any comment, Professor Spicer?

A. Spicer (The Lord Rank Research Centre, High Wycombe, Bucks): No, not really—except to agree with Dr Cookson that it is a great pity the public could not have heard what Dr Widdowson had to say. The BBC may be making contact with her tomorrow.

E. M. Widdowson: Thank you for warning me!

J. J. Groen (Leiden University, Holland): You Dr Widdowson and Mr Chairman showed that to eat white or brown bread made no difference to the growth of children, but now claims are being made of a different nature about these breads. We must try to solve these problems by carefully planned experiments, just as you did in the past. The arguments put forward are indirect ones. One is that new diseases are arising in our population likely to be connected with new eating habits, the worst being the consumption of white bread. The new diseases, of course, may be due to something other than a decline in the quality of the bread eaten, whether brown or white; they may be related to the increase in the amount of saturated fat and in the amount of sucrose consumed. These problems will have to be solved.

E. M. Widdowson: May I thank Dr Kodicek for clarifying some remarks I made in my paper and remind the audience that they were quoted from a paper given by Dr Burkitt at a Symposium organised by the British Nutrition Foundation in 1972.

Chairman: We've got to stop because we've over-stepped our time. I can only finish by thanking the speakers for their papers and the audience for their tolerance and participation.

Session V

IMPROVEMENT

The Fortification of Flour

G. A. H. ELTON

Chief Scientific Adviser (Food),
Ministry of Agriculture, Fisheries and Food, London, UK

INTRODUCTION

Since man ceased to be a hunter-gatherer and came to rely on agriculture, cereals or root crops have formed the bulk of his food. In Asia the predominant cereal is rice, in Central America it is maize (corn), in much of Africa it is millet, but in the West wheat predominates. In fact it is understood that when we say flour, we mean wheat flour.

TABLE I

PERCENTAGE OF RECOMMENDED INTAKES OF SOME NUTRIENTS MET BY
SUFFICIENT FLOUR TO SATISFY ENERGY REQUIREMENTS OF UK WOMEN

Flour	Amount needed (oz/day)	Energy	Protein	Calcium	Iron	Thiamin	Riboflavin
Wholemeal	25	100	156	52	199	307	52
Breadmaking white (fortified)	22·6	100	137	187	110	221	14

From unpublished analyses by the Laboratory of the Government Chemist.

Flour is such a good source of nutrients that it is possible to live for long periods on bread (and water) alone. It can be calculated, for example, that if the 'average UK woman' were to eat sufficient wholemeal flour (equivalent to about 1·5 large loaves per day) to meet her energy requirements, she would also obtain (Table I) 156% of the protein, 52% of the calcium, 199% of the iron, 307% of the thiamin and 52% of the riboflavin which has been recommended by the Department of Health and Social Security (1969), and these recommendations contain generous safety margins. She would also obtain ample quantities of some other vitamins and minerals for which there are as yet no recommended intakes in the

249

UK; the limiting nutrient would probably be vitamin C. Table I also anticipates later sections of this paper by including comparisons with fortified white flour.

NUTRIENT LOSSES IN MILLING

If the grain is milled to produce white flour—a process which has been commonplace for centuries, and certainly since the 16th century for rich Englishmen—significant proportions of many trace elements (contaminants as well as nutrients) and vitamins are discarded. This is because they are concentrated in the pericarp, testa, aleurone layer and embryo of the wheat grain, while the remaining endosperm is richer in starch. The effects of extraction rate on nutrient levels have already been dealt with in this symposium by Dr Widdowson, and it is sufficient for my purpose to indicate (Table II) the small proportions of a wide variety of nutrients which are retained during the production of American 70% extraction flour.

TABLE II

PERCENTAGE OF NUTRIENTS RETAINED DURING
PRODUCTION OF AMERICAN 70% EXTRACTION FLOUR

Vitamins		Minerals	
Pantothenic acid	50	Selenium	84
Folic acid	33	Chromium	60
Vitamin B_6	28	Molybdenum	52
Thiamin	23	Calcium	40
Riboflavin	20	Copper	32
Nicotinic acid	19	Phosphorus	29
Vitamin E	14	Iron	24
		Potassium	23
		Zinc	22
		Sodium	22
		Magnesium	15
		Manganese	14
		Cobalt	12

Adapted from the Millfeed Manual, Millers National Federation, Chicago, 1967.

Not only is there this loss of nutrients during the milling process, but there may also be further losses from the action of flour improvers and other additives, and during subsequent baking of any flour into bread or other products. Some of the additives allowed in UK flour, other than wholemeal, are in fact nutrients, e.g. L-cysteine as an improving agent, and calcium phosphate and other salts as raising agents or yeast stimulators. Others, however, such as sulphur dioxide or the oxidising agents benzoyl peroxide, chlorine and chlorine dioxide (some of which are used only in cake or biscuit flours) may assist in the destruction of some of the vitamins. In practice the effects are small, the most important probably being the partial destruction of vitamin E by bleaching agents.

TABLE III

CONTRIBUTION OF SOME CEREAL PRODUCTS TO AVERAGE
HOUSEHOLD DIET IN GREAT BRITAIN

| Year | Consumption (oz/person/week) | | | Percentage of total energy derived from bread |
	White bread	Wholemeal bread	Flour	
1957	40·9	1·4	7·8	18·8
1962	36·1	0·8	6·2	16·8
1967	33·8	0·6	5·8	15·6
1972	29·6	0·45	5·4	14·4

From the Annual Reports of the National Food Survey Committee.

TABLE III(A)

PERCENTAGE OF UK INTAKE OF SOME NUTRIENTS
PROVIDED BY (FORTIFIED) FLOUR—AS SUCH,
AND IN FLOUR PRODUCTS, 1971

Calcium	22
Iron	23
Thiamin	29
Nicotinic acid	15

Derived from the National Food Survey.

Because of the considerable, although decreasing (Tables III and III(A)) importance of white flour in the British diet, it is possible that the losses of nutrients from the whole grain during milling may be important, not only with respect to bread but also in the whole mixed diet. Should this be the case, flour becomes an appropriate vehicle for fortification. Such fortification may be made on either of two principles:

(1) to restore to the level found in higher extraction or wholemeal flour those nutrients which are important; or

(2) to use flour as the means of rectifying nutritional deficiencies in a nation's diet, even if wheat is not ordinarily a major source of the nutrient in question.

In the UK, flour has been fortified by law with nutrients for both these reasons, and it is appropriate here to trace very briefly the history and the reasoning behind this fortification up to the present time, when the Food Standards Committee has just completed its Second Report on Bread and Flour.

HISTORY OF UK FLOUR FORTIFICATION

After the suppression by law of the adulteration of flour with chalk, bone, etc., in 1758, no nutrients were added to flour until after the beginning of the Second World War. Although millers had previously planned to add thiamin because of known generally low intakes, it was not until 1940 that this vitamin was required to be added, at the level of 200 mg per 280 lb sack of white flour (0·16 mg per 100 g). At this time, the extraction rate was raised in order to save valuable shipping space, the minima being 70% in September 1939, 73% in October 1939, 75% in April 1941, 85% (with minor exceptions) from March 1942 and 90% in May 1946. The higher levels followed recommendations of the Medical Research Council's Accessory Food Factors Committee which also recommended that bleaching agents and alkaline baking powders should not be used in case they impaired the nutritive value of the flour, and that calcium carbonate be added. This last recommendation was intended to counteract the action of phytic acid in the high extraction flour (for this constituent was thought to reduce calcium absorption) as well as to improve calcium intakes at a time when other calcium-rich foods, such as milk and cheese, were in short supply. From August 1943, then, after some initial trials, creta preparata was compulsorily added to flour at the rate of 7 oz per 280 lb (156 mg per 100 g) and when the extraction rate was raised to 90%, this quantity was doubled.

In January 1945, the Ministry of Food convened a 'Conference on the Post-War Loaf' which concluded that, because the amounts of four critical nutrients (thiamin, riboflavin, nicotinic acid and iron) which had been provided in the restricted war-time diet appeared adequate for health, intakes of these should be maintained. This could be achieved by fortification of flour. The levels required, if families derived one-third of their energy intake from bread, would be (per 100 g flour): thiamin 0·24 mg; riboflavin 0·14 mg; nicotinic acid 1·60 mg; and iron 1·65 mg. Except for riboflavin, for which wheat is not a major source, these additional standards (which are reached in 80% extraction flour and thus make the measure one of restoration rather than fortification) were required from 1953 when the extraction-rate of flour was again allowed to fall below 80%.

In 1960 the Food Standards Committee of the Ministry of Agriculture, Fisheries and Food reported on whether there should be more extensive control over the composition of bread and flour. Its nutritional conclusions, with advice from the then Ministry of Health, were that no changes were necessary, i.e. that thiamin, nicotinic acid and prescribed forms of iron should continue to be added at the same levels, that calcium addition should also continue although the evidence for its usefulness was not strong, and that there was no case for adding riboflavin, pyridoxine or any other nutrient. These conclusions were accepted, and the Bread and Flour Regulations (1963) became law and, as amended in 1972, are still in force.

FOOD STANDARDS COMMITTEE REPORT (1974)

In May 1974, the Food Standards Committee produced a Second Report on Bread and Flour, with nutritional advice from the Department of Health and Social Security. Its recommendations include:

(1) that fortification of all flour other than wholemeal with iron and thiamin should continue at present levels;
(2) that calcium addition to flour other than wholemeal, wheat malt flour and self-raising flour be continued at present levels, although not now to counteract generally poor intakes, nor to compensate for reductions in vitamin D supplements (two previous reasons) nor to replace the calcium lost in milling (Table II), but rather to maintain the present situation until the question of the association of softness of water supply and incidence of ischaemic heart disease is clarified;
(3) that there is no longer any need for addition of nicotinic acid when the diets of all sections of Britain already contain ample amounts; and
(4) that there is still no case for the addition of further nutrients, including lysine.

The last two recommendations were based on the general adequacy of the UK diet, which contains many nutritious foods beside bread, and not a simple comparison of the nutrient contents of white and higher extraction flours. This difference can be illustrated by comparing the total intakes of some nutrients when white flour is fortified and when it is not. This is shown in Table IV for families with four or more children with low incomes, for these not only have generally lower nutrient intakes than average, but also rely more heavily on bread. The prima facie case for continued fortification with iron and thiamin, and discontinuance of fortification with nicotinic acid, can clearly be seen. The Committee was aware that the nicotinic acid naturally present in wheat, as in other

G. A. H. ELTON

TABLE IV
PERCENTAGE OF RECOMMENDED INTAKES OF SOME NUTRIENTS
ACHIEVED BY LARGE LOW INCOME FAMILIES IN THE UK IN
1971 WHEN FLOUR IS, OR IS NOT, FORTIFIED

	Flour fortified as at present		All flour unfortified
Calcium	156		135
Iron	102		92
Thiamin	112		93
Nicotinic acid equivalents	165		157
Protein		105	
Riboflavin		117	
Vitamin C		147	
Vitamin A		175	
Vitamin D		63	

cereals, is largely unavailable, but that tryptophan can be converted into nicotinic acid. Furthermore, many trace nutrients are less well absorbed from wholemeal flour than from white flour.

PROBLEMS IN FLOUR FORTIFICATION

Fortification of flour in this way has posed two major problems. The first is that the form of calcium carbonate used has not been easy to add accurately to flour. This has been recognised in the Regulations, which specify the wide range of 235–390 mg per 100 g, but even then the Government Chemist found in 1965 that between 25 and 64% of flour samples, depending on mill capacity, were outside this range. The Food Standards Committee has endorsed a recommendation that a revised form of calcium carbonate be investigated.

The second problem is over the 'biological availability' of the iron used. The 1956 and 1963 Regulations specified the use of reduced iron or ferric ammonium citrate, and the 1972 amendments changed the specification for powdered iron and allowed ferrous sulphate, but the former has been used almost invariably in many other countries as well as the UK. That it is available to some extent was shown as long ago as 1936 by its ability to cure anaemia in dogs, but it is probably not as readily available to man as ferric ammonium citrate or ferrous sulphate (although the latter might also tend to induce development of rancidity in the flour). Factors affecting the availability of these forms of iron have been extensively studied in this and other countries (Ministry of Health, 1968), although more research is still needed. In mixed diets all appear poorly absorbed, especially metallic iron, and the absorption becomes almost negligible if the meal includes egg. If, however, higher concentrations of a more soluble iron compound were to be used there could be some risk, as is being widely discussed in the USA at present—for iron is also poorly excreted and diseases of iron excess are known. If the anaemia which occurs especially in women responds only little to the level of iron in flour, and is not generally harmful, it may be that in future iron therapy will be left to the medical profession.

INTERNATIONAL ASPECTS

In developing countries, where dependence on cereals is sometimes much greater than in the UK and where nutritional deficiencies occur with some frequency, fortification of the predominant cereal may be considered. This is difficult with polished rice, which is particularly deficient in thiamin; unless it is first parboiled, it would be necessary to coat the grain with a nutrient 'skin' which cannot be washed off, and added riboflavin may impart an unacceptable yellow colour. Maize (corn) is particularly deficient in nicotinic acid, but its lysine content at least can be increased by selective breeding. But beyond the replacement of those nutrients in which the cereal is deficient, there may be a case for adding nutrients in which the diet as a whole is deficient. This should not, of course, be the only action taken to improve a country's diet, but it can be one of the quickest and simplest.

Guidelines for food fortification have been laid down by the FAO and WHO (1971). It is noteworthy that cereals are among the recommended vehicles for all the nutrients considered (vitamin A, thiamin, riboflavin, nicotinic acid, vitamin C, vitamin D, calcium, iron, protein and amino acids) except one (iodine); this is especially appropriate for vitamins A and D, which are toxic in excess. In practice, however, although fortification of wheat flour with vitamin A and amino acids has been studied, the usual nutrients added are thiamin, nicotinic acid, iron and often riboflavin and calcium (Chopra, 1974).

Thanks are due to my colleague, Dr D. H. Buss, for his help in the preparation of this lecture.

REFERENCES

Chopra, J. G. (1974). 'Enrichment and fortification of foods in Latin America', *Amer. J. Public Health*, **64**, 19.
Department of Health and Social Security (1969). *Recommended Intakes of Nutrients for the United Kingdom*, HMSO, London.

FAO/WHO (1971). *Food Fortification*, World Health Organisation Technical Report Series No. 477.

Food Standards Committee (1974). *Second Report on Bread and Flour*, HMSO, London.

Millers National Federation (1967). *The Millfeed Manual*, Chicago.

Ministry of Agriculture, Fisheries and Food, *Household Food Consumption and Expenditure* (Annual Reports of the National Food Survey Committee), HMSO, London.

Ministry of Health (1968). *Iron in Flour*, HMSO, London.

DISCUSSION

Chairman: Will the possibility of shortages of milk and cheese in the near future be likely to influence the Ministry in their fortification policy for bread flour?

G. A. H. Elton: As far as calcium is concerned the average person in this country gets vastly in excess of their total recommended daily intake, something of the order of 180%, so it would have to be quite a severe deficiency before it was felt that we ought to put still more chalk into the flour.

D. Hollingsworth (British Nutrition Foundation, London): There are other nutrients like pyridoxine and folic acid and some trace elements too that nutritionists are beginning to worry about. I wonder whether the Food Standards Committee gave detailed consideration to these: indeed whether it is thinking about recommending the need for more experimental work?

G. A. H. Elton: As you know, the Food Standards Committee referred this whole question of supplementation of flour to the Committee on Medical Aspects of Food Policy. They themselves did not make the recommendation to which you refer but it was the expert committee which was appointed to advise them on this, that did consider such nutrients, for which at the moment there are no recommended daily intakes. There were no recommended daily intakes on which to base the view that more of these particular nutrients should be put in the flour. I believe that Sir George Godber, who was until recently Chief Medical Officer, considered that there is need for more information and research on nutrients in the diet other than the ones which I referred to and I imagine his successor, Dr Yellowlees is in agreement.

M. A. Cookson (RHM Bakeries Ltd, London): To the best of my knowledge, most other European countries, leastways in the Common Market, do not practise fortification of flour. I would very much welcome views on why this is not so.

G. A. H. Elton: I have explained why we consider it is necessary, but as we have delegates from other EEC countries in this room they might care to explain why it is not.

J. J. Groen (Leiden University, Netherlands): The problem I would like to raise, and which has been discussed repeatedly in the Netherlands, is the problem of calcium deficiency. It is customary in most committees, when we discuss questions like supplementation, to take the figure for daily requirements of a certain nutrient and then make a pronouncement whether or not the average allowance necessary for this should be achieved by supplementation. I do not know of a single nutrient where, if you only go by average figures, we get away so far from individual reality. It is the elderly which show signs of calcium deficiency as a prominent feature, even in our so-called affluent Western society. In them there is frequently widespread osteoporosis. I know that it is debatable whether all osteoporosis is the result of straight calcium deficiency or whether there is some additional factor, but it does mean that the recommended intake for calcium will not necessarily provide the net requirement of absorbed mineral in some elderly individuals. We have also to give special attention to the requirements of iron for women during their reproduction period.

G. A. H. Elton: Fragility of the neck of the femur in the elderly does worry medical authorities in this country and our Chief Medical Officer has again called for further research on the causes of this disease. This brings up one rather difficult philosophical point. Should we, in supplementing flour with nutrients, also be aiming to do a therapeutic job by, for example, attempting to cure everyone who has got iron deficiency anaemia with what we put into bread: should we put in enough calcium too, if it indeed proves to be the case that the elderly can be helped by specific prescription. My personal view is that it is best to aim to give a good general level of nutrition to the population as a whole, and to treat specific cases of diseases in minorities through the normal mechanism of the medical profession.

J. Edelman (R H M Research Ltd, High Wycombe, Bucks): Dr Elton, we have heard in two previous papers that the consumption of bread has fallen dramatically over the last decade or two. Does the Food Standards Committee feel that it now needs to have regulations about fortification of foods which are replacing bread in the British diet?

G. A. H. Elton: The phenomenon of falling bread consumption is one generally associated with increasing affluence normally. It is happening in this country, the USA, Canada, Australia and others. They are all apparently at different points on the same downward slope, and this is even true in countries where they make good, crusty bread such as in France. The average working class housewife is buying for her family fish fingers and baked beans and instant TV dinners and so on, and there just isn't enough room for the bread which you used to have in the old days, although I think the quality of our diet as a whole is probably increasing for the average person, for some children who live largely on lemonade and crisps it is not. The Food Standards Committee does not have any immediate intention to require supplementation of any other foodstuffs.

E. Kodicek (Strangeways Research Laboratory, Cambridge, U K): Further to the remarks of Professor Groen. As yet there is insufficient clinical evidence of a true calcium deficiency ever developing where there is adequate Vitamin D supplied. Secondly, osteoporosis of the elderly is a very vexed question which does not appear to depend on the amount of calcium supply. New observations indicate that there is a very low absorption of calcium by the elderly, which is not improvable by ordinary Vitamin D supplementation. This is the problem.

Advances in Breadmaking Technology

N. CHAMBERLAIN

*Baking Technology Group, Flour Milling and Baking
Research Association, Chorleywood, Herts, U K*

INTRODUCTION

The purpose of breadmaking is to present cereal flours to the consumer in an attractive, palatable and digestible form. At its simplest this is achieved by baking portions of a kneaded mixture of crushed grain and water, usually with salt added to enhance flavour, and cereals are still consumed in this form in many communities. However, credit for the first great technical innovation, the introduction of leavening, seems to belong to the Egyptians and may date from about 4000 B C. The superior palatability of yeast raised, or leavened, bread led to the almost universal adoption of the necessary breadmaking procedures in those countries where bread became the staple cereal based food.

It is extraordinary that there were no further notable technological innovations for nearly 6000 years. In 1857, Eliza Acton (Acton, 1857) published a book with the splendid title page: 'The English Bread Book for Domestic Use, Adapted to Families of Every Grade: containing the plainest and most minute instructions to the learner; practical receipts for many varieties of bread; with notices of the present system of adulteration, and its consequences; and of the improved baking processes and institutions established abroad'. She quoted the following passage from a contemporary French scientific review called 'The Cosmos':

'We might refuse to believe, if the fact were not forced on our conviction, that the most important and the most ancient of all the arts is the one which at the present day is the least advanced, and we might almost say, which is still in the rudest and most barbarous state; but enter into the first baking establishments of the capital, and follow in all its details the conversion of flour into bread! You will be grieved to see that, though incessantly repeated for thousands of years, the process has remained absolutely devoid of improvement; and you will turn away from the sight of it with a saddened spirit, even if it should not have inspired you with deep disgust.'

However, Eliza Acton went on to refer with approval to the recent

259

introduction in France of the first powered dough mixer, and a new type of oven in which the floor could be rotated by means of a winch to bring each section in turn to the oven mouth for loading and unloading. These were the first steps towards mechanisation of the traditional process, which was to dominate breadmaking technology for the next hundred years.

For mechanisation to reach the point where bread could be continuously manufactured on a series of inter-linked machines, working on fixed time cycles, parallel developments were necessary to control the natural variability of the raw materials. Important examples were the introduction of standardised yeast especially suitable for panary fermentation, the breeding of new wheats, the development of advanced milling techniques, and the rapid and controlled ageing of flour by the use of low levels of chemical oxidising agents.

The extent to which these measures have been adopted varies from country to country, depending on the type of end-product required, sociological attitudes and the pattern of retailing. For instance, a powerful consumer preference for fresh crusty bread, allied with a necessary willingness to buy it at least daily and pay a relatively high price, militates against centralised mass production and distribution over wide areas, and leaves baking in the hands of many thousands of small craftsmen.

Eliza Acton would have appreciated the irony that this picture is now more typical of France than of Britain.

BULK DOUGH FERMENTATION

It is convenient to illustrate a mechanised bakery, making bread by a process involving fermentation of the bulk dough after mixing, by describing a typical English plant bakery as it would have appeared 10–15 years ago.

Dough is first mixed from its basic ingredients of flour, yeast, salt and water in a low speed machine designed to imitate the action of the human hand and arm (Fig. 1). Mixing takes 15–20 min and the dough is then set aside to ferment in its bowl for 3 h at about 80 °F (27 °C). At the end of this period the dough is divided mechanically into pieces of the desired weight, moulded into a ball shape and allowed to rest for 15–20 min in what is known as first proof. The dough piece is remoulded into its final shape, placed in a baking tin if desired, and allowed to ferment for a further 45–60 min in a closed chamber with a controlled temperature of 100–120 °F (38–48 °C) and high relative humidity. This final proof is followed by baking for about 30 min at 430–450 °F (220–230 °C) in a tunnel, or 'travelling', oven. The baked loaves are removed from their tins and, especially if required for slicing and wrapping, cooled in an air-conditioned chamber to a centre crumb temperature of about 80 °F (27 °C) in a time of $2\frac{1}{2}$–3 h.

Many variations of detail from this procedure can be found, both within the UK and in other countries. In the USA, for example, the recipe commonly contains relatively high levels of fat, sugar and milk solids. The bulk dough fermentation stage is split into two parts, the 'sponge', which may contain about three-quarters of the total flour, two-thirds of the water and all the yeast, and is allowed to ferment for 4–5 h, and the dough, which results from mixing the rest of the ingredients into the sponge and is given a further 30 min of fermentation. The rest of the process is broadly similar to that already described, but the end-product is a sweet, soft loaf with a very high specific volume, perhaps 7 ml/g of bread compared with the 3·6–3·8 ml/g of the standard English loaf.

FIG. 1. Low speed mixer for bulk fermented doughs with lid raised. The single mixing arm moves backwards and forwards with a kneading action while the removable bowl revolves. Bowls full of fermenting dough occupy the foreground.

A different approach is illustrated by the 'Green Dough Process' of Holland (Smit, 1964), where bulk fermentation times are traditionally shorter than in the UK. The dough is given an extended mixing and is then divided and moulded into balls immediately. There then follows a greatly extended first proof of about 70 min, interrupted half-way through by a remoulding of the dough. Bulk dough fermentation has disappeared but has been replaced by extended fermentation of discrete lumps of dough. Total process time is not much reduced compared with traditional Dutch practice.

The ultimate in mechanisation of traditional bulk dough fermentation was reached in the Soviet Union in the form of the Rabinovich process (Goroschenko, 1957). Ingredients are continuously metered and mixed into a dough which is fed into the upper end of a sloping trough. The dough is propelled slowly down the trough by the intermittent rotation of a screw type impeller, taking about 4 h to traverse the full length. The fully fermented dough is then fed directly to the hopper of the mechanical divider.

It can be seen from the examples quoted that a breadmaking procedure involving long fermentation of the dough occupies a great deal of time and space. It is also wasteful, in that a proportion of the carbohydrate content of the flour is the substrate for the yeast fermentation and is being converted to volatile products, principally ethanol and carbon dioxide, which never appear as bread. Nevertheless, there is general agreement that if the bulk dough fermentation stage is merely omitted, and the dough taken straight from the mixer to the divider, then the bread is of inferior quality, being characterised by low volume, coarse crumb structure and poor keeping qualities. The bulk fermentation must therefore exert some beneficial effect on the properties of the dough which is subsequently reflected in the quality of the bread.

It is now generally agreed that the major beneficial effect is on the rheological properties of the dough. When it leaves the mixer it is 'short' and inelastic and cannot be inflated by gas. As fermentation proceeds it becomes more elastic, and able to hold entrapped gas in the form of finely dispersed, discrete bubbles, even during the rapid expansion that occurs in the oven. On the other hand, if fermentation is too prolonged, the dough again loses gas retaining ability. At the critical point, when the dough has the optimum combination of properties, it is said to be 'ripe' or 'mature' or 'developed'. This property is essential to the production of a bold, well-risen, fine-textured and resilient loaf. It was the discovery of the fact that dough could be developed by means other than yeast fermentation that eventually led to the explosion in breadmaking technology which has characterised the last 20 years.

MECHANICAL DOUGH DEVELOPMENT

The seeds of revolution were sown as far back as 1926 by the American workers Swanson and Working (Swanson and Working, 1926), who published a paper with the title: 'Mechanical modification of dough to make it possible to bake bread with only the fermentation in the pan'. They used a specially designed laboratory-scale mixer to demonstrate that intense mechanical working of the dough modified its structure in such a way that bulk fermentation could be omitted without loss of bread quality. A rapid commercial process was suggested but later withdrawn (Working, 1928), probably because success seemed to depend on the particular design of mixer and there was no known way of controlling the extent of the intense mechanical working.

The 'Do-Maker' process

It was not until the early 1950s that this principle of mechanical development was successfully exploited commercially, fittingly in the USA, as a result of research extending over a number of years by Dr J. C. Baker (Baker, 1954) of the Wallace and Tiernan Process Company. He called his process, and the mixing machinery devised for it, the 'Do-Maker'.

Dr Baker went one step further than simple mechanical development by combining it with continuous mixing in a two-stage process. The first step is to pre-ferment a sugar solution with yeast for a period of 2–4 h. This 'brew' also contains a number of other ingredients including, these days, a large proportion of the total flour in the recipe.

FIG. 2. A Wallace and Tiernan 'Do-Maker' plant. Fermented brew and melted fat are metered from tanks on the right, and flour from above, into the central continuous mixer. Dough is pumped through the pipe to the developer on the left and divided into the pans on the track below.

The brew is combined with the flour and melted fat in a continuous mixer to form the dough. The dough is pumped at a constant rate through a closed developer chamber, full of dough, in which revolve two large impellers. The dough absorbs a considerable quantity of mechanical energy during its passage through the developer, and this, together with the rapid action of added chemical oxidising agents, permits it to be extruded directly into the tin ready for final proof and baking.

A 'Do-Maker' plant is shown in Fig. 2 and comparison with Fig. 1 gives a strong impression of change from almost cottage industry to high technology.

The 'Do-Maker' process abolishes a number of traditional dough processing steps and clearly offers considerable savings of time and space. The 'Do-Maker' and closely related 'Amflow' (American Machine & Foundry Company, 1959) process are now reputed to be responsible for the manufacture of 30–40% of American bread and have been installed, though not always successfully, in a number of other countries having bakeries large enough to justify the high capital cost.

The first 'Do-Maker' was introduced into Britain in 1956, but considerable experimentation was necessary to find the best operating characteristics for producing bread more British in character than American. In particular there was no simple quantitative basis for controlling the all-important mechanical development stage at that time.

The 'Do-Maker' loaf had a characteristically fine and even crumb structure which did not prove widely popular with the British consumer and, though the equipment has now been modified to allow greater control of crumb structure, only a few 'Do-Makers' are now operating in Britain.

The Chorleywood bread process

In 1958, the British Baking Industries Research Association at Chorleywood, now absorbed into the Flour Milling and Baking Research Association, began to examine quantitatively those factors which seemed to be important in the mechanical development of bread doughs. An early and vitally important finding was that the quantity of mechanical work expended on the dough during mixing and development appeared to be fairly critical for optimum results. Furthermore, this optimum quantity of work was independent of the design of the mixer, provided it was imparted rapidly, and could be applied in a high-powered batch mixer just as effectively as in a continuous mixer. It was also sensibly constant over a wide range of flour properties and recipes.

Further discoveries followed which defined other conditions which had to be fulfilled for the production of good quality bread, and eventually these were collected together into a set of rules and published to the baking industry in 1961 under the name of the Chorleywood Bread Process (CBP). The CBP has now been described publicly on a number of occasions (e.g. see review by Chamberlain, 1969) but in addition to the total omission of bulk dough fermentation, its characteristic features are as follows:

(1) A work input during dough mixing of about 5 Wh/lb (11 Wh/kg) applied in a time of less than 5 min, preferably between 2 and 4. This quantity of energy is about 5–8 times that consumed in mixing a dough destined for bulk fermentation in a machine such as that illustrated in Fig. 1, and is applied in about a fifth of the time. This necessitates the use of a specially designed, high-powered batch or continuous mixer.

(2) The presence in the dough of 75 ppm (based on flour weight) of ascorbic acid, or its equivalent, as oxidising improver.

The use of low levels of oxidising agents has already been referred to, and their addition to flour and dough has been common practice for many years in traditional processes. An earlier effect is needed in rapid bread-making processes and the requirement can be met by using relatively high levels of slow-acting agents such as ascorbic acid or potassium bromate, or lower levels of fast-acting agents such as potassium iodate or azodicarbonamide, having proper regard to the legislation in each country. Ascorbic acid at 75 ppm was first used in Britain but was rapidly superseded by mixtures of ascorbic acid and potassium bromate to a similar total level, usually compounded with other ingredients such as fat, enzyme active soya flour and permitted emulsifier.

It may seem odd to refer to ascorbic acid as an oxidising agent whereas chemically it is a reducing agent. It takes an oxidising role in flour dough due to its rapid enzymic conversion to dehydroascorbic acid, the true oxidising agent (Melville and Shattock, 1938).

(3) The presence in the recipe of fat at a level of 0·7% of flour weight.

Fat has always been a common, but optional, ingredient of British bread. In the CBP its improving effect on gas retention by the dough during baking, and hence on loaf volume and crumb softness, is dramatic, and its presence is therefore necessary for good quality bread. The required level of the effective fraction of the fat may be as low as 0·05% of flour weight (Chamberlain et al., 1965).

(4) The absence of any brew or pre-ferment.

It has not been found that the use of a brew makes any appreciable contribution to the structure or flavour of British bread. The flavour aspect has been examined with particular care (e.g. Collyer, 1966) as the finding strikes a blow at the traditional view that bulk dough fermentation makes a vital contribution to bread flavour.

(5) The addition of extra water.

This is a necessary consequence of the retention of flour solids normally lost during bulk fermentation and the absence of the dough softening which takes place during that period. The extra water is needed to maintain normal dough consistency.

(6) The raising of the yeast level.

The yeast is fermenting less rapidly at the beginning of final proof in the CBP due to the absence of bulk fermentation. Sufficient extra is added to maintain final proof time constant.

The CBP is simple to operate by virtue of the precise automatic control which is substituted for the craft skill needed to judge the optimum development of a fermenting dough. Batch mixers are fitted with a watt-hour meter and counter unit and the circuitry is arranged in such a way that the mixer is switched off automatically when the dough has absorbed the optimum quantity of energy. Modern mixers have a completely automatic sequence of ingredient weighing and addition, mixing and development, and discharge of the dough, initiated by a demand signal from the divider.

Adoption of the CBP was rapid in the UK. The first large commercial mixer began operation in 1962 and 10 years later 75–80% of all British bread was being made in this way. The CBP is in use in about twenty other countries, though adaptations are sometimes required and it is not always successful as yet, notably in the commercial production of the standard pan bread of North America.

The advantages of the CBP over the traditional British 3-hour bulk dough fermentation system, described earlier, can be summarised as follows:

(1) A saving of about 60% of time in the conversion of raw materials into bread.

(2) A saving of about 75% of space in the dough room, previously occupied by fermenting dough.

(3) A reduction of 75% of the quantity of dough in the course of processing at any time, and hence a reduced risk of loss in the case of plant stoppage.

(4) An increased yield of about 4% of bread due to retention of flour solids, extra water and yeast, and increased accuracy in dividing the denser, more uniform dough.

(5) A net cash saving on raw material costs stemming from the increased yield.

(6) Flour of lower protein content can be used without loss of organoleptic bread quality.

(7) A lower rate of staling in the bread.

The first five of these advantages have now been verified in practice but were predictable. Advantages (6) and (7) were an unexpected bonus of considerable importance.

The CBP had been developed, and was first used commercially, with typical British bread flours of about 12% protein content, milled from grists containing about 60% of strong Canadian wheat and a mixture of weaker wheats, about half of which was also imported. Commercial experience, backed up by detailed experimental work, led to the conclusion that the CBP could produce better bread in terms of volume, rate and extent of staling (Axford *et al.*, 1968), and other characteristics than could bulk fermentation, especially from weaker flours (Collins, 1966). The effect was such that when changing to the CBP the baker could simultaneously change to a flour containing 1·0–1·5% less protein without significant loss of bread quality. This meant that, given good parent wheats, the milling grist for British bread flour need only contain about 35% of imported strong wheat and 65% of the weaker wheats, most of which could be drawn from domestic or west European sources in good harvest years. The resultant flour would have a protein content of about 10·5%. In practice, flours from the CBP still contain about 11% protein, though the content of English wheat in the grist may now be about 50%.

Weaker flours usually have lower water absorbing powers, due to lower contents of protein and starch granules damaged in the milling process, and frequently have higher levels of α-amylase activity. The water absorption can be restored to some extent by careful adjustment of milling techniques to bring about a judicious increase in damaged starch, but a high level of α-amylase activity is at least as damaging to the quality of CBP bread as it is to bulk fermented bread (Collins, 1971).

This ability of the CBP to allow the use of greater proportions of weaker wheats in the bread grist has assumed very great economic importance to the UK in recent years, due to the large price differences which exist between strong American and Canadian wheats and the cheaper wheats available in western Europe.

CHEMICAL OR ACTIVATED DOUGH DEVELOPMENT

At much the same time that mechanical development was being quantified in Britain as the CBP, a second alternative to bulk fermentation as a means of developing dough made its appearance in the USA. First introduced by Henika and Zenner (1960) as 'instant dough development', it made use of a balanced blend of reducing and oxidising agents added as dough ingredients. It appeared that the beneficial reactions within and between flour protein molecules, which occurred slowly during the course of bulk dough fermentation, could be made to occur rapidly by this combination of chemicals.

Though a variety of reducing and oxidising agents could be employed (Henika and Rodgers, 1962) the first proprietary additive, named 'Reddi-Sponge', contained a mixture of the reducing amino acid L-cysteine and potassium bromate, together with a large proportion of whey powder. The dough containing the additive is mixed on a conventional machine for a carefully controlled time, allowed a short period of 30–40 min of bulk fermentation and processed immediately. The 4–5 h of sponge fermentation, conventional in the USA, is entirely omitted.

The principle of chemical development was further explored in Britain (Chamberlain *et al.*, 1966; Coppock, 1966) and modifications made to suit local circumstances. L-cysteine, at about 35 ppm of flour, remained the reducing agent of choice, the preferred oxidant was a mixture of potassium bromate at 40 ppm and ascorbic acid at 50 ppm, and the whey powder of 'Reddi-Sponge' was omitted. The Chorleywood workers christened the process 'Activated Dough Development' (ADD) (Chamberlain, 1969; Collins, 1972). They confirmed that low speed mixers, such as that in Fig. 1, could be used, that a short rest period before dividing was beneficial, and that a number of features of the CBP were also applicable, for instance, the requirements for fat and extra water and yeast.

The advantages of ADD over bulk fermentation should be the same as those of the CBP in terms of time, space and yield, though mixing times are still long. The baker can avoid the purchase of a special mixer for the CBP, and this should make ADD attractive to the smaller baker. However, producing bread of the highest quality is not easy with ADD and it is not now believed that a change can be made to a weaker flour without noticeable loss of bread quality, an important feature of the CBP.

THE FUTURE

Figure 3 summarises, in diagrammatic form, the processing stages and the times that they occupy of four major breadmaking processes to which reference has been made. Fermentation of the dough is shown as ceasing after 10 min of baking, and the dramatic reduction of total process time from raw materials to baked bread, which has resulted from the application of mechanical and chemical development, is clearly seen.

The diagram shows that second proof, during which the vital inflation of the dough piece before baking occurs, though at the expense of fermentable carbohydrates, has remained constant throughout. It has already been suggested (Oakes, 1961) that this could be replaced by injecting gas under pressure into the dough during mixing, though there are severe technical problems in presenting the product in conventional loaf form and in restoring the flavour lost by the removal of the yeast from the recipe.

The largest block of time and space occupied in a modern plant bakery, which is not shown on the diagram, and is common to all the processes, is the bread cooler. This is a particularly important processing stage where the bread is to be sliced. The constraints imposed in Britain by the dimensions of the loaf and the required slice thickness mean that slicing is accomplished with difficulty at loaf centre temperatures above 80 °F (27 °C), when the crumb is still very soft. Bread is a poor conductor of heat and cooling takes $2\frac{1}{2}$–3 h in Britain. Times are shorter and slicing can be carried out at higher temperatures in different circumstances, such as prevail in the USA. It is not surprising, therefore, that many attempts have been made to accelerate cooling, and the possibilities of cooling under vacuum, thus making use of the latent heat of vaporisation of water, are currently being re-examined.

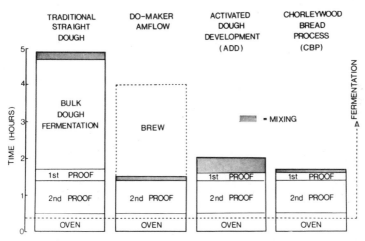

FIG. 3. Processing stages and times for four breadmaking processes.

One of the most severe limitations on the use of many wheats for breadmaking is the high α-amylase activity of the flours milled from them. Excessive α-amylase activity is highly deleterious to bread quality as it breaks down starch gelatinised during baking to produce sticky dextrins and release previously bound water. If the dough could be heated evenly and rapidly throughout its bulk, instead of waiting for the heat to penetrate slowly from the outside as in conventional baking, then it was reasoned that α-amylase could be rapidly inactivated. A unique means of heating in this way is offered by high frequency electromagnetic radiation, and experiments are now actively in progress to perfect a method of baking by a combination of microwave radiation and radiant or convected heat (Chamberlain, 1973). Preliminary results are encouraging and cost considerations favour the process in those areas, such as Britain, where wheat of high α-amylase activity is cheaper and relatively abundant.

It is tempting to speculate that if the process could be perfected then wheat breeders would no longer need to regard high natural α-amylase as an adverse feature in their new strains, and a wet harvest would not be regarded by farmers and millers as a total disaster.

CONCLUSION

It has only been possible, within the time and space available, to deal with the most significant advances that have taken place in breadmaking technology.

It is hoped, however, that enough examples have been quoted of the startling progress made during recent years to refute the 19th century accusation of 'The Cosmos' that: 'the most important and the most ancient of all the arts . . . is still in the rudest and most barbarous state'.

REFERENCES

Acton, E. (1857). *Acton's Bread Book*, Longman, Brown, Green, Longmans and Roberts, London.

American Machine & Foundry Company (1959). 'A Method and Apparatus for Developing Dough', British Patent No. 808,836.

Axford, D. W. E., Colwell, K. H., Cornford, S. J. and Elton, G. A. H. (1968). 'Effect of loaf specific volume on the rate and extent of staling in bread', *J. Sci. Fd Agric.*, **19**, 95.

Baker, J. C. (1954). 'Continuous dough mixing', *Bakers Wkly*, **161** (11), 60.

Chamberlain, N. (1969). 'Baking: the significance of modern processing methods', in *Proteins as Human Food* (Ed. R. A. Lawrie), Butterworths, London, p. 300.

Chamberlain, N. (1973). 'Microwave energy in the baking of bread', *Food Trade Review*, **43** (9), 8.

Chamberlain, N., Collins, T. H., Dodds, N. J. H. and Elton, G. A. H. (1966). 'Chemical development of bread doughs', *Milling*, **146** (13), 319.

Chamberlain, N., Collins, T. H. and Elton, G. A. H. (1965). 'The Chorleywood Bread Process: improving effects of fat', *Cereal Sci. Today*, **10**, 415.

Collins, T. H. (1966). 'Flour properties and the Chorleywood Bread Process', *Milling*, **146** (12), 296.

Collins, T. H. (1971). 'The importance of damaged starch', *Milling*, **153** (4), 21.

Collins, T. H. (1972). 'The uses of L-cysteine and azodicarbonamide in bread-making', *Br. Baker*, **164** (26), 18.

Collyer, D. M. (1966). 'Fermentation products in bread flavour and aroma', *J. Sci. Fd Agric.*, **17**, 440.

Coppock, J. B. M. (1966). 'The use of L-cysteine in no-time doughs', *Milling*, **146** (13), 317.

Goroschenko, M. K. (1957). 'Continuous dough making', *Backer u. Konditor*, **11** (6), 11.

Henika, R. G. and Rodgers, N. E. (1962). 'Process for Making Yeast Leavened Bakery Products and Composition Therefor', US Patent No. 3,053,666.

Henika, R. G. and Zenner, S. F. (1960). 'Baking with the new instant dough development process', *Bakers' Digest*, **34** (3), 36.

Melville, J. and Shattock, H. T. (1938). 'The action of ascorbic acid as a bread improver', *Cereal Chem.*, **15**, 201.

Oakes, E. T., Corporation (1961). 'Improvements in the Manufacture of Bread Dough', British Patent No. 867,428.

Smit, J. A. P. (1964). 'Green dough method of breadmaking', *Br. Baker*, **148** (16, 20.

Swanson, C. O. and Working, E. B. (1926). 'Mechanical modification of dough to make it possible to bake bread with only the fermentation in the pan', *Cereal Chem.*, **3**, 65.

Working, E. B. (1928). 'The action of phosphatides in bread dough', *Cereal Chem.*, **5**, 223.

DISCUSSION

J. G. Ponte (ITT Continental Baking, New York): I wonder if you can make any comments on the ability of the Chorleywood process to make bread, because you know bread in USA—50–60% is made by the old 'Sponge and Dough' process.

N. Chamberlain: The CBP has its failures, which is hardly surprising, and one of the failures which is of the most concern to us is that it has by and large failed to make the standard of pan bread required by the USA.

In fact we can take all American ingredients and pans, indeed everything American, and bring all these back to Chorleywood and use a small scale mixer and make bread which Americans agree is indistinguishable from their classical pan bread. Mr Collins, the head of our bread bakery—whose name should certainly be coupled with my own and Dr Elton's in the development of the CBP—and I have worked on a number of occasions in commercial bakeries in the USA. We have always achieved the specific volume that is required and the bread has had all the desirable qualities, with the exception of one and this is the necessary desired fineness of the crumb cell structure. I suspect that this is basically a problem of mixing action, because as J. C. Baker showed the yeast cell is incapable of originating its own gas cell in the dough. The mixer has to put in the gas cell nuclei which are expanded by fermentation, and we have got a mixer basically which puts in the number and size distribution of gas cells which are expanded to the specific volume of British bread, and that is fine. But in American bread you expand up to twice the volume and it is inevitable that the texture will open up just beyond the point at which it is acceptable. If one could devise a mixing action which could give you many more gas bubbles, I think the problem might well be solved.

T. Jakubczyk (Warsaw University): In the ADD process the reducing agent is in the form of cysteine and then an oxidising agent is added. In my opinion, they probably should not be added together or, if so, they should be added in sequence? Probably first the reducing and then the oxidising agent, am I right?

N. Chamberlain: They are in fact put in together, although some precautions have to be taken. If you put the cysteine and the oxidising agents together in solution and leave them in solution, then one is likely to run into trouble. Not least that if it dries out the bakery might well go up in flames, but in fact you can use them in a solid diluted form. You can have this mixture of oxidising and reducing agents and the thing works very well indeed. The assumption is, I think, that cysteine acts quite rapidly to break disulphide linkages which are subsequently encouraged to reform by the action of the chosen combination of oxidising agents. It is interesting, I think, that if you choose as the oxidising agent something which is very rapid, potassium iodate or azodicarbonamide, then you do run into real difficulty and I imagine that one is getting an interaction between the reducing and the oxidising agent rather than their sequential action on the protein.

P. W. Russell Eggitt (Spillers Ltd, Cambridge, UK): I would suspect as, Dr Chamberlain says, that it is one particular aspect of the mixing action in America that is different. The Americans have become used to the type of bread produced by the 'Do-Makers' and the 'Amflow'. In their developer—the mixing takes place under very considerable pressure, something like $40 lb/in^2$, so some of the gases in the dough are going in to pre-solution to be released when the dough comes out of the developer in the form of very minute points which form the nucleus of the gas and from which you get a very fine structure—the reverse happens in Britain of course, which is the reason why that bread failed commercially over here.

N. Chamberlain: Yes, well, thank you very much Dr Russell Eggitt, but in fairness, I think I will add that the fineness of texture that we failed to match was not in fact, from a 'Do-Maker' or 'Amflow' process in the USA. We failed to match the fineness of texture from a straightforward Sponge and Dough classical traditional process and I think the reason is that the structure is put into that sort of dough by the action of the moulder which is very sophisticated in the USA.

Chairman: In conclusion we would like to express to our two speakers, and all those who have taken part in this discussion, our very sincere thanks. This has been a very fine series of papers.

Session VI

WHEAT AGRONOMY

Wheat Agronomy—North America

E. G. HEYNE

Department of Agronomy, Kansas State University,
Manhattan, Kansas, USA

Wheat (Triticum spp.) is not a native of the Western Hemisphere. It was first brought to North America by early Spanish settlers in the 16th century. English colonists seeded wheat soon after landing at Jamestown, Va., USA, in 1607. Many immigrants to North America brought wheat with them, mostly from northern European countries. A major introduction was in the 1870s by Mennonite immigrants from Southern Russia who brought Turkey hard red winter wheat with them (Quisenberry and Reitz, 1974).

TABLE I
RECENT WHEAT PRODUCTION IN NORTH AMERICA[a]

Country	Hectares (1000)		Metric tons (1000)	
	1967–71	1973	1967–71	1973
Canada	9 421	10 021	15 106	17 112
Mexico	715	720	2 005	2 000
USA	20 363	21 803	40 694	46 577
Other	37	48	32	45
Total	30 536	32 592	57 837	65 734
World	215 507	216 218	314 787	366 950

[a] Source: World Agriculture Production and Trade, FAS, US Department of Agriculture, March 1974.

Wheat is now the major cereal grain in the Great Plains of North America, from east of the Rocky Mountains to about the 750 mm rainfall region. Winter wheat (fall sown) predominates in the southern Great Plains; while spring sown wheat predominates in the northern Great Plains (Fig. 1).

North America generally produces about one-sixth to one-fifth of the world wheat (Table I), with about half available for export. The USA, in recent years, has been the world's largest exporter of wheat, and

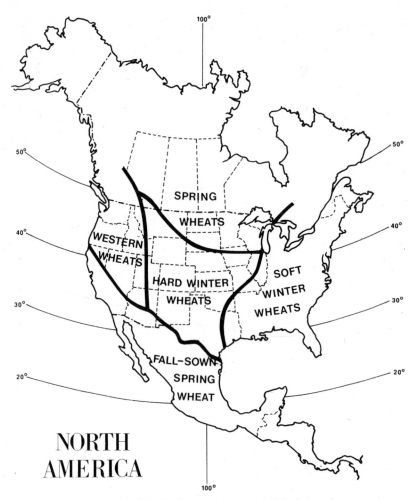

FIG. 1. Distribution of wheat-types in North America.

Canada always is a top exporter. Wheat, a plant immigrant to North America, has made good on its vast Great Plains prairie lands.

All types and species of what have been grown in North America, but the common wheat, *Triticum aestivum* L. em. Thell. spp. vulgare (Vill., Host) MacKey; club wheat, *T. aestivum* spp. compactum (Host) MacKey; and durum wheat, *T. durum* Desf. are the only ones now grown commercially.

Percentages of each type grown in the USA in 1969 were (Reitz *et al.*, 1972):

	%
T. vulgare, Hard Red Winter	59·5
T. vulgare, Hard Red Spring	13·4
T. vulgare, Soft Red Winter	11·5
T. vulgare, White Wheats	7·7
T. compactum, Club Wheats	1·3
T. durum, Durum Wheat	6·6

Most Canadian wheat is hard red spring. The Mexican crop has been a mixture but the harder spring-type wheats have increased there.

Hard red spring and winter types are the classes most available for export. White wheats grown in the Pacific Northwest and durum wheat from the northern Great Plains also enter world markets.

The variation in climate and soils in North America results in wheat qualities for many uses, but primarily in food products. That used as animal feed varies annually with prices and quality. Relatively little is used for industrial purposes.

The soft wheats and Pacific Northwest wheats are generally low in protein content (8–10%). Wheats grown in the drier areas (Great Plains) generally have higher contents. The protein content of hard red winter wheats in lower rainfall areas varies from 9 to 13%. Winter wheat grown farther north in Montana and Alberta has protein content as high as 16%. In the northern Great Plains spring-sown wheats average from 11 to 15% protein.

Wheat is a cool season crop but it is one of the better domesticated species for the hot, semi-arid regions because its major growth takes place during the cooler season. In southern North America ((Mexico and southwestern USA) where winter hardiness is not a factor) spring wheats are seeded in the fall. Farther north fall-sown wheat must have cold hardiness to survive the winter. These fall-sown types that survive the winter yield better than spring-sown types.

Cool nights permit spring-sown wheat in the northern Great Plains to grow through the hot summer months.

Three reference books on wheat in North America give many details on the wheat plant: Leonard and Martin (1963); Peterson (1965); Quisenberry and Reitz (1967).

MANAGEMENT

Because of climatic diversity where wheat is grown, different cultural practices have developed (Schlehuber and Tucker, 1967). The total potential value of wheat production generally is lower than for maize, sorghum, cotton, or soybeans, where those crops do well, wheat is included only in rotations to help distribute labour or because wheat production generally requires less input: seedbed preparation, weed control, and harvest costs. Large efficient machines are well suited to wheat production. The 1974 Kansas wheat crop of 900 000 metric tons on 444 400 hectares was harvested as it matured and most of the land for the 1975 crop was cultivated at least once within one week of harvest. Such management makes wheat a competitive crop, especially in the Great Plains.

In the humid areas of 750 mm rainfall or more, wheat or some other crop is grown annually. Where it is fall-sown wheat has been difficult to use in rotations because it is on the land 8–9 months. However, early maturing cultivars and late seeding now permits crop rotation. Winter wheat generally does well after soybeans but poorly after maize. Wheat responds well to fertilisers; phosphorus and nitrogen are required to produce satisfactory crops in humid areas. Amounts vary, so soil tests should precede nutrient purchases. Thirty-five to 57 kg of phosphorus and 43–115 kg of nitrogen per hectare are common in humid areas.

Continuous wheat is common in the Great Plains where rainfall varies from 600 to 800 mm. Early seedbed preparation, complete or partial incorporation of stubble, and added fertiliser have been successful for the last 30 years. Twenty-two to 43 kg of phosphorus and 35–70 kg of nitrogen per hectare generally are sufficient.

Where rainfall is from 200 to 600 mm summer fallow is common. In the southern Great Plains 200 mm of rainfall is not enough to produce wheat because evaporation and transpiration are too high, but well-managed summer fallow schemes in the northern Great Plains produce wheat with 200 mm of rainfall.

Even in the drier areas wheat responds to N and P fertilisation and high applications are required for maximum results under irrigation. Use of N and P fertilisers in lower rainfall areas has increased greatly. In 1945 42 200 Mton of all fertilisers were used in Kansas, while in 1972 1 131 800 Mton or an increase of 27 times more (Hargett, 1973). In the USA, fertilisers used increased only 3 times from 1945 to 1972. A large percentage of fertiliser in Kansas is used on wheat. One hundred and ninety-three times more N was applied in Kansas in 1972 than in 1945; for P_2O_5 it was 15 times the 1945 level. Occasionally N depresses wheat yields in drier areas, but I expect use of both N and P to increase in such areas.

Dryland wheat yields vary from failures to about 55 quintals per hectare in the Great Plains. Yields are consistently 27 or more quintals per hectare in the humid areas, like the maize belt (Indiana).

Much wheat is irrigated in western Mexico and western USA. The greatest increase in wheat production in North America likely is in Sonora, Sinaloa, and Baja California, states of Mexico. Irrigation, fertiliser, and new cultivars are responsible for Mexico's progress.

However, water is the key input. Wheat production in Mexico went from less than 1 200 000 Mton in 1960 to more than 3 200 000 Mton in 1969 without an appreciable change in acreage (CIMMYT Annual Report, 1970–71).

Irrigation results have been less dramatic in other North American areas because irrigated wheat does not compete with maize, sorghum, cotton, and alfalfa where those crops are adapted.

Where the climate is suitable and the proper cultivars and cultural practices are used, consistently high wheat yields are obtained. In some areas of the Pacific Northwest, 100 quintals per hectare are expected with irrigation. The record 133 quintals per hectare was produced in the state of Washington in 1965 (Reitz, 1967). In the southern Great Plains high temperatures limit farm yields, under irrigation, to generally less than 50 quintals per hectare. Farther north, especially in the inter-mountain areas, similar genotypes often exceed 68 quintals per hectare.

Young wheat plants, high in protein (20–28%), are a highly nutritive pasture crop. Texas and Oklahoma have extensive cereal pasture-livestock programmes based on wheat used only for forage. When weather conditions are favourable, some is left and harvested as a grain crop.

Farther north (Kansas) winter wheat is grazed during November–March when sufficient growth occurs. Some years as much as 60% of the acreage is grazed but in other seasons none is available. Wheat offers an excellent supplement for sheep and cattle grazing when available and, if properly managed, its grain yield is reduced little or none by grazing. Plant breeders are developing cultivars that are suited for this dual purpose that are especially effective under irrigation.

Cereal crops are grazed in southeastern USA but wheat in that area is generally plagued with diseases so other cereals are used.

PROTECTION PRACTICES

Weed control in wheat generally is managed through good cultural practices. Winter wheat competes well with most weeds because it is seeded in the fall and covers the soil rapidly in the spring. Winter annual grasses that can become problems, include cheat, *Bromus secalinus L.* and occasionally other Bromus spp., and jointgrass, *Aegilops cylindrica.* Mustards and corncockle, broadleafed winter annuals, grow with wheat. Perennial weed species are common in some areas, especially bindweed, *Convolvulus arvensis* and Canadian thistle. They require special eradication methods or chemical control. *Avena fatua*, wild oats, is a problem in the northern Great Plains. Like wheat, bindweed and jointgrass (*Aegilops*) were introduced into North America by immigrants.

Likewise, nearly all wheat diseases and several insects have been introduced. Chemicals (Rowell, 1972) and breeding for resistance are controls as detailed in ASA Monograph No. 13, Wheat and Wheat Improvement, Chapters 8–12.

WHEAT CULTIVARS

Wheat culture began along the Atlantic coast early in the 17th century and moved westward with settlers. Earliest settlers brought wheat from England, Netherlands and Sweden. Spanish wheats also came into North America, and the cultivar Sonora persists today through progeny in Mexico and southwestern USA.

The two most important cultivars responsible for the development of Great Plains prairie lands were Marquis hard red spring wheat and Turkey hard red winter wheat. Marquis was bred in Canada (Saunders, 1912); but Turkey was introduced directly from southern Russia (Quisenberry and Reitz, 1974).

Marquis originated from the cross Hard Red Calcutta/Red Fife at the Dominion Department of Agriculture at the Central Experimental Farm, Ottawa, Ontario, Canada. An Ontario farmer selected Red Fife in 1842 from a lot of winter wheat obtained from Europe. A. P. Saunders made the cross in 1892 at the Agassiz farm but progeny were transferred to Ottawa for further study. The final selection in 1903 was released to farmers in 1909. Because Marquis was earlier than most other spring wheats and the growing season in western Canada was short, this one cultivar increased wheat production phenomenally. It was the leading hard red spring wheat in Canada and the USA until the 1930s.

Turkey wheat's introduction into Kansas in 1874 had no immediate impact in the southern Great Plains as Marquis did in the northern Great Plains because many of the earlier settlers continued to grow the soft red winter and spring wheats they brought with them. During the 1890s Turkey wheat's winter hardiness was recognised by farmers and acreage increased rapidly. The first reliable survey of cultivars in 1919 (Clark et al., 1922) reported Turkey on more than 840 000 hectares in 33 US states (about 30% of the US wheat acreage). It was the leading US wheat cultivar until 1944.

We see that two cornerstones of wheat production in the Great Plains dominated the wheat area that was earlier called the Great American Desert, said to be unfit for cultivation, uninhabitable by people depending on agriculture, and fit only for grazing.

Marquis and Turkey, through their progeny, still dominate the cultivars in the Great Plains so most of the export wheats of North America have these two cultivars in their parentage.

Reciprocal exchange of germplasm began when John H. Parker at the

Kansas Station crossed a selection of Turkey with Marquis and developed the winter cultivar Tenmarq. H. K. Hayes and others (1936) used Kanred wheat, a selection from Turkey, to develop the spring cultivar Thatcher. The cross was Marquis/Iumillo × Marquis/Kanred. Thatcher was extensively grown in the northern Great Plains and was used as a parent of many crosses. Tenmarq became the leading hard red winter wheat in the USA and it was also used extensively in crosses.

All hard red winter wheat cultivars grown in the southern Great Plains trace their parentage to Turkey. Turkey was also used widely in the western wheat region because it resisted bunt, so its germplasm is represented in many cultivars grown in North America. Turkey wheat is also related to the 'Green Revolution' cultivars (Reitz and Salmon, 1968) as one of the parents of Norin 10, the Japanese semidwarf cultivar that has been used so widely to introduce short stature into worldwide breeding programmes. Marquis is also included among the 'Green Revolution' cultivars through hard red spring wheats used in the CIMMYT programme in Mexico. From Mexico, semidwarf cultivars carrying germplasm from Marquis and Turkey have gone to many other countries, especially Pakistan and India.

Of the 85 or more hard red winter cultivars grown, Scout and related types, Centurk, and Triumph-types comprise about half of the acreage in 1973. Of about 60 cultivars of hard red spring wheat, Neepawa, Manitou, Selkirk, Chris and Fortuna are among the leading cultivars.

Many cultivars introduced early were soft red winters. Their special use in pastries, crackers, and other similar products makes them the third most important class of wheat in North America. The Indiana Experiment Station has been the centre of high quality breeding of soft red winter wheats. There are many soft wheat cultivars, because the environmental variability increases the advantages of locally adapted types. Monon, Arthur and Blueboy II are grown extensively. Recent releases from Indiana are Arthur 71, Abe and Oasis. They probably have more protective genes than any other cultivars as they resist leaf rust, stem rust, Septoria, smuts, soilborne mosaic virus, and Hessian fly. Also they are tolerant to aluminium, and have excellent strong short straw, good quality, and they yield well.

Many types are grown in the western region, including winter wheats that are hard or soft with red or white grain; club wheats; and hard red and white spring wheats, and durum wheats are now being encouraged. NuGaines, a white wheat, is one of the most extensively grown cultivars in the western region.

Durum wheat has been largely concentrated in small areas in Saskatchewan and Manitoba, Canada, and in the states of North Dakota and Minnesota, especially in the Red River Valley. North American durums have good quality but smaller grain than desired by export markets. Wells, Leeds, Hercules, Wascosa and Stewart 63 are among the leading durum cultivars. Semidwarf durums will soon be produced commercially. Many semidwarf cultivars developed by CIMMYT in Mexico are grown almost exclusively in Mexico and southwestern USA. Among them are Siete Cerros, Inia 66, Sonora 64, Cajeme 71 and several Bluebird related lines.

The development of wheat agriculture in the last 100 years in the Great Plains has been an outstanding contribution to the never ending struggle for food production. Its development brought native lands under cultivation; spurred organised research in plant, soil and water management; cultivar development; plant protection practices; and machinery improvement. Several disciplines made significant inputs and no one segment of wheat production could have succeeded without the other.

More than 200 years ago Jonathan Swift, in Gulliver's Travels, had the King of Brobdingnag say, 'That whosoever could make two ears of corn or two blades of grass to grow upon a spot of ground where only one grew before, would deserve better of mankind, and do more essential service to his country, than the whole race of politicians put together'. Agricultural research, through basic and applied sciences is doing that in many areas of the world. But much remains to be done with wheat and other crops.

REFERENCES

CIMMYT, *Annual report on maize and wheat improvement*, 1970–71.

Clark, J. A., Martin, J. H. and Ball, C. R. (1922). *Classification of American Wheat Varieties*, US Dept. Agric. Bulletin 1074.

Hargett, Norman L. (1973). 1972 *Fertilizer Summary*, National Fertiliser Development Centre, Tennessee Valley Authority, Muscle Shoals, Alabama.

Hayes, H. K., Ausemus, E. R., Stakman, E. C., Bailey, E. C., Bramberg, H. K., Markley, R. H., Crim, M. C. and Levine, M. N. (1936). *Thatcher Wheat*, Minn. Agr. Expt. Sta. Bul. 325, 36 pp.

Leonard, W. H. and Martin, J. H. (1963). *Cereal Crops* (Part III. Wheat), Collier-Macmillan, New York, Chapters 11–16, pp. 275–446.

Peterson, R. F. (1965). *Wheat—Botany, Cultivation, and Utilization*, Leonard Gill Books, London; Interscience Publishers, New York.

Quisenberry, K. S. and Reitz, L. P. (1974). 'Turkey wheat: the cornerstone of our empire', *Agric. History*, **48**, 98–114.

Quisenberry, K. S. and Reitz, L. P. (Eds) (1967). *Wheat and Wheat Improvement*, Monograph No. 13, American Society of Agronomy, Madison, Wisconsin, USA.

Reitz, L. P. (1967). 'World distribution and importance of wheat', *Wheat and Wheat Improvement* (Eds. K. S. Quisenberry and L. P. Reitz), ASA Monograph No. 13, Madison, Wisconsin, USA, pp. 1–18.

Reitz, L. P., Lebsock, K. L. and Hasenmyer, G. D. (1972). 'Distribution of the varieties and diseases of wheat in the United States in 1969', US Dept of Agric., Statistical Bulletin No. 475.

Reitz, L. P. and Salmon, S. C. (1968). 'Origin, history, and use of Norin 10 wheat', *Crop Sci.*, **8**, 686–689.

Rowell, J. B. (1972). 'Fungicidal management of pathogen populations', *J. Envir. Quality*, **1**, 216–220.

Saunders, C. E. (1912). *Report of the Dominion Cerealists*, Canada Expt. Farm Repts, 1911–12.

Schlehuber, A. M. and Tucker, Billy B. (1967). *Culture of Wheat* (Ed. R. S. Quisenberry and L. P. Reitz), ASA Monograph No. 13, Madison, Wisconsin, USA, pp. 117–179.

DISCUSSION

H. S. Darling (Wye College, Kent): Could you comment on the influence of climate on the post-harvest storage of wheat in the USA? You seem to be able to get away with storage periods a lot longer than elsewhere.

E. G. Heyne: Generally there is no problem in the Great Plains. At harvest time, although there are rains these are followed usually by wind, and moisture content falls. Very seldom is it necessary for us to dry wheat in the southern Great Plains. In the hard red spring wheat area, particularly the northern part, they do run into frost problems and have some wastage. But our wheat comes in very often $12\frac{1}{2}$–13% moisture content right off the combines. Our problems with storage in the southern part are primarily insects.

Chairman: The point to be made here, Professor Heyne, that is so familiar to you but not to us, is that the wheat is swarthed or windrowed in much of the Great Plains, not combined directly.

E. G. Heyne: Well, in the southern Great Plains it is combined directly, and then as you move north it is windrowed.

P. W. Russell Eggitt (Spillers Ltd, Cambridge, UK): Is there not a danger that you will turn the Great Plains into desert or are you beginning to think about growing complementary crops like timber?

E. G. Heyne: I know we've learnt our lesson. We have an expression: 'The dirty thirties'. To many this just means depression, to others it means that the air was continually full of soil. Wind erosion taught us some lessons and the very wind erodible lands at the present time are tied down. It has to be with grass; it can't be with timber, because we can't support the timber growth. But I think you're right: we could denude the whole area very easily if we go through those kind of times, like we did in the 1930s.

Wheat Agronomy—the Netherlands

J. MESDAG

*Cereal Department, Foundation for Agricultural Plant Breeding,
Wageningen, Netherlands*

It is quite different to come from countries with very big areas like the USA and Finland to a country with very small areas, not only for wheat, but for the whole agricultural crop. To give you an idea, the area of agricultural crops in the Netherlands in 1973 was about 670 000 ha and about twice that area of grass.

The area of agricultural crops has decreased since 1967 by 11%! During the same period the area of meadow decreased by 2·5%. This is a fast decrease, due mainly to the increase of the population density. The difference in pace between decrease of the area of agricultural crops and that of meadow is due to the relatively better prices in cattle holding and milk.

Wheat was grown on 20% of the area but there was a decrease of spring wheat (from 8% to 3%) and an increase of the higher yielding winter wheat. In the 5 years since 1968 the acreage of rye has halved, and oats decreased to nearly $\frac{1}{3}$! On the sandy soils these changes were very drastic, where rye decreased from 27% of the area to 13% and oats from 17% to 5%.

In the place of rye and oats now much maize for ensilage is grown on the sandy soil, and this came up from nearly nothing in 1967 to 23%, that is 7·5% of the area for the whole country.

Going more into details for wheat, it is evident that the differences between parts of the country with a light sandy soil and a very good sea clay soil are large. In the greater part of the sea clay soil about one-third of the agricultural crops is wheat. This is a relatively healthy situation, where we grow other crops during two years after one year with wheat. Such a rotation is possible due to a relative high proportion of potatoes ($\pm 20\%$) and about 25% of sugar beets.

With respect to the *varietal situation* the figures given in Table I are of interest.

Some recent figures for the production and destination of the wheat in the Netherlands may be of interest. Table II gives production figures and the destination of the home grown wheat harvest from 1972 is shown in Table III.

The first conclusion from these figures may be that the use of home

TABLE I

Number of varieties cultivated in 1973	Origin of these varieties	% of the area under varieties of each origin
Winter wheat 11 (of which 4 cover an area greater than 5% of the total winter wheat acreage)	Netherlands Germany Belgium France	56 39 4 1
Spring wheat 6 (of which 3 cover an area greater than 5% of the total spring wheat acreage)	Netherlands Belgium Germany	83 11 6

TABLE II

	Area harvested (hectares)		Yield (tons/ha)		Total yield (tons)	
	1972	1973	1972	1973	1972	1973
Winter wheat	135 300	116 300	4·4	5·4		
Spring wheat	21 000	21 600	3·6	4·4		
Total wheat	156 220	137 880	4·3	5·3	673 500	724 600
Total cereals	331 070	291 824			1 318 700	1 359 000

TABLE III
DESTINATION OF THE HOME GROWN WHEAT HARVEST

	1972	1971
Milling for consumption	12·6	16·7
Fodder purposes	49·6	38·2
For sowing	3·4	3·3
For sale in foreign countries (from which 70% within EEC)	30·0	32·6

grown wheat as bread wheat is very restricted. The second conclusion is that a great part of the wheat produced goes for fodder purposes. The point of view of a breeder is that we try to increase the varietal situation by breeding for superior baking quality.

From the point of view of a Dutch farmer it is a question of EEC price setting, productivity and crop rotation that he grows wheat for fodder purposes and only a little oats.

TABLE IV

RAW MATERIAL USED BY THE MILLS DURING
THE 1972–73 SEASON

Dutch home grown wheat	8%
Wheat from another country within EEC	48%
Wheat from countries outside the EEC	44%

(In total 1 197 000 tons of wheat were milled.)

I will now go a little bit more into detail about the situation in the Dutch milling industry (Table IV). It is useful to give some explanation to these figures of raw material of the mills.

(1) For the types of bread eaten in the Netherlands (which are not so different from those in Great Britain) a part of the raw material must have an excellent baking quality: these types of wheat are imported from different countries outside the EEC (± 40–45%).

(2) The other 55–60% of wheat comes from NW European countries, and the Dutch millers are free to buy this wheat inside the Common Market which they prefer to do and where the price is favourable for them. From the experiences in the last years we must conclude that the French wheat seems to be more attractive than the Dutch wheat. One cannot say that French wheat has a distinctly better baking quality, but we know that small differences between French and Dutch home grown wheat do exist, e.g. a small difference in protein content; the French wheat is offered in bigger homogeneous lots; in certain years the damage caused by sprouting in French is lower than that in Dutch wheat. Another factor is financial, where in different years the French franc was relatively cheap for a merchant having Dutch guilders.

SOME TRENDS IN WHEAT GROWING

Under Dutch environmental conditions the nitrogen supply of the wheat plant is one of the first limiting factors for the production. In different surveys you may find extremely high figures for the mean nitrogen level/ha for the whole country, and also such figures for the wheat crop. For many years we have been proud of such figures, for we have seen them as an indication of the intensity of wheat growing in our country.

But there is a strong tendency to think again about this and a discussion is going on about the usefulness of these very high N applications, and this discussion is not only caused by the actual high prices of fertilisers.

More and more attention is being paid to a gradual uptake of N during the whole development of the plant. Therefore attention is paid to:

(1) The amount of nitrogen available in the soil at the beginning of the spring before top dressing.
(2) The amount of nitrogen added as a fertiliser.

The amount of nitrogen before top dressing in the soil in early spring depends to a high degree on the amount of rain in the preceding autumn and winter: much rain means that a greater part of the nitrogen will be washed away to deeper soil layers and this will not be available to the roots of cereals.

Using this principle, an indication can be given to the farmers each year about the level of nitrogen fertilisation in comparison to the amount of rain in the preceding year. A newer development in the Netherlands is to have more exact information about the amount of mineral nitrogen in the soil at the beginning of the growing season.

We have to learn whether it will be possible to give the same advice to the whole country, and there are doubts about this. Another possibility in future will be to follow the N mineralisation on certain fields which are spread over the regions and to use the figures as a basis for regional advice about the amount of N for early application and for a second application.

This more exact knowledge about the amount of N which is available in the upper soil layers, together with a more exact dosage of nitrogen, eventually in two or three applications, is being studied by not only the agronomists but the phytopathologists also. The reason that phyto-pathologists are interested in the Netherlands (and Belgium) is that the amount of nitrogen which is available in the plant during the tillering stage is influential in the spreading of leaf and ear diseases.

So, the more exact dosage of nitrogen to the grain plant will be profitable to prevent lodging and to prevent a too luxurious growth of the plant, which will be conducive to widespread disease development. This is one trend in modern cereal growing in the Netherlands.

According to official sources the amount of seed used varies from 130 to 190 kg/ha for winter wheat, and for spring wheat from 150 to 190 kg/ha.

I should explain that 160 kg of seed/ha means that when the 1000 kernel weight $= 40$ g -400 kernels/m^2 at a row distance of 25 cm, there is a distance between plants of 1 cm, while 200 kg of seed/ha means a distance between plants of 0·8 cm.

Often this high sowing rate is used partly as an insurance against the loss of plants by diseases in the early stages, or by frost in the seedling stage. But in research some people came to the conclusion that they cannot find a decrease of yield when the amount of seed is decreased. Under certain conditions they even find an increase in yield with a lower seed rate.

TABLE V

EFFECT OF SOWING DENSITY IN WINTER WHEAT

140 kg of seed per ha		200 kg of seed per ha	
Yield (kg/ha)	% of lodging	Yield (kg/ha)	% of lodging
6 400	56	5 840	70
	mean of 5 types of sowing		

For example, Ten Hag and Darwinkel at the Research Station of Arable Farming gave me some results of such a type of trial (Table V). The trend in these figures is clear: a higher seed rate has produced a number of plants which was too high for the conditions. In this case it would have been wise to use less seed (and thus to pay less for the seed) and to get a higher yield.

TABLE VI

EFFECT OF SOWING METHOD

	140 kg of seed/ha		200 kg of seed/ha	
	Yield (kg/ha)	% of lodging	Yield (kg/ha)	% of lodging
Row distance 25 cm	6 250	80	5 650	95
Row distance 12·5 cm	6 500	50	6 050	80
Broadcast	6 830	37	6 280	40

In the same trial a variation in the sowing method was introduced: partly in row distance, partly by sowing it broadcast (Table VI). A lower row distance induces a lower tendency to lodging, and we may suppose that more lodging induced a lower yield. It is rather remarkable that the optimal spreading of the kernels over the area by sowing the wheat broadcast induced much stiffer plants which yielded more.

A warning against too quick a conclusion is that the same trial was repeated this year, and that no lodging appeared at all, and that no differences in yield were found. Nevertheless the trial in 1973 is very useful to demonstrate the way of thinking.

Most breeding work is done by private plant breeders; the breeding activity of the governmental institutes is only research. These private plant breeders range from relatively small firms through to large co-operative organisations. A number of breeding firms have a complete programme on cereals: some of them in co-operation with one of the others.

The first purpose in wheat breeding is high *yield*, this is not useful without resistance against different *diseases* as mentioned by Dr Moore. Stripe rust, mildew, eyespot and lately a certain resistance against *Septoria* and *Fusarium* are useful. It is desirable to have resistance to physiological damage from frost, sprouting in the ear, and eventually tolerance to high acidity present in sandy soil. During the 60 years of breeding activity the interest of the breeders in baking quality was very restricted, the Dutch farmer didn't ask for varieties with baking quality, for he, the farmer, is paid for the number of tons of yield, and not for protein content or for baking quality. In our position of a country at the border of the sea with much trade, traditionally we imported good baking wheat from continental areas, and we mixed that with home grown wheat; our mills do the same at this moment. Nevertheless the Dutch government and the farmers' organisations have stimulated a breeding programme for better baking quality. More precisely defined as a breeding programme with the aim of combining a normal yield level with better baking characteristics. To stimulate this type of breeding work a premium was promised to the breeder who could bring such a variety of wheat on the market.

The government gave help in this work by financing a baking quality programme in the cereal department of the Foundation for Agricultural Plant Breeding. In this programme useful genetic sources were looked for, a crossing and selection programme was started and half-way products were offered to the private plant breeder for further use in their programmes.

The point we have arrived at now is that we (as Foundation for Agricultural Plant Breeding) have made lines which yield nearly 100% of the varieties used in practice and which have a good baking quality (comparable to that of the best Swedish spring wheats). Having these lines and having grown them in bigger trials and after testing them in the test baking of one of the biggest mills, we are sure that it is possible to grow in the Netherlands wheat of a much better baking quality than that of the varieties which are sown now.

For winter wheat we have not yet reached the 100% yield level, but I can't see any major difficulty in reaching that combination in winter wheat.

No major difficulty, but I see practical hindrances and one is that we do not know what the exact demands of modern baking technology are. In our breeding programme we have worked with the micro-baking test and we are very pleased with this method; but it is rather expensive. One of the important things of this micro-baking method is that the correlation of the loaf volume with that determined in the standard baking test is good ($\simeq 0.85$) and such a useful correlation is, in my opinion, missing between so-called indirect methods and loaf volume.

DISCUSSION

Chairman: Well Ladies and Gentlemen, any questions which are specific to Dr Mesdag's paper, I will accept but remember that we have time for general discussion at the end of the afternoon.

A. Spicer (The Lord Rank Research Centre, High Wycombe, Bucks): You expressed a certain amount of confidence that given appropriate information from the bakery side you don't foresee any particular technical reasons, at least in your country, why yield and quality should not be combined. May I ask you the basis of this confidence?

J. Mesdag: Some years ago we thought we can't breed for higher protein percentages but we thought we could breed for a better protein quality. There is little evidence that yield and protein quality are in conflict. So we must concentrate on the amount of protein. Now Atlas 66 and Nap Hal show that there is appropriate genetic variation and more such varieties may be found. This may provide the means of increasing protein contents.

Hilkka Suomela (Helsinki University): Do you not think that Holland has too many varieties for high quality production to be possible?

J. Mesdag: Yes, there are different points of view on this. The pathologist would not agree with you. But the quality people in wheat and in barley prefer to have one variety. Under our conditions with many leaf diseases, this is too dangerous especially when we look at the similar resistance of the varieties.

Wheat Agronomy in Australia

W. V. SINGLE

*New South Wales Department of Agriculture,
Tamworth, New South Wales, Australia*

INTRODUCTION

The Australian wheat industry is based on an extensive system involving relatively large areas and small marginal returns per hectare. Distance from the seaboard and from most markets imposes a heavy freight penalty, which is only partially offset by a moderate level of government subsidy when prices are unfavourable. The generally low economic return for the crop has largely excluded it from the limited irrigated areas, and from the high rainfall districts where dairying, wool and higher value crops are more profitable. Because labour costs are high, the industry is well mechanised, with a history of some success in the pioneering of machinery design and development. The average wheat farm is some 300–400 ha, cropping 200 or more hectares annually. Recently the tendency has been for amalgamation of holdings and the cropping of some new land on a large scale, areas up to 10 000 ha being farmed as a single entity. The norm, however, is a family unit, self-sufficient for machinery and to a large extent for labour, which combines the growing of wheat with sheep and/or cattle raising. Production has varied recently from 6·4 to 14·8 million tonnes, from an average sown area of 6·5–10·8 million ha. Usually more than two-thirds of the crop is exported.

Research in agronomy is undertaken principally by the state governments on a network of research stations throughout the wheat areas. Several universities with strong commitments to agricultural teaching are also active, particularly in crop improvement. The Commonwealth Scientific and Industrial Research Organisation is heavily involved in research in soil fertility, and work on plant physiology occupies a significant place in the nebulous area which distinguishes agronomy from other disciplines. Product testing, research and demonstration by private companies is undertaken on a moderate scale, although reduced somewhat several years ago by a general recession in rural incomes.

All research, including that of the state government based on research stations, relies heavily on farmers who provide land, machinery and,

293

frequently, ideas. The innovative and developmental role of progressive land-holders is difficult to assess but is obviously of major importance.

CLIMATE AND TOPOGRAPHY

The location of the wheat belt is shown in Fig. 1, with some appropriate annual rainfall isohyets. The inner boundary in the south approximates the 250 mm line, but in northern NSW and Queensland this does not hold. This is because in Western Australia, South Australia and Victoria the wheat areas enjoy a Mediterranean-type climate of moist, mild winters

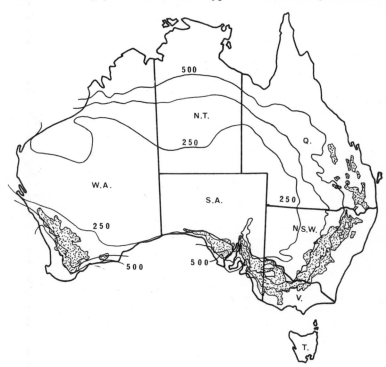

FIG. 1. The Australian wheat belt. Stippled sections indicate the main areas of wheat production. Annual rainfall isohyets are shown for 250, 375 and 500 mm.

and hot dry summers. In the north rainfall has a predominantly summer incidence and cropping relies to a significant extent on moisture stored in the subsoil during a short summer fallow. Nix (1974) has quantified this by defining the marginal areas for crop growth as those which can supply 152 mm of water during the period May to September in 8 years out of 10. This moisture may fall as rainfall during the period, or be stored in the fallow, assuming 20% efficiency of conservation. The wheat belt is also defined on its interior boundary by the hydric value, precipitation/evaporation$^{0.7}$ = 0.25–0.5, for the period July to October (Gentilli, 1971), although this fails to take account of stored fallow moisture.

Whichever method is used, it serves to highlight the fact that water stress is the major limiting factor in wheat production. In the dry areas it is present in practically every season, and even in the more favoured areas, the erratic nature of precipitation ensures that fear of drought colours the approach to every agronomic decision.

Lack of rain is exacerbated by high evaporation and surface run-off which further reduce the effectiveness of what moisture is available. Run-off and consequent soil erosion become a large factor in the higher, more hilly terrain which borders the wheat belt to the eastern and western seaboard, and help to confine wheat growing to the flat and gently undulating inland areas.

PERIOD OF CROP GROWTH

Lack of moisture, or high temperature, or both, combine to prevent active growth during summer, so the end of the grain filling period occurs in quite a narrow range, harvest commencing in the north in November and finishing in Victoria in January. The major constraint which determines the beginning of grain growth is frost. In early spring, radiation and daytime temperatures are often ideal for plant growth, but night temperatures of $-3.0\,^{\circ}$C and below can prove lethal to crops in the heading and later stages (Single and Marcellos, 1974). Nix (1974) has defined the approximate safe ear emergence date as the mean date of the last screen reading of 0 °C plus one standard deviation. Farmers achieve this by sowing in April–May in the south, where winter growth is relatively slow, but seed as late as July or even August in northern areas. Because harvest takes place in early summer, grain is usually of low moisture content and artificial drying is rarely necessary.

SOILS AND NUTRITION

Soil types cover an extremely wide range, from acid podzolics over almost pure sand in Western Australia to alkaline black earths of basaltic origin in NSW and Queensland. Between them is a variety of soils derived from alluvial and wind blown deposits.

McGarity (1974) gives a comprehensive description of wheat growing soils within the great soil groups as defined by Stace et al. (1968) under the following headings.

Red-brown earths were the first soils utilised and constitute major portions of the wheat areas in Southern Australia. They are of moderate fertility with initial surface nitrogen levels of about 0.1%, falling to 0.05 after prolonged cropping. As with most Australian soils, phosphorus is inherently low and application of 5–12 kg/ha of P as superphosphate with the seed is almost universal. On these soils, and others of moderate to low initial fertility, the use of subterranean clover in a pasture ley rotation, involving 2–5 years of pasture followed by three or more successive wheat crops, has had a dramatic effect. Areas which 40 years ago were virtually exhausted by continuous cropping and weed infestation have been restored to the point where excellent yields are obtained without the use of nitrogenous fertiliser. High returns of mutton and wool from the grazed pasture phase ensure a balanced and diversified farming system.

Solodised solonetz—solodic soils.
Solonised brown soils.
Yellow earths.
Red earths.

These descriptions cover a wide range of the poorer soils used for wheat growing. They are generally characterised by moderate to strong profile development and leached surface horizons. Some have reasonably retentive clay subsoils but many are seriously lacking in moisture holding capacity. This is true in particular of the sandy soils of Western Australia. On many of the latter soils, successful wheat growing depends on the combination of leguminous leys with up to 110 kg/ha of applied nitrogen, plus phosphorus, copper, zinc and occasionally manganese and molybdenum (Halse, 1969; Gilbey *et al.*, 1970; Jessup and Tuohey, 1973).

Black earths derive their name from the colour of the moist soil. They are uniform, heavy textured, ranging from clay loams to clays in the surface to medium to heavy clays with depth. They are strongly cracking, usually with a soft-crusty, self-mulching surface. Organic matter and nitrogen are inherently high, as is pH, with values up to 9.0 in surface layers.

Phosphorus usually appears adequate initially, partly because of an inherently low buffer capacity. Reserves are not high, however, and application of phosphoric fertiliser (up to 40 kg P/ha) becomes necessary after intensive cropping (Holford, Pers. comm.). These soils are common in the north, when they initially produce high yields of grain of high nitrogen content. A really stable system for their use has not, however, been established as yet. Because of the high pH and summer rainfall incidence, subterranean clover does not thrive. Naturalised and introduced medics, particularly lucerne (*M. sativa*) are used to a limited extent only, despite the large contributions to soil nitrogen which this species can make (Holford, 1968). The very stable surface structure of these soils has played a part in reducing the need for ley farming. They do not depend entirely on organic matter to prevent surface crusting or clodding, so the correction of nitrogen deficiency by chemical means provides, superficially at least, a stable management system.

The only micro-element found to be lacking occasionally is zinc. This is strongly adsorbed by the soil and applications of up to 12 kg/ha elemental zinc every 3–4 years are required to overcome deficiency where it occurs (Storrier, 1974).

Grey, brown and *red clays* make up the bulk of the remaining wheat soils in NSW and Victoria. Many of them have much in common with the black earths, being self-mulching and inherently high in fertility although lacking in phosphorus and zinc. The Wimmera soil of Victoria, which consistently produces the highest wheat yields in the country, belongs to this group.

WEEDS

Australia has its share of weeds, both introduced and native, covering a side spectrum of plant species which are too numerous to list here. Clean fallowing is the traditional method of control but the use of pre- and post-emergence herbicides is essential under some circumstances. Because of the relatively low yields and risk of droughts, chemicals are often too costly for general use. Two major weeds stand out as having attracted concentrated attention by agronomists. These are, first, the ubiquitous wild oat, *Avena ludoviciana* and *A. fatua*, and skeleton weed (*Chondrilla juncea*).

Wild oats are best controlled by careful farming in a ley rotation. A period of 3 or 4 years under pasture has been found to be sufficient to break dormancy, the majority of seeds germinating when the land is cultivated.

Skeleton weed is also kept in check by ley farming, subterranean clover and lucerne both being successful competitors. This weed was introduced from Europe, and prior to the advent of subterranean clover and 2-4D almost eliminated wheat growing in many areas. Recently rust (*Puccinia chondrillina* Bubak and Syd.) has been introduced to Australia and shows real promise of eventually reducing the weed to the minor place it occupies in European agriculture (Cullen *et al.*, 1973).

SOIL PREPARATION AND PLANTING

Techniques of seedbed preparation and planting have gone through a number of phases and are still evolving. Methods were borrowed initially from English farmers and involved deep ploughing followed by a series of workings designed to break up clods and produce a firm seedbed. Upon this was superimposed the system of dust mulch farming introduced from the USA early in this century. Credited with conserving moisture (a doubtful proposition on the soils to which it was applied) it was certainly effective in improving yields through mineralisation of nitrogen and destruction of weeds. The concomitant mechanical damage to the soil was not immediately apparent, although subsequently dust storms and wind erosion brought the message home all too clearly (Callaghan and Millington, 1956).

Agronomists are now concentrating attention on methods of establishing crops with least disturbance to the soil, bearing in mind the need to control weeds, provide adequate levels of available nitrogen and in the north to maximise pre-sowing water penetration and retention. Progress in this direction has been hampered by lack of suitable machinery and a sufficiently cheap, wide spectrum herbicide. Reeves and Smith (1973) and Pearce (1969) have shown that paraquat can be used to replace cultivation, but the cost of approximately $4/ha must be considered in the light of the average gross return of $50/ha which the farmer received until the recent world price rises. By the same token, it has proved cheaper and more convenient to burn the stubble from the previous crop than to attempt to incorporate it or work through it.

And so a fairly general pattern is accepted. If heavy stubble is present it is burned or stocked with sheep to help break it down, worked to a shallow depth with a disc plough or tyned scarifier (rarely a mouldboard plough), and again at intervals as required to control weeds. Seeding is done with the ubiquitous 'combine', a spring- or rigid-tyned light scarifier with seed and fertiliser boxes attached. The system cannot, however, be regarded as satisfactory. Although an improvement over the dust mulch practice, serious problems of water erosion are present on all but the flattest land, and soil organic matter levels are in jeopardy.

PESTS AND DISEASES

It is not proposed to give a comprehensive description of pests and diseases here, as with one or two exceptions these do not influence crop management practices to a very significant extent. From time to time, insects and mites attack crops as part of their general diet and can usually be controlled by spraying. The stem saw fly and hessian fly are mercifully absent. In southern areas the cereal cyst nematode (*Heterodera avenae*) causes serious yield losses and enforces a period of clean fallow or rotation with resistant crops. Similar measures are also employed occasionally in attempts to control soil-born fungi attacking roots and crowns, notably *Fusarium*, *Helminthosporium* and *Gaeumannomyces* spp. (Brown, 1974).

At one time flagsmut (*Urocystis agropyri*) threatened the wheat industry on many soil types, but is now under control through the efforts of plant breeders. Control of stem rust (*Puccinia graminis tritici*) has been achieved in northern areas through resistant varieties, but in the south, where susceptible cultivars are normally satisfactory, severe losses can still be sustained in unusual seasons.

It was stem rust which initially stimulated William Farrer in 1889 to undertake his pioneering efforts in plant breeding. Although he failed in his attempts to produce a cultivar with what is now called 'specific' resistance he was spectacularly successful in the production of the variety Federation. By virtue of its early maturity, Federation escaped rust damage in many years and pushed wheat growing into the drier, less rust-liable, areas.

Leaf rust (*P. recondita*) is prevalent in most years but is not usually credited with causing severe reduction in yields. Yellow stripe rust (*P. striiformis*) has not been recorded.

PLANT BREEDING AND VARIETIES

Australian cultivars have all been produced locally and are of generally similar constitution. Despite the spread of the wheat belt over more than 14 degrees of latitude, the same varieties can be successfully grown in all states. They are relatively insensitive to photoperiod to enable them to grow and develop in the short days (11–12 h effective photoperiod) of winter and early spring (Marcellos and Single, 1971). Various degrees of response to vernalisation are present but true winter wheats are too slow in maturing for most districts and are only used to a very limited extent where very early sowing and grazing are possible. Although short strawed by previous European standards, Australian varieties are considerably taller than the Norin type semi-dwarfs. Recently this character has been introduced and several recent releases, notably Kite and Condor, have Norin 10 in their parentage.

Grain is universally white and the quality varies from that of Timgalen, which is the equal of the best Canadian hard types, to soft biscuit wheats. A reasonable degree of success has been achieved in restricting varieties to areas suited to their grain quality and disease resistant characters, and so far the very poor quality varieties of Mexican origin have been excluded, despite their high yield potential and resistance to stem rust. The leading varieties in Australia are currently Gamenya, Heron, Falcon, Insignia, Robin, Timgalen, Olympic, Halberd, Gamut and Eagle. Durum wheats are grown, but the area is insignificant at present.

CROP YIELD

Agronomists in Australia have spent considerable effort in attempting to understand why, despite good soils, abundant sunshine and (on occasions) adequate moisture, the best yields even in experimental plots rarely exceed 5000 kg/ha, and the highest recorded average for the country is a mere 1500 kg/ha. Farmers and experimenters, using both local and imported varieties under irrigation have attempted to achieve the magical figure of 6700 kg/ha (100 bushels per acre) but to the best of the author's knowledge this has only once been achieved on anything approaching a commercial scale.

The obvious major constraint is water, at least in determining average yields. Water tends to be readily available only early in the life of the crop, producing excessive vegetative growth and tillering, which cannot be supported during the grain filling phase (Fischer and Kohn, 1966a). Fawcett (1964), working in northern NSW, attempted to control tiller number by using seed rates as low as 6 kg/ha. Under extremely dry overall conditions, the lowest rates were the best, but these yielded only 400–600 kg/ha. For more normal seasons, producing economic returns, very low rates cannot produce optimum yields and at least 15 kg/ha is recommended, with most farmers favouring 20–30 kg/ha. In southern and western areas, 30–80 kg/ha are sown, higher rates being used partly to overcome winter growing weeds.

The problem of late tiller death, or 'haying-off', is compounded by excess nitrogen which may increase vegetative growth and depress grain yield (Taylor, 1965; Russell, 1968). The result is clearly expressed as an extremely low harvest index in the mature crop.

The second part of the problem involving the low ceiling on potential yield is less easily understood. The more northern sections of the Australian wheat belt are similar in latitude to Sonora in Mexico, where yields of up to 9000 kg/ha are reported for control plots (Anon., 1970). As Australia's wheat ripens a little later in the season than that in Mexico, and therefore receives longer days, solar radiation seems unlikely to be the limiting factor to ultimate yield.

The remaining major constraint is temperature. Field observations leave little doubt that unusually cool springs and early summers are associated with good crops and it is equally clear that the decline in yield brought about by late sowing involves high temperature as an associated factor (Doyle and Marcellos, 1973; Fischer and Kohn, 1966b). A similar situation obtains in Mexico. This is obviously a fruitful field for further research (Donald and Puckridge, 1974; Single, 1974).

REFERENCES

Anon. (1970). 'International Maize and Wheat Improvement Centre', Annual Report 1970–71. Londres 30. Mexico 6. D. F. Mexico.

Brown, J. F. (1975). 'Diseases of wheat—their incidence and control', in *Australian Field Crops* (Ed. Alec Lazenby and E. M. Matheson), Angus and Robertson, Sydney, pp. 304–363.

Callaghan, A. R. and Millington, A. J. (1956). *The Wheat Industry in Australia*, Angus and Robertson, Sydney.

Cullen, J. M., Kable, P. F. and Cott, M. (1973). 'Epidemic Spread of a Rust Imported for Biological Control', *Nature*, **244**, 462–464.

Donald, C. M. and Puckridge, D. W. (1975). 'The ecology of the wheat crop', in *Australian Field Crops* (Ed. Alec Lazenby and E. M. Matheson), Angus and Robertson, Sydney, pp. 288–303.

Doyle, A. D. and Marcellos, H. (1973). 'Time of sowing and wheat yields in northern New South Wales', *Aust. J. Expt. Agric. An. Husb.*, **14**, 93–102.

Fawcett, R. G. (1964). 'Effect of certain conditions on yield of crop plants', *Nature*, **204**, 858–860.

Fischer, R. A. and Kohn, G. D. (1966a). 'The relationship between evapotranspiration and growth in the wheat crop', *Aust. J. Agric. Res.*, **17**, 255–267.

Fischer, R. A. and Kohn, G. D. (1966b). 'The relationship of grain yield to vegetative growth and post-flowering leaf area in the wheat crop under conditions of limited soil moisture', *Aust. J. Agric. Res.*, **17**, 281–295.

Gentilli, J. (1971). 'Climates of Australia and New Zealand', in *World Survey of Climatology*, Vol. 13 (Ed. J. Gentilli), Elsevier, Amsterdam, p. 175.

Gilbey, D. J., Greathead, K. D. and Gartrell, J. W. (1970). 'Copper requirements for the south-eastern wheat belt', *J. Agric. West. Aust.*, **11** (4), 70–72.

Halse, N. J. (1969). 'Legumes or artificial nitrogen?', *J. Agric. West. Aust.*, **10** (2), 79–81.

Holford, I. C. R. (1968). 'Nitrogen fixation by lucerne on several soils in pot culture', *Aust. J. Expt. Agric. An. Hus.*, **8**, 555–560.

Jessup, R. S. and Tuohey, C. L. (1973). 'Zinc is essential for Wimmera and Mallee crops and pasture', *J. Agric. Victoria*, **71** (8), 273–274.

McGarity, J. W. (1975). 'Soils of the Australian wheat growing areas', in *Australian Field Crops* (Ed. Alec Lazenby and E. M. Matheson), Angus and Robertson, Sydney, pp. 227–255.

Marcellos, H. and Single, W. V. (1971). 'Quantitative responses of wheat to photoperiod and temperature in the field', *Aust. J. Agric. Res.*, **22**, 343–357.

Nix, H. A. (1975). 'The Australian environment and its effects on grain yield and quality', in *Australian Field Crops* (Ed. Alec Lazenby and E. M. Matheson), Angus and Robertson, Sydney, pp. 304–363.

Pearce, G. A. (1969). 'Chemical ploughing', *J. Agric. West. Aust.*, **10** (4), 134–137.

Reeves, T. J. and Smith, I. S. (1973). 'Wheat without cultivation', *J. Agric. Victoria*, **71**, 74–75.

Russell, J. S. (1968). 'Nitrogen fertilizer and wheat in a semi-arid environment. II. Climatic factors affecting response', *Aust. J. Expt. Agric. An. Hus.*, **8**, 223.

Single, W. V. (1975). 'Frost injury', in *Australian Field Crops* (Ed. Alec Lazenby and E. M. Matheson), Angus and Robertson, Sydney, pp. 364–382.

Single, W. V. and Marcellos, H. (1974). 'Studies on frost injury to wheat. IV. Freezing of ears after emergence from the leaf sheath', *Aust. J. Agric. Res.*, **25**, 5 (in press).

Stace, H. C. T., Hubble, G. D., Brewer, R., Northcote, K. H., Sheanan, J. R., Mulcahy, M. J. and Hallsworth, E. G. (1968). *A Handbook of Australian Soils*, Rellim, Adelaide.

Storrier, R. R. (1975). 'Wheat nutrition', in *Australian Field Crops* (Ed. Alec Lazenby and E. M. Matheson), Angus and Robertson, Sydney, pp. 256–287.

Taylor, A. C. (1965). 'Wheat crop surveys in southern New South Wales. 2. Haying off in commercial wheat crops', *Aust. J. Expt. Agric. Anim. Husb.*, **5**, 491.

DISCUSSION

Chairman: The thing that impressed me, looking at wheat agriculture in Australia, was the extent to which it is dependent on sheep in many areas. This relationship is interesting and possibly unique. It reminded me of an English proverb which says that 'The hoof of the sheep turns sand to gold'.

M. V. Rao (Indian Agricultural Research Institute, New Delhi): Dr Single, you mentioned the spring wheat frost resistance and its importance. Can you find genotypes resistant to spring frost? This is also important in India: but we don't know resistant genotypes.

W. V. Single: The best spring wheat that we have found in a laboratory test is Frontana. Cheyenne has this character although it may not seem so to North American breeders.

V. A. Johnson (Nebraska University): A brief comment to Dr Single. You mention the variety Cheyenne: earlier today you heard from Dr Heyne that the Turkey-type was the backbone of the hard red winter wheat industry in the United States. Cheyenne is a selection from Crimean which is one of the Turkey types of wheat.

Wheat Agronomy in India

M. V. RAO

Wheat Research Co-ordination Centre,
Indian Agricultural Research Institute, New Delhi, India

INTRODUCTION

Wheat is the second most important cereal crop of India, contributing nearly a quarter to the total food grain production and is surpassed only by rice in area and production. In recent years after the identification and popularisation of semi-dwarf wheats there was a steady increase in acreage, total production and yield per unit area of wheat resulting in more than doubling of the wheat production in a short span of 5 years. The multidisciplinary approach in simultaneously tackling different problems connected with wheat cultivation played a crucial role in this achievement coupled with the enthusiastic co-operation of the farmers, policy makers and extension personnels. A brief account of results of the scientific research covering some of the major disciplines and carried out by a number of my fellow workers connected with wheat production, is presented here.

CHARACTERISTICS OF INDIAN WHEAT CROP

Four species of Triticum are known to be cultivated in India. Out of these *T. aestivum* Linn. is the most important, occupying nearly 87% of the total acreage, followed by *T. durum* Desf. with 12% and *T. dicoccum* with less than 1% of the acreage, respectively. *T. spaerococcum* was at one time under cultivation but now it has practically disappeared from the Indian countryside. While *T. aestivum* is grown all over India the distribution of *T. durum* is confined to the non-yellow rust, dry areas of Central and Peninsular India. *T. dicoccum* because of its disease resistance and grain type, is grown on a very limited scale in Peninsular India and Gujarat. The most intensively cultivated areas of wheat are in the north covering the states of Uttar Pradesh, Punjab, Haryana, Madhya Pradesh, Bihar and Rajasthan. Without exception all the wheats grown in India belong to the spring type although they are sown in October–November and

harvested in April–May. Most of the wheats grown in India are fully
awned with amber, hard grains. The wheat straw is an important cattle
feed. Out of the 19 million ha put under wheat half of the area has to
depend on natural precipitation which is often scanty and irregular.

LANDMARKS IN THE WHEAT IMPROVEMENT WORK IN INDIA

The firm foundations for the systematic improvement of the Indian wheat
crop can be said to have been laid towards the beginning of this century
with the establishment of the Imperial, now Indian, Agricultural Research
Institute (I A R I) and the departments of agriculture in the different states

TABLE I
COMPARATIVE PERFORMANCE OF TRADITIONAL TALL INDIAN WHEATS
(Data from Dr Mahabalram, 1965)

Variety	Yield (Quintal/ha)	Variety	Yield (Quintal/ha)
NP 4	14·68	C 281	17·54
NP 52	13·81	C 286	16·27
A 115	14·52	C 306	16·35
NP 165	16·74	C 518	15·87
NP 718	15·87	C 591	15·55
NP 823	16·90	Hy 65	16·35
NP 824	15·63	RS 31-1	16·74
NP 825	15·16		

of India. Sir Albert Howard and Lady Howard, the Imperial and the
Second Imperial Economic Botanists at the I A R I, can be said to be the
pioneers in the wheat improvement work. The efforts made by these and
other notable scientists like Sir Geoffrey Evans, T. Milne, H. M. Leake
and Ram Prasad resulted in the isolation of superior pure lines like I P 4,
I P 12 (now NP 4, NP 12), Pb. Types 8, 8A, 9, 9D and 11, C 13, A O 13,
etc., which surpassed the local mixtures in yield and grain quality. Pure
line selection among the indigenous material was followed by hybridisation work which resulted in wheats like NP 52, NP 165, Pb. C. 591, etc.,
which occupied considerable acreages in the country for a long time.
From the mid-1930s to the early 1960s emphasis was given to disease
resistance particularly to the rusts and loose smut. This line of work
resulted in the production of a number of wheats, the more important of
which are the wheats of the NP 700 and NP 800 series, C 285, C 286,
Hy 65, H 633 and Kenphad wheats. Since the work of this long period

of 60 years was concentrated on the tall wheats which were unable to stand intensive agricultural practices, the yield advances were very marginal (Table I).

TABLE II
CHANGES OVER DECADES IN AREA, PRODUCTION AND YIELD PER HECTARE OF WHEAT IN INDIA

Decade	Area (ha × 10⁶)	Production (tonnes × 10⁶)	Yield/ha (kg)
1931–32	13·5	9·0	660
1941–42	13·6	10·0	770
1951–52	9·4	6·2	650
1961–62	13·6	12·1	890
1971–72	19·1	26·4	1 380

During the decade 1932–42 there was some increase in production although the area remained unchanged. Due to partition of the country in 1947 there was a sudden drop in acreage as reflected by the data of 1951–52. The acreage, production and yield per unit area showed real advance in the decade ending by 1971–72 and this is the year when the dwarf wheats were widely grown and new agronomy widely practised.

From Table I it is clear that the yield increases by way of varieties, over a period of half a century, are marginal. In the review made by the wheat workers in the early 1960s it was fully realised that it is difficult to increase yields with the traditional tall wheats. A programme to introduce short stature from some Italian wheats which were available at that time, into the Indian wheats was initiated. Meanwhile the Mexican dwarf wheats developed by the Rockefeller Foundation programme in Mexico were located in the International Spring Wheat Rust Nursery of 1963 supplied

TABLE III
PRODUCTION, ACREAGE AND YIELD/HA OF WHEAT IN RECENT YEARS IN INDIA

Year	Production (tonnes × 10⁶)	Acreage (ha × 10⁶)	Yield/ha (kg)
1965 (base year)	12·3	12·6	827
1968	16·6	14·9	1 103
1969	18·6	15·9	1 169
1970	20·1	16·6	1 208
1971	23·2	18·2	1 299
1972	26·4	19·1	1 380
1973	24·9	19·9	1 254

by the USDA. By collaborative efforts between the Indian scientists and Dr Norman E. Borlaug and his colleagues in Mexico a number of superior types were selected suitable for Indian conditions. These new dwarf wheats and the new technology in growing them revolutionised wheat production in India. The changes in trends of production, acreages and yield per hectare are depicted in Tables II and III.

The new wheats acted as catalysts and triggered off a number of changes in the countryside. The farmers, who were considered to be tradition bound took to the new wheats and technology most enthusiastically after seeing the advantages. The wheat revolution was partly responsible for provoking changes in other crops also.

OBJECTIVES AND ORGANISATION OF WHEAT RESEARCH

The plant breeding objectives in wheat, as in any other crop, are generally very clear: yield, adaptation, disease and pest resistance and, quality being the primary goals. In India few other objectives also become important such as non-shattering character of the grain, resistance to drought, particularly under unirrigated rainfed conditions and early maturity not only to ripen before the hot desiccating winds that start in March–April but also to fit into the multiple cropping system. Since most of the wheat is consumed in the form of unleavened pan baked breads called 'chapatis' the preference of consumer for amber, hard grain has to be kept in mind by the breeders.

With nearly 19–20 million ha planted under wheat in India under widely differing soil and climatic conditions with varying problems, our approach is to solve problems on a regional or zonal basis. The country is divided into five wheat zones, the areas in each zone having more or less similar conditions and problems. Strong research centres are present in each of the states of each zone to carry on research on a multidisciplinary basis. The research efforts made in each zone are reviewed in the annual meetings of the wheat workers of India and programmes are drawn up for the following season. The disciplines of breeding, pathology, agronomy, quality, physiology, nematology, entomology, agricultural engineering, dry land technology are strongly represented at these meetings. In addition to the annual meetings which are generally held in the month of August every year, the wheat workers in each zone meet during the crop season at zonal meetings. The involvement of different wheat workers of different disciplines is the major strength of the wheat research efforts in India. Four major centres in wheat pathology strategically located at hot spots of diseases, screen the breeding material developed all over the country. At present three laboratories located at Delhi, Pantnagar (in the state of

Uttar Pradesh) and Ludhiana (in Punjab) screen the wheat material for quality. In the 5th Five Year Plan more research centres and more facilities are envisaged, to strengthen the present efforts. The Indian wheat project also has two excellent off-season nurseries located in the high Himalayas in the north and, in the hills in the south. These centres not only help in advancing generations but also aid in screening breeding material against diseases and also in initial multiplication of the most promising strains.

PROGRESS IN VARIETAL IMPROVEMENT

The Mexican varieties Sonora 64 and Lerma Rojo 64-A which were responsible for initiating the wheat revolution in India were quickly replaced subsequently, because of their red grain colour, by amber grained

TABLE IV
MAJOR WHEAT VARIETIES IN INDIA

Species	Name of the variety	Height	Special features	Area(s) of adaptation
T. aestivum	Kalyansona	Double dwarf	High yield and adaptation under normal sowings	Irrigated conditions of North, Central and Peninsular India
	Sonalika	Single dwarf	High yield and adaptation for late sowings	Irrigated conditions of North, Central and Peninsular India
	Sharbati Sonora	Double dwarf	High yield and adaptation for late sowings	Central and eastern India
	Choti Lerma	Double dwarf	High resistance to stem and stripe rusts	Southern hills
	Safed Lerma	Single dwarf	High resistance to stem and stripe rusts	Southern hills
	Moti	Triple dwarf	High yield	North-western India where stripe rust is not a problem
	Hira	Triple dwarf	High yield	North-western India
	Girija	Tall	High resistance to all three rusts	High hills of North India

Species	Name of the variety	Height	Special features	Area(s) of adaptation
	Janak	Double dwarf	High resistance to leaf rust	Eastern India
	UP 301	Triple dwarf	High resistance to all rusts	Peninsular India
	UP 215	Double dwarf	High resistance to all rusts	Peninsular India
	WG 357	Double dwarf	Good grain quality	Punjab
	NI 747-19	Tall	Rainfed conditions	Peninsular India
	NI 5439	Tall	Rainfed conditions	Peninsular India
	K 65	Tall	Average fertility conditions	Uttar Pradesh
	K 68	Tall	Average fertility conditions	Uttar Pradesh
	NP 824	Tall	Average fertility conditions	Gujarat
	Narbada 4	Tall	Rainfed conditions	Madhya Pradesh
	C 306	Tall	Average fertility conditions	North India
	Ridley	Tall	Average fertility conditions	Northern hills
	NP 846	Tall	Average fertility conditions	Northern hills
T. durum	A 9-30-1	Tall	Rainfed conditions	Central India
	Bijaga red	Tall	Rainfed conditions	Karnatak
	Bijaga yellow	Tall	Rainfed conditions	Karnatak
	N 59	Tall	Rainfed conditions	Maharashtra
	MACS 9	Tall	Rainfed conditions	Peninsular India
	Malavika	Triple dwarf	High fertility conditions	Peninsular India
T. dicoccum	NP 200	Tall	Low fertility conditions	Southern hills

Recently a number of strains have been identified, combining yield with resistance to rusts, and these are now under pre-release multiplication.

selections such as Kalyansona, Sonalika, Choti Lerma, Safed Lerma, Sharbati Sonora. Kalyansona and Sonalika are now the most dominant wheats under irrigated agriculture having high yield potentials up to 6–7 tonne/ha. Certain triple dwarfs like Moti and Hira were released which had still higher yield potential but recent fertiliser shortages and their susceptibility to one or other of the rusts did not permit their spread.

Information on the characteristics of some of the most important wheat varieties and the areas of their adaptation are given in Table IV.

Recently a number of strains were identified, combining yield with resistance to rusts, and these are now under prerelease multiplication.

Since 1967 a programme to develop multilineal varieties of some of the major commercial wheats like Kalyansona, Sonalika and Sharbati Sonora was started and the lines that resulted from this programme are now in the advanced stages of testing. Data on some of the promising lines of Kalyansona are given in Table V. Similar promising lines are now available in two other commercial varieties Sonalika and Sharbati Sonora.

TABLE V

PERFORMANCE OF NEW LINES OF KALYANSONA AT DEHLI DURING 1972–73

Strain	Yield (Quintal/ha)	Reaction to rusts		
		Stem	Leaf	Stripe
IWP 2	44·7	F	TX	F
IWP 8	46·1	TS	F–LX	TS
IWP 17	48·5	F	TR	F
IWP 18	51·5	F	TR	F
IWP 19	51·9	F	TR	F
IWP 25	46·0	TS	TR	F
IWP 33	50·6	TS	F	LS
IWP 40	48·6	TS	F	F
IWP 44	47·2	F	F	TS
IWP 45	41·4	F	TR	F
Multiline	45·8	F–TS	F–LS	F
Kalyansona (check) CD 7·5	41·7	TS	HS	TS

One significant development in Indian wheat breeding work in recent years is the development of dwarf durums with (1) high yield potential and (2) high resistance to rusts. The durums so far cultivated in India besides being very tall are highly susceptible to yellow rust with the result their yields were poor and their cultivation was restricted to the drier areas of Central and Peninsular India. In 1973 a dwarf durum, Malavika, was released for Peninsular India which combined resistance to rusts with high yield under high fertility conditions. Certain dwarf durums which are now in final stages of testing are doing well in North India also and it is envisaged that in the next few years, durum production would go up as a result of cultivation of yellow rust resistant dwarf durum in the northern bread bowl of India.

While good progress has been achieved in increasing yields under areas of assured water supply, the yields under rainfed areas which constitute 50% of the total wheat acreage in India, more or less remained stagnant. Besides the conventional breeding using varieties and species it is felt that agronomy, water conservation and plant protection have to play a significant role in stepping up yields in these areas. In recent years the possibilities of introducing the triticales in rainfed agriculture are being explored. Other lines that appear to hold promise are the utilisation of winter wheats in spring wheat breeding and development of dwarf wheats with long coleoptile.

PROGRESS IN CULTURAL PRACTICES AND PRODUCTION TECHNOLOGY

Innumerable simple fertiliser experiments carried out all over India during the late 1950s and early 1960s on farmers' fields, had shown that it is not economical to apply more than 20 kg of N per hectare to wheat. However, to get high yields the dwarf wheats needed higher fertiliser inputs, different management and cultural practices.

Agronomic research carried out by our researchers enabled us to draw up recommendations to be followed by farmers for a variety of conditions, namely, irrigated high and medium fertility, normal sowing and late sowing and rainfed conditions. The agronomists actively collaborate with the breeders under the All India Co-ordinated Wheat Improvement Project in testing the new wheats under different agronomic conditions and developing production agronomy suitable for each newly released wheat variety.

Based on the agronomic research done, the following recommendations are made for getting the best out of the existing wheats.

(a) For rainfed conditions
(1) Levelling and bunding of fields before monsoon.
(2) Conservation of moisture by deep ploughing towards the end of the monsoon.
(3) If white ants and other pests are a problem, application of pesticides like BHC, Aldrin, etc., to soil and ploughing it in.
(4) One or two light cultivations before sowing
(5) Sowing of seed in the second fortnight of October.
(6) Drill sowing of seed at the rate of 100 kg/ha and with a spacing of 23–25 cm from row to row.

(7) Application of fertiliser at the rate of 40 kg N and 20 kg of P_2O_5 per hectare. Both N and P should be placed 10 cm deep at or before sowing.

(b) For irrigated seasonably sown conditions
   (1) Long duration varieties should be sown in the first fortnight of November.
   (2) Depth of sowing: 5–6 cm.
   (3) Seed rate: 100 kg/ha for wheats with average grain weight;
                 125 kg/ha for bold seeded wheats.
   (4) Row spacing: 22·5 cm.
   (5) Irrigation: 4–6 irrigations. First irrigation should be given at crown root initiation stage which is generally 20–25 days after sowing. Other irrigations should be given at late tillering, late jointing, flowering, milk and dough stages.

      If water is available for a limited number of irrigations then the most important stages when the water should be given are at the crown root initiation, followed by irrigations at intervals of about 5–7 weeks each.
   (6) Fertilisers: At the rate of 100–120 kg N/ha.
                       50–60 kg P_2O_5/ha.
                       25–30 kg K_2O/ha.
Phosphorus and potash should be applied on the basis of soil test. Half N and full quantities of P and K should be drilled about 5 cm below the seed at the time of sowing. The remaining half of N should be top dressed at first irrigation.

(c) For irrigated late sown conditions
   (1) Choose early maturing varieties.
   (2) Sowing wheat beyond the 3rd week of December is not economical.
   (3) Give seed rate of 125 kg/ha (higher seed rate).
   (4) Give a row spacing of 15–18 cm (close spacing).
   (5) Fertilisers should be applied at the rate of 80 N : 50–60 P_2O_5 : 25–30 K_2O in kg/ha.

As in irrigated timely sown conditions all recommended doses of P and K and half of N should be applied at the time of sowing and the remaining half quantity of N should be top dressed at first irrigation.

    In addition to what is stated about the production technology for irrigated and rainfed conditions there are a number of special situations in the country for which answers are to be found. These are: (1) proper agronomy for multiple cropping where it is found possible to grow three crops and in special circumstances four crops per year on the same piece of land; (2) companion cropping of wheat with crops like sugar-cane which are planted in rows; (3) about 7·0 million ha in India have alkalinity-salinity problems out of which 2·8 million ha are located in the highly productive Indo-Gangetic plains alone. The work done at the Central Soil Salinity Research Institute at Karnal has shown that it is possible to get 4–6 tonnes of wheat/hectare by leaching of salts in April, judicious application of gypsum to a green manure crop like Sesbania and frequent light irrigations to wheat. Varieties like HD 1944, Kalyansona, Kharchia, etc., were found to be more tolerant to alkaline conditions than certain others; (4) micro-nutrient deficiency which was never a limiting factor in crop production in India has of late become important in certain areas. Zinc deficiency was found to adversely affect wheat production in the highly productive areas of Punjab and the submountainous areas of Uttar Pradesh. Application of zinc sulphate at the rate of 25–50 kg/ha was found to substantially increase wheat production in these areas. Similarly in the last 2 years sulphur has been found to be limiting in some soils of Punjab.

Weed control through chemicals, aerial spraying of fertilisers, targeting of yields on the basis of available resources, conduct of agronomic experiments and national demonstrations on farmers' fields, are some of the other areas of production technology followed in India.

PROGRESS IN PLANT PROTECTION

The wheat crop in India is attacked by a number of fungi, nematodes, pests and bacteria and these include the three rusts, stinking smut, loose smut, partial bunt, flag smut, powdery mildew, Alternaria leaf blight, Helminthosporium leaf spot and seedling blight, ear-cockle, tundu, molya, stem borers, cut worms, white ants, brown mites, army worms, etc. In some humid areas in the hills Septoria glume and leaf blotches are also met with. Fortunately many of these diseases and pests are not serious and generally they are of local importance. None of the field pests, except occasionally, are serious on wheat crop. The stored grain pests on the other hand are more serious. The rusts, the smuts and the leaf blights are the most serious, while powdery mildew is a problem in the hills and submountainous areas.

All the attempts to protect the wheat crop are co-ordinated at the All India level by senior scientists. Besides strong plant pathological stations, a number of trap nurseries, plant pathological screening nurseries and National Genetic Stock Nurseries are planted every year in different parts of the country to know what is happening to the new varieties, genetic stocks, etc. There is disease surveillance work at the national level to keep a watch on the disease situation in different parts. Diseased wheat samples are collected from all over the country and the physiological races of the infections are identified to guide the breeding work. All the rust races identified in India since 1930 are maintained by single spore culturing.

Our strategy for control of the pathogens can be broadly divided into the following categories: (1) development of resistant varieties; (2) identification of suitable chemicals; (3) identification of suitable cultural practices; and finally (4) reduction of the inoculum from where it is coming.

As an adjunct to breeding for resistance, particularly against rusts, all the breeding material at the main centres is exposed in the field to all the races prevalent in the country. Genes which govern resistance to the races of rusts are identified. It is found that Sr11, Sr6, Sr8, Sr17, Sr5; Lr9, Lr19, Lr12, Lr10 and a number of Yr genes govern resistance to a number of Indian races of the rusts.

The extensive survey and surveillance carried out by the plant pathologists has indicated that there are two main foci, one in the northern hills, i.e. Himalayas, and the other in the southern hills (Nilgiri and Palni), from where the inoculum of rusts comes to the plains to attack the wheat crop. While varieties are being bred for the plains that are resistant to rusts, our efforts are also aimed at saturating the northern and southern hills with rust resistant wheats with a view to reducing the initial inoculum. Two such varieties have been found—Choti Lerma (resistant to stem rust) for the southern hills, and Girija (resistant to all the three rusts) for the northern hills. More such strains are now under initial multiplication.

PROGRESS IN RESEARCHES ON QUALITY OF WHEAT

More than 90% of the wheat in India is consumed in the form of 'chapatis' —unleavened pan baked bread. Amber, hard grain capable of giving creamish-yellow 'chapatis' with good flavour, taste, puffing and keeping qualities are preferred. In the early stages of wheat improvement work in India the grain samples used to be sent for quality analysis to Sir Albert Humphries of the National Association of British and Irish Millers. Subsequently a quality laboratory was set up at Lyallpur, now in Pakistan. Recently well equipped quality testing laboratories are available at the I A R I, New Delhi, Ludhiana (Punjab), Pantnagar (Uttar Pradesh) and at the Central Food Technological Research Institute, Mysore. The former three centres help the breeders in screening their materials for different quality characters. They also test all the strains in the All India Co-ordinated Trials. In the 5th Five Year Plan it is envisaged to set up three more quality testing laboratories.

While for breadmaking purposes strong wheats are needed, for 'chapatis' medium strong wheats are used. The breeders selections as well as the strains in preliminary trials are screened for protein and pelshenke values while the promising strains in the advanced tests are subjected to all quality tests including amino acid contents. Based on tests carried out over the years, varieties suitable for different purposes have been identified. Some of such wheats are given in Table VI.

TABLE VI

SOME INDIAN WHEATS SUITABLE FOR DIFFERENT PURPOSES

For bread	For pastries and biscuits	For blending	For chapatis	For semolina	For uppumav[a]
K 65	Choti Lerma	C 306	C 273	Bijaga-	NP 200
K 68	Pissi Local	RS 31-1	C 281	yellow	NP 201
NP 880	NP 832	Narbada 4	C 591	Bansi	Samba
NP 890	Safed Lerma	Hy 65	C 286	Amrut	Khapli
Sharbati-	Sonalika	C 303	NP 824		Popatiya
Sonora		NI 5439	Kalyansona		
UP 301		NI 747-19			
UP 319					

[a] Southern Indian dish made with semolina. Eaten with vegetables and/or beef. Has the consistency of a doughnut.

The demand by the baking industry in India at present is of the order of 1 million tonnes but the demand is increasing very rapidly.

FUTURE PROSPECTS

As the population increases the demand for more wheat is obvious. It is estimated that the requirement for wheat in India in 1975, 1980 and 1985 will be of the order of 24·23, 30·05 and 36·66 million tonnes respectively. If fertiliser, water and good seed are in ample supply the above targets can easily be achieved under the climatic conditions of India. The fact that even 3 years before 1975, wheat production had reached 26·2 million tonnes indicates the scope and potentialities. That it is possible to produce 7–8 tonne/ha in a short growing period of 5–6 months is quite evident from the data of the national demonstrations where inputs were not limiting (Table VII).

While the potentialities for high yields under irrigated conditions are well appreciated the possibilities of increasing production under rainfed conditions with better management are equally bright though not of the same order as for irrigated wheat. The early maturity of most of the Indian wheats enable them to be used in multiple cropping thus stepping up production substantially in a year.

TABLE VII
YIELDS OBTAINED IN NATIONAL DEMONSTRATIONS (T/HA)
(Data of Dr S. K. Sharma)

Year	Average of the country	Average of the national demonstrations	Highest of the national demonstrations
1966	0·83	3·96	6·80
1967	0·9	3·65	8·41
1968	1·13	4·18	9·60
1969	1·17	4·04	10·20
1970	1·21	4·07	9·35
1971	1·31	4·08	9·00
1972	1·38	4·51	8·70

The diseases, nematodes and pests, however, have to be controlled in any future strategy for wheat production. Varieties having different genes for resistance have to be produced to avoid large-scale epidemics of rusts. The present programmes are already geared in this direction. Timely availability of inputs in adequate quantities should enable us to produce more wheat in the coming years.

DISCUSSION

J. M. Hirst (Rothamsted Experimental Station): Could you comment on the significance of *Septoria* and *Alternaria*?

M. V. Rao: *Septoria* is only a problem in the southern hills in the rainy season. *Alternaria* is a big problem and could be devastating but we have tolerant varieties, some semi-dwarf, in agricultural use. *Helminthosporium* causes concern in the east but it could be controlled chemically.

J. T. Walker (Nickerson Group): Have you found any indications of genetic variability giving resistance to waterlogging and salinity?

M. V. Rao: Yes, we are using a number of wheat varieties which are tolerant, or perhaps you would say resistant, to these conditions. One is a local variety grown in Rajasthan in the area adjacent to Pakistan.

E. Bullen (Ministry of Agriculture, Fisheries and Food, London): The yield of 10 t/ha to which Dr Rao referred is fantastic on a world scale. Is this a very small plot multiplied up, or is this a field yield?

M. V. Rao: These are field yields. In our National Demonstrations the minimum plot size is 1 ha but we follow all the latest technologies, including variety, drilling, fertiliser and water use. Our agronomists have found that the time of irrigation is crucial for wheat production. This is the crown root in the initial stage which is generally 21–28 days after planting. The most crucial irrigation is 21–28 days after planting; if you skip it, you may lose 20% of yield. When we follow the best practices in the National Demonstrations we get 9–10 t/ha.

Wheat Agronomy in France

J. HÉBERT

Station Agronomique de l'Aisne, Lâon, France

CONDITIONS FOR SOFT WHEAT PRODUCTION

Wheat is still the most cultivated cereal in France. About half the French farms (700 000) produce it.

Table I shows the trend in wheat cultivation. Production has almost doubled whereas the areas cultivated decreased by 45%, in 70 years, this is related to an important gain in productivity, especially in the last 15 years.

TABLE I
TREND OF WHEAT PRODUCTION IN FRANCE

	Area		Yield		Production	
	1 000 ha	*Index*	*kg/ha*	*Index*	*1 000 t*	*Index*
1900–09	6 740	100	1 310	100	8 876	100
1920–23	5 255	78·0	1 380	105·3	7 291	82·1
1930–33	5 442	80·7	1 400	106·9	7 491	84·4
1950–53	4 289	63·6	1 800	137·4	7 747	87·3
1960–63	4 244	63·0	2 680	204·6	11 376	128·2
1970–73	3 705	55·0	4 000	305	14 903	167·9
1973–74	3 807	67·0	4 650	355	17 368	195·7

TABLE II
USES OF WHEAT IN FRANCE
(millions of metric tons)

	Volume	*%*
Production	14·7	100
Farm consumption	2·8	19
Animal nutrition	1·8	12
Agricultural and food industries	5·4	37
Exports	4·6	31

Although bread consumption has greatly fallen (68 kg/capita/Y in 1972 versus 95 kg/capita/Y in 1962), it remains the main outlet for wheat. The uses are shown in Table II. Thus, France is the first European producer and the fourth world exporter.

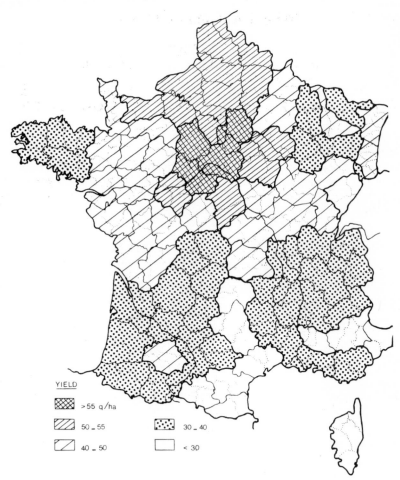

FIG. 1. Distribution of wheat yields in France in 1972.

Soft wheat production in France is carried out under oceanic climate conditions, without any systematic dry month or severe winter. Table III gives some climatic data. The annual rainfall of the great wheat areas varies from 550 to 750 mm with a mean annual temperature of between 9·5 and 12·5 °C. The eastern areas have severer winters with

TABLE III

CLIMATIC DATA FOR SEVERAL FRENCH STATIONS

		J	F	M	A	M	J	July	A	S	O	N	D	Annual average
St-Quentin	t°C	1·7	3·0	6·3	9·5	12·9	15·5	17·3	17·1	15·2	10·7	6·1	3·3	9·9
	R	52	46	42	46	50	60	54	75	63	47	58	64	658
	PET				53	78	74	90	84	74				
Dijon	t°C	1·3	2·6	6·9	10·4	14·3	17·7	19·6	19·0	15·9	10·5	5·7	2·1	10·5
	R	64	42	42	46	64	81	58	77	72	60	76	57	739
	PET				79	97	91	90	99	76				
Tours	t°C	3·5	4·4	7·7	10·6	13·9	17·3	19·1	18·7	16·2	11·7	7·2	4·3	11·2
	R	64	55	49	48	63	49	49	61	59	60	64	68	689
	PET				65	100	76	98	94	69				
Toulouse	t°C	4·5	5·4	9·0	11·4	14·8	18·6	20·8	20·7	18·0	13·0	8·3	5·3	12·5
	R	49	46	53	50	75	61	44	54	64	45	51	67	659
	PET				102	107	154	159	113	64				
Clermont-Ferrand	t°C	2·7	3·5	7·3	10·1	13·7	17·2	19·2	18·8	16·1	11·0	6·7	3·5	10·9
	R	25	25	29	43	67	72	51	68	61	49	40	33	563
	PET				16	32	17	72	48	30				

more frost hazards than elsewhere. The south-western area enjoys a
higher temperature, allowing an earlier growth. In the south-east, hard
wheat would be better adapted.

The moisture deficit in the early summer is not very high in the coastal
areas. However, it is sometimes high for the whole southern part of the
Paris Basin (Beauce, Orleanais, Berry, Poitou), which may induce very
severe premature ripening.

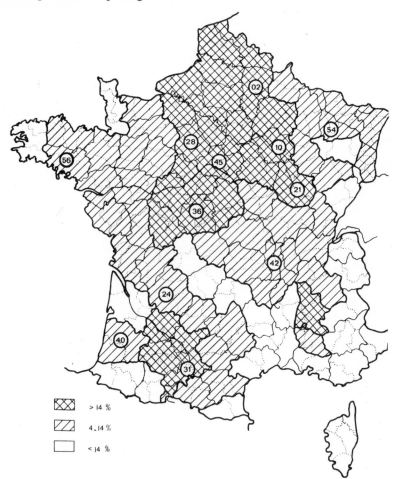

FIG. 2. Soft wheat acreage in the regions (% U A S) (1971–1972–1973).

Independently of its present price, wheat cultivation is attractive
because of the possibility of complete mechanisation. Then, too, as well

as favourable climatic conditions this crop is better suited for the big fields and rolling lands of the large sedimentary areas which are the great producing regions; that is the Paris Basin, the Aquitaine Basin and the great valleys between the mountains.

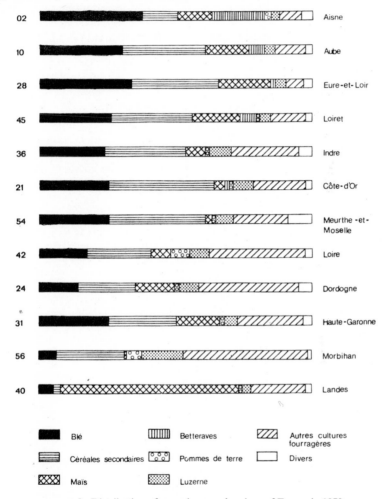

FIG. 3. Distribution of crops in several regions of France in 1972.

Figure 1 gives the yields for the French regions. They are relative to 1972, a good year for cereals in the whole country but which on account of the rapid extension of technical progress for these crops, is fairly representative of the French situations.

High yields are found in the Paris Basin, the best in the south of Paris (Beauce). Around this nucleus, a broad zone with average yields extends to the Charentes, the Massif Central Plains and the East of France. South of a line from Bordeaux to Geneva, yields are more irregular, more prone to premature ripening (the worst situated in mountainous or arid zones).

Figure 2 shows that the importance of soft wheat areas (as a percentage of the agricultural region—SAU in French) follows pretty well the map of yields.

CROP SEQUENCES

Figure 3 shows for several regions, representative of certain cultural situations, the importance of wheat on arable land. The first four lines are relative of regions of intensive cultivation. The department of Aisne, an example of the loam area of northern France, has always had an

TABLE IV

AVERAGE LOWERING OF THE YIELD OF WHEAT IN THE PARIS BASIN, AFTER DIFFERENT PRECEDING CROPS AS COMPARED WITH THAT FOLLOWING POTATOES
(OCCAS, 1972)

Length of survey Preceding crop	Yield of wheat after potatoes less yield of wheat after crop		
	Over 16 years *(kg)*	*Over 10 years* *(kg)*	*Over 5 years* *(kg)*
Lucerne	40	0	100
Sugar-beet	100	50	20
Peas	150	110	160
Rape-seed	290	270	210
Maize	470	450	230
Wheat	750	550	510

important acreage of root crops, forming an excellent entry crop for wheat. Maize is partly replacing oats and barley, but does not cut into the acreage of root crops. In Champagne (represented here by Aube), coarse grains have been increased but sugar-beet and maize are developing fast. To these good entry crops, we may add a not inconsiderable acreage of lucerne for dehydration. In the south of Paris (Eure-et-Loir, Loiret) there was traditionally a lack of 'heads of rotation'. There are not many sugar-beets but maize is spreading considerably, it is further more irrigated in part. But these mainly cereal rotations are not without problems.

In the areas with a stock production (and with a large fodder area), wheat finds quite easily a valid entry crop among fodder crops (fodder maize, fodder beet, legumes . . .) and also oil seed crop. Nevertheless, in certain intermediate areas (ex. Meurthe-et-Moselle, Côte-d'Or, Indre), wheat after wheat is quite frequent. The importance of wheat is very slight in the areas essentially used for animal breeding, such as the department of Morbihan and in the Landes, an important part of which is used for what is almost a maize monoculture.

For the north of the Paris Basin, the Office Central de Comptabilité Agricole de Soissons (OCCAS, 1972) indicates (Table IV) that the best entry crop for wheat is potato; then come: lucerne, sugar-beet, peas, rape seed, maize, wheat. But differences in yields become less as the years go by, probably due to a better adjustment of growing practices for every entry crop.

DISEASES, A MAJOR INFLUENCE ON ANNUAL YIELDS

Though the farmer is not very conscious of this, the success of wheat in different crop sequences is above all at the moment, a problem of health conditions. The other factors may at the present time be quite well controlled by the choice of varieties and cultivation methods according to local conditions.

High yield varieties were selected with satisfying resistances to some fungi:

Black rust: Capitole, Etoile de Choisy, Hardi, Talent . . .
Yellow rust: Remois, Hardi, Heima, Maris-Huntsman, Talent . . .
Loose smut: almost all
Foot rot and take all: Atou, Cappelle, Joss, Remois
Powdery mildew: Cappelle, Champlein, Maris-Huntsman, Talent, Top.

On the contrary, no selection was carried out against brown foot rot and ear blight nor speckled leaf blotch. At least for the north of the Paris Basin yields depend mainly on the climatic and cultural conditions which promote more or less these two pests, chiefly fusarium. The higher yields in the south of Paris, with a drier spring than in the north does not seem to have any other explanation.

Spraying during growth with systemic fungicides (Benomyl, Carbendazim, methyl-thiophanate associated or not with manebe and mancozebe, ethyrimol, tridemorphe) carried out in the last three years has controlled pests. But an efficient protection costs the equivalent of 500 kg/ha of wheat, with a percentage of success from 30 to 50%. Then the advisability of spraying has to be studied very carefully. Light and chalky soils, certain varieties (Joss, Talent, Courtot, Hardi . . .), mild winters, cereals as preceding crop, 'rich' preceding crops and excessive nitrogen doses, sowings carried out too early and too concentrated make spraying more likely to be profitable. But the farmer must be able to reach yields higher than 5500 kg (Lescar *et al.*, 1973).

Possible damage by nematodes, exists chiefly in high cereal rotations, but its actual importance is unknown.

OTHER VARIETAL CHARACTERS

Rather varied climatic conditions in the wheat production areas in France have led to a great diversifying of selection relative to early maturity and suitability for alternative winter or spring sowing.

Early maturity
Very early: Etoile de Choisy, Talent
Early: Brennus, Capitole, Chrismar, Top
Less early: Champlein, Heima, Joss, Maris-Huntsman.

Later varieties such as Cappelle are less sought after now. However, Atou gives good results in northern areas whereas very early wheats are used in southern areas to escape premature ripening.

Alternateness
The following popular varieties are listed in order of latest sowing date:
Winter varieties, 15 January: Capitole, Heima, Maris-Huntsman, Remois, Top
Half winter varieties, 15 February: Hardi
Half winter varieties, 1 March, half alternative: Champlein, Talent
Alternative, 15 March: Charles-Peguy, Magali.

Spring varieties, whose yields are lower than for varieties sown in winter are much less used. However, substantial advances have been made. Now the farmer is giving up frost resistant varieties (Alsace 22, Cote d'Or, Heima . . .), with a lower productivity than usual varieties and prefers, if the wheat is frostbitten, to sow again a spring wheat. Moreover, the baking capacity of these is often good and they are used as 'improving' wheats. Thus we have: Aronde, Atys, Cesar, Florence-Aurore, Kolibri, Rex . . .

RESISTANCE TO LODGING

Most of the present varieties have an average to very good resistance to lodging. Their height is less than 1 m with a more lignified stalk. This allows heavier doses of nitrogen fertilisers, particularly if the farmer is able to avoid too great a number of tillings. Furthermore, the use of CCC should practically eliminate the hazards.

Nevertheless, INRA is doing research on half-dwarf wheats. The variety 'Courtot' (very early and alternative to spring) was registered. This type seems more suited to central and south of France.

Other characteristics such as tilling, resistance to shattering and out-growth are being worked on by breeders.

Though some work is being carried out on hybrid wheats, they are not expected to be used in practice for the next few years.

Now, about forty-five varieties are registered by the 'Permanent Technical Committee of Breeding' (CTPS). Production control and certifications of seeds are made by the 'Official Commission of Certification (COC)' and the 'Official Service of Control (SOC)'.

TILLAGE

It is known that wheat needs a rather firm seedbed for numerous reasons (depth of sowing, tilling, health conditions). But, in light soils, hazards of 'glossing' the surface during winter are high. Then, it is difficult to specify the sequences of tillage, which varies according to soils. One tries to leave light soils cloddy enough and to thin heavy soils. Usually, the soil is ploughed 10 cm deep in autumn, or more in the late winter.

According to the soil conditions, sowings are made directly on the ploughed land or after harrowing or crosskilling, seed drills being force sunk to insure a shallow (0·5–1 cm) and regular drilling.

In autumn, rotary cultivators are also used (particularly after maize) in very well levelled soils, with the sequence rotavator-drill or with a combined machine (semavator), the sowing being made in the front of the rotor. The main advantage of this method is the speed of the sowing at a period when the time saving is very important. Its drawbacks are the danger of poor sowing if conditions are bad and, perhaps, an increase of pests in the case of a mild winter.

In spring, wheat is crosskilled in limestone and clay soils, harrowing being totally abandoned.

SEED DENSITY AND NITROGEN FERTILISATION

The interdependence of these two factors is still poorly understood by growers. The best yields would be obtained with about 600 ears/m^2, if lodging were not a danger, moreover, seedling misses are higher according to lateness in sowing. But, too early sowings favour take-all root diseases and lodging. Thus, the farmer is led to choose seed-rate in accordance with the quality of the seed and also the variety (with more or less tillering capacity), the time of sowing and the soil conditions. For example, he may get very good results with a 120 kg/ha rate of Capitole on about the 20th of October and a 200 kg rate of Champlein in January.

According to the winter climatic conditions, the seedling density is variable. One of the roles of nitrogen fertilisation is to act on the more unfavourable yield component. If the plant density is low, one increases tilling by a maximum dose at this time. On the other hand, if it is too high, the nitrogen fertilisation is delayed as long as possible. If the early spring climate favours tilling nevertheless, CCC makes it possible to lower the risks of lodging. But it is considered that for normal shoot densities, high nitrogen doses can be used without shortener sprays.

It is estimated that wheat takes up 3 kg of N to form 100 kg of grain. A target of 7000 kg/ha supposes the absorption of 210 kg of N. The N fertilisations must provide in quantity and at the required time, the complement of the supply from the soil.

This supply depends on:

The nitrogen residues after the previous harvest (higher after potatoes than after beets or maize);
the nitrate leaching during the winter, related to rainfall, and its distribution;
the soil mineralisation during the spring;
the organic manures sometimes ploughed in.

Particular attention is brought to bear on the assessment of these supplies for different types of soils, cropping systems and years. This allows one to give an approximate dose of nitrogen fertiliser, the time of dressing being influenced less by the soil than the conditions of the field and the crop in spring. A local advice system for nitrogen fertilisation is now being studied.

On an average, doses vary from 50 kg/ha after 'rich' entry crops in fertile soils to more than 150 kg after poor entry crops in badly mineralising soils. Field trials show that the surest division is $\frac{1}{3}$ tilling $\frac{2}{3}$ shooting, with ammonium nitrate fertilisers. With nitrogen solution ($\frac{1}{2}$ urea, $\frac{1}{4}$ ammonia, $\frac{1}{4}$ nitrate) doses are usually raised by 10–15 kg/ha, with a higher first dressing or one dressing only at the height of tilling. In some areas with drier winters, nitrogen is dressed before winter.

Usually, P and K are dressed on wheat crops but doses are fixed according to the whole rotation.

WEEDING AND PESTS

Combine harvesting and cereal rotations make weeding of wheat necessary and the techniques are various. The problem is a very real one in the control of gramineae and of several dicotyledoneae (common fumitory, scratch grass, gipsy weed, scarlet pimpernel, chickweed . . .) the farmer is confronted by a wide variety of herbicides none having a total selectivity or efficiency and whose use must correspond to quite precise phases of wheat and weed growth. He must also plan these treatments within the weedkilling process of the other crops of the rotation. This question is not without risks, according to toxicity hazards, not only for wheat but also for soil microflora and the fate of residues.

From time to time, hessian fly and wheat midge cause damage.

QUALITY OF FRENCH WHEAT PRODUCTION

At the present time, wheat is bought from the farmer only on the basis of yield and weight per hectolitre. So, the French farmer tends to choose the high productive varieties. The definition of quality for wheat is very difficult because, according to the climatic characteristics of the year, the average of French wheats is more or less satisfactory for the area of production. Although good bread can be made with nearly all flours, mechanisation of bakery demands a standardisation of lots, as do increasing exports.

French millers assess the wheat value by Chopin alveograph. According to W and the feature of the curve, the wheat lots are classified for biscuit processing, rusk processing or French bakery. 'Improving' wheat lots (high W for Common Market) are mainly dependent on the variety.

The 'National Interprofessionnel Office for Cereals' (ONIC), which controls the trade in France, strives to promote a policy of quality by perks according to the class of the lots put on the market. For this, the Zeleny sedimentation test, Hagberg's falling times, protein content and impurities are used. Current production is in class II or III according to the year (Z:25–30, H:160–220, P:11–12·5), improving wheats not being graded.

Every year a survey on a sample at random is carried out in the main departments of wheat production and samples are analysed by three groups of methods: alveograph, ONIC classification and breadmaking tests. Features of the last harvest are known as early as October, for the French flour industry and exporters.

REFERENCE

Lescar, L., Bouchet, F. and Poussard, C. Trois années de lutte contre les maladies des organes aeriens du blé tendre d'hiver. Institut Technique des Céréales et Fourrages. 'La Lutte contre les maladies des céréales', Versailles, February 1973, 211–221.

DISCUSSION

Chairman: In British conditions early sowing may lead to excess disease problems. Would you think it would lead to excessive susceptibility to rust in France?

J. Hébert: Mildew is usual in France. Other than this the main problem is *Fusarium* not rust. It is necessary to have a high root crop rotation to restrict disease. It seems that *Fusarium* increases with high doses of nitrogen. On the average the dose of nitrogen on the whole rotation was carried from 90 kg/ha up to 140 kg/ha/year in approximately 6 years.

M. V. Rao (Indian Agricultural Research Institute, New Delhi): You said you are applying CCC spray to the wheat crop. Do you advocate CCC application over a wide scale over the whole country? If so, does it delay the crop and cause it to be more liable to infection? This is our experience in India.

J. Hébert: CCC is a saving practice because, if we have low densities, it is not necessary to use CCC; but with late sowing with high densities, or high rate sowing with a mild winter, we must apply CCC, but we do have more diseases.

F. Lupton (Plant Breeding Institute, Cambridge, UK): Three small points. What about the *Septoria* picture? Secondly, have you any evidence that late applied nitrogen goes into the grain? Thirdly, are awn wheats popular in some parts of France.

J. Hébert: *Septoria* is an annual problem. We have had years without and some years with *Septoria*. Systemic sprays are useful in case of *Septoria*. I suppose in southern France they have awned wheats.

Nitrogen is divided for purposes of tilling or nutrition. We make applications to avoid too much tilling; but if we want high yield, it is necessary to apply nitrogen, and we do this at shooting. But applications of nitrogen at earing or flowering does not pay, because the wheat is not bought on the basis of protein. Probably it is difficult to improve grain proteins because the nitrogen does not get into the soil, and it is immobilised by microbiological activity.

Chairman: Perhaps you could emphasise a point you made in the last answer. You say that there is no payment in France for grain quality?

J. Hébert: No. For the farmer there is no payment, but there is for the co-operative.

Chairman: But the co-operative then transfers the payment back to the farmer?

J. Hébert: No, it is impossible because wheat is received in bulk. Probably if Maris-Huntsman is successful in France, that will induce payment for quality!

Chairman: I think with that remark you had better leave the platform!

General Discussion

Chairman: We have heard from these five papers a fascinating description of the enormous diversity of conditions in which the wheat crop is grown—from the highly intensive treatment in France and Holland with very high production levels, to the almost marginal cultivation of the crop in some parts of Australia.

I wonder whether, at this stage, I could ask Mr Edward Bullen to make some comment on the agronomy of the crop in Britain.

E. Bullen (Ministry of Agriculture, Fisheries and Food, London): First I should say that I speak as an agronomist and not as a representative of my Ministry. I would like to comment on the UK position as I see it, dealing with a few problems loosely defined as agronomic.

In the UK we grow about one million hectares of wheat, which is fairly small compared with some of the countries we have heard about. But it is second in arable acreage to barley. The acreage is small compared with that of grass which on a day like this you may think is better suited to our climate!

Ninety per cent is winter sown—October or November—because there is about a 20% superiority in yield over spring wheat. The UK only produces about two-thirds of its cereal requirements. We import a substantial amount, not merely wheat for bread, but also of maize for animal feeding and other purposes.

Wheat is grown mostly in the east of England; rainfalls varying from 500 to 700 mm. A statistical point which is important is that August is the wettest month in our main cereal growing counties. Economically cereals have been, until the last year or two, a low return crop so it has been grown on a low cost basis, with conservative use of the more expensive sprays and techniques. There hasn't effectively been any worthwhile quality premium for the British farmer since 1939. The farmer has felt that he would be better served by growing a heavier yield of something acceptable, considering that a large amount has gone for feed in many years. It may be better not merely for the farmer but for the country, that we should produce a high yield of wheat of feeding quality, and cut back on maize imports rather than pursue the possibility of high breadmaking wheats which may be impossible in some years. This is a controversial point about which no doubt I shall be chased.

The other point which is significant is that, although the wheat acreage has tended to creep up in the last 20 years and at the same time yields have increased rapidly, markedly fewer farmers are producing it. The scale of enterprise on the individual farm is increasing quite dramatically. Nitrogen maturing, in particular, is the key to a high yield of wheat in the UK. I shall not mention disease because it was thoroughly discussed by Dr Joan Moore.

The cost of the man and his machine has gone up at a frightening rate. These, so-called, fixed costs have taken off and there is a somewhat limited scope for restoring them by changed farm structure. Farm structure and field structure limit to some extent the use of the sort of tackle which we heard about from America. But there is, however, some scope for economies in tillage work. Because so much of our wheat is sown in October and November, when arable farmers are harvesting sugar-beet and potatoes, we must go towards reduced labour input. Direct drilling is practised and is being investigated, but there are problems with slugs, with couch grass and of getting the right machinery to give a decent plant so there is preference for reduced tillage, replacing the plough with tined implements, or discs, and perhaps halving the labour and fuel inputs. Other problems in eastern counties are the grass weeds *Avena fatua*, *Avena ludoviciana* and *Alopecuris mysuroides*—black grass. If current prices are maintained the more routine use of herbicides against weed grasses will be possible. This may be just as well because some of the semi-dwarf varieties provide favourable ecological niches for the wild oat because crop competition is a major factor in keeping grass weeds under control. In contrast to many other countries, storage is normally on the farm in the UK. The farmer has the responsibility for drying his grain and of keeping it in good condition until sale. The use of propionic acid, etc., avoids the need for drying of grain for feed but is a major cost and a major problem. Yields have increased faster than the improvement and replacement of dryers, giving difficulties.

The average yield of wheat is about 4 t/ha in the UK. We achieve, with the best conditions, yields of 6–8. I don't think we would claim to go as high as 10 t, which Dr Rao referred to. The challenge is to push these yields from 4 t/acre to something which we would now consider optimistic but which our children will have to consider realistic. Remarks have been made about farming 'at half-cock' and they are appropriate to UK cereal production, even though our yields are not low.

M. Cookson (RHM Bakeries Ltd, London): Despite what the last speaker said, I think economically the British miller making breadmaking flour will be using the maximum amount of home-grown wheat. And as I am a baker I am naturally interested in getting the most consistent flour.

Various remarks have been made on what millers and bakers can do to get over this problem of variability in wheats and flour quality. There were some suggestions that air classification in milling could help correct a number of deficiencies, and there was talk that microwave baking can overcome other problems. But as I see it, we still want as consistent a wheat for breadmaking as we can have in this country. I would not like wheat breeders to go away from here thinking that millers and bakers can swing changes, and no matter what the wheat is like they can make a good bread-making flour from which the baker can make good consistent bread.

I would like to ask one question, on the subject of yield. In Britain you cannot have both yield and protein content and quality yet, in America and the Netherlands there is no relationship between the two! Could somebody please reconcile these differences of what appears to be happening here and what is happening in America and the Netherlands?

F. Pushman (Plant Breeding Institute, Cambridge, UK): We have not been intensively breeding for high protein qualities but for yield. If you look at the varieties grown in Britain in a constant environment, the higher yielding varieties have less protein. If we look at a range of early selection, we could probably select for higher protein without necessarily losing the yield advantage. We have in fact found some varieties in our collection at the Plant Breeding Institute which do have additional protein above their yield potential. However, without the necessary impetus this was not our major objective. Other countries have been positively trying to get a high yield of protein as well as a high yield of grain. If we start to look for this more actively in Britain, with the encouragement of both the Milling and Baking Industries, we shall probably attain it. It won't happen overnight! Therefore, we are looking actively at the relationship of baking quality and protein content to fertiliser application, so that we know what we can do with the present varieties while in the process of increasing the yield on protein in newer varieties. The two things must go together. But we must know what *all* varieties are capable of doing, and whether it is economically worth putting more nitrogen on some varieties than on others. In the case of Maris-Huntsman it is doubtful; in the case of Maris-Widgeon it gives a very useful increase in quality.

E. Sanchez-Monge (Polytechnical University, Madrid): It is often said that Spain has a Mediterranean climate, but this is true for only part of the country. The central high plain is very dry, with cold winters and hot summers. The northern coast is very humid with no extremes in temperature in the winter or in the summer. The southwestern region is more humid than the central, with mild winters and very hot summers. We even have a small area of sub-tropical climate round the Malaga coast where sugar cane is cultivated. Both common and durum wheats are grown, and the total acreage is about 3·5 million ha. Durum wheat is grown in about 100 000–300 000 ha, mainly in the south. Sowing time starts in early October and extends until late December according to when the rain comes.

More than three-quarters of the varieties used are of recent Spanish, Italian or French origin. Recently some Mexican wheats from C I M M T T have become popular, especially in the south. Fertilisation is required only for phosphorus and for nitrogen in accordance with the spring rainfall. It is difficult to advise many farmers of the necessity for potassium fertilisation.

Most varieties are early enough to escape infection with black rust. Yellow rust seldom occurs. Moisture conditions are such that no severe epidemics of mildew or *septoria* are produced. Hesian fly can be a problem about once in every ten years, especially in the Ebro valley, when there are early rains and sowing. The worst accident that can happen is scorching during the milky stage of the grain because of strong, hot, dry winds. This year we have had a very big crop reduction in central and southern Spain due to this. The difference in price for durum does not compensate the farmer for its lower yield in comparison with bread wheat. The quality of all durum varieties is excellent but breeding of durum has been neglected until recently. The varieties are too tall and the straw weak.

Chairman: There is no English word for the grain drying you describe in France, it is called 'enchaudage'.

Hilkka Suomela (Helsinki University): Crop year studies of wheat quality have been made in Finland by the Grain Research Committee since the year 1966. The Committee has 10 members representing the Ministry of Agriculture, Flour Industry, Grain Research, Education, Crop Husbandry, State Granary, etc. Finland has the most northerly cultivated areas of wheat in the world. Spring wheat areas are in general three or four times larger than the areas of winter wheat because of the severe winter. Finland is self-sufficient in bread grain and generally in feed grain too. The quality of Finnish wheat has been very good in the 1970s because we have had several years with favourable weather conditions for grain production. High protein content is typical of Finnish wheat. In some years, for example in 1972, winter wheat had nearly the same potential content (15%) as spring wheat. Finland has many winter wheat cultivars with a good baking quality. Falling number and protein content are the principal quality parameters.

V. A. Johnson (Nebraska University): I would like to take up a point raised earlier by Dr Russell Eggitt. After the First World War a very extensive acreage of marginal land in the extreme western edge of the Plains area was taken out of grass, largely for wheat production. In the ensuing years a lot of that land has moved back again into grass. And I think that, as Dr Heyne said, we have learned a lesson and much is done with the idea of conserving the Plains and keeping it in a reasonably productive state. That means controlling wind erosion as well as water erosion.

I should like to make another comment. It seems to me that we breeders need guidance from members of the industry as to what represents reasonable breeding goals, keeping in mind that we have a great array of characteristics or traits with which we must be concerned, and we cannot adequately deal with all of them. Consequently, a rigid system of priorities must be assigned. The breeder is forced into this: and so I would make a plea to you to engage in a speculation with us as to what represent reasonable breeding goals for wheat quality—not for tomorrow, not for next year, but for a decade from now.

Chairman: This is the guidance which the breeder surely needs, his response cannot be quick—he has to have adequate guidance. Perhaps at another session the processors would be prepared to tell us what sort of flour we're going to need in 10 or 15 years' time. It would be interesting for us to learn from Elmer Heyne or Virgil Johnson what are going to be the consequences of the return to production of the 'set aside' area—both in relation to the type and quantity of production and what are going to be the consequences for American agriculture.

E. G. Heyne (Kansas University): The restrictions were relaxed and although the acreage is large, it is spread over a large area, and it includes all crop production—only part of it is related to wheat. So we did have an increase in wheat acreage—there's no question about that. There is an increase in the maize acreage; but there was a decrease in the soya bean acreage. The farmer says: 'I'm not going to jump in'. But more is going into summer fallow—that is, the actual conservation acreage, not necessarily all the set aside acreage. But I expect, as far as wheat production is concerned, we'll see more in summer fallow, and I think this will be welcome.

D. B. Pratt (Pillsbury Company, Minneapolis): I thought it might be appropriate to point out that in the United States and in Canada there is a great deal of co-operation between plant breeders, millers and bakers through our Crop Counsel Association of the Great Plains Wheat Association. As new varieties are brought up to the point of release, or increased for release, adequate quantities of these are milled and evaluated against controls, and portions of the finished flour are distributed to some 30–45 cereal chemists or bakery laboratories for evaluation of the chemistry and physical properties as well as the breadmaking properties. This results in the grading of a new variety as being equal to standard or superior to standard on a number of different factors. This then, hopefully, provides the plant breeder with some steering in terms of what the market really needs. A constant question of the plant breeder is 'What do you want?' As a miller, it is a constant question for me. I talk to a bakery customer and ask him: 'What do you want?' But he really can't tell you: he says: 'Well, it's got to make a good loaf of bread, but it's got to make it my way'. It's a tremendous enigma to figure out.

D. J. Samborski (Canadian Department of Agriculture, Winnipeg): We don't have problems in Canada with quality, because of the legislation dealing with licensing of varieties. Our priorities are on quality: we must have disease resistance and quality; we have not bred for yield at all. Our present day varieties are not yielding one iota better than Marquis was: all that we have is disease resistance and we maintain our quality.

G. N. Irvine (Canadian Grain Commission, Winnipeg): In connection with Dr Johnson's comment, we face the same problem: What is it that the world is going to require, in terms of the export market particularly, in 12–15 years from now? Our response so far has been, within the limitations of our handling system, to try a belt-and-braces approach to this. That is, we are continuing to develop the equal-to-Marquis wheats: we have now got a high yielding wheat which is overly strong, which probably might find a place in the European market as a supporting wheat. We also have a series of grades now which will take wheats which are weaker than Marquis, but which perhaps give the plant breeders the possibility of producing higher yielding types, if anybody in the world wants it.

The biggest problem we have is that these grades must be identifiable so that you can segregate them and not end up with one great mishmash of all the different types together.

Session VII

SUMMING UP

Concluding Remarks

K. L. BLAXTER

Rowett Research Institute, Bucksburn, Aberdeen, U K

During our discussions in this unique symposium we have ranged very widely from anthropology to electron microscopy and from the technological complexity of modern industrial grain processing to what Professor Riley has called 'Cytogenetic trickology'. The progression has been orderly; from the genetic origins of the grain, its biochemistry and physiology through its response to disease, its agronomy and its effect on man to wider consideration of the economic world in which grain is bought and sold. To summarise the detailed factual information presented in the papers we have heard is not necessary, for all have been presented with the utmost clarity. More profitable is to attempt to integrate the information and views which have been presented. Any integration, however, has to consider a context. What we should now do is to look forward at the alternative options which are open and consider the actions that might be taken.

The central problem which has emerged in the symposium is the relationship between yield and quality and I intend to deal in the main with these aspects. Yield and quality are very different attributes. Yield is an absolute measure readily determined and easily compared on a country to country basis. Quality, however, is an aggregation of attributes and to define it entails defining a purpose. During the course of the symposium we have distinguished many different types of quality. Thus, we have considered nutritional quality in a wide sense in that we have dealt with the overall value of bread as a source of the many nutrients man requires. We have also dealt with the specific quality of the proteins of the wheat grain, with baking quality, milling quality, organoleptic quality and even that quality of being a preferred item in diet which Professor Mary Douglas told us may well be very deeply rooted in our social origins. How best to collate all these various aspects of quality so as to arrive at some simple statements of value to agronomists, plant breeders and others who need to know what cognisance they should take of the relative importance of yield and quality is clearly difficult. We can, however, commence with a logical analysis of the nature of quality by asking in the first place what does man himself require of the bread he eats.

We can distinguish four primary requirements; bread must meet his nutritional needs, bread must be safe, it must be culturally acceptable and it must be adequate in amount. We can consider each in more detail.

The basic concern of nutrition is to meet the overall dietary needs of man. Man is not a weanling rat nor does he live by bread alone. In the UK only 14% of the energy of the diet of the population is provided by bread and while there might be a greater reliance on the bread grains in some countries as evidenced by Dr Carpenter's very revealing description of Indian diets, it appears highly improbable that experiments carried out on weanling rats in which bread is the sole food have any real relevance to man's need. It follows that to improve bread by either genetic manipulation of the composition of the grain or by adding nutrients to flour or bread in the course of manufacture is not necessarily the only way of improving diets for people. Because of its ubiquity in diet, however, bread becomes a very convenient vehicle for the addition of nutrients to the diet of man. In this respect it is similar to table salt which for long has been a convenient vehicle for adding iodine to the diet.

As far as the safety of bread is concerned, the experience of generations has been that bread is remarkably safe. Certainly care has to be taken to make certain that the sclerotia of ergot are not present in grain and in some areas of the world it may be necessary to consider whether or not the levels of selenium in grain grown on seleniferous soils are not too high for human consumption. Of more concern to people at present, however, is the possibility that residues of pesticides and herbicides might affect health. While this concern is undoubtedly real, it seems highly probable that it can be dissipated by better information and education of those who express it.

The food habits and food mores of populations are of extreme importance in a designation of quality in bread. Several examples can be given. First, we have the complete irrelevance of yeast-raised breads in Middle Eastern countries, an aspect which clearly has considerable implications with regard to the importance attributed to gluten quality. Similarly, the old controversy regarding the merits of white and brown bread appears, on deeper analysis, to be largely a matter of culture and aspiration and, as Dr Widdowson showed us, has little nutritional significance. In highly urbanised societies different aspects of quality emerge. Most of these are associated with what is commonly called convenience in food and this in turn relates to the whole of the structure of an industrial society. More specifically, people in industrialised countries require that their bread must either be sliced or is of such a texture that it can be readily sliced. Bread must also keep for long periods without going stale since such is the pressure on time that there is no opportunity to savour the market place and to shop once or twice a day. Finally, there is a curious requirement which may well reflect the conservative nature of man, namely that bread should be a standard and reproducible product so that what is bought one day can also be purchased the next.

With regard to the demand that bread should be adequate in amount and freely available at all times, this may again relate to the culture in which we live. Individuals are, of course, only concerned about supplies when there are shortages but they are also increasingly aware of the fact that world population increases and that more people will need more bread. Even though the *per capita* consumption of bread is falling in Western societies, it may well be that because of other factors affecting the supply of alternative foods the demand for bread may well stabilise. It is, however, doubtful whether those things which man requires of bread can necessarily be measured by demand. The evidence of the market place is not the only expression of man's needs and wants.

A consideration of these four aspects of what man requires of the bread he eats suggests very strongly that it is virtually impossible to arrive at a single specification of an aggregated series of attributes which specify a quality in bread. Rather we have to recognise the inequalities between populations and sectors of populations so as to arrive at not one but many specifications of quality in bread. In any specific context, however, it would seem possible to arrive at such a specification.

Given that a particular specification for the final product can be given, the baker in turn can specify what attributes he requires in flour. The problem here is that the attributes which the baker requires in flour depend to a large extent on the technology which he adopts. For example, the Chorleywood Process can produce good keeping bread which slices readily even from low protein flours. Given another technology, high protein in flour would be essential to give a well risen loaf. Again, the presence of α-amylase in grain may well not be a problem if the method of baking involves a very rapid heating process such as has been developed in the microwave oven. Lastly, if all homes were equipped with facilities for low temperature storage of food then we could avoid the problem of staling altogether by the simple expedient of storage at low temperature. Given a specification of the final bread it would seem sensible for the baker to assess baking quality in flour by test-baking procedures possibly associated with consumer acceptability tests. These would enable the baker to discriminate between flours in terms of the quality of the final product. Quality of final product, however, is not the sole criterion the baker applies. He has several additional problems with which to deal, all of which are concerned with the profitability of his business. Time and space are expensive and accordingly he needs to economise in mixing time and equally he needs to minimise power consumption. Since adjustments in technology are equally expensive in terms of time he also needs a standard product as his input. Indeed, the options open to the baker confronted with a variety of input flours are three-fold. He can adjust his technology to suit, he can exert a choice on the materials he purchases which, of course, he does, and in the longer term he can specify what he wants subject to the restraint of the capital investment in his plant.

Just as the baker is bound by his investment in plant so too is the miller. The critical test which he can apply is, as Dr Irvine reminded us, the yield of flour of an acceptable colour and texture. Flour is not, however, the only output from a mill. Cereal by-products have also to be considered and the adjustment of the output from a mill may well, as Dr Russell Eggitt reminded us, be in some measure dictated by the relative prices of millers' offals, other feedingstuffs and wheat grain. Happily perhaps the farming community and the compound feedingstuffs manufacturers have not yet themselves specified quality in milling offals! The miller, because he is a businessman, can equally specify a series of desiderata in grain which are of importance specifically to him and only indirectly of importance to the final consumer of bread. An example is the central role of hardness in the grain, the morphology of the crease which determines aspects of yield, and other attributes which make the preparation of a flour difficult. Like the baker, the miller has two options open to him; he can adjust his technology even to the extent of replacing it with a new technology, a problem which involves very considerable capital investment, or alternatively, he can exert a discriminatory pressure on the farming industry against wheats which are difficult or expensive to handle with his existing plant.

It would seem, from this analysis, that to define quality in wheat as distinct from quality in bread, even when there is the possibility of a close specification of what is desired as the final product, is extremely difficult indeed. The additional factors that have to be considered are those which relate to the suitability of different flours and different wheats to particular technical processes used in milling and in baking. The question inevitably arises about how far new technologies will arise in milling and baking so as to enable less desirable wheats to be used more expeditiously or, conversely, how far should cultural, manurial and breeding programmes be designed simply to provide wheats better suited to current industrial technology, realising that further revolutions in that technology may come about. Such a consideration now involves the dimension of time. Here we must adduce the evidence that it takes some 10–15 years to move from an initial genetic isolate of a wheat plant to the introduction of a new variety on a wide scale. In order to give the plant breeder a specification of quality which he can take in to his breeding programmes we have to undertake predictions. I would like to suggest that the discussion following this paper should attempt certain predictions. Recognising that quality is not a single concept common to all countries, we can simply keep our consideration to the UK. We clearly need: (1) a prediction of the rate of change in the ultimate demand for bread and an estimate of whether the nutritional, safety and cultural aspects which I have outlined will undergo any appreciable change; (2) a prediction of the rate of change in the technology of breadmaking and how far this might affect the specification of flours; (3) a prediction of the rate of change in milling technologies and in by-product demand bearing in mind that entirely new technologies based on wet processing might emerge.

It is perhaps reasonable to expect one who has stated that he will attempt to integrate to give his opinion of the situation rather than to ask others to do so! I think that it is grossly unfair to blame the plant breeder for failing to satisfy all the various demands which are made upon him for quality in wheat grain, whatever that might be. Furthermore, it has to be pointed out that there are alternative ways of reaching ends. One can add materials to flour or even to bread at the baking stage rather than incorporate them genetically. Until the millers and bakers and those representing consumer interests can specify far more precisely than at present what will be the attributes of quality in 10 years' time then there is every reason for the breeder simply to concentrate on yield, on the elimination of known defects and possibly set a desirable level of, let us say, 12% for the protein content of the grain. It has to be recognised that the breeder in some respects has far more important things to do than to cater for matters which could more readily be dealt with by mechanical ingenuity. He has to make a plant capable of producing grain in an intrinsically variable climate. He has to consider the hardiness of the plant, its resistance to drought and its resistance to pests and diseases which are both subject to mutation and change. In addition, he has to increase yield per unit land per unit time. It would be unfortunate in the extreme, in my opinion, to reduce the emphasis on all those factors which affect yield for the sake of relatively small advances in quality attributes which may be rendered nugatory by advances in the technology of milling and baking. If, however, we could designate what Dr Lupton called an idiotype in terms of definable attributes of quality and be reasonably certain that these would be unchanged over a period of 10–15 years, then there would be merit in pursuing them, but only if yield is not jeopardised.

Having discussed quality at length perhaps we should say something about the aspects of yield. At various times in the discussion questions have been raised about the limits to the improvement of yield and the additional resources which are needed to extend still further the productivity of land sown to wheat. The remarks in discussion by Professor Aylward, Dr Edelman, Sir Ernst Chain and also some of the less hilarious ones by Dr Angold are very relevant here. So too are those by Dr Samborski and Dr Moore in their presented papers. We can consider questions of ultimate productivity by a dissection of the restraints which affect the wheat crop.

It is clear that our knowledge about the rate-limiting steps in the synthesis of the carbohydrates and proteins of the wheat grain is severely limiting. We do not know whether the rate-limiting steps are at the stage of amino acid synthesis, amino acid activation and transport, or at the level of the ribosome. We do, however, know something about the limits of the photosynthetic capability of the wheat plant as judged by studies of the isolated leaf. These indicate that the wheat plant shows light saturation unlike the maize plant which is, of course, a C4 rather than a C3 plant. It has been suggested that present limits in yield could be achieved by using varieties with shorter straws and by taking cognisance of analysis of the dynamics of growth. There is, however, clearly an absolute limit to the productivity of wheat. More important perhaps is the fact that wheat is grown in monoculture. An incredible toll is taken in the field by diseases and pests and these are not fully documented in terms of their quantitative effect. Certainly, as Dr Cooke pointed out, there is wisdom in nature even in monocultures since many of the soil-borne diseases in cereals eventually achieve a curious ecological balance. Even so, it is very obvious that there are considerable restraints placed by disease, by pests and by the fertility of the soil on the realisation of the biological potential of the wheat plant.

There are, however, particularly in the developed countries and to a growing extent in the developing ones, additional restraints on the productivity of wheat and indeed on the productivity of agriculture generally. The work by Pimental on the maize crop illustrates this very well since it shows that considerable inputs of energy not as solar radiation but as fossil fuel are required to support the modern mechanised and fertiliser-dependent culture on which wheat production depends. For the UK most calculations show that for every joule recovered in terms of wheat grain 0·5 J has been expended in terms of primary fuel equivalent to meet the fuel costs of cultivation, grain drying, on-farm transport, the manufacture of fertilisers and the application of agrochemicals. The balance in this instance is positive but calculations for the whole of British agriculture which, of course, has a very large livestock sector, shows that to produce 1 J as human food entails the expenditure of some 2·5 J of fuel energy. If an estimate is made of the energy cost of the secondary processing of farm produce—that is the milling of wheat, the manufacture of bread and all other aspects of modern industrial processing of farm produce—then it appears that every J we purchase from the shops as food entails the consumption of 6·5 J of fossil fuel. No doubt such a calculation and those made by others will lead to an acceleration of research to find new sources of power for modern agricultural technologies. Such a search may take very long and in the interim it may well be that we have to take very considerable risks concerning the future of man's food supply. Certainly, in the developing countries, it is hardly

conceivable that the solutions to their food problems will come about
by an investment in modern fossil fuel energy dependent agricultures.
We can, perhaps, in closing quote Ralph Hodgson's poem which deals
with wheat, and you will note that I have altered but a single word.

I saw in vision the oil in the wheat,
And in the shops nothing for people to eat,
Nothing to eat in stupidity street.

DISCUSSION

Chairman: Thank you very much for your excellent review of what we have
discussed in this symposium. You have called our attention to the problems we face
in the future and posed three questions.

G. A. H. Elton (Ministry of Agriculture, Fisheries and Food, London): I would
like to have a shot at answering some of the questions that Dr Blaxter posed. You ask
what we feel is going to happen to the demand for bread, the quality of bread, safety,
processing technology and milling technology so as to arrive at guidance for the
plant breeders. I predict that consumption of bread will go down, there may be some
hesitation before that decline takes place, but inevitably it will occur. As far as safety
of bread is concerned, I think we are going to see an increase of public concern. This
is true of all foods. All the additives which are used in breadmaking have, of course,
been tested thoroughly. Many of them need to be more thoroughly tested as do new
additives which will have to be developed to enable us to handle new types of wheat
in the future. On the question of advances in technology, obviously one can have two
main approaches. You can either decide that one is to breed wheat to fit the technology, or one can try to change the technology to fit the wheats that can be grown
well. It is almost impossible to say whether we are going to have microwave baking
in 5 or 10 years' time, and thus we have got to use both approaches. We want the plant
breeders to produce wheats that will be suitable for existing technology, and they
should have up their sleeves wheats that would be suitable for the new technologies,
particularly for microwave baking, which could work with low protein content.
When one comes to what sorts of wheat, one would want to specify them in terms
of existing farming technology. We want a hard wheat and a low amylase wheat.
I would put those as the two highest in priority and in front of a high protein content
judged by the technology of turning our wheat into bread. If one can have a high
protein as well, that's good, but I think it has got to be hard wheat and low amylase
wheat.
    Finally I think we must specify in more precise chemical or biological terms to
the plant breeders and millers and bakers what is wanted. It is no good just saying
we want wheat that when baked gives a good bread because this means that the
plant breeder has to use large quantities of wheat in order to test. We want chemical,
physical and biochemical specifications of parameters that can be applied to a single
wheat grain or to single ears of wheat.

P. W. Russell Eggitt (Spillers Ltd, Cambridge, UK): I would not disagree with anything that Dr Elton said regarding the sort of specification and instructions we should provide for our wheat breeders in the UK. Clearly we want a better wheat and a higher yield. In considering how baking technology can change in 15 years, we have, however, to take into account the enormous capital invested in our present plant and the likely life of that plant. Although we might have microwave baking in the future, I believe it will be far more distant than 15 years. We have, obviously, a great sense of responsibility in what we ask our plant breeders to do because they will be looking for their F.1 cultivars in the immediate future, and it will take 10 years to bring one to fruition. I would suggest, yes, we want a winter wheat as hard as possible, but we have to be realistic in setting our targets. We want first a wheat which will on average produce a protein content of 12% in the United Kingdom. Secondly it should have what Dr Lupton calls 'a milling texture' at least comparable to the best we have at the moment and thirdly, although one has yet to devise the tests, I would like to be able to assess what the baking quality is likely to be on very small quantities.

A practical test of its value is that one should mill the flour from this new wheat and mix 70% of this flour with 30% of the flour from a strong Northern Spring wheat of North America and bake it. The baking tests should be related to the CBP process. If that test gives excellent bread, I think everything else is looked after, the amylase and the so-called protein qualities. We are not quite so much concerned at the present moment with the baking quality of any individual variety baked on its own.

F. H. Ellis (Spillers Ltd, Cambridge, UK): Dr Russell Eggitt has covered my main point which is that the very recent capital investment at the Chorleywood Bread Process is certainly going to have a 20–25-year life before it is replaced. In addition to Dr Elton's comment on microwave baking, direct carbon dioxide injection is another experimental approach which has been held in abeyance because of the capital investment involved, and which will materially alter the whole fermentation process if it really does come to be a practical proposition. One can visualise in the future plant bakery an operation from which is eliminated the whole of the final proof system with its requirements for temperature and humidity control after the normal mixing process. This is feasible with the activated dough development recipes which we now have.

K. Blaxter (Rowett Research Institute, Aberdeen): We have just contemplated replacing a biological means of leavening bread by an input of fossil fuel energy. This used to be done by yeast free, gratis and for nothing and of course we had to spend a little time. Carbon dioxide injection is likely to be equally expensive, if not more so in terms of fossil fuel.

D. A. Doling (The Lord Rank Research Centre, High Wycombe, Bucks): I do commend Dr Blaxter on his review and particularly for his comments on the energy situation. If I may criticise slightly I regret that his sympathy stopped with the plant breeder. In my view it should go to the farmer as well and the farmer is an element that is perhaps a little bit missing in our discussion. We can congratulate the Rank Prize Funds on the blend of people here today, but I think we could have done with one or two real farmers! A number of us are close to the farm gate, but as far as I know, none of us actually earns a living from the land. May I make a plea that the milling and baking industry do something to sell the Chorleywood Process to the English farmer. To the best of my knowledge he is unaware that it exists and when you talk to farmers about Chorleywood, very few of them know where it is and what it is, and although I have been associated with farming for a very long time I myself had to go to Manitoba to hear about it! The reason for this is that the English farmer is a rather suspicious individual. He can carry on for quite a while despite brewers and millers stating that his grains are no good for anything! Last year up to 500 000 t more went into the mix quite happily. The farmer would be very glad to hear about that, but I think his suspicions would be aroused if this goes on without his being aware that those very same wheats, though not perfect, can be used in this new process. I would suggest that as a practical measure something should be done by bakers and millers to sell this process to the farmer more directly than has been done in the past. To me one of the great values of this get-together has been the level of communication enjoyed, and I would indeed like to thank the Rank Prize Funds for arranging it and to commend further commodity meetings of this kind.

M. A. Cookson (R H M Bakeries Ltd, London): I would like to follow on from the last speaker, and to say that the wonderful thing about this symposium has been the blend of experts who, to the best of my knowledge, have never sat down in one room before to give their different points of view. I sincerely hope that this is going to be followed up in some way. We shouldn't just go away from here in an hour's time and say that 'that was a good idea' and that nothing further should be done about it. The challenge has been given. What can the baking industry and the milling industry put down in finite terms to guide the plant breeders and the farmers? Dr Elton has indicated some points and Dr Eggitt has indicated others. I started writing a speci-fication last night on what you might call 'Selsdon Wheat'. This hotel gave rise to Selsdon Man, so why not Selsdon Wheat? And we can be very finite and quite scientific in defining what characteristics we want. We can define for Britain and the U K what we want for the batch bread of Scotland and Northern Ireland as well as for pan bread. The definition is very much the same as that required in North America and in Europe.

I do not think, however, that this is the time or the place to read out my definition because it is technical and because representatives of the industry from major groups, and indeed other bodies connected with the matter, should get together with wheat breeders to thrash out a definition. We will probably want another week long conference to do that.

K. Blaxter: I have the specification of Selsdon Wheat in front of me and despite Dr Cookson's protestations I think it should be duplicated and given out here. The specification includes no less than 10 attributes. Now how do we put these together, how do we weight them? Eventually the plant breeder has got to be told what priorities he gives to these characteristics. Is it, for example, more important to have a good colour or a good gluten quality and what exactly do we mean by a good gluten quality? Here we are back to definitions which are still slightly ambiguous though partly biochemically defined as Dr Elton would like.

M. A. Cookson: I have no objection to the specification being handed out; it is just my personal view and something I know I would like to change if I was spending an hour on the thing. The indefinable terms I put down can be defined and I could place my order of priority to guide the breeders in the order of one to eight. I am sure that Dr Russell Eggitt would also put a backing order to it, and I am sure that Dr Elstow would do the same. I am sure we could hammer out a list of priorities.

Guidance to wheat breeders for preparation of future breadmaking varieties of

'The Selsdon Wheat'

1. *General*

It should be recognisably different either by shape, colour or some other feature from feed wheats, to avoid unscrupulous mixing of the two.

2. *Milling Quality*

(a) It must give a good yield of flour (min. 72%).
(b) The flour must have good colour (FGC max. 2·5).
(c) The wheat must be capable of giving reasonable starch damage on roller milling (25–35 Farrand units).

3. *Baking Quality*

(a) Low α-amylase (max. 5 Farrand units) and low proteolytic activity.
(b) Minimum 11·0% protein content in the flour.
(c) Good gluten quality.
(d) Good baking quality (this can be defined).
(e) A long term target would be to avoid millers/bakers having to use oxidising improvers.

A. Spicer (The Lord Rank Research Centre, High Wycombe, Bucks): What Dr Blaxter has done in his comments is to stress that on one side of the scale we have the plant breeders and the farmers, who face a number of imponderables in their endeavour to produce the end product, and on the other side we have the miller and the baker, who I think in many ways do not face these imponderables. They merely have a technology, and a mill, or a bakery, which can be air-conditioned. Many things can be introduced so that their process is independent of the weather, the sunshine and the pests that come to the farmer to make all his calculations go haywire. He makes all possible predictions and then at the last minute rain will ruin his expectations.

When the semi-mechanised processes of milling and baking on a large scale were developed, one thing that was totally ignored by engineers was the flexibility that the small baker had who could put his hands into the trough and if he found that the water wasn't quite right, in went a pound of flour, out came half a pint of water and he still had his bread. In a large plant this is no longer possible. You press a button and in its eventual form down comes the flour and the water and out comes the wrong bread because the amylase content was too high.

So I think what we have got to see in the next 10–15 years is that in the construction of our plants and in the development of our technology we must take into account that we take a live product, not a chemical. Technology has to be the flexible thing and if you follow this argument to its right conclusion then within the next 15 years we can face the Huntsman or the other types in a much calmer attitude than we can face it today. Having shifted the task from the plant breeder, we have to some extent given it to the chemical engineer who, will be prepared to give us the answers much more readily.

For two or three thousand years bread has been a political issue. Were wheat to decrease, however little, the protein content of our daily bread by any new technology, the outburst that we would have to face could be tremendous. And, therefore, what we want to see in British wheat is a protein content around 12%. I think the amylase part is not so important, because flexible technology in time should cope with that.

Give us a protein content, give us a fair amount of hardness so that we can incorporate the starch damage, so that we absorb the water that we need for economy and for the storage life of the bread, and I think when that is done we can face with confidence the next 10–15 years in our milling, baking and farming activities.

R. Riley (Plant Breeding Institute, Cambridge, UK): Some comment is needed from a plant breeder to the helpful advice that has been given. I think it is important to recognise that although this symposium is called 'Bread' and is about wheat and bread, wheat is used for other purposes than making bread.

Nevertheless, it clearly is of the utmost importance that since the major direct use of wheat is for making bread for our populace, we try to develop the crop so that it can be most efficiently exploited in this way.

I welcome Dr Cookson's suggestion that we should all sit down together on some other occasion and look at what the definition might be and how we can reconcile our various objectives and the possibilities that it is feasible for us to follow in arriving at criteria for producing the Selsdon Wheat.

K. Blaxter: I think there are 2 main things to come out from this discussion. One is, that wheat breeders can go away and say quite categorically 'We want wheat with 12% protein, we want wheat which is uniform and we want wheat which does not involve too much alteration from day to day, or from time to time in the operation of the plant. We can equally well say that we want a wheat that is hard, which gives minimal starch damage and possibly also wheat with a low amylase content. And I think quite frankly that is as far as one can go.

Chairman: In arranging a symposium, many preparations are necessary and for that reason I would like to thank first the Rank Prize Funds, and especially the Trustees, who gave the money and in this way made the conference possible.

To organise a symposium it is also very necessary to have a title and in this respect I know that we have to thank Dr Blaxter, who at one of the meetings of the Advisory Committee put forward the idea to have a symposium on 'Bread'. Of course, the success depends very much on the speakers discussing the topic and I would like to thank once more the speakers in the discussions we have had, which have made our symposium so lively.

Besides these scientific activities, the administration is very important and in this respect I would like to express our gratitude to Mr Hadley, who put a lot of work into the organisation of this symposium. Then, of course, the people behind the scenes, and as an example of the male and female I would like to say thank you to Mr Brown and Miss Gookey. So I think we should summarise all our thanks and I hope I can speak on behalf of you all, in the usual way. Thank you very much (Applause).

H. C. Pereira (Ministry of Agriculture, Fisheries and Food, London): Mr Chairman, I have the pleasant task of reinforcing your thanks on behalf of all the guests of the Lord Rank Prize Funds. In particular to Professor Arnold Spicer, who has masterminded this whole procedure and has given us a truly memorable week. I echo your thanks to James Hadley, to Mr Brown and all the others who have supported us and to Sir John Davies for the splendid evening that we had at the Mansion House last night.

The breadth of imagination in assembling this unusual group to discuss both the scientific and the technical and economic subject is really a memorable experience. We meet most often in disciplines and discuss subjects on a rather specific group of interests and in this assembly we have really unusual geographical, scientific, technical, commercial and economic and even administrative experiences, all mixing in to give us a quite unusual opportunity to appreciate the other man's point of view.

So on behalf of my fellow delegates, I offer my sincere thanks to the Lord Rank Prize Fund Foundation and all those who have contributed to this conference.

Index

3 0081 009 881 107